Praise for *Kay Thompson*

A *Vanity Fair* magazine "Hot Type" Selection
A Book-of-the-Month Club Alternate Selection
A *Kirkus Reviews* Best Biographies of 2010 Selection

"The greatest gift my parents ever gave me was my godmother, Kay Thompson. No one was as brilliant or as funny, and Sam Irvin's book manages to capture that lightning in a bottle. Hang onto your hair!"

—Liza Minnelli

"Kay Thompson was the most important influence on me and my musical career. Sam Irvin's wonderful book is right on the mark."

—Andy Williams

"Kay Thompson never ceased to amaze. It is high time someone wrote a comprehensive book about her extraordinary life and Sam Irvin has done just that."

—Angela Lansbury

"Isn't it wonderful that Sam Irvin was able to capture this fantastic lady on paper?"

—Robert Wagner

"Hilarious, jaw-dropping, and hugely inspiring. I was swept aboard, like being on a train: the Atchison, Topeka, and the Santa *Kay!*"

—Tommy Tune

how business biography; chock full of outrageous stories, accurate history, insight and, of course, a fabulous subject."

—Charles Busch

"This informative book details Kay's and my collaboration. Like some very special unions it produced a child: the ageless, guileless, indomitable and endearing Eloise. Thank you, Kay, and especially Sam Irvin for this astounding story."

—Hilary Knight, illustrator of *Eloise*

"Awesome, overwhelming, breathtaking, and terrifying, but always, *always* hilarious."

—Mart Crowley, playwright of *The Boys in the Band*

"Sam Irvin has preserved an authentic legend in amber . . . . It's got bazazz!"

—Rex Reed

"Irvin's brilliantly detailed book captures the lady in all her compelling contradictions. His book is really *quelque chose*!"

—Michael Musto

"Smart, dishy, and full of fascinating show-business stories. I loved every bit of it."

—Leonard Maltin

"A brilliant job of research, judgment, insight and style."

—Kevin Thomas

"Auntie Mame, Cleopatra and Madonna could all take lessons from Kay Thompson. To borrow a word once used to describe her work, Irvin's book is *Thompsensational*."

—Robert Osborne, Turner Classic Movies

"Sam Irvin illuminates the supercharged life of the entertainer and author."

—Megan O'Grady, Vogue.com

"Mr. Irvin has done his homework and then some . . . [and he] writes with intelligence and insight about the development of *Eloise*."

—Dwight Garner, *The New York Times*

"A revealing look at this complex and contradictory woman."

—Susan King, *Los Angeles Times*

"Wildly fascinating. Readers will be hard pressed to forget it."

—Nora Dunne, *The Christian Science Monitor*

"Kay Thompson's status as a show business cult figure is bolstered by . . . this new biography about the zany, irascible dame behind Judy & Liza & Eloise."

—Joe Meyers, *Connecticut Post*

"Sam Irvin, producer and director, has written a biography of one of the most influential and perhaps underappreciated figures in show business."

—Scott Simon, *NPR*

"Spectacular. One of the best biographies I have ever, ever, *ever* read. From the moment I finished, I read it again. And then I went back and read it a *third* time."

—Peter Filichia, *Broadway Radio*

"Rollicking humor and infectious enthusiasm . . . An extremely entertaining chronicle of one of the most distinctive and absurdly gifted personalities in show business."

—*Kirkus Reviews*

"A superbly crafted portrait of one of the least appreciated giants of 20th-century American show business. Irvin fully grasps Thompson's Auntie Mame vivacity."

—Christopher Loudon, JazzTimes.com

"Irvin preserves Thompson's star-studded exploits with the attention to detail that Thompson would approve of."

—Joanne Latimer, *Maclean's*

"Sam Irvin tells the life story, quirks and all, of this wildly talented and hilariously eccentric woman."

—Evelyn Renold, *AARP Magazine*

"Thompson gets a long-overdue examination in this breezy bio. Her feud with Fred Astaire makes for some of the book's most entertaining passages."

—Advocate.com

"Raucous and rollicking story. Thoroughly entertaining."

—Kathleen Hughes, *Booklist*

"Comprehensive, yes. But could we truly understand this ridiculously complicated whirlwind without all these details?"

—Steven Suskin, Playbill.com

"Hollywood director Sam Irvin writes an entertaining biography describing Thompson's dynamic personality and wild personal lifestyle."

—Andrea Tullman, DowntownMagazineNYC.com

"Film and television producer Sam Irvin brings Thompson lovingly, yet well-lit, to this thoroughly researched and stylishly written biography."

—David Marshall James, *Yahoo! Shine*

"The beauty of a biography of a lesser-known but influential figure like Kay Thompson is their Zelig-like appearances in the lives of other celebrities, and here Irvin delivers."

—Brent Hartinger, AfterElton.com

"Funny, sad, shocking, entertaining, and always riveting . . . this thoroughly fascinating showbiz biography is a must-read."

—Steve Weinstein, Edge.com

"Sam Irvin captures the essence of Kay Thompson in this page-turning biography . . . including her scandalous love-affair with a teenage Andy Williams and her mentorship of goddaughter Liza Minnelli."

—Zachary Stewart, TheaterMania.com

"Irvin did an incredible amount of research for this book, and he provides meticulous details and firsthand accounts of encounters with Thompson that really make her personality and the show business world come alive."

—Claire Kelley, *[TK] Reviews*

Kay Thompson

From
Funny Face to Eloise

Sam Irvin

SIMON & SCHUSTER PAPERBACKS
New York   London   Toronto   Sydney   New Delhi

Simon & Schuster Paperbacks
1230 Avenue of the Americas
New York, NY 10020

First Simon & Schuster trade paperback edition November 2011

SIMON & SCHUSTER PAPERBACKS and colophon are registered
trademarks of Simon & Schuster, Inc.

For illustration credits see page 390.

For information about special discounts for bulk purchases,
please contact Simon & Schuster Special Sales at 1-866-506-1949 or
business@simonandschuster.com.

The Simon & Schuster Speakers Bureau can bring authors to your live event. For
more information or to book an event contact the Simon & Schuster Speakers
Bureau at 1-866-248-3049 or visit our website at www.simonspeakers.com.

Designed by Nancy Singer

Manufactured in the United States of America

10 9 8 7 6 5 4 3 2 1

The Library of Congress has cataloged the hardcover edition as follows:
   Irvin, Sam.
   Kay Thompson : from Funny Face to Eloise / Sam Irvin. — 1st Simon & Schuster
hardcover ed.
      p. cm.
   Includes bibliographical references and index.
   1. Thompson, Kay, 1909–1998. 2. Authors, American—20th century—Biography.
3. Singers—United States—Biography. 4. Actors—United States—Biography. I. Title.

PS3570.H642355Z78 2010   2010020530
813'.54—dc22
   [B]

ISBN 978-1-4391-7653-5
ISBN 978-1-4391-7654-2 (pbk)
ISBN 978-1-4391-7655-9 (ebook)

To my mother, Mary,
and my sisters,
Janet and Anne,
for introducing me to the
Eloise books when I was young
and impressionable

CONTENTS

Part Six

The Doyenne

Introduction

PRECOCIOUS GROWNUP

Kay Thompson is a thrilling showbiz secret,
a kind of skeleton key to mid-century Broadway and Hollywood.
—*Emily Nussbaum*, New York *magazine*

The lights dimmed, pianist-conductor Billy Stritch struck up the band, and Liza Minnelli burst onstage with four boys singing "Hello, Hello," the first of several songs from Kay Thompson and the Williams Brothers' 1947 breakthrough gig at Ciro's. The scene was a private workshop recital of Liza's re-creation of her godmother's nightclub act sixty years after the original took Hollywood—and then the country—by storm. The invited audience was filled with a few potential investors but mostly Minnelli's devoted fans and friends, including entertainer Michael Feinstein, actress Arlene Dahl, critic Rex Reed, Turner Classic Movies' Robert Osborne, and the producers of *Chicago*, Craig Zadan and Neil Meron.

The performance was much more than an homage to a legendary entertainer of yesteryear. There were so many ghosts crowded on that stage, the living artists barely had room to maneuver. Kay Thompson, Judy Garland, Vincente Minnelli, and the whole of MGM, *Eloise*, and *Funny Face*. It was the culmination of everything.

As the show progressed, however, there were some technical problems. The radio mikes went haywire and the choreography was still rough around the edges. Nevertheless, it was plain to see that Liza meant business and, allowing for polishing and fine-tuning, this work in progress had enormous potential—though not everyone concurred. After the show, a television exec told Liza point-blank, "We'd only be interested if you sang 'Cabaret' and 'New York, New York.' Our audience doesn't know Kay Thompson."

Aghast, Liza shot back, "Well, then we need to teach them."

Indeed. Not to name-drop or anything, *but* . . . Kay Thompson was Judy Garland's mentor and best friend and Frank Sinatra's and Lena Horne's vocal coach. She went to school with Tennessee Williams and got her first big break from Bing Crosby. She created a nightclub act for Ginger Rogers, and played charades with Gene Kelly. Bette Davis learned from her, Diana Vreeland was portrayed by her, and Danny Kaye masqueraded in drag as her.

She auditioned for Henry Ford, trained Marilyn Monroe, channeled Elvis Presley, rejected Andy Warhol, rebuffed Federico Fellini, and got fired by Howard Hughes. Prince Aly Khan made a pass at her and the Beatles wanted to hold her hand.

She costarred in a whodunit with Ronald Reagan, gave pointers to Eleanor Roosevelt, and directed John F. Kennedy's Inaugural Gala.

She was a member of the Rat Pack and she managed to dazzle the likes of Queen Elizabeth, King Juan Carlos of Spain, and Princess Grace (Kelly) of Monaco.

She was, in short, a massive overachiever. With nothing but her wits and talent, she decamped for Hollywood and New York in the 1930s, working her way up in radio to become one of the country's most popular singing stars. In the 1940s, she expanded her range, becoming the head of MGM's vocal department, a powerful position at a time when the studio was at the nexus of Hollywood. In the late forties and fifties, she emerged as the highest-paid nightclub entertainer in the world, with her act Kay Thompson and the Williams Brothers, featuring her nineteen-year-old protégé (and secret lover), Andy Williams.

Then she wowed audiences in 1957 when she costarred in *Funny Face*. Playing the role of the no-nonsense fashion magazine editor, critics declared that Kay had stolen the film right out from under Audrey Hepburn and Fred Astaire.

In a stunning feat of reinvention, Thompson became the bestselling author of *Eloise* (with those unforgettable drawings by Hilary Knight), chronicling the rascally adventures of the beloved six-year-old mascot of The Plaza, a book that spawned an industry that is still going strong today.

Her love life was just as adventurous: she was married twice but rumors of affairs with both men and women were as ubiquitous as they were star-studded.

In the aftermath of the tragic passing of Judy Garland in 1969, Thompson took Liza Minnelli under her wing, advising and guiding the young actress throughout her meteoric rise to superstardom.

In her twilight, Thompson retreated into Garbo-like seclusion, but just when it appeared that her larger-than-life story was headed for an uneventful conclusion, an astonishing final act was yet to be played out.

The Kay Thompson saga swells from small-town wannabe to international headliner, then dissolves into self-destruction and madness—the story line usually reserved for a rags-to-riches potboiler—yet with unexpected twists, outlandish turns, and a surprise ending that, even by Hollywood standards, is nothing short of preposterous.

But that is Kay Thompson—wildly talented and hilariously eccentric, yet with an exasperating underbelly of neuroses that deprived her of the recognition she so richly deserved. Until now.

Part One
RADIO DAYS

Chapter One

THINK FINK

Kitty Fink Becomes Kay Thompson
(1909–32)

In a year Which Shall be Nameless
In east St. Louis
This vunderkind,
This enfant prodique,
This miracle, lyrical,
Slightly hysterical Gal Was Born.

—*Roger Edens,*
The Passion According to St. Kate, Opus 19, #46

Like Eloise at The Plaza, Kay Thompson was a figment of the imagination. Both were dreamed up by Kitty Fink as whimsical escapes from a mundane and sometimes painful childhood.

Kitty's father was Leo George Fink, born on January 12, 1874, in Vienna, Austria, the son of Mark Fink, a Jew from Norway, and Antoinette "Antonie" Steiner, a Christian from Vienna. Troubled by anti-Semitism and interfaith bigotry, the Fink family immigrated to America in 1886 with high hopes for a safer and more prosperous future. Unfortunately, anti-Semitism existed on both sides of the Atlantic and so, like many others, the Finks submerged their Jewish heritage in order to assimilate into mainstream society.

When Leo arrived in the United States at the age of twelve, he was teased by bullies for his broken English and foreign ways. Afraid to draw attention to himself, he kept his mouth shut and faded into the background. As he sat on the sidelines, Leo's youth passed him by, and when it came to dating girls, he was a late bloomer. How Leo ended up in St. Louis is not known, but it was love that anchored him there.

The object of his affection was a waitress named Harriet Adelaide Tetrick, an attractive WASP from the Midwest. Most people called her Hattie, but Kay later nicknamed her Flavia, the Latin word for "yellow-haired," because of her bleached-blond tresses (a look Thompson later adopted). Though her ancestors were German, Hattie was as American as apple pie. Born in 1888 in Eureka, Kansas, she was raised 140 miles northwest in Abilene, home of future President Dwight D. Eisenhower, two years her junior. She also lived for a time in Iowa, but by the age of eighteen ended up in St. Louis, where she got a job waiting tables at a local restaurant. It was there that she met a shy, thirty-two-year-old admirer named Leo Fink.

For Leo, Hattie was stylish, youthful, and outgoing, an appealing manifestation of everything he was not. And that was just fine with Hattie. Though he was fourteen years her senior, she admired his gentle demeanor and saw him as a responsible man who would provide well for her and their intended family. Smitten, Leo wanted to "rescue" Hattie from the workplace, so he proposed marriage on the condition that she quit her job and become a stay-at-home wife. She agreed and they tied the knot.

Emulating family trades he knew from Vienna, Leo had opened L. G. Fink, Inc., Jeweler and Pawnbroker, at 719 Pine, on the corner of North Eighth Street, where three balls, symbolic of pawnshops, hung over the door.

The first Fink residence was a modest apartment in a lower-income neighborhood at 3966 Laclede Street. Hattie was musical at heart, so even though space and money were tight, she convinced her husband to acquire an upright piano—probably an orphan from his pawnshop.

Sociable with all the neighbors, Hattie offered piano and singing lessons to friends while her husband managed the store in town. Leo didn't like this arrangement one bit. He believed a wife should be making babies, not earning money; that was the man's job. Unfortunately, Hattie's passion for fashion exceeded her spending allowance, so she saw no reason why she couldn't help fund her expensive taste in clothes. This rebellious behavior was a constant source of conflict—with Leo assuming the role of strict disciplinarian.

The solution to their differences came on January 28, 1907, when the stork delivered a baby girl named Blanche Margaret, a dark-haired beauty. To Leo's great relief, Hattie would now have no time for anything except being a mom. And the job title stuck.

Hattie may have acquiesced to her duties as a housewife, but when it came to religion, her Presbyterian background prevailed. However, no matter how much Leo may have desired to blend in as an American Protestant, he was never able to erase his Yiddish accent. Regardless, there were no menorahs to be found at holiday time; their house had the requisite Christmas tree and stockings were hung by the chimney with care.

On November 9, 1909, the stork made a second stop at the Fink residence, this time armed with a blue-eyed, redheaded, freckle-faced bundle of joie de vivre named Catherine Louise, but everyone called her Kitty—until the time when she left home to become Kay Thompson. Her middle name, Louise, was inspired by her city of birth, St. Louis, and it became the basis for the name of her alter ego, Eloise.

Having outgrown their tiny home, the Finks relocated three miles northeast to a slightly larger dwelling at 5965 Maple, in a more family-oriented, middle-class neighborhood. Hattie busied herself with a rapid succession of additions to the family: first, on March 20, 1911, a boy christened Leo George Fink Jr., known to everyone as Bud, and then, on August 20, 1912, a girl named Marian Antoinette.

The Fink kids were welcomed into the neighborhood, with frequent compliments on how cute Blanche, Bud, and Marian were. The comments about Kitty were not quite as enthusiastic—and it was painfully apparent why: she wasn't blessed with beauty. Even as a toddler, Kitty could sense that her siblings got more notice than she did. She quickly learned that if she wanted to vie for attention, she would have to do something to earn it. So, she made faces. She grimaced. She stuck out her tongue, messed up her hair—whatever silliness came to mind. Hardly a coincidence, Kitty pulled the same sort of attention-grabbing stunts that later turned up in all those Eloise books—like putting toe shoes on her ears or wearing a cabbage leaf as a hat. And it worked. People began to notice her. They thought she was funny. In the midst of laughter, Kitty was no longer second fiddle. She was a self-made star.

She was also a daredevil, often climbing trees and roughhousing with the neighborhood boys. But she loved fantasizing with dolls and playing dress-up, too. This split personality—half tomboy, half girlie girl—would prove to be just one of her many dichotomies.

"I was different from my siblings," Thompson later reflected. "I used to lie awake nights, trying to think up ways of keeping up with brilliant Blanche and good-looking Marian . . . whom everyone admired while they disregarded me."

As feelings of insecurity and alienation intensified, Kitty often retreated into her own world, where, in her solitude, she developed an imaginary friend—the first signs of an alter ego that later evolved into Eloise. While others played games, Kitty played God. She created characters, not only fictional ones but flesh-and-blood personas like Kay Thompson—a calling she continued throughout her life, both for herself and for many others.

She was also obsessed with music. Before she could walk or talk, Kitty merrily banged away on the piano, composing her own discordant cantatas. To preserve the family's sanity, her mother began giving Kitty piano lessons when she was three. To Hattie's astonishment, the toddler took to classical music like a duck to water. Neighbors clamored to hear for themselves what this precocious youngster would master next—Bach? Beethoven? In no time flat, Kitty's reputation switched from clown to prodigy and, with her tiny legs dangling off the piano stool, she got her first taste of applause, a genuine appreciation that she liked much more than mere attention.

The day after her fourth birthday, Kitty was enrolled in kindergarten at Dozier Elementary School, where she boasted that she was going to be an actress, "Not sometime, mind you, but right away!" And, frankly, they had no reason to doubt her.

When a larger house nearby went up for sale, Leo grabbed it and moved his family to 17 Parkland Place, the residence that became their permanent home.

Kitty's childhood friend Virginia "Ginny" Farrar Ruane, ninety-three years old when interviewed for this book in July 2002, could still picture it vividly: "It was a very nice house, nicely furnished, on a lovely, gated cul-de-sac with a fountain."

Despite the fact that World War I had broken out in Europe in the summer of 1914, the Finks were living out the Norman Rockwell ideal; everything on their horizon was looking bright.

Convinced that Kitty was a budding genius, Hattie and Leo enrolled her in first grade on September 21, 1914, when she was several weeks shy of five years old—even though school regulations required children to be six. A close look at her school records reveals how this rule was fudged.

Kitty's entrance form lists her birth date as November 19, 1908—wrong day *and* wrong year—making her appear to be a year older than she really was. Given the precocious nature of the child in question, the administration either never bothered to check or turned a blind eye. It wasn't until Kitty was entering college that the awful truth finally surfaced.

The transfer-of-records form from Soldan High School to Washington University owns up to Kitty's correct birth date, November 9, 1909,

finally in agreement with her certified birth record and the City of St. L
birth registry, making her a full year *younger* than her peers had been led t
believe.

After that, Kitty kept everybody in the dark about her age and it became a
running joke among friends. During her years at MGM in the 1940s, legendary joint birthday parties with her colleague Roger Edens featured endless rib-
bing on the subject, as evidenced by the lyrics to "The Passion According to St.
Kate, Opus 19, #46," a satiric birthday cantata Roger composed in Kay's honor:
"She drove an ambulance in the First World War," sang MGM orchestrator
Conrad Salinger. In a teasing reference to "The Trolley Song" in *Meet Me in
St. Louis*, Judy Garland chimed in, "All I know is, she was on that goddamned
trolley ride I took. That was 1903."

The natural aging process, coupled with too much plastic surgery, did her
no favors. In 1954, Cecil Beaton and Kenneth Tynan wrote that she was "skeletal" and "hatchet-faced," and the 1976 *Who's Who in Hollywood* blithely described her as "cadaverous."

Thompson's lack of candor about her age backfired completely after her
death. In her obituary, *The New York Times* had egg on its face when it cautiously
guesstimated that she was "between 92 and 95." The truth is that Thompson
was born on November 9, 1909, and died on July 2, 1998—at the ripe *young*
age of eighty-eight. Case closed.

In early 1915, five-year-old Kitty Fink breezed through first grade so fast,
she was promoted to the second grade in April, completing a quarter of the
curriculum by the time school let out in June. But schoolwork was just a distraction from what she really loved—playing piano. It was decided that Kitty
would benefit from more advanced training than her mother could provide, so
she began taking outside piano lessons.

"I practiced four or five hours a day," Kay remembered. "When I was six, I
wrote a piece and called it 'The Billy Goat in the Woods.' It was just eight bars."

As teachers and adults paid more and more attention to Kitty, resentment
grew among her classmates. Suddenly, her red hair, her freckles, her oversized
nose, even her last name became the butt of cruel jokes.

"I had an inferiority complex," Kay later admitted. "I always felt, when I
was little, that I was ugly. My sisters and my mother were so gorgeously beautiful. If people asked my mother what she thought the children would grow up
to be, she used to say that [Blanche and Marian] would probably be a writer
and an artist—they were so talented—that her son might be President. Then

d Kitty has a lovely personality. All this must have waked the
me to do something outstanding."

f seven, Kitty advanced to the fourth grade on April 6, 1917,
e United States entered the First World War by declaring war
on Germany. This must have been an uncomfortable time for Leo and Hattie,
both of whom had family ties in enemy territory.

Things were not peaceful in St. Louis, either. That summer, racial unrest
erupted into devastating riots and fires that frightened an eleven-year-old Josephine Baker into dreaming of a life where the color of her skin did not matter. Josephine would eventually abandon St. Louis in favor of Paris, where she
became the highest-paid entertainer in Europe—a hometown success story
that later proved empowering and inspirational to the *other* St. Louis femme
phenom.

But, during her youth, Kitty's world was sheltered from the hell of war and
race riots—even though she would suffer some minor injuries on her own turf.
She got plenty of spankings because she was "as freckle-faced and mischievous
a brat as ever caused a mother gray hair."

"I always was theatrical, and lickings were a nuisance," Kay admitted to a
reporter. "So I tried a little trick."

In the dead of night, Kitty woke everyone up, screaming uncontrollably,
claiming that she was haunted by thoughts of being whipped. "It's the idea, not
the pain, that frightens me so much," she sobbed, wiping away crocodile tears.

"I must have done a good job," Kay recalled, "for that night I heard my
Mother tell Dad she had never realized what a sensitive child I was, and that it
was best not to strike me ever."

Kitty may have saved her behind from further corporal punishment, but
she continued to suffer from injuries of her own making. At the age of eight,
she developed a crush on a neighborhood boy named Harry. Her heart sank,
however, when she saw him flirt with her older sister, Blanche. When he finally
looked in her direction, Kitty couldn't help herself. She sneered and stuck out
her tongue. Unfazed, Harry did the worst thing imaginable: he ignored her.
Infuriated, Kitty suddenly ran halfway up the staircase and blurted out, "I can
jump more than anyone!"

All the children turned as Kitty shrieked like a banshee and leapt from
the sixth step, landing at the foot of the stairs. Unscathed, Kitty taunted Harry,
"'Fraidy cat, 'fraidy cat!"

Then she scrambled up the stairs again, this time jumping from the seventh step, crashing with a thud that must have hurt, but she wasn't about to
admit it. When she threatened to go even higher, Harry finally took the bait,

proclaiming, "You can't. *I* can. It's a cinch for a boy." Harry climbed to the eighth step, jumped to the floor, then gloated at Kitty.

"I can do nine," she retorted.

What happened after that was not pretty. Kitty landed flat on her face, breaking her nose. If her snout was considered unsightly before the calamity, now it was a bona fide eyesore. But, as far as she was concerned, her death-defying leap was worth the pain and disfigurement because, a few days later, Harry offered to carry her books to school. That episode encouraged further flights of folly, resulting in a broken arm and a *second* broken nose.

"My method as a kid was wrong," Kay later admitted, "but the idea was right. Because I was homely, I learned I'd have to bestir myself and try extra hard to make the grade."

Doctors' visits to fix her wounds were so painful, she developed a phobia that many of her friends believe was the underlying motivation for her later conversion to Christian Science, a faith that bans medical intervention. And yet, exemplifying her many contradictions, she eventually came to rely heavily on the medical profession for nips, tucks, and pick-me-ups.

Broken body parts and interest in boys did not mix well with schoolwork. When her academic momentum imploded during the fifth grade, Leo took away her vacation privileges. He enrolled her in summer sessions at Emerson, another St. Louis school, where she began the sixth grade on June 16, 1919, still only nine years old. This sobering turn of events did not bring Kitty closer to her father, and their relationship would forever remain strained.

On April 5, 1920, Kitty transferred to Ben Blewitt Intermediate Junior High School, entering the seventh grade at the age of ten. During her two years of junior high, Kitty's grades were highly erratic except in music and athletics, where she routinely excelled. Interestingly, she found a unique way to combine her passions. "At twelve, I wrote 'The Tuberculosis Ball Game Benefit,'" Kay recalled in 1936. "I thought [it] was just grand. I had a record made of the 'Ball Game.' When last I was home and heard it, I was amazed at my nerve!"

She had nerve to spare. Her friend Ginny Farrar Ruane recalled, "Each class during the semester would put on some kind of show for the entertainment of the rest of the school, and Kitty's class did a high-stepping cakewalk, complete with blackface, and it brought down the house. In a cakewalk there is not much choreography—you just *strut your stuff*! Needless to say, Kitty was the highest stepper of all. Kitty's costume, made by her mother, was entirely of red bandannas." (Kay's affinity for red bandannas would endure.)

Kitty was supposed to graduate from Blewitt Junior High in June 1922, but her grades were just not good enough. She was finally promoted to Soldan

High School on January 26, 1923, and it took the rest of that school year and all of the next to scrape through her freshman year. So much for accelerated learning.

Protesting the threat of summer school, Kitty begged Leo to let her go with Ginny to girls' summer camp. With the help of her mother, she got her way and spent eight weeks during the summer of 1924 at Minne-Wonka Lodge in Three Lakes, Wisconsin, her first time away from home—a much needed cooling-off period between father and daughter.

"Every Saturday night we'd have skits and musical things," Ginny enthused, "and of course Kitty was so fun, so full of pep, and the life of everything. We'd have canoe trips that took three to five days. We all did lifesaving together and things like that. It was just grand."

With growing independence and maturity, Kitty was determined to make her life at home more enjoyable, too.

"We had a little pitiful high school sorority," Ginny recalled. "Xi Delta Sigma. We'd all get together, sing, sit around, gab, and have dumb fun."

Another favorite distraction from homework was attending movies, although it wasn't exactly for the love of cinematic arts. "We went to 'em all, didn't matter which ones," Ginny chuckled, "because we just wanted to see who else was there."

On Saturdays, Kitty and her friends would go shopping in downtown St. Louis. When Kitty needed to get her five-dollar weekly allowance from her father, however, she never let anyone come with her to his "office." She was so ashamed of her father's pawnshop, she'd make her friends wait several blocks away. Even Ginny, her closest confidante, did not discover this secret until years later.

"The malign exercise of snobbery in 'middle American' life"—as Tennessee Williams labeled it—was alive and well in St. Louis. Kitty worried that her social standing would be irreparably stigmatized if her father's profession were known. Even later in life, she steadfastly characterized Leo as "a jeweler," never once admitting the pawn brokerage side of his trade. It is telling that as far back as high school, Kitty was carefully crafting an idealized public image.

Keen to be up on the latest fashion trends, Kitty was a shopaholic. "There's one department store that we'd always hit called Vandervoort's," Ginny related, referring to Scruggs-Vandervoort-Barney. "It was a big deal. We'd look at all the clothes."

Kitty and Ginny became fast friends with one of the store's young employees—a vivacious new girl in town named Mary Lorena "Billie" Cantrell, who worked as a sales clerk in women's sportswear. Department stores must've been in Billie's blood, because later, in 1932, she would marry Stanley Marcus of Neiman-Marcus in Dallas, the most prominent and influential department store outside of New York City.

In St. Louis, Billie's family lived in an apartment building on Maple, just four blocks from the Fink residence. Jerrie Marcus Smith, daughter of Billie and Stanley Marcus, recalled hearing stories about the Finks' wild child. "Kitty came over to my mother's house to *pound* on the piano all the time," Jerrie said, laughing. "My grandmother was always worried about the neighbors complaining."

Among her late mother's personal effects, Jerrie found a 1926 handwritten invitation "to pledge membership" with Xi Delta Sigma, signed "Catherine L. Fink." And the sorority bond they pledged never ended. In later years, Kay kept in close touch with Billie, bringing her nightclub act to Dallas—twice—and making several personal appearances at the flagship Neiman-Marcus store, where she promoted *Eloise* and also served as a creative consultant on its International Fortnight expositions.

So, it was only fitting that Kitty had first become acquainted with Billie at a department store—and Scruggs-Vandervoort-Barney was *the* favorite haunt among Kitty's group of high school friends.

"It had a lovely tearoom," Ginny recalled, "and we'd always end up having lunch there. Then we'd go and listen to the records in the music department. They had several listening booths. We just listened, though. We never bought 'em."

"I'm a miser at heart," Kay later admitted. Recalling her youth, she added, "I'd deprive myself of a lot. I'd much rather have money in the bank than anywhere else." And at the age of sixteen, Kitty's bank balance was about to increase.

Lalla Bauman, who ran a nearby dance school, suddenly found herself without an accompanist, so she called Kitty and asked how much she would charge.

"Three dollars an hour," Kitty boldly replied.

"Why, that's preposterous!" the woman responded. "The usual rate is a dollar-fifty at the outside."

"Not *my* usual rate," Kitty lied, never having worked a day in her life. "I always get three dollars."

"Goodness," said Miss Bauman. "Who do you think you are? Paderewski?"

Aware that the teacher was in a tight spot, Kitty held firm: "That's my price."

After a prolonged silence, the woman finally caved: "O.K., you little Big Shot. I'll have to give it to you."

"That was the first money I ever earned," Kay later recounted. "It seemed so easy to make forty-five dollars a week." In no time, she had saved six hundred dollars, a tidy reward for her brazen negotiation. It would not be the last time she drove a hard bargain.

While tinkling ivories at the dance studio, she came down with a serious case of dance fever. She enrolled at Clark's Dance School, where she took lessons alongside Ruth Elizabeth Grable, seven years her junior, who later changed her name to Betty Grable and became the famous movie and pinup star. One of Grable's other teachers at Clark's was Robert "Bob" Alton, and, although Kitty only met him in passing back then, he later became her indispensable choreographer for stage, screen, and nightclub appearances.

Like Toad in *Wind in the Willows,* Kitty was mesmerized by motorcars. They made her shoulders tingle—a feeling she always got when something was especially thrilling.

Kitty's automobile fixation led to dating a fellow classmate named Krenning Duncan "Dunc" Dorris, son of George Preston Dorris, founder and chairman of the Dorris Motor Car Company. First introduced in 1906, the Dorris was a St. Louis–made luxury car, and when Kitty turned sixteen, there was nothing she wanted more than to get behind the wheel of the latest model. And Dunc had exactly the equipment she craved. Not to be outmaneuvered, Ginny was dating Dunc's older brother, Pres (George Preston Dorris Jr.), so between the two, these industrious young ladies had managed to just about corner the high school market on automobile access. And, according to Kay, Dunc was one of several boys who tried to corner the market on her.

"I've been telling men I don't want to get married ever since I was sixteen," Thompson later bragged, "but they just wouldn't believe me!"

The question is, should we believe her? Although she later made two trips to the altar, it is hard to imagine marriage proposals coming her way during adolescence, a time when even she freely admitted, "I was the official ugly duckling of the family."

Far more believable is the anecdote in which Kitty and Ginny had a typical Lucy-and-Ethel moment. "One time we borrowed another boy's car," Ginny said with mischief in her voice. "His name was Chester Wolfe, a friend of the Dorris boys. While he was doing football, he let us borrow it. That was his big mistake. We slammed the door and accidentally broke the grind-up window on one side. Oh my Lord. We ran to some place that fixed windows and cried and carried on. It is just embedded in my memory how we had to sweat that out until they fixed it." But, with impish satisfaction, Ginny added, "Chester never knew about it at all."

Everyone thought they were such angels. When asked about Kitty's churchgoing habits, Ginny said, "I went to Westminster Presbyterian Church and she went to West Presbyterian. I'm not sure how often they went, or even *if* they went."

As it was only a five-minute stroll from her address, Ginny was a frequent visitor to the Fink home. "The whole family was fun," she recalled. "They enjoyed each other. They always seemed to have such a good time together—a wonderful, close family."

However, when pressed, Ginny admitted that the men of the house were decidedly on the fringe. "Mr. Fink was a lot older than Mrs. Fink," Ginny remarked, "and I think he was just overwhelmed by them all and he'd take a backseat. The women were all so extroverted—entertaining and singing and having such fun— he didn't know what hit him! He just shook his head and paid the bills."

Kitty's brother, Bud, also made himself scarce. "He was a nice kid," Ginny recalled, "but I mean, you know, nobody wants a little brother hangin' around. I know. I had one, too."

Ginny's memories of Kitty's mother, Hattie, were especially fond: "Oh, she was quite sharp, always dressed up, looked so nice. She liked to sing and when you would go over there, she was like one of the girls. So much fun."

Most of Ginny's time in the Fink home was spent around the piano. In adolescence, Kitty's voice developed a squeaky quality that had become the butt of family jokes, so she stuck mostly to the keyboard while her mother sang along with Blanche, Marian, and visitors like Ginny.

There was never a need for sheet music. "Kitty played by ear," Ginny marveled. "Anything you wanted to hear, she'd come up with it—all the popular songs, current jazz, musical comedy tunes, whatever was current at the time. 'Tea for Two' was a favorite."

"Kitty could play serious music, too," Ginny added. Her accomplished classical skills pleased her father and he hoped that she would find her calling as a concert pianist. To that end, in early 1926, during her junior year in high school, sixteen-year-old Kitty made her debut as a piano soloist with the St. Louis Symphony Orchestra for a performance of Franz Liszt's "Hungarian Fantasy" at the Odeon Theatre on Grand Boulevard. Making the event all the more momentous was the fact that the concert was broadcast live over KWK, Kitty's very first radio exposure.

For her big night, she wore a very special new dress. "It was the kind of thin white stuff," Kay later told a reporter, drawing the shape of it in the air with her manicured index talon. "It wasn't long enough and it wasn't short enough, and it had scallops around the skirt. But my mother thought I looked grand."

In preparation for the performance, Kitty had to memorize the entire ninety-page concerto. "[My mother] sat in the front row," Thompson recalled, "and she was more nervous than I was. I told her to hold her breath till I came to an eight-bar passage I had to play alone. If I got past the place where I crossed my hands, she could go on breathing—the worst would be over."

Just before her solo, however, the unimaginable happened: Kitty went blank. The distinguished conductor, Frederick Fischer, knew something was dreadfully wrong when he glanced over to the piano and saw the expression of a deer caught in the headlights. All Kitty could do was whisper, "Go right ahead, Fred."

Balding, plump, and bespectacled, Mr. Fischer was not accustomed to brain-dead pianists any more than he was used to being addressed as "Fred." He stared back at her in utter disbelief.

Kitty shrugged. "I'll join you later."

Somehow, the maestro managed to wing it through Kitty's solo without missing a beat. After sixteen measures, when her next cue came up, Kitty hopped on board and gave the performance of her life. By the end, the audience was on its feet, cheering.

Kitty took her bows to thunderous applause, especially thrilled to see her father beaming with pride. It wouldn't last long. As she stepped back toward the wings, Kitty stumbled into a row of potted palm trees, which fell like dominoes. The poor creature ended up sprawled on the floor amid a hopeless tangle of chiffon and palm fronds.

Kay later claimed to have made the decision then and there to renounce all aspirations of classical keyboarding. "I wanted to have long fingernails!" was her practical excuse.

In truth, the renunciation took quite a bit longer, due to strict orders from her father. Though she was loath to admit it, Kitty continued as the pianist for the St. Louis Symphony for three full years.

Despite the pressure to be a classical musician, Kitty favored popular tunes—which she handily parlayed into social invitations. "She was always the life of the party," Ginny remembered, "because she'd sit down at the piano and that was it. She was just great."

"I was always the one to play the piano while the others danced," Kay confirmed. "Of course the ones that danced got the men. So I hit on this scheme: I'd sit down at the piano and sing blues. The tempo was impossible for dancing.

Pretty soon all the men would be grouped around the piano—and the other girls would be thinking of forming an organization to work for the repeal of the existing laws governing homicide."

Kitty's transformation to torch songstress did not happen overnight. She longed to be taken seriously, like Fanny Brice, an ugly duckling Jewish girl from New York's Lower East Side who had become a national sensation singing weepy ballads. They may have shared homely looks, but Kitty didn't have Fanny's distinctive voice or range. One night at a local vaudeville show, however, Kitty heard something that made her shoulders tingle: a female African-American blues singer with a deep, husky voice. Kitty announced that her latest goal was to be a blues singer, an aspiration met with considerable skepticism by her family.

"If my sisters hadn't made fun of my voice," Kay later explained, "I would never have buckled down to taking singing lessons seriously. And if they weren't so sure I could never become a singer, I wouldn't have fought for a career!"

Seething with resentment, Kitty set out to prove them wrong. "Mother, who gave singing lessons, had often said you could change the range of your tones," Kay recalled. "I decided to get rid of my squeak and develop a lower range for blues singing."

Using the keyboard as her guide to the depths of hell, Kitty groaned, growled, and grunted guttural sounds that could wake the dead. Eventually, the nightmare paid off. Incredibly, she had developed a lower register—an entire octave—rich and throaty. Not only did she sound great singing blues, the full range of her voice had miraculously *arrived*.

Stretching her newfound talent, Kitty landed a supporting role in, of all things, an operetta—the Soldan High production of *The Bells of Beaujolais*, performed on April 16, 1926. Since the entire student body was required to attend, she had a captive audience—including a schoolmate named Tennessee Williams.

Born on March 26, 1911, in Columbus, Mississippi, Thomas Lanier Williams and his family had moved to St. Louis when he was eight years old. Thomas would eventually be nicknamed Tennessee because of his thick hillbilly drawl, but back then, Kitty and his other neighborhood friends knew him as Tom. For three years starting in 1918, Tennessee resided in a furnished six-room apartment at 4633 Westminster Place, just a few blocks southwest of the Fink's Parkland Place home. (The apartment would later be the setting for Tennessee's play *The Glass Menagerie*.)

"[My sister] Rose and I made friends," Tennessee recalled, "and we had an agreeable children's life among them, playing 'hide-and-seek' and 'fly, sheep, fly,' and bathing under garden hoses in the hot summer."

Tennessee's older sister, Rose, was the same age as Kitty and Ginny. "We would run around together," Ginny recalled, "and Tom would tag along, trying to keep up with us." More often, he hung out with Kitty's brother, Bud, his senior by only six days. Tennessee's father worked for Ginny's father at the Friedman-Shelby branch of the International Shoe Company in St. Louis (a factory where Tennessee later worked).

"Our mothers were co-joiners in the UDC, United Daughters of the Confederacy," Ginny explained. "Once a month there was a meeting of 'the children of the C' and my brother and I were dragged kicking and screaming to a get-together where we sang 'Dixie,' had refreshments, and listened to another member play the cello. Kitty, Rose, and Tom were victims, too, but they seemed to enjoy it."

Kitty was the local ham and Tennessee's keen interest in student theatrical productions kept him abreast of her rise to stardom—first at Blewitt Junior High, then at Soldan High, and finally at Washington University. After leaving St. Louis, they would cross paths on many occasions around the world.

Another famous graduate of Soldan High was actress Agnes Moorehead. She was nine years older than Kitty and, by 1926, had left St. Louis. Nevertheless, they later became friends and shared stories about their Missouri upbringing. There was also Vincent Price, born in St. Louis two years after Kitty. But even though the two grew up just a couple of miles from each other, they were worlds apart in terms of social standing. Born into a wealthy family, Vincent was sent to private schools and attended Yale. Still, Kay and Vincent became friends as adults via showbiz circles and their shared passion for fine art.

Sans silver spoon in a class-conscious society, Kitty used her musical skills to parlay herself into a higher bracket. In the middle of her junior year at Soldan High in February 1926, Kitty was elected to serve as librarian of the Chaminade Glee Club, the fifty-member girls' choral group, known for singing songs like "S'wanee River." And that summer, for the third year in a row, she returned to Minne-Wonka Girls' Summer Camp, this time leading all the campfire songs.

That fall, Kitty entered her senior year at Soldan High and involved herself in just about every extracurricular activity on campus: Song Committee, Orchestra, Chaminade Glee Club, the Athenaeum (a twenty-five-girl debate and speech club), Scrippage Committee (the school newspaper staff), Dancing Club, and the Girl's Athletic Association, where she excelled in hockey, tennis, and swimming. And, in addition to her regular gig as pianist for the St. Louis Symphony, she somehow found time to star in the school production of Gilbert and Sullivan's *Iolanthe*.

All this took its toll on her schoolwork; by the time she graduated in June, she mustered an average of only 67 (out of 100), ranking 209th in a class of 214 students. Diplomatically, the quote in her yearbook focused on her strengths: "A friendly maid and likewise gay is she; her touch upon the keys is heavenly." But by then, she'd given up piano lessons—another thorn in her father's side. On the verge of burnout, she insisted on recharging her batteries at Minne-Wonka Summer Camp.

In the fall of 1927, Kitty enrolled at Washington University in St. Louis, which offered a broad range of academia. But the social whirlwind of sororities was what girls like Kitty and Ginny craved. "I became a Kappa Alpha Theta," Ginny said. "Kitty became a Delta Gamma first—her sister Blanche's sorority—and then broke that pledge and joined Kappa Kappa Gamma." After a freshman year best described as one long party, Kitty and Ginny spent the summer of 1928 at Minne-Wonka again—their fifth annual retreat to Wisconsin—this time as camp counselors.

Once they returned to school for their sophomore year, however, Ginny didn't hang out with Kitty as much. Differing sororities played a role. "We sort of grew apart," Ginny lamented.

There were other gravitational pulls. Kitty was devoting more of her time to the music and theater departments. Surrounded by scores of extroverted actors and ambitious singers, Kitty had her hands full trying to elbow her way into these highly competitive cliques.

"While other girls posed in front of mirrors trying to look like Norma Talmadge and Vilma Banky," Kay later mused, "I wore myself out working for personality."

Don't let her fool you. Kitty was equally concerned about her looks. She had matured early into her adult size: 121 pounds, five feet five-and-a-half inches tall. "I know that I give the impression of being tall," she was later quoted, "so I avoid stripes especially. When I have my shoes on, with their higher heels, I am about five feet six-and-one-half or seven inches." She may have had the body of a woman, but she still had the face of a kid with red hair, freckles, and an unfortunate nose. This mug worked fine for comedic performances, but if she was going to be taken seriously as a torch singer, she needed sophistication.

"Make me like Carole Lombard," Kitty told flummoxed hairdressers and makeup artists at the Scruggs-Vandervoort-Barney cosmetics counter, showing them magazine photos of her favorite actress. At that time, the young

Lombard was a teen idol who, after a disfiguring automobile accident, had just undergone her very own makeover with the aid of advanced plastic surgery, state-of-the-art makeup, and a tireless publicist. Lombard's ordeal was great fodder for fan magazines and Kitty attentively followed her every move on the road back from tragedy. Details from Lombard's life story—dropping out of school, her use of a stage name, her hair and makeup techniques, even her plastic surgery—all eventually became essential to the creation of Kay Thompson.

However, even after her accident and recovery, Lombard was still a knockout, so Kitty's wish to look like her was a very tall order indeed. Without the aid of Hollywood magicians, Kitty had to rely on St. Louis hair and makeup folk to do the best they could.

When she turned eighteen, Kitty got the first of many nose jobs—a battle zone that would forever remain a work in progress.

"With my new appearance, my collection of fraternity pins jumped by leaps and bounds," Kay later boasted. "I've got more than fifty tucked away at home." It also helped her land a part-time singing job with a band, earning a whopping $125 per week. She ran home and reported the news to her stunned father.

"I won't need my allowance anymore," Kitty proudly announced.

"What?" Leo said, shocked by her good fortune. "They pay you for making those noises that drove us crazy? Something is wrong somewhere." In spite of her father's hurtful cynicism, Kitty had become a campus celebrity.

In June 1929, her sister Blanche graduated from Washington University with flying colors, but Kitty's sophomore year made a crash landing. After she'd skipped three-quarters of her classes, there was no way Kitty could pass. When she sat down to take her Greek exam, the only thing she knew were her sorority letters. After several minutes of painful squirming, she decided to write the teacher a note, in plain English: "Dear Mr. Durfy, I am very sorry I will not be able to answer these questions today. Mother has been ill and I haven't been able to concentrate. This is no reflection upon your teaching. Sincerely Yours, Catherine Fink."

Concerned, Mr. Durfy contacted Kitty's parents, and soon discovered that Mrs. Fink was in perfect health. Leo grounded his daughter, canceled her annual trip to Minne-Wonka, and ordered her to take Greek lessons all summer for a reexamination in September, which, by the skin of her teeth, she managed to pass. "My days as a Greek student, though, were over," Kay later expressed with no regrets.

Unfortunately, Kitty had to repeat most of the other courses from her sophomore year. So, in the fall of 1929, she was back for a third year at Washington University as a half-baked sophomore while Ginny and her other contemporaries were already juniors. Unfazed, Kitty kept her sights set on the stage, volunteering to produce the annual *Co-Ed Vodvil* show. Delegation was not her strongest suit; after appointing herself director, writer, composer, choreographer, chorus leader, pianist, and stage manager, she had no time to appear in her own show. That unintended deprivation would be rectified when she landed the female lead in *Ten Nights in a Bar-Room*, the melodramatic story of a self-destructive alcoholic.

"Oh, at seventeen," Kay reminisced, "I decided I was going to be another Sarah Bernhardt."

That ambition, however, was not embraced by her peers. The school yearbook, appropriately named *The Hatchet*, sliced and diced the production in its review and, even worse, ran an unflattering photograph of Kitty with a severe expression and a hideous black wig.

Undaunted, she appeared in another production that same school year, *Si, Si, Señorita*, the story of a Mexican ghost rider and his schemes to scare off gullible American tourists. She also served as assistant musical director and was the lead singer of the Trio, alongside Harriet Ingalls and Louise LaRue. The yearbook review stated, "From the overture to the final curtain the whole concoction was grade A sour goat milk. The chorus wasn't bad in its dances but *ouch!* when they sing."

On October 29, 1929, eleven days before Kitty's twentieth birthday, Wall Street hit rock bottom. It was Black Tuesday, the inauguration of the Great Depression.

As the Fink family's income plummeted, Kitty figured out a way to twist the dilemma to her advantage. She was more than happy to drop out of school in the spring of 1930 in order to go to work. Even though Leo disapproved of career women, he did not have the financial luxury to stand on ceremony. Completely out of character, he casually suggested, "I thought it would be nice if one of you girls would sing on the *Capitol Family* program someday—ballads, you know." Broadcast from New York, *Major Bowes' Capitol Family* was a nationally heard amateur hour that provided early exposure for such rising stars as Frank Sinatra, Bob Hope, and a seven-year-old Beverly Sills.

Overjoyed by her father's seeming enlightenment, Kitty announced, "I'll sing . . . but not ballads. Right now I'm going to get myself a radio job as a blues singer."

Although the genre is today considered mainstream, back then blues was still ghettoized as "Negro music"—the very last thing Leo had in mind for his daughter. But her mind was made up. "Blues singers have done for the radio what the self-starter did for the automobile," she declared.

In the spring of 1930, Kitty began singing on KWK, but her insistence on blues numbers did not go over well with station management or listeners. Frustrated, she decided to resurrect her singing group, the Trio, with her sorority sisters Harriet Ingalls and Doris Shumate (replacing Louise LaRue). A few local gigs came their way, but once the money was split three ways, it hardly seemed worth the effort. Times were getting tougher by the day and Kitty needed to get a real job.

After sending a bunch of applications to every summer camp advertised in the classified section of her favorite magazine, *Harper's Bazaar*, Kitty lined up a job as a counselor at Toyon Summer Camp, a ritzy girls' enclave on Catalina Island within eyeshot of Los Angeles. In addition, she wangled the hiring of her singing partners, Harriet and Doris, so the Trio went west for the summer of 1930. Earning $175 for the season, Kitty proved to be a skilled swimming, diving, and sailing instructor, and she led the campfire songs.

"Finky was one of the favorite counselors," recalled celebrity biographer Cynthia Lindsay at the age of eighty-eight in 2003, identifying Kitty by the nickname for which she was known at Toyon. "She was funny, friendly and darling. We all absolutely adored her." In 1957, Cynthia wrote a profile of Kay Thompson for *McCall's* magazine.

"Finky wanted things done *her* way," Cynthia observed, "and they were done her way or else there was a lot of trouble. But she was the best disciplinarian I have ever known—never mean, never without humor. To reprimand campers, she would break into the voice of a little girl and say things like, 'You better do what I say or you'll have to answer to me, Eloise."

The official story has always been that Eloise extemporaneously came into being in 1947 when Kay was late for a rehearsal with the Williams Brothers. Asked why she was tardy, Kay had supposedly improvised in the high-pitched voice of a little girl, "I am Eloise and I am six." Debunking that mythology, however, Cynthia testified she'd heard the prehistoric voice of Eloise ages before the sanctioned chronology.

When the summer was over, Kitty found herself longing to be at school again, missing the social outlet campus life provided. Hardship or not, her father was thrilled to have Kitty resume her studies—as if that were her true intention.

"I did have one ambition unfulfilled," Kay later explained. "I didn't have a Phi Beta Kappa to my credit. I managed to get back into school again and set about getting one. In the process I developed my first real 'crush'—on an assistant instructor. He was terribly attractive and the Phi Beta Kappa key on his watch chain was like a piece of hamburger in front of a kennel. Our first date was a terrific success. He quoted Shelley and Swinburne and I thought I'd found romance for sure. We drove into the country, and under a full moon he stroked my cheek. He whispered, 'Your skin is as smooth as velvet,' which was hot stuff for St. Louis in those days!"

However, when Kitty discovered that he'd said the exact same thing to her sister Marian, she saw red.

"So the next day, when he called up," Kay explained, "Marian got on the upstairs extension and I got on the downstairs phone. 'Oh, darling, your skin is as smooth as velvet!' we both shouted at the top of our lungs. He hung up—and that was the last we ever heard of him."

Once she'd gotten her fill of fraternity pins, Kitty set her sights on another sort of prey. She got herself all dolled up and marched over to the Mayfair Hotel in downtown St. Louis, where, on the second floor, she found the headquarters of KMOX, the top radio station in the city. Without an appointment, Kitty demanded to see George Junkin, the managing director and announcer, adding haughtily, "and I haven't much time to give him."

The bluff got her ushered right into his office because everyone assumed Junkin already knew her—including Junkin himself.

"All you have to do is to keep 'em guessing and you've got 'em!" Kay later remarked. "That goes for men—and everything." It was a mantra she lived by.

Once she was inside Junkin's office, it became clear what was up. Intrigued, he gave her the once-over and said, "So you think you can sing."

"I *know* I can sing," Kitty replied.

"Go ahead." Junkin waved his hand, granting her an impromptu audition. With a bluesy style, she sang Hoagy Carmichael's "Rockin' Chair" a cappella. Moved, Junkin pondered, "You sound a little like Libby Holman." Deciding the time was right for a St. Louis knockoff of "the first great white torch singer," Junkin said, "All right, we'll take you on at twenty-five dollars a week."

"That's not enough," she said. "Look how much Libby gets and you said I sound just like her."

"Keep still or I'll make it twenty dollars," Junkin countered, flabbergasted by her chutzpa.

"Go ahead," Kitty shot back. "I'll be making more than you will, someday."

By all rights, he should have kicked her sassy ass right out the door, but cooler heads prevailed. After caving to his "insulting" offer, Kitty joined the ensemble of *The Anheuser-Busch Antics,* a hit variety show for CBS, the first national radio series broadcast from St. Louis, sponsored by the local

Anheuser-Busch brewery. (During this time of Prohibition, Anheuser-Busch had switched from beer to producing ginger ale, yeast, and sarsaparilla.)

On Kitty's debut show, she began by singing "Rockin' Chair." Unfortunately, the height of her microphone had been adjusted for a much taller person and so, while teetering on tiptoe, she fumbled with the screws on the stand, trying to lower the darn thing to her level.

Suddenly, the delicate crystal microphone toppled off its perch and crashed to the floor, exploding into a million tiny particles. While conductor Ben Feld kept the band playing, Kitty charged over to host Tony Cabooch's podium, commandeered his mike, and finished the song.

As soon as the show went off the air, Junkin bellowed, "That mike cost us three hundred dollars! How did you ever dare touch it? You'll have to pay for it."

"Pay you three hundred dollars?" Kitty scoffed. "You can't draw blood from a turnip." Nevertheless, her pay was docked for the next three months.

Other than her grumpy boss, Kitty was well liked by her colleagues, especially Ted Straeter, a pianist four years her junior. His first association with the Fink family came at the age of eight when he passed by the window of L. G. Fink, Inc., and a secondhand Victrola caught his eye. Like a dog in heat, he sold Christmas cards door-to-door until he had earned enough money to buy the record player. In his teens, he worked as a pianist and bandleader at KMOX, where he accompanied Kitty on countless occasions. (Years later, when they both had migrated to New York, Kay would help Ted land jobs as the choral director for *The Kate Smith Show* and as the house conductor for the Persian Room at The Plaza.)

In late 1930, not long after Kitty's twenty-first birthday, KMOX added her to the cast of *The Phillips 66 Flyers* variety series, sponsored by Phillips Petroleum, and broadcast Monday through Saturday at 6:00 p.m. One hot Saturday afternoon in the spring of 1931, Kitty and one of her many fraternity escorts—this one named Jimmie—were at a big party at Creve Coeur Lake, northeast of St. Louis at the end of the electric trolley-car line. Caught up in the fun, Kitty lost all track of time until Jimmie happened to point out the beautiful sunset. Glancing at her watch, Kitty realized *The Phillips 66 Flyers* was due to go on the air in only *ten minutes!*

"We made forty miles in thirty minutes, doing 80 an hour," Kay remembered vividly. "Sure we got there late, but the broadcast was still on."

Realizing she had not rehearsed the song the band had prepared for her, she scribbled a note and passed it to the conductor, Mike Child: "Play 'Some of These Days' in G Minor."

"He just glared at me," Kay said, shuddering at the memory. Mike winged the number well enough, but her performance was dreadful. Not only was Junkin fit to be tied, so, too, was the president of Phillips, who shot off a telegram: KEEP THE BAND BUT DISMISS VOCALIST. On Sunday, Kitty got eighty-sixed.

"I was young and foolish," Kay later admitted. As long as Mr. Junkin was the managing director at KMOX, Kitty would remain persona non grata. With bridges smoldering at the only St. Louis radio station that really mattered, she was left with no choice but to focus on other endeavors.

Kitty's 1930–31 school year at Washington University was spent mainly in the drama department, where she performed in *Princess Nita*, a musical comedy about a young royal in ancient Egypt, with such intriguing song titles as "Sahara Sarah" and "Jazz Rhythm Strut." She also served as assistant music director under Edmund L. Hartmann, the show's librettist, lyricist, and composer, who later went to Hollywood, where he wrote and/or produced nearly fifty movies, including two Sherlock Holmes adventures starring Basil Rathbone, five Abbott and Costello vehicles, and seven Bob Hope comedies.

When the academic semester ended in June 1931, Kitty decided to quit school for good. Having accumulated barely enough credits to qualify her as a junior, she never came close to graduating.

Fed up with St. Louis and her stifling father, twenty-one-year-old Kitty announced her intention to head for Hollywood. Leo refused to finance her trip, but that would not stop her from going. Toyon, the girls' camp on Catalina Island, wanted her back for the summer, offering to increase her pay to $250 for the season. Kitty could not have packed her bags faster.

*U*pon arriving in California, Kitty used every second of her free time to pound the pavement in Hollywood. In July 1931, she stormed the headquarters of KFI (part of the NBC Pacific Coast Network), one of the top radio stations in Los Angeles—owned by Earle C. Anthony, who also happened to be "the largest Packard automobile dealer in California." She bamboozled a meeting with the station's thirty-three-year-old programming director, Glenn Dolberg, and to her surprise and delight, he agreed to give her a shot on an amateur talent show. But he made it clear that to get a regular slot on the schedule, she would have to impress his mother, who always listened to the show at home. Kitty thought this was a peculiar stipulation, but who was she to argue? She sang her heart out on the program and apparently made a good impression on Mama Dolberg, because her son offered Kitty a job as a staff singer—to start in eight weeks, as soon as her summer camp commitment was done.

Finally, things were looking up, so she rented a $75 flat in La Marquise (later a residence of Errol Flynn), a brand-new apartment building on Gramercy Place, just northwest of the Wiltern—the highly anticipated Art Deco theater at the intersection of Western and Wilshire that would open in October.

With her luxury address all set, Kitty got another nose job, had her teeth capped, bought fancy cosmetics, and acquired a new wardrobe. Brimming with confidence, she reported to Dolberg's office at KFI on the prearranged date in early September, only to find that things were not quite what they seemed.

The mama's boy had come down with a serious case of bad memory, claiming he had never met Kitty and that he was unaware of any job promise. Dazed and confused, Kitty was politely ushered to the sidewalk. With wobbly legs, she made it back to the new apartment she could no longer afford, wondering if she had stepped into some sort of alternate universe.

Later reconnaissance revealed the raison d'être for Dolberg's sudden amnesia. During a routine background check, Dolberg had called George Junkin, the KMOX station manager in St. Louis, and gotten an earful about the notorious Miss Kitty Fink. Consequently, she was blacklisted at KFI.

Realizing that her sullied reputation had followed her all the way to California, Kitty decided that now would be a very good time to assume a new name. And so, henceforth, she called herself Kay Thompson (although the stage name was not made legal until fourteen years later on September 25, 1945). "Kay" came from the pronunciation of the letter *K*, the first letter of Kitty. No one knows where she came up with "Thompson," but it certainly suggested Waspier breeding. Together, "Kay Thompson" rolled off the tongue emphatically, with an authoritative, staccato beat. In addition to providing a clean break from her checkered past, the new identity would forever erase her Jewish surname. Tellingly, she never again mentioned it to the press. As far as she was concerned, Kitty Fink was dead and buried.

Even though Leo Fink had spent a lifetime rejecting his own heritage, he was deeply offended by his daughter's repudiation of his family name. His reaction to the KFI debacle was summarily unsympathetic: an "I told you so" followed by a command that she return to St. Louis at once. Kay did not want to crawl back home with her tail between her legs, but she was down to her last dime.

Her confidence reached an all-time low. "I was a singer, [but] I wasn't a good one of them," Kay told her old Camp Toyon chum Cynthia Lindsay for her 1957 article in *McCall's*. "It took a close friend, a black Irishman he was, to wise me up to what I did have—musicianship. 'Kiddo,' he said, 'you have creative talent obviously, so if you're not getting it across there's something wrong.

There's a reason.' As soon as he spoke the whole thing unfolded and I knew the reason. I was doing the wrong thing."

Up until then, Kay had been copying other singers. What she lacked was a style of her own. At the same time she was changing everything on the outside, it clicked in her brain that she had to reinvent herself from the inside, too.

Providence also intervened. "At a party, I met the daughter of the President of Union Gas Company," Kay explained in *Radio Stars*, referring to oil baron L. P. St. Clair. Not letting on that she was all but destitute, Thompson "kidded around, and sang and played for the guests, as though she were on top of the world."

One of those guests was Don Forker, a thirty-seven-year-old Iowan go-getter who created radio shows sponsored by the Union Oil Company of California (makers of Union Gas and 76 Gasoline), for which he served as manager of advertising and publicity. Forker was impressed with Kay and decided on the spot that she would be just the talent to revitalize their flagship radio program.

"I got the job," Thompson recalled, "singing for the Union Gas Company on the air, at ninety dollars a week."

With an orchestra conducted by Gus Arnheim, Kay would sing, play piano, and arrange songs on *The Kay Thompson–Union Gas Show*, broadcast from KTM, the local Santa Monica station. The miraculous timing saved her from financial ruin and her father's wrath.

She obviously made a good impression on Arnheim, too, because he invited her to perform with his red-hot, fourteen-piece dance band, appearing nightly at the Cocoanut Grove, the mythic ballroom in the Ambassador Hotel—coincidentally within easy walking distance of her apartment.

Not only was Kay suddenly performing in front of the rich and famous, but Mondays through Fridays, from ten o'clock to midnight, her singing was broadcast live over the radio. The remote was heard throughout the West over the Warner Brothers station, KFWB, and the program had already gained considerable fame as the place to hear tomorrow's stars, like the young Bing Crosby, member of the Rhythm Boys trio with Al Rinker and Harry Barris.

In November 1931, Arnheim left to go on tour, leaving his arranger, Jimmie Grier, to wave the baton. Without missing a beat, Kay continued having a grand ole time, delighting Cocoanut Grove patrons as well as KFWB radio listeners, until it was announced that the broadcasts of *Jimmie Grier's Cocoanut Grove Orchestra* would switch to, of all the rotten luck, KFI. When Glenn Dolberg discovered that Kay Thompson was really just Kitty Fink in sheep's clothing, he barred her from appearing on the show.

• • • •

Humiliated, Thompson decided to skip town and spend the Christmas holidays with her family in Missouri. "When one door closes, another one always opens," Kay told her California chums as she waved good-bye at the train station. And she was right. Upon arriving in St. Louis, she was greeted with the news that her hometown nemesis, George Junkin, had just quit KMOX. Not only that, but starting January 1, 1932, the station was moving to brand-new headquarters in the St. Louis Mart Building, featuring five state-of-the-art broadcasting studios.

With its increased capabilities, KMOX was looking to launch a number of new shows that its parent company, CBS, might pick up for national broadcast—reaching a sizable percentage of the nearly 17 million homes then equipped with radios. With her two sisters, Kay immediately formed a new vocal trio called the Debutantes. In no time flat, the girls were headlining their own radio show two nights a week. "The Debutantes, a regular feature of KMOX, are one of the most popular girl trios in the Middle West," read a promotional brochure. "The trio features modern renditions of the latest popular tunes in a unique style of presentation."

Just when things were settling in, however, Kay got word from Los Angeles that, "having established herself in the hearts of followers," she was being sought to host *Brighten-Up with Kay Thompson*, a new morning show being mounted by, to her great surprise, KFI. Kay thought it was a cruel joke until it was explained that Glenn Dolberg had been persuaded to give her a second chance. She soon discovered, however, that his about-face had, in fact, been motivated by the almighty dollar. It turned out that the sponsor for the series would be Union Oil, thanks to that company's marketing whiz Don Forker, Kay's most ardent supporter. Forker's vote of confidence—and the vast riches he brought to the table—trumped Dolberg's concerns about Thompson's murky past.

And so, when her thirteen-week commitment to *The Debutantes* series on KMOX in St. Louis ended on April 8, 1932, Kay replaced herself with Louise LaRue (formerly of the Trio) and raced back to California, where she signed a thirteen-week contract for *Brighten-Up* on KFI. From April 18 to July 15, the half-hour wake-up call was broadcast Monday, Wednesday, and Friday mornings from the Cocoanut Grove, featuring Kay's singing and piano playing (sandwiched between histrionic news updates on the Lindbergh kidnapping). A press release, written by Don Forker and issued by the Union Oil Publicity Department, noted that Kay's "blue" singing style was "devoid of the moan affected by so many other blue singers." Kay was accompanied by the backup vocals of seventeen-year-old Jack Smith (later host of ABC-TV's *You Asked for It*), Martin Sperzel, and Johnny Smedburg, better known as the Three Ambassadors—the first of many male backup groups Thompson would utilize.

On August 30, Kay joined the cast of *KFI's Fun Factory*, a nighttime sketch comedy series that mined her comic abilities. The very next night, however, she committed something akin to treason by appearing on rival station KHJ, the local CBS affiliate. Though, contractually speaking, she was nonexclusive to KFI and free to moonlight elsewhere, Dolberg took it as a personal affront.

Nevertheless, Kay accepted an offer to be the featured singer and piano soloist for Tom Coakley and His Orchestra during their three-month gig in the Blossom Room overlooking the roof patio at the Roosevelt Hotel in Hollywood. On September 9, 1932, KHJ broadcast a live special from the Roosevelt featuring Coakley and company to coincide with one of the biggest social events of the year: the Gala World Premiere of *Rain* (United Artists, 1932) at Grauman's Chinese Theatre. All the stars and klieg lights in Hollywood were shining for the highly anticipated Joan Crawford vehicle, with much of that glitter and excitement spilling right across the street into the Roosevelt, where the after-party was taking place. This gave Thompson and Coakley a captive audience of A-list celebrities. After that enchanted evening, their stock rose dramatically. So, beginning Monday, September 26, the orchestra "featuring Kay Thompson" was broadcast over KHJ six nights a week through the end of Coakley's engagement on October 25.

Kay could not help but notice Coakley's handsome eighteen-year-old saxophone player and vocalist, an affable fellow by the name of Alvin Morris, who, in 1936, would change his name to Tony Martin and become a big-time singer and movie star. Kay alternately called him "Mr. Suede" (because he always wore it), or simply "Mr. M.," nicknames she was still using on the air in 1939 when she and Tony co-headlined the series *Tune-Up Time* (CBS Radio).

Kay quickly became known for her startling vocal arrangements. She loved to take a song, do the first verse straight, then reinvent it, changing the tempo, adding lyrics, and improvising improbable flourishes that spiraled into the wild blue yonder. Her groundbreaking swing arrangements oozed Thompsonian gusto at every fast-and-furious turn. Not everyone appreciated her tampering, however. To the ears of übercolumnist Walter Winchell, she crossed the line by reinventing Hoagy Carmichael's "Stardust." Appalled that Kay had "messed around with it on the air," Winchell chastised her for being "sacrilegious." Winchell did not forgive and forget, either. In 1937, he declared, "Kay Thompson simply spoils lovely hits by re-writing them."

The Winchell-Thompson controversy fueled an onslaught of cover versions of "Stardust" from just about every band and vocalist on the map. In his autobiography, Carmichael credits Winchell for turning "Stardust" into the standard it is today, though it was Thompson's "desecration" that got the fire started.

During the fall of 1932, three young male singers caught Thompson's eyes and ears. They were eighteen-year-old Hal Hopper, a tenor from Oklahoma City (later the father of actor Jay North of *Dennis the Menace* fame), eighteen-year-old Woody Newbury, a tenor from Dallas, Texas, and seventeen-year-old Chuck Lowry, a baritone from Los Angeles. They called themselves the Three Rhythm Kings, inspired by Bing Crosby's recently defunct trio, the Rhythm Boys. Kay took them under her wing and helped them create special arrangements to showcase their three-part harmonizing. Kay adopted the Three Rhythm Kings as her new backup singers, succeeding the Three Ambassadors.

Building on the group's exposure with Coakley's orchestra, Warner Brothers' radio station, KFWB, launched a new series called *Kay Thompson and the Three Rhythm Kings* on Sunday night, October 2, 1932. Amazingly, with concurrent radio shows broadcasting over KFI, KHJ, and now KFWB, Kay had managed to become the belle of West Coast radio.

As Kay turned twenty-three that November of 1932, Franklin D. Roosevelt was elected president, to serve the first of four terms, a regime that would lead the nation out of the Great Depression and into the Second World War.

Kay had been so busy in California, she hadn't made it back to St. Louis since April. The Finks were laying the pressure on thick for her to come home for Thanksgiving, but Kay replied that she was too busy to get away. Then, in mid-November, just minutes before one of her radio shows, Kay received a telegram from her mother: FATHER TERRIBLY ILL COME HOME AT ONCE.

"I stayed for the whole broadcast," Kay recalled. "I couldn't walk out on them." As soon as it was over, she boarded the next train to St. Louis only to find that the seriousness of her father's condition had been greatly exaggerated. Leo had been diagnosed with a heart condition known as angina pectoris, but he clearly was not on his deathbed. The panic had been a ruse—a rather sadistic one—to get Kay home for the holidays.

While Kay had been away, her St. Louis–based trio, the Debutantes, had morphed into Three Best Girls, featuring Blanche Fink, Louise LaRue, and Georgia Erwin, regularly featured on *KMOX County Fair* with pianist Ted Straeter. Marian Fink, who did not have as strong a passion for showbiz as her sisters, had decided to leave the group but would occasionally fill in when needed. Kay was happy to see them and enjoyed getting caught up on all the local gossip.

Jimmie, the young man who had partied with Kay the day she got canned from KMOX, asked her out on a Saturday night date to the Beaux Arts Room, a fancy dinner/dance club at the Coronado Hotel in downtown St. Louis. After the first course, he proposed.

"I don't want to get married," Kay responded. "My place is at a microphone in front of an orchestra like that one. Now, be a good boy and wangle me an introduction to that bandleader." The puppy dog obeyed and, a short time later, Jimmie formally introduced conductor Al Lyons to his non-fiancée, "Kitty Fink."

Winking at Jimmie to keep his mouth shut, Kay took over the conversation: "I have a friend who was a sensation at the Cocoanut Grove and she'd love to sing with your band." With devil horns practically growing out of her head, Kay added that her "friend" was a West Coast singer named Kay Thompson, in town for the holidays.

Mesmerized by two magic words—"Cocoanut Grove"—Lyons said, "Send her around to the Fox Theatre tomorrow for an audition."

The next day, when Kay came sauntering down the aisle at the Fox, Al asked where the Cocoanut Grove vocalist, Kay Thompson, was.

"Here I am," she said with a smirk, sashaying over to the piano. "I'm the girl."

The hoax went over better than the audition itself. Suddenly, Kay was stricken with stage fright. Her voice cracked through the first eight bars of "Underneath the Harlem Moon."

Thinking fast, she exaggerated the deterioration in her voice, whispering pathetically, "I've got laryngitis. But I'm really very good."

"I'll never forget it! It was horrible!" Kay later recalled. "But he said to return to work, to my astonishment."

Pulling herself together, Kay performed with Lyons regularly at the Fox Theatre, the Coronado Hotel, and the Meadowbrook Country Club, plus two nights a week on KMOX.

Around Christmas, however, after she'd been back home only a month, fate dealt Kay a card that took her right back to Hollywood for her biggest break yet.

Chapter Two

A FACE FOR RADIO

Thompson on the Air
(1933–37)

To us, she was the Statue of Liberty.

—*Bea Wain, of Kay Thompson's Rhythm Singers*

"*N*ext came a wire from Los Angeles," Kay told a reporter, "asking me to sign up with Columbia." Offered an eye-popping $200 per week, Kay was being recruited by Don Lee's KHJ radio station, the Los Angeles affiliate of the Columbia Broadcasting System (CBS). "A horseshoe must have appeared over my head!" Kay recalled. "My lucky day had come! So, away I swished myself."

Kay settled back into her La Marquise apartment in Los Angeles—just three miles from her new place of employment in the eight-story Don Lee Building at 1076 West Seventh Street (at the corner of Bixel). A Cadillac dealership, also owned by Lee, took up the ground floor, with KHJ occupying several of the floors above.

Wasting no time, Lee placed her on a new program, *The Merrymakers Hour*, which premiered on January 1, 1933. It should come as no surprise that the sponsor was the Union Oil Company, arranged by marketing manager Don

Forker, whose undying loyalty to Kay was surely a factor in Lee's decision to hire her in the first place.

The show's ensemble of comic performers was led by Sterling Holloway, twenty-eight, a redheaded Georgian with a raspy falsetto who would later supply the voice of Walt Disney's Winnie the Pooh. Though Sterling was a gay man, he and Kay had columnists thinking they were a couple. For instance, after the April 7 congressional vote to end Prohibition, the *Los Angeles Evening Herald and Express* reported that Kay and Sterling were the first to raise their mugs at the Cocoanut Grove on the night beer started flowing once again.

Thompson and Holloway were not the only diamonds in the rough at KHJ. "The first show on which I worked was *The Merrymakers*," noted Sylvester "Pat" Weaver, the future president of NBC-TV (and future father of actress Sigourney Weaver). Although officially hired as a comedy writer, Pat was a jack of all trades. "I was allowed to write, direct, announce, and sometimes even act in programs, many of which I conceived and developed."

Because Pat reminded her of a bird, Kay affectionately nicknamed him "Weaver Feathers"—a moniker she used for decades to come.

A few weeks after *Merrymakers* got under way, Kay was added to *Laff Clinic* and *The Happy-Go-Lucky Hour,* the latter of which paired her with thirty-one-year-old vaudeville performer Frank Jenks. With his shock of wavy red hair slicked back tight on his head, Frank had an infectious Irish grin and a salty delivery that delighted audiences. From the moment Kay and Frank shared a microphone, hilarity ensued, and so, starting March 6, they were given their own song-and-comedy series, *Thompson and Jenks.*

Kay also joined *California Melodies,* the most popular of KHJ's broadcasts because, each week, the show featured big-name Hollywood guest stars such as Jean Harlow, Boris Karloff, Claudette Colbert, Edward G. Robinson, Mae West, and Dick Powell, who became Kay's lifelong friend. Unlike some of her starstruck colleagues, Thompson impressed celebrities with her blasé ease and charm. Throughout her life, Kay would be most comfortable mingling with the glitterati—even though she was often the least famous among them.

Thompson was accompanied on all five of these series by KHJ's thirty-two-piece orchestra conducted by Raymond Paige, who encouraged her to create unique vocal arrangements that he would then orchestrate. "Paige was already well known," recalled Pat Weaver, "though not as famous as he would become in New York as the Radio City Music Hall conductor. He fit perfectly into our jocular style at KHJ."

• • •

Touting its new starlet, KHJ got the *Los Angeles Times* to run a headshot of Thompson on March 11, 1933—the first time her photograph appeared in a major publication. It caught the eye of Leonard Sillman, who asked her to join his first "New Faces" stage revue, *Low and Behold!* at the Pasadena Community Playhouse, scheduled for a one-week limited engagement starting May 16.

Bound by her exclusive contract with KHJ, Kay had to get special permission from Don Lee to do the show. In exchange for agreeing to work around her performance schedule, the station would collect 20 percent of her outside earnings. She was already giving up 10 percent of her income to an agent the station had forced on her, Thomas Lee, son of her boss. The conflict of interest was astounding.

But for Kay, doing *Low and Behold!* was not about the money. She hoped the exposure would lead to movies and/or Broadway.

The cast of *Low and Behold!* would include such unknowns as Eve Arden (then billed as Eunice Quedens), Teddy Hart (brother of lyricist Lorenz Hart), Charles Walters (who later became a top choreographer and director at MGM), Lois January (who later appeared in *The Wizard of Oz*), and, last but not least, Leonard Sillman's hunky nineteen-year-old chauffeur, Tyrone Power.

On March 13, three days after the devastating Long Beach earthquake, rehearsals got off to a shaky start at a dance studio on Highland Avenue in Hollywood. "A lot of professional gnashing" was how Lois January described the rehearsals. "Fighting and feuding and 'we don't like this and that'—I was so unhappy with it. Kay, on the other hand, was a delight. She brought stability to the mishmash. She kept it together. She was always fun and games, you know? A very talented, very bright person. So, I just took to her right away. I listened to her more than anyone."

While *King Kong* was premiering in Hollywood, *Low and Behold!* was Pasadena's behemoth run amok. Ascribing to the "bigger is better" philosophy, the final dress rehearsal contained a staggering seventy-five numbers exhaustively performed in two hundred costumes from 8:30 p.m. to 2:00 a.m. By opening night, an hour and a half had been mercifully amputated, reducing its girth to merely mammoth proportions.

"There are enough clever ideas to furnish three revues," wrote W. E. Oliver in the *Los Angeles Evening Herald and Express.* "What *Low and Behold* needs to give it a professional fillip is a doctor not afraid to use the scalpel."

Thompson had some choice bits in the show. During scene changes, Kay, June Shafer, and Dorothy Dee, billed as the Low and Behold Trio, would roll out a cocktail cart in front of the curtains and mix highballs for themselves while singing three-part harmonies. With each new appearance, however, they progressively became more and more sloshed until finally they could barely stand. "It was a very funny routine," Sillman recalled, "but Miss Thompson had to sacrifice her artistry for a laugh. That she did, and bless her."

More daring was "Piano in the Parlor," in which a somber Tyrone Power quietly stood next to Kay at an elegant grand piano, turning the pages of her sheet music as she played a concerto. Attracted to this strapping young man, Kay begins to flirt. At first, her advances are subtle, but when he shows no interest, she becomes increasingly more determined. Tyrone breaks his concentration only when he catches sight of a sexy chorus boy crossing the stage, at which point he becomes so flustered, he misses his cue to turn the page.

For 1933, *Low and Behold!* had a surprisingly progressive queer eye, unabashedly cultivated by its flamboyant creator, Leonard Sillman, who perhaps had never been asked if he was a homosexual simply because everyone already knew the answer. His in-your-face bravado was evident in the homocentric casting of Larry Armstrong, a three-hundred-pound drag queen, and the Rocky Twins, the notorious gay courtesans from Europe who were among the trailblazers of the Pansy Craze of the early 1930s—and, according to historians Samuel Marx and Jan Clayton, were "rumored to have been protégés of Adolf Hitler."

Kay had been exposed to plenty of discreet gay men and women in the arts, but never before had she witnessed a group of people who were so open about it. Each night, after wholesome spaghetti dinners cooked for the cast and crew by Sillman's mother, the more adventuresome members of the troupe would migrate to the Rocky Twins' rented Beverly Hills mansion, where moderation and clothes were checked at the door.

As word spread among Hollywood's bohemian elite, *Low and Behold!* suddenly became the hottest ticket in town. With the likes of Joan Crawford, Charlie Chaplin, and Barbara Stanwyck clamoring for seats, the revue had to be extended from one to three sold-out weeks, until a logjam of incoming shows forced its closure on June 3.

When Sillman made arrangements to remount the show in July at the Music Box in Hollywood, however, everybody wanted a raise.

"I had the unions to contend with in one corner of hell," Sillman recalled, "the actors in another, and a select band of lunatics in the men's lounge, the balcony and the boxoffice. We had come down from Pasadena in orderly fashion with our little flags flying, [but] as soon as we hit Hollywood our rehearsals looked like something Max Reinhardt might have done with *The Inferno*. Kay Thompson came to me one afternoon and announced that she was a properly brought-up young lady and couldn't stand all the obscene talk going on in the theatre."

As an ultimatum, Thompson warned, "If people don't stop saying 'hell' and 'God damn,' I'll have to quit."

So, when Sillman responded, "What the hell has gotten into you?" it was the last straw.

Kay wasn't the only one fed up. "Very few people in that show stayed," recalled Lois January, herself included. "I'd had too much of Leonard." But Thompson must have wondered if she'd made the right decision when the show was moved successfully to Broadway as *New Faces of 1934*, where it launched the careers of Henry Fonda and Imogene Coca.

Settling back into her routine at KHJ, Kay was awarded her own series, *The Kay Thompson Show*, and was assigned to join three others as well: *The Late Night Concert*, *Fun Frolic*, and *The 76 Gasoline All-Star Revue*. The last was sponsored by Union Oil—courtesy of Don Forker yet again.

According to Pat Weaver, Forker became Thompson's "boyfriend." But it was complicated. First of all, there was the age difference; Don was forty and Kay was only twenty-three—an even wider gap than the fourteen years that separated her parents. Then there was the minor detail that he was married—though that inconvenience quickly evaporated when his wife filed for divorce. The next thing Kay knew, Don asked her to marry him.

"That was the first time I ever was tempted to take the plunge into matrimony," Kay confided to a reporter for *Radio Stars*. "He was quite a bit older than I and if he'd been—well, a little more impetuous, it would have happened. But he wanted me to give up my career—which really hadn't started yet, anyhow. He was a brilliant man and I admired him immensely. But I was doing a lot of radio work on the coast, and I was sure I'd found my groove. I certainly didn't want to quit."

Kay had witnessed how her own father had stifled her mother's musical aspirations, and she was not about to let the same thing happen to her. Despite their differences, Thompson's relationship with Forker was far from over. But for now, the only serious love in Kay's life was Mr. Chips, her new black thoroughbred Scottish terrier, who, she proudly boasted, had "won a prize at a dog show." She absolutely adored the pooch and took him with her wherever canines were allowed—as well as many places they weren't.

Beginning August 29, 1933, Kay and Frank Jenks headlined five daily stage shows, seven days a week, at the Paramount Theater in downtown Los Angeles, produced by the leading vaudeville booking organization, Fanchon and Marco. The *Los Angeles Times* called it "an unusually good stage revue." After each live show, the silver screen would be lowered and on it projected a newsreel short subject, a cartoon, coming attraction previews, a featurette of the Mills Brothers performing a song, the sixth chapter of the *Tarzan the Fearless* serial starring Buster Crabbe, and, finally, the feature presentation *One Sunday Afternoon*, starring Gary Cooper and Fay Wray—all for only twenty-five cents.

Incredibly, while the movie unspooled, Kay was required to race eight blocks to the KHJ studio and sing numbers on various radio shows. Then she had to dash back to the Paramount for her next scheduled live performance. If the nerve-racking schedule wasn't enough to drive her batty, the repetition certainly was. By the end of the first week, Kay had performed the exact same revue thirty-five times. On the verge of coming unglued, she decided the vaudeville biz was for the birds. Accepting her resignation, Fanchon and Marco replaced Kay with her former colleagues Leonard Sillman and his sister, June, billed as "Stars of *Low and Behold!*"

In November, the Brunswick record label granted Kay an audition demo recording session for "My Galveston Gal," a chipper ditty with backup barbershop harmonies by the Three Rhythm Kings. The label execs must have liked what they heard, because she was signed to an exclusive two-year deal. But, for reasons hard to fathom, the company chose not to make any records with her right away. At the same time, the pact restricted her from recording for other labels. Feeling like a caged animal, Kay would think twice before ever again signing long-term agreements.

Meanwhile, big things were afoot at KHJ. Bing Crosby, then the most popular voice on radio and the seventh biggest box-office movie star, was hired by Woodbury Soap to host a new CBS series beginning October 16, 1933. In order for Bing to continue his day job at movie studios in Hollywood, the network agreed to base the series at KHJ, where it would be written and directed by staffers Pat Weaver and Jack Van Nostrand.

Practically overnight, *The Bing Crosby–Woodbury Show* became one of the top programs in the country, and to Kay's delight, Bing invited her and the Three Rhythm Kings to be his guests on the November 20 installment. When asked by the *Los Angeles Times* how things went, Thompson said she was most proud of the fact that "Bing tapped his foot" when she sang.

The foot tapping must have been sincere, because Kay and her boys were invited back the following two weeks, and then, "as a result of listeners' response," signed as regulars for a thirteen-week commitment through March 5, 1934—far and away Thompson's most important national exposure to date.

And yet, she didn't have much in the bank to show for it. While Crosby was raking in $1,750 per show (plus additional earnings for movies and records), Kay was limited to her all-inclusive salary of $200 as a KHJ staff artist.

As the popularity of the series grew, Bing rapidly gained an enormous amount of power and, for better or worse, took control of all creative aspects. He also demanded that the station pay him the entire $5,800 weekly budget, from which he would pay all salaries and expenses, then pocket the rest.

Although Crosby had been offered the use of conductor Raymond Paige and the KHJ orchestra, he insisted on hiring his own, cheaper accompanists. The first was Lennie Hayton and his sixteen-piece band. Musically, Lennie and Kay's arranging styles melded perfectly and they became instant friends. Unfortunately, their collaboration was cut short in January 1934 when Lennie was offered more money by NBC in New York to conduct *Town Hall Tonight* starring Fred Allen. Kay was very sad to see him go, but her connection with Lennie was far from over. Not only would they find themselves working together on many future projects, Thompson would help pave the way for Hayton's marriage to Lena Horne.

Lennie's replacement was none other than Gus Arnheim, with whom Bing and Kay had worked (separately) at the Cocoanut Grove. However, the network was unhappy, not only with the change of orchestras but with Crosby's mismanagement and ever-increasing demands. The behind-the-scenes drama got so bad, William S. Paley, chairman of CBS, finally intervened, sending in one of his big guns, Burt McMurtrie, to handle the situation.

Both natives of the state of Washington, Burt and Bing had worked together before Bing was a star. But now the dynamics of their relationship had changed and Crosby was not about to take any orders from his old friend. Unable to tame the lion, McMurtrie did manage to fall head-over-heels in love with Thompson—an unexpected distraction that may have kept him off point.

Redirecting his energies, Burt decided to capitalize on the revved-up national recognition of Kay Thompson and the Three Rhythm Kings by creating a new show for them. *Pontiac Surprise Party,* a CBS network series broadcast from KHJ on Saturday nights, was sponsored by General Motors to the weekly tune of $17,500—triple the budget of *Crosby-Woodbury.*

General Motors was represented by the Batten, Barton, Durstine, and Osborn advertising agency (BBDO), where twenty-seven-year-old William "Bill" Spier was the golden boy of the radio department—revered for his development and direction of *The March of Time* for *Time* magazine (another BBDO client).

For *Pontiac Surprise Party,* Spier negotiated a special tie-in with Walt

Disney, securing exclusive "first radio rights" to original songs from his *Silly Symphonies* cartoon featurettes. On the February 10 premiere broadcast, "The World Owes Me a Living," from the brand-new Disney short *The Grasshopper and the Ants*, was performed by Kay as the Queen Ant and Pinto Colvig as the Grasshopper. Colvig had provided the same voice in the film and went on to be the original voice of Goofy, Pluto, and two of the Seven Dwarfs (Sleepy and Grumpy).

After *Radio Guide* hailed the broadcast performance as "a brilliant novelty," Victor Records cut a disc of the melody with Raymond Paige and his orchestra featuring Colvig and the Three Rhythm Kings—though sadly, because of her exclusive contract with Brunswick Records, Kay was not allowed to voice the Queen. Nevertheless, her vocal arrangement was utilized and, as always, she coached the Rhythm Kings' harmonics.

On subsequent installments, other familiar cartoon voices dropped by to sing with Kay, including Walt Disney as Mickey Mouse and Clarence Nash as Donald Duck.

Although Spier was based in New York, he traveled to California to seal the deal with Disney. It was then that he came face-to-face with Thompson for the first time. From the moment he laid eyes on her, Bill was smitten, but because he had a wife back home in New York and Kay had Burt McMurtrie and Don Forker vying for her affections, the timing just wasn't right. Not yet.

Despite its promise, the ratings for *Pontiac Surprise Party* did not live up to the high-octane expectations of General Motors. Expensive Hollywood guest stars such as W. C. Fields and George Raft were hired for added oomph but the results were negligible, so the series was canceled after the show on March 17.

Just two days later, when Kay and the Rhythm Kings asked for a raise to continue making appearances on *Crosby-Woodbury*, the request was denied and they were dropped from the series "to free up time for more Crosby solos."

In a fit of rage, Kay and her trio went on strike, refusing to appear on any of their other scheduled KHJ shows. The conflict of interest between her agent, Thomas Lee, and his father's radio station had never been more evident, and she went public with her grievances in local newspapers. Late in the day on Friday, March 23, Don Lee caved, demands were met, and the walkout ended.

"Everything is rosy now between KHJ, Kay Thompson and the Three Rhythm Kings," reported the *Los Angeles Times* on March 24. Or at least that was the party line.

"I expected to love Hollywood—but it was awful," Kay later reflected. "I thought it would be gay and interesting, but I found myself hating it." Disillusioned, she was itching for a change of scenery.

In June, Kay received a telegram from Tom Coakley, begging her to come to San Francisco and perform with his orchestra for a two-week gig in the Rose Room at the Palace Hotel. Kay had loved working with Tom and his guys at the Roosevelt in Hollywood back in 1932, and the offer was just the excuse she needed for a getaway.

On June 16, 1934, the *Los Angeles Evening Herald and Express* announced, "Kay Thompson was booked by Thomas Lee to sing with Tom Coakley's organization for two weeks beginning today."

Although KHJ would collect a 20 percent commission on her outside earnings, Don Lee was not going to make life easy for her. "Kay Thompson will be heard nightly at the Palace, except Sunday," explained a report in the *San Francisco Call-Bulletin*. "Over the weekends she'll fly to Los Angeles [to be] on *The Merrymakers* broadcast."

Not only would she have to fly back-and-forth to KHJ in L.A., but Kay was also assigned two series on KFRC, Don Lee's San Francisco station: *The Kay Thompson Show* and *The Blue Monday Jamboree*, both featuring Meredith Willson and his orchestra, and overseen by Pat Weaver (who had just been sent to San Francisco as reinforcement).

What she had hoped would be a San Francisco getaway had turned into a whirlwind of commitments. Of her opening night at the Palace Hotel with Coakley's band, Kay recalled, "I was terrible. *Really* bad." Despite her external exuberance, Thompson had recurring bouts of stage fright. The pattern is easy to trace—her teenage memory loss at her debut with the St. Louis Symphony, her sudden laryngitis attack at the audition with Al Lyons, and so on. Frequently nauseous before performances, she utilized many backstage tricks to calm her anxiety—such as a shot of whiskey or improvising comic conversations as Eloise. Unfortunately, none of those worked when she went onstage with Coakley. The hotel manager was so upset, he told the bandleader to get rid of her.

"You can imagine how I felt," Kay said, shuddering from the memory.

Compassionately, Coakley insisted on giving her another chance, and the second night went well enough to convince the manager to let her stay. Now Kay had something to prove: "It was do or die." Miraculously, she regained her footing and the breezy, self-confident Thompson was back in action.

One night she blithely announced to the audience, "I cannot sing unless I wear a scarf." This was the sort of nonsensical bon mot Kay had perfected over the years as a way to drum up attention—humorous, eccentric, and self-glamorizing, conveyed with an economy of words. When an interviewer later nailed her to explain the predilection, Kay couldn't "tell you why to save her life." But it got plenty of ink.

Less savvy was her decision to sleep with the enemy. Coakley's band was being nationally broadcast daily by NBC via their local affiliate, KECA, the initials of owner Earle C. Anthony, who also owned KFI in Los Angeles and twenty Packard dealerships throughout California. In both radio and automotive sales, Anthony was Don Lee's archrival.

So, it was beyond brazen for Kay to think she could get away with belting her pipes out on NBC, and yet that's exactly what she did. When Lee lodged an objection, he assumed that would be the end of it, but Thompson, stubborn as a mule, kept right on singing, figuring she would solve the problem by using a pseudonym. Her voice had become so recognizable, however, few were fooled.

"Kay Thompson is singing with Tom Coakley's Orchestra under the name Judie Richards," scooped the *San Francisco Call-Bulletin* on June 22. The following day, the *San Francisco Chronicle* insisted that her alias was not Judie Richards at all, but rather "Judy Rich."

Whether her name was Judy Rich, Judie Richards, or Kay Thompson, Kitty Fink's goose was cooked. Don Lee not only fired her, he canned the Three Rhythm Kings as well. Predictably, their agent, Thomas Lee, dropped them as clients.

Finally free to do as she pleased, Kay decided to stay with Coakley's band at the Palace and appear as Kay Thompson on their nightly NBC broadcasts. "There is no thrill that compares with it," Thompson later reminisced. "There's something about having a swell orchestral background designed especially for your own torching which few songbirds can resist."

Her notices were good, too. "When she sings a number," columnist Carroll Nye wrote in the *Los Angeles Times*, "the dancers gather around the band stand to give her a cheer—especially when she's singing 'Here Come the British.'"

"I was jealous of Kay when she did 'Here Come the British,'" said Virginia Haig, another of Coakley's vocalists, "because I thought I should have had that song. Thank God she didn't go with us on tour! She was extremely talented and that's why I was losing it. I was jealous. I could sing, but not like Kay. She was a real star."

All of Coakley's singers and musicians were given free accommodations at the Palace, which naturally led to some late-night shenanigans.

"Kay and one of the guys in the band made goo-goo eyes at each other and fell in love," Haig recalled. "His name was George Kinney. He was from Oakland and he played clarinet and saxophone. Sometimes he sang, too. This affair he had goin' with Kay developed into a pretty hot thing. It was the talk of the band, you know. Everybody was teasing them but Kay and George just laughed it off. They were very sharp with the double entendre. Of course, there was the sex angle, but I think they had a wonderful rapport as far as humor was concerned. They laughed a lot."

"In love?" Kay pondered, responding to gossip about her many romances. "I'm in love all the time! It's fun! It's the salt and pepper of life—and I adore salt and pepper! I want my whole life to be highly seasoned. Oh, I've been in love, all right—but so far, I haven't got beyond the stage of being in love with love."

Victor Records invited Kay to be the featured vocalist on several of Coakley's sessions for the label, but Brunswick would only grant a "loan-out" for Kay to do one side. Recorded on September 25, 1934, "Take a Number from One to Ten" (Victor 24744-A) became Thompson's first record. When it was released the following month, *Variety* called it "a brace of brisk foxtrotology."

While Kay was hanging out with Coakley in 1934, New York–based radio star Jane Froman dropped her manager, Danny Winkler, leaving a vacancy at the Morrison-Winkler Agency for a female singer on the rise. Danny had been keeping close tabs on Kay's career ever since she had shared the KHJ airwaves with his client Lennie Hayton. Now that Kay was no longer represented by Thomas Lee, Danny began actively courting her to sign with Morrison-Winkler and advised her that, if she was really serious about a career in radio, she'd have to move to New York, where the major networks were based. Kay told him she'd consider it if he got her a New York radio gig first.

It just so happened that Danny was friendly with Burt McMurtrie and was well aware of the romantic fireworks that had ignited between them in Los Angeles. No longer with CBS, Burt was now head of programming for WMCA, the New York hub of an upstart rival network, Associated Broadcasting System (ABS), where he was creating a whole new slate of programming. When Danny informed him that Kay was available, Burt promptly signed her up to headline a show.

Just hours after recording her Victor record with Coakley, Thompson grabbed her dog, blew a kiss to George Kinney, and flew to New York, where, starting September 30, *The Kay Thompson Show* would air three nights a week from the WMCA studio in the Hammerstein Building at Fifty-third and Broadway.

Unsure if her relocation would be permanent, Kay—and Mr. Chips—moved in with her younger sister, Marian, who as luck would have it was studying painting in Manhattan. When Blanche, the eldest Fink sibling, got wind that Kay had joined Marian in the Big Apple, she took a break from St. Louis and boarded a train for a little sightseeing/family reunion.

The exposure on ABS was nothing to sneeze at, but the network trailed far behind CBS and NBC in the ratings. Wary of becoming an indentured servant again, Kay refused to sign a long-term contract for *The Kay Thompson Show*, opting for a single thirteen-week season commitment.

That hard bargain prompted McMurtrie to affectionately call Thompson "a bitch," a term of endearment that stuck. In fact, nineteen years later, in a wistful love letter to Burt (by then, a top radio personality in Tacoma, Washington), Kay nostalgically wrote, "I have never forgotten you. Years come and days go merrily dancing into the blue beyond, but I still think of you when I hear the word bitch (which of course is very often now that I'm all grown up and all). I am more than delighted that you are Mr. Tacoma. I am not in the least surprised. You have always been twice as bright as anybody else in the world. And you know it."

But in 1934, McMurtrie was essentially a lovesick puppy caving to Thompson's demands. Leaving her options open suited Kay's manager, too, because in the grand scheme of things, working for WMCA was not a step up—it was merely a stepping stone that got Thompson to New York.

Sure enough, in less than a month, Winkler orchestrated a major coup for her: "What if I told you I could get you a meeting with Fred Waring?"

At that time, Fred Waring was the No. 1 bandleader on the airwaves, host of CBS's phenomenally successful program *The Fred Waring–Ford Dealers Radio Show*, broadcast weekly from Manhattan. Today, Waring is a household name mainly because of a bartender gadget he invented and patented that earned him his greatest fortune: The Waring Blender.

"Fred Waring's program was one of the best, and nothing but the best for Thompson was my slogan," Kay boasted to a reporter. "He'd heard me on the air in California and wanted me to come to New York for a talk."

Three thousand miles for a tête-à-tête? Hardly. In truth, Kay was just an elevator ride away from Waring's office in the Hammerstein Building—the same location where her WMCA show originated. On the day of the fateful appointment in late October, Waring was about to leave town on a six-week tour.

Fred explained that he wanted to incorporate more female vocalizing into his arrangements. "If you can find sixteen girls and train them in six weeks," he proposed, "you're hired."

Directing a choir of sixteen would be a cinch for Kay; the daunting part of the task would be *finding* them. "I didn't know a soul in New York," she recalled.

To make matters more difficult, Fred had a litany of provisos. Each girl had to be young, pretty, refined—no drinkers or smokers, no loose morals—and above all, they had to be *untrained*. He hated "longhaired" voices. His progressive pop style was the inverse of everything taught in formal singing lessons, and he was fed up with trying to undo the damage. Upon returning from his tour, he would audition them. If they passed the test, each girl would make $25 a week, with Kay earning a robust $350.

The job seemed impossible, the Mt. Everest of tall orders, but Kay was ready for the challenge. "I said, 'Yes,'" she recalled, "just because I wanted to go with him." Taking a gulp, Kay told Fred, "When you come back, we'll be ready for you."

Kay rushed to Marian and Blanche: "You two kids are caught in the draft. Art can wait, and so can Grant's Tomb. Right now you're going to sing." Thus, the Debutantes were reunited, with additions soon to follow.

Kay marched to the Capitol Theatre, the site of her father's favorite radio amateur hour, *Major Bowes' Capitol Family*. There, she found two dancers in ghastly stage makeup who seemed interested—she gambled that they looked human beneath the greasepaint.

Next, she accosted girls in hotel lounges, department stores, and theaters, leaving no clone unturned. Blanche and Marian scouted candidates, too, among passersby on streets and in stores—anyone who was eye-catching and eager.

At Macy's, Kay hijacked a salesgirl who looked the part. Although the young woman had never sung a note outside her own bathroom, Thompson made her chirp right there in the store in front of astounded customers. "You're hired," Kay declared, to a round of applause. Moving on to a fashionable store on Fifth Avenue, Kay kidnapped a model who fit the bill.

Three Texas girls were found singing at the New York Roosevelt Hotel, a trio named Dot, Kay, and Em who had been featured regularly on *The Fleischmann's Yeast Hour* starring Rudy Vallee.

Another girl named Janet Ayres popped up in the lobby of a song publishing company, where she had been hanging out with hopes of being discovered. She recommended Elizabeth Newburger, who would later marry Al Rinker (Bing Crosby's boyhood friend and a founding member of the Rhythm Boys). "I was the only one who was classically trained," Elizabeth explained, "but I learned to fit in with something different. She hired me right away."

Eventually, Kay had her sweet sixteen. It would've been too crowded to hold rehearsals in Marian's modest flat, so Kay rented a larger apartment on Park Avenue in the mid-Fifties, complete with piano, and enough bedrooms to house all three Fink sisters plus Mr. Chips.

"The most nightmarish weeks of my young life," was how Thompson dramatically characterized the ordeal to reporters. But, by the time Waring returned in December, Kay had a rock-solid group.

For the audition, Thompson and her girls first sang "Wistful and Blue," with Kay on piano and lead vocal. Poker-faced, Fred made a few suggestions and they performed it again, incorporating his adjustments. Enigmatically, he asked for the next number, "I Got Rhythm." They not only nailed it but at the very end, they broke into a little synchronized tap dance routine Kay had taught them.

A smile curled up on Fred's face and he said, "Swell"—the highest praise imaginable for this perfectionist of few kind words and even fewer happy emotions.

But the hard part wasn't over. Waring informed Thompson that she would have to get the final thumbs-up from someone more powerful than he: Henry Ford, founder and chairman of the Ford Motor Company—the show's sponsor.

Wrapping the seventy-one-year-old tycoon around her elongated index finger, Kay showed off her surprising knowledge of cars and made it a point to mention her teenage romance with Dunc Dorris, the son of Ford's former competitor in St. Louis. Ford was charmed and the deal was done.

To celebrate, Kay let her girls have Christmas off, but then it was throats back to the grindstone in preparation for their debut broadcast on Thursday, December 27, 1934. They were an instant hit, measured by a large influx of fan mail.

Kay insisted that Blanche and Marian use "Thompson" as their stage name, further suppressing "Fink" out of existence. Henry Ford's highly vocal anti-Semitism may have been a motivating factor. In any case, this must have been hard on their father, especially when his local newspaper, the *St. Louis Globe-Democrat,* did a proud story on the hometown girls who had hit the big time in New York without a single mention of Leo and Hattie Fink. For Kay and certain species of sharks, it was all about forward motion.

Aside from her vocalizing on the show, Waring allowed Thompson to show off her skills as a pianist and arranger. One night, she presented a stunning, semiclassical arrangement of "My Heart Stood Still," with no lead vocal, spotlighting Kay on piano, accompanied by the male and female choral groups. The number went over so well, it was repeated the following week.

A struggling vocal coach named Jule Styne, thirty, was so impressed with Kay's unique arranging style that he went to the broadcast one night, introduced himself, and struck up an enduring friendship. Later, after hitting it big as a songwriter and theatrical producer, Jule sought Thompson's services and/or advice on practically everything he did.

On a talk show in 1957, Styne declared, "Kay Thompson, in my estimation, is one of the most talented people I've ever met in my life."

As pleasant as things may have appeared to Waring's listeners, behind-the-scenes politics were cutthroat. Fred devoted more airtime to other female acts, like Stella and the Fellas and the Lane Sisters (Rosemary and Priscilla). Not satisfied with one measly number per broadcast, Kay began campaigning for more.

With Thompson's thirteen-week contract coming to an end in March, Waring should have realized he'd have a problem if he did not do something to appease her.

Meanwhile, back in September 1934, Don Forker quit his job as manager of advertising for the Union Oil Company of California and, as if following Kay's lead, migrated to New York the very same month she did.

"A few weeks ago, he came east," Kay confessed to a reporter. "We had dinner together—and we both agreed that maybe it was best, after all, that we hadn't married. Maybe we'd both have been unhappy."

The romance between Kay and Don may have cooled, but their professional relationship was about to heat up like never before.

In Manhattan, Don had taken a high-powered position at the Lord and Thomas advertising agency, where his mandate was to create radio shows for clients—particularly the American Tobacco Company, makers of Lucky Strike cigarettes. The tobacco giant was controlled with tight-fisted impunity by George Washington Hill, an infamously brusque tyrant who would stop at nothing to promote his product. When Frederic Wakeman spoofed the advertising business in his bestselling novel *The Hucksters,* it was no secret that the irascible tycoon Evan Llewellyn Evans was a caricature of Hill—and actor Sydney Greenstreet had a field day skewering him in MGM's 1947 movie adaptation.

In March 1935, with American Tobacco on board as the sponsor, Forker instigated *The Lucky Strike Hit Parade,* a new Saturday night program for NBC. Each week, the broadcast would present performances of the fifteen most popular songs in the country, rankings based on sales of sheet music, phonograph records, and airplay requests. Nowadays, countdowns of the top hits of the week are a staple of radio and television, but back then, the concept was new, at least on a national level.

Forker essentially stole the idea from *The Big Ten,* a local San Francisco radio program he'd heard while working on the West Coast. Conductor Meredith Willson had come up with the idea in the fall of 1933, after his boss complained he was playing too many oldies. "Just to quiet him down," Willson explained, "I took the ten most-played songs of the week out of *Variety's* list and made them into a show." Willson later became famous for writing the Broadway hit *The Music Man*, but in 1935, he was still a fringe commodity.

Although *The Big Ten* was produced by NBC's San Francisco affiliate, KECA, and therefore could have been picked up by the network for national broadcast, Forker advised NBC that it was not slick enough and needed a complete overhaul with better singers and musicians.

Naturally, Forker wanted to hire Thompson and he proposed a package that included more money, more airtime, more creative input, and star billing.

Kay asked, "Who is going to conduct the orchestra?"

Don replied, "Who would you recommend?"

"Lennie Hayton."

"Done."

And so, along with singers Johnny Hauser, Gogo DeLys, and Charles Carlisle, Kay would be a regularly featured vocalist on the one-hour series, guaranteed a minimum of four out of the fifteen songs per show. For her backup singers, Kay got NBC to import the Three Rhythm Kings from California and she would also continue using her choir, renamed Kay Thompson's Melody Girls, all of whom would jump ship—no apologies to Waring.

Fred went ballistic. After he threatened legal action, a compromise was struck to keep Kay and her choir with Waring, nonexclusive, for an additional thirteen-week season on CBS. In return, the network agreed to allow Kay and her Melody Girls to simultaneously appear on NBC's *Lucky Strike Hit Parade*.

The big winner in all this, of course, was Kay. Starring in two major prime-time shows on competing networks was unheard of. As her income and notoriety skyrocketed, so did Waring's resentment. Tolerance deteriorated into pettiness and he made life hell for Kay and her girls.

"He would say scathing things to us," Elizabeth Newburger Rinker recalled. "I know Kay couldn't stand him. Who could?"

When renewal time came up again in June, Waring let them go—a relief for all concerned.

Kay focused on *Lucky Strike Hit Parade*, where she and Lennie Hayton had a field day experimenting with offbeat arrangements. One of the more notable novelties was inviting Fred Astaire to tap-dance selections from his brand-new movie, *Top Hat*, including its No. 1 hit, "Cheek to Cheek."

Describing Astaire's historic appearance, Kay told writer Stephen M. Silverman, "He was dancing on the radio, if you can imagine it. Well, why not?"

No exaggeration. They built a little wooden stage and set up "table microphones" at his feet to capture the rhythm of his tap shoes. Kay later dubbed the platform their "Astaire-way to Heaven." The stunt went over so well, Fred was brought back for three more consecutive weekly appearances before the month was out. Then he was off to Hollywood to begin rehearsals for *Follow the Fleet*, so that was that. When the September 7 broadcast aired without Astaire, however, there was a flood of complaints. Surrendering to the public outcry, George Washington Hill decided that if Fred could not come to *Hit Parade*, then *Hit Parade* would just have to go to Fred.

To contain costs, several of the show's soloists were dropped, leaving only Kay and Charles Carlisle to divvy up songs with Fred. Kay's Melody Girls were left behind, with only her Three Rhythm Kings on board as backup singers. Forced to use mostly L.A. musicians, Hayton did manage to persuade the powers that be that he needed to bring a few of his key sidemen—including his star trombonist, Jack Jenney. That was just fine with Kay because, by then, she and Jack were an item.

Five feet eleven inches tall, with brown eyes, dark, slicked-back hair, and a thin William Powell moustache, Jack Jenney was a handsome twenty-five-year-old from Mason City, Iowa, who dressed snazzy and played jazzy. His father, John Jenney, was a horn salesman who, according to family legend, was the basis for Harold Hill in *The Music Man*, the Broadway musical written by fellow Mason City native and family friend Meredith Willson. That's why, in later years, Kay often referred to Jack as "the son of the Music Man."

By the mid-1930s, Jack had become a top trombonist, highly sought-after for radio, recording, and club gigs. "Jenney could match anyone in the business," wrote swing historian Campbell Burnap, "including Tommy Dorsey." In fact, in the aftermath of the infamous breakup of the Dorsey Brothers Orchestra in May 1935, Jack was called in to replace Tommy.

Immediately upon meeting Jack, Kay was besotted—and the feeling was mutual. Hughie McFarland, Jack's band boy, later told friends that Jack and Kay had a "highly charged sexual relationship." But Jack had his issues. He was a devil-may-care "bad boy," who drank hard, smoked reefer, womanized, and neglected the wife and child he'd all but abandoned back home in Iowa. Either Kay was in a dreamy state of denial or she was hell-bent on living dangerously, because any fool could see this was headed for disaster.

Kay, Mr. Chips, and the other *Hit Parade* transplants arrived in Los Angeles by express train on September 15. Jack did not show up until two days later in a car that had acquired extra baggage along the way.

"In 1935, my father picked me up in Cedar Rapids, Iowa, driving a Packard convertible," recalled John Jenney, Jack's son. "He also picked up his mother—in other words, my Grandma Ada—and he took us both to Hollywood. We stayed at the Ambassador Hotel. Kay Thompson was out there already, staying in the same hotel. They were busy doing a radio show but she really wanted to be in movies and she wanted to see if my father could get into them, too. He was a good-looking man, but he was not an actor."

The presence of Jack's mother and six-year-old son put a damper on romance, but Kay made the best of it by making a good impression on her potential mother-in-law and, more important, on little John.

"I remember she used a lot of makeup," John recalled. But regardless of how exotic a creature Kay must have appeared to a wide-eyed country bumpkin, John warmed up to her immediately. "She was a very nice person," he admitted.

Although Kay loved kids, she definitely preferred them in manageable doses—perfect aunt material. And she made no bones about it, admitting to a reporter, "I'm not the maternal type." True to form, Kay would never have any children of her own, unless you count Eloise.

"I've always wondered," John speculated, "if Kay might have based a little bit of Eloise on me from my experience living in the Ambassador Hotel when I was out there with her in California. I was six years old and I raised hell in that place, let me tell you."

While Little John was pouring water down mail chutes and ordering room service, Papa Jack and Auntie Kay were busy jammin' with Fred Astaire. But, after just four weeks of shows, without advance warning, Astaire announced on the air that the program would be his last. Citing exhaustion and overexposure, he simply up and quit.

"I vowed I would never try it again," Fred declared, "regardless of the monetary attraction."

Infuriated, George Washington Hill ordered that the show be hauled right back to New York and demanded that it get back to basics. Outraged that Astaire had so easily hijacked the franchise, he banned future guest stars. *Radio Mirror* reported that the sponsor did not want *any* performer "to become too closely identified with the show."

Hill wanted a program in which the *concept* was the star: straight-ahead performances of the top hit songs. He changed the name of the show to *Your Hit Parade* and instituted strict new creative guidelines, aimed directly at Kay and Lennie, insisting that the songs be performed "without variations or new ideas."

"I don't want attention diverted by French horn gymnastics," Hill railed. "Let's give the public what the public wants and not try to educate them. We should not be concerned about introducing new numbers and novelties."

Don Forker and NBC executives tried to defuse the situation but there was no changing Hill's petulant mind-set—and, since he controlled the purse strings, he called the shots. When the broadcast on November 2 failed to adhere strictly to the new rules, everyone was fired including Kay. It was a startling turn of events for an extraordinarily popular program, a decision that bewildered the industry, press, and listeners.

Nevertheless, Hill stuck to his guns, and if longevity is the barometer of success, history is on his side. Remarkably, *Your Hit Parade* lasted twenty-four years and spawned a smash television series. As a founding member of the phenomenon, however, Kay only got to enjoy the first twenty-nine weeks of it. But she never would have been happy stifling her own creativity in favor of a purely pedestrian formula.

"That's *impossible* for Kay to do," chuckled Norman Jewison, who started his career directing *Your Hit Parade* (CBS-TV, 1958–59) and later worked with Thompson on projects with Andy Williams and Judy Garland. "Kay will change *every* note if given the opportunity. She'd get all excited and say, 'Let's do this in the bridge!' And then she would fly off on a riff and create a whole new song. But some of the stuff was just terrific. She was a really, *really* creative person."

The same week she got the boot from *Hit Parade*, Kay got word that Brunswick Records had decided it had better get her into a recording studio before her contract expired at the end of the year. It wasn't exactly a ringing endorsement, but given that she was unemployed, at least it was something. She was assigned to record four songs from new movies: "You Let Me Down" (from *Stars over Broadway*), "You Hit the Spot" (from *Collegiate*), plus "Don't Mention Love to Me" and "Out of Sight, Out of Mind" (both from *In Person*). For the sessions, Kay asked Jack Jenney to blow his trombone and conduct a band that they assembled from the ranks of New York's top sidemen, including ace trumpeter Manny Klein and drummer Johnny Williams (father of movie maestro John Williams). Recorded on November 11, the numbers were released on two 78 rpm discs in time for the Christmas buying season—the first records Thompson could truly call her own.

To promote the records, Kay made a series of guest appearances on *The Harry Richman Dodge Show*, where she performed the numbers with Louis Katzman and his orchestra. To her delight, the sponsor offered her a free car in exchange for appearing as the Dodge spokeswoman for ads in magazines such as *Better Homes and Gardens*. Nice work if you can get it, but as a career move, it was spinning wheels. Making matters worse, none of her records broke out as hits, so Brunswick let her renewal option expire.

Kay had a tempestuous, almost childlike temper, and when things were not going her way, she tended to take out her frustrations on other people, often those working hardest on her behalf. The fall guy this time around was her manager, Danny Winkler. She accused him of concentrating entirely too much of his time on a hot newcomer named Milton Berle while her career was going down in flames. When the smoke cleared, Danny discovered that she'd left him for Mark Hanna, whose showbiz clients included bandleader Benny Goodman.

The first thing Hanna did was get Thompson a nightclub booking in the King Cole Room at the St. Regis Hotel, backed by Emil Coleman and His Orchestra. For five weeks, February 13 to March 18, 1936, Kay performed for the upper crust of Manhattan's café society—including William S. Paley, president of CBS, who was known to frequent the joint. Of course, that was precisely the reason Hanna had chosen the spot in the first place and the scheme worked like a charm.

Awestruck by Thompson's versatility and musicianship, Paley decided that she was just the commercial ingredient they needed to team with renowned Russian conductor André Kostelanetz and his forty-five-piece symphony orchestra for a new Friday night series. The program would be called *The Chesterfield Radio Show,* sponsored by Liggett and Myers Tobacco Company, makers of Chesterfield cigarettes. Although Kostelanetz was associated with classical fare, the idea for this new show was to present big-band rhythm and swing tunes augmented by lush orchestrations. But there was a caveat. Paley wanted Kay as well as her large chorus.

That was easier said than done. By then, the Melody Girls and the Three Rhythm Kings had gone their separate ways. Even Kay's sisters had given up the business and gone back to St. Louis (where Blanche was now married and expecting her first baby). But, with an offer of $1,000 per week on the table for her and her group combined, Kay agreed to deliver whatever CBS wanted.

In Kay's new choir, there would be three males and a dozen females. She would pay them each a flat weekly salary of $31.75 and pocket the remaining $500 for herself.

Elizabeth Newburger was her first recruit—the only carryover from the original lineup. Thompson let it be known that she was interested in combining several existing groups into one superchorus, to be billed as Kay Thompson and the Rhythm Singers. The components would include the Vass Sisters (Jitchy,

Weezie, and Sally), the Blue Flames (Helen Jackson and Jude and Beverly Freeland), two members of the Symphonettes (Loulie Jean Norman and Marjorie Miller), plus Marion Jernigan and Jessie Mahr from other groups. For the twelfth girl, Jack Jenney recommended eighteen-year-old Bea Wain.

"Jack had me go to Kay's apartment and talk to her about joining the choir," Wain recalled. "Kay said, 'I'd love to have you in my group.' And I said, 'There's only one problem. I'm in a quartet, Bea and the Bachelors, with Al Rinker, Johnny Smedburg, Ken Lane, and me.'"

Problem? For Kay, it was manna from heaven. She knew all three of the guys and adored them. Rinker was a former member of the Rhythm Boys with Bing Crosby; Smedburg was a former member of the Three Ambassadors who sang backup for Thompson at the Cocoanut Grove in 1931–32; and Ken Lane was not only a singer but an expert pianist who demonstrated songs for top publishing companies. Wasting no time, Kay awarded them all the final slots on her all-star team.

Next, she spread the word that she was looking for a rehearsal pianist. Loulie Jean Norman recommended a twenty-one-year-old friend from Birmingham, Alabama, named Hugh Martin. When Hugh came to audition at Kay's apartment, he met an Oklahoman singer named Ralph Blane and, subsequently, they joined forces to become one of the most successful composing teams of the 1940s ("Have Yourself a Merry Little Christmas," "The Trolley Song," among others). In the meantime, though, Hugh would collect $25 a week playing piano for Kay—and Ralph would join her choir the following year.

"We rehearsed every single day," Elizabeth Newburger recalled. "The hours were unbelievable." Even though Kay was the red-nailed dominatrix of a vocal chord sweatshop, the Rhythm Singers were having too much fun to hold it against her. And the results were astonishing.

"I have never heard anything like the sound that came out of them," Hugh Martin rhapsodized. "It actually made me ill. All the blood went to my feet and I had to lean against the wall for support. It was such a thrilling sound."

In addition to rhythm, swing, and jazz, Kay specialized in comic novelty songs, like "Us on a Bus" and "The Old Man in the Mountain," for which she'd have her singers doing sound effects, funny accents, and silly voices. "I Can Pull a Rabbit Outta My Hat" featured imitations of Betty Boop, Portland Hoffa, and a chicken.

And there was a certain mascot who often popped up unexpectedly during rehearsals. "Kay always used to do the Eloise bit," Bea Wain recalled. "She would come into the room and do the voice: 'How's everybody? Well, I was late today because I did so-and-so and so-and-so.' And we used to be hysterical."

"Kay used to do Eloise a lot," Elizabeth Newburger confirmed. "It was as if her freedom gave us permission to come up with crazy things of our own."

"Kay used to use her Eloise voice to quiet us down when we were not behaving or singing the right note or something," Virginia "Jitchy" Vass explained. "She would say, 'I'm Eloise and I think Jitchy and Loulie are talking too much and I'm gonna report them to the management.' Then we'd all stop and laugh and get to work again."

Another habitué of their rehearsals was Mr. Chips. Unfortunately, he was not always a gentleman. "I wasn't crazy about Chips," recalled Loulie Jean. "He got on my leg once, and well, he lost me there."

"Kay also had a housekeeper," Bea explained, "which was *very* impressive. Her name was Mamie. She was young and black, a sophisticated Lena Horne type, who did everything from cooking to cleaning to secretarial duties."

In the mornings, Kay would rehearse the small army at her place, then march everyone over to CBS at 485 Madison Avenue (between Fifty-first and Fifty-second Streets) for afternoon and evening sessions with Kostelanetz—Kosty, as they called him. In addition to his regular musicians, the maestro brought in a number of top jazz sidemen, including, quite conveniently, Jack Jenney—who, by then, was "living in sin" with Kay at her apartment.

"Kosty was crazy about our group," Bea remarked, "which was quite something because he was really a very cultured conductor."

They charmed other starched collars, too. "This very dignified gentleman came to one of our first rehearsals," Bea recalled. "He was a big shot. And our little Southern girls, Jitchy, Weezie, and Sally Vass, shouted, 'Cousin Willie!'"

It turned out that William Randolph Carmichael, vice president of Liggett and Myers Tobacco Company, was a cousin of the Vass sisters. Jitchy's diary entry understated the obvious: "Kay is so thrilled that we're kin to the Vice President." No kidding.

Thompson was very careful not to offend Cousin Willie and his Chesterfield colleagues. "Kay only smoked Camels," Bea said, "so she would take all her Camels out and put them in the Chesterfield package."

The Chesterfield Radio Program made its debut on May 1, 1936, and the reaction was seismic—especially for Kay and her Rhythm Singers.

"I have to tell you," Bea reflected, "Kay was a mentor and a goddess and everything else. To us, she was the Statue of Liberty."

The show was such a smash, Paley expanded it to two nights a week, Wednesdays and Fridays, starting July 1. It became one of the hottest tickets in town, especially for composers and musicians enraptured by Thompson's unique vocal arrangements. Cole Porter, Richard Rodgers, George and Ira

Gershwin, Harold Arlen, and E. Y. "Yip" Harburg were but a few of the avid fans who considered *The Chesterfield Radio Program* inspirational.

The great jazz vocalist Mel Tormé was only 11 years old when he first discovered Kay on *Chesterfield*. He was enthralled by her innovative use of voices and the fact that her group was the very first "to approximate a band."

"Kay knows more about vocal-group writing than any other person alive," Tormé wrote in his book *My Singing Teachers*. He particularly loved one of her signatures. "Kay's tag endings to her arrangements were a hoot. She made a specialty of starting a line, adding to it, adding a bit more to it, then saying the whole line. Example: In *Back in Your Own Backyard*, she would wind up the arrangement with: *Back . . . Back in . . . Back in your . . . Back in your own . . . Back in your own back yard.*"

When Vincente Minnelli directed his first Broadway musicals, *The Show Is On* (1936) and *Hooray for What!* (1937), he wanted the scores to emulate the "marvelous André Kostelanetz arrangements on the radio," and ended up borrowing Kay and Gordon Jenkins from Kosty's staff to re-create that magic formula. This was just the beginning of a lifelong family bond between Thompson and Minnelli (later extending to his daughter Liza).

Initially, *The Chesterfield Radio Program* was staged at CBS's Forty-fourth Street Playhouse, but as demand for seats intensified, the series was moved in September to a larger facility, the newly acquired CBS Radio Theater 3 (at Broadway and Fifty-third), later rechristened the Ed Sullivan Theater.

Unfortunately, double weekly doses were perhaps too much of a good thing. As ratings for the series began to soften, the folks at Chesterfield got spooked and, by the end of September, the Wednesday night installment was changed to classical music featuring opera singer Lily Pons (Kostelanetz's future wife). The expectation was that the Friday night ratings would rebound, but when that did not happen, the maestro became the fall guy.

Although Kostelanetz's orchestral treatments were critically acclaimed and had a major impact on Broadway and movie musicals, the biggest dance hits of the day continued to be those with the stark, brassy arrangements of the big band sound. When it was clear that a more youthful and hip bandleader was being sought, Kay recommended Lennie Hayton or Jack Jenney. Ultimately, the Chesterfield execs settled on Hal Kemp, who, with his thirteen-member ensemble, had not only been voted "Favorite Dance Band of 1936" by the readers of *Radio Guide*, but had also dominated the pop charts that year with two No. 1 records, "There's a Small Hotel" and "When I'm with You."

With such sweeping renovations, Kay feared she might get thrown under the bus, too, but her impressive rankings in popularity polls apparently saved her. The year-end Hearst Newspaper Radio Editors Poll ranked Thompson as the No. 2 Best Female Vocalist (behind Frances Langford) and her Chesterfield program was voted No. 1 Best All-Round Musical Show.

Bob Hope was offered the job of master of ceremonies, but that dream quickly faded when he demanded the moon. Instead, it was decided that the modestly priced announcer Paul Douglas could handle the introductions just fine. (Ten years later, Douglas would star opposite Judy Holliday in *Born Yesterday* on Broadway.)

Renamed *It's Chesterfield Time*, the stripped-down version of the series was launched on January 1, 1937. Billed by CBS as "Our First Lady of Rhythm," Kay remained the overall driving force as star vocalist, choral director of her Rhythm Singers, and vocal arranger.

"I rehearse my group and make the arrangements," she told a reporter, "and then give them to Hal Kemp, who fits his orchestra into it the way he wants to. But my arrangements of tunes are set and are the basis for any elaboration the orchestra makes."

Kemp's elaborations were the antithesis of Kosty's—light on symphonic flourishes, heavy on blasts of brass and percussion. "It was better for Kay with Kostelanetz," Hugh Martin believed. "I liked it better because I liked the rich, plush sound that Kostelanetz got. But, it was good both ways. Kay seemed to get along fine with both of them." And according to all accounts, Kemp got on well with Kay.

Thompson's popularity was at an all-time high but, of course, being a radio star did not necessarily translate into being mobbed on the street. Other than the occasional fan magazine spread and print ads for Dodge and Chesterfield, the general public had rarely glimpsed what Kay looked like. With any luck, that was about to change.

Herbert J. Yates, the cigar-chomping honcho of Republic Pictures, the Poverty Row movie studio, offered Kay the lead in *Hit Parade of 1937*, a musical scripted by Bradford Ropes, author of *Forty-second Street*. Despite the dubious pedigree of the low-budget quickie, it was just the sort of showcase she needed to springboard her way into major studio pictures. And the part was not a stretch. Kay was set to play Ruth Allison, an aspiring radio singer who becomes an overnight sensation via the guidance of talent agent Pete Garland (Phil Regan), with whom she falls in love. All would be perfect except that Ruth has a secret criminal past that threatens to ruin her career and her relationship.

Although Kay was announced for the role in the *Los Angeles Times* on January 18, 1937, her commitment to *It's Chesterfield Time* prevented her from being available for the West Coast shoot in February. Her appeal to William Paley for a leave of absence was denied and so, to her great dismay, she was replaced by Frances Langford, her top radio rival.

On a brighter note, Kay was enjoying the riches of steady employment. She moved into a bigger, more luxurious apartment at 520 Madison Avenue between Fifty-third and Fifty-fourth Streets—within sneezing distance of CBS.

As *Radio Mirror* reported, "Kay took an entire floor, so that her three dogs could have plenty of room."

Indeed, Mr. Chips had acquired two roommates, a pair of cocker spaniels named Nooky and Mooey (after characters in Mazo de la Roche's novel *The Master of Jalna*). The additional space would also provide more elbow room for the human members of Kay's entourage—boudoir companion Jack Jenney and maid Mamie—not to mention ample expanse for entertaining. Kay decorated the place herself, the first time she really had the money and a canvas large enough to serve as an outlet for one of her latent talents.

"She had a stunning apartment," Bea Wain recalled. "Highly styled, very dramatic."

So much so, it got ink. A radio trade paper reported, "The woodwork is largely white and there is a particular fireplace that is the delight of Miss Thompson's heart. At the first venture with a real log fire, the mantelpiece looked as though it had been held over a Pittsburgh blast furnace. But that's fixed now."

Then, quite unexpectedly on January 27, 1937, Kay eloped with Jack Jenney, tying the knot in a secret New York ceremony, witnessed by her manager, Mark Hanna, plus chorus members Elizabeth Newburger and Loulie Jean Norman. Everyone else found out after the fact, including their families. Some friends believed that the bigwigs of CBS and Chesterfield may have pressured them into matrimony to avoid a brewing media scandal about their live-in arrangement. Whatever the true motivation, the bride and groom were back at work the very next day. The honeymoon would have to wait.

Shortly thereafter, Kay signed a deal with Victor Records, under the aegis of Eli Oberstein. A 1930s version of Clive Davis, Oberstein was a formidable figure in the platter biz, with an eye for new talent and an uncanny ability to cultivate hit records. He got Kay to record four sides on April 13, accompanied by Her Orchestra and Her Rhythm Singers. As with her prior Brunswick sessions, Kay's so-called orchestra was a hastily assembled gathering of crème de la crème musicians conducted by her husband.

Oberstein chose the blues ballad "Carelessly" as Kay's first single. But there was stiff competition from the twenty-two-year-old legend-in-training, Billie Holiday, who released her own version of the song on Brunswick. Snubbing the African-American singer, the song publisher settled on a photo of Thompson for the cover of the sheet music—perhaps racially motivated, but more likely an honest gamble that Kay's version would be the bigger hit. However, buyers leaned the other way, giving Holiday her very first No. 1 pop hit on the *Billboard* chart. Oberstein was furious.

It got worse. The flip side of Kay's single was "There's a Lull in My Life," a song from an upcoming movie, *Wake Up and Live*, starring Kay's fiercest detractor, columnist Walter Winchell. Quite predictably, Winchell sharpened his poison pen. "Kay Thompson certainly spoiled the recording of 'Lull,' didn't she?" he fumed in his column. "All I know is that it didn't sound like Gordon and Revel's lovely hit at all [and it] makes me so irritable."

Kay's follow-up single, the up-tempo "It Had to Be You," backed with the bouncy "Exactly Like You," had all the earmarks of a double-sided crowd-pleaser. Kay promoted them both on *It's Chesterfield Time*, but the disc just never took off. Irate, Thompson blamed Oberstein, claiming he didn't support the records because "he thought they were awful." But realistically, with Winchell on the rampage, Oberstein must have decided to cut his losses.

None of this went down well with the producers of *It's Chesterfield Time*—especially when, during the same time period, Hal Kemp racked up his third and fourth No. 1 records ("This Year's Kisses" and "Where or When"). With Kay's contract up for renewal in June, pressure was building for her to shine like never before.

But catering to the tastes of Joe Q. Public would never be Kay's strong suit. She could only do what she did best—and, whether mainstream listeners got it or not, she ended up churning out some of the most progressive swing numbers of the era. On the April 30 installment of *It's Chesterfield Time*, for instance, Kay and her chorus performed a high-energy song called "Whoa Babe," written by Larry Clinton, that advanced the notion of singers as musical instruments to a new level—with "da-dee-da's" and "bada-bada's" replacing the entire brass section.

"I have a special place in my heart for 'Whoa Babe,'" recalled Hugh Martin. "I was singing in the group the night she did it on *Chesterfield* and it was almost a supernatural sensation . . . like flying. People talk about cloud nine—it was something like that, singing this wild, unshackled, yet controlled little gem of jazz."

Kay's chorus member Al Rinker had been moonlighting as one of the producers of another CBS radio show, *The Saturday Night Swing Club*. On

June 12, he booked Kay to sing "Whoa Babe" on *The Saturday Night Swing Club First Anniversary Special* as part of an all-star lineup that included Duke Ellington, Benny Goodman, and Lionel Hampton.

"That was the big night for Kay," recalled CBS publicist Gary Stevens, who was there to witness it. "That was her shining hour. That's when Kay electrified musicians, critics, CBS, *everybody*. That's when Kay became a big leaguer. Everybody was there—Goodman, Ellington, an all-star group—and she was startling. They idolized her. She was like a god to these guys. She was the patron saint of scat, of singing, of everything. She just won everybody over. When she opened her mouth and moved, well . . . that was *it*."

One of Kay's quirkiest signatures was introduced in "Whoa Babe." "We used to have musical breaks," Bea explained, "and whenever we needed to fill in something, Kay would have us just sing, 'Simone, Simone, Simone.' And the orchestras all knew it. They'd wait for us to do it."

Down Beat dubbed it her "famous 'Simone Simon' break." But where the heck did it come from? It was, in fact, a reference to the gorgeous French starlet Simone Simon, who had started making pictures in Hollywood that year.

"Simone Simon was very 'hot' at the time," Hugh Martin recalled, "and her studio ran ads telling the public how to pronounce her name. 'SEE-MOAN SEE-MOAN,' the advertisements advised us. Kay thought it was ridiculous, which it was, and worked it into the arrangement in a most marvelous way."

Although *Down Beat* raved that Kay's rendition of "Whoa Babe" was "plenty hot," it was apparently not the sort of heat the Chesterfield people were after. A short time later, it was announced that starting in July, Hal Kemp and his band would be relocated to the West Coast for *Chesterfield's Music from Hollywood* starring Alice Faye (aka Mrs. Tony Martin). The services of Kay Thompson and the Rhythm Singers were no longer required.

"Exhaust pipe!" was the expression Kay always used when she'd had it. Reeling from the ups and downs of the past few months, she needed a breather to focus on herself and her marriage, which had been on the back burner ever since the January "I dos."

So in early July, Kay and Jack boarded the *Queen of Bermuda* for a belated honeymoon. As they sailed out of New York Harbor, Kay waved good-bye to chorus members who had come to see them off. As the luxury liner drifted by the Statue of Liberty, a feeling of newfound freedom washed over her. She looked at Jack, a glint of mischief in her eyes. With nothing more to hide, she cracked open a fresh new pack of Camel cigarettes.

Chapter Three

HOORAY FOR WHAT?

Broadway Bound-and-Gagged
(1937–42)

The screaming and the sobbing were something you can't imagine
out of Kay—she went to pieces in such a spectacular way.
—*Hugh Martin*

*I*n July 1937, while Kay and Jack were on their belated honeymoon in Bermuda, Republic Pictures' Herbert J. Yates cabled an offer for Thompson to appear in a new movie musical called *Manhattan Merry-Go-Round*. Unlike the leading role he'd wanted her to play in *Hit Parade of 1937*, however, this new opportunity would only be a guest appearance as herself—along with her Rhythm Singers—wedged among a cavalcade of cameos by the likes of Gene Autry ("the singing cowboy"), the Cotton Club's Cab Calloway, and, to cover all bases, Joe DiMaggio, the Yankees baseball champ. Even though her screen time would be limited to just two songs, Thompson accepted an offer of $5,000 on the condition that her husband be hired as her on-screen bandleader—a move she hoped would help Jenney launch his own orchestra. Yates agreed.

Because the budget of the picture was poverty-stricken, both of Kay's numbers would have to be completed in one day of shooting on August 4. And, to save the cost of transporting her ensemble to Hollywood, her sequences would be filmed at the decidedly less glamorous Biograph Studio on East 175th Street in the Bronx. What's more, Kay's scenes were being relegated to an uncredited "second unit" director named John H. Auer—remembered today for having helmed nineteen-year-old Frank Sinatra's featurette debut in *Major Bowes' Amateur Theater of the Air* (RKO, 1935) on the exact same stage.

Cutting their vacation short, the Jenneys sailed on the first ship back to Manhattan. Upon arrival on July 26, Kay learned that half her Rhythm Singers had flown the coop, but replacements were quickly rustled up. With less than a week to go, Kay had to create vocal arrangements for two new songs, "All Over Nothing at All" and "I Owe You," plus rehearse her new group to perfection.

Manhattan Merry-Go-Round tells the story of how a mobster muscles his way into the music business by strong-arming major artists into joining his new record label.

"We need stars," he demands, "like Ted Lewis, Kay Thompson and her singers, and Cab Calloway!"

The Mob boss sends a couple of his thugs over to a radio station, where the marquee announces "Kay Thompson and Guest Star Joe DiMaggio."

"Joe DiMaggio?! The ballplayer?" asks Thug #1. "I'm laying off him. He hits too hard. Besides, the boss only wants Kay Thompson."

Once inside the studio, the gangsters watch Kay and her chorus performing "All Over Nothing at All" in front of a live audience. After a straightforward rendition of the first verse, the ensemble launches into what can only be described as an aural roller-coaster ride, slowing for anticipatory rises, then whiplashing into supersonic free falls. Incredibly, there are no fewer than seven tempo shifts within the last two minutes of the song, deliriously careening up, down, under, and way over the top. Never had an arranger broken so many rules in such a short span of time—and with such gleeful abandon.

The only thing Kay's motion picture debut lacked was a visual presentation as kinetic as her arrangement. With Thompson nailed to a piano stool and her chorus members rigidly standing on their marks, it truly was a radio performance caught on film. The song screamed out for choreography, camera movement, *anything* but the dull, static direction it got. Kay had perfected her sound, face, hair, and wardrobe, but without body language, it was all for naught. Her latent abilities as a dancer would not be put to the test until a decade later when she exploded onstage with the Williams Brothers. For now, heaven would have to wait.

Following Thompson's first number, the script called for DiMaggio to warble the first verse of "Have You Ever Been in Heaven?"—someone's idea of funny shtick. The director had presumed that Kay would remain in her position at the piano to accompany him. At the appointed time, however, Miss Thompson suddenly became indisposed. DiMaggio found her sulking in her dressing room.

"Joe asked Kay to play for him," recalled chorus singer and rehearsal pianist Hugh Martin. "But she said to Joe, 'Nah, I think I'd rather not. I want to look like a star in this movie. Maybe Hugh will do it.' So I played for Joe."

DiMaggio may have been one of the greatest baseball sluggers in history, but on the movie soundstage, he struck out big-time. Even though he only had a few lines of patter, it required twelve takes to get something remotely usable.

With so much time wasted, the most obvious casualty of compromise was Jack Jenney, whose close-up coverage was jettisoned. As a result, he is only vaguely discernible in crowded wide shots conducting the orchestra for Thompson's and DiMaggio's numbers. So much for a career boost.

Kay's second number, "I Owe You," popped up later in the movie, visible on the screen of a "Remote Control Short-Distance Television Set." This product placement—one of the very first live television broadcasts documented on film—served to introduce the newfangled technological wonder of TV. It would be more formally introduced by RCA at the 1939 World's Fair, but here was Kay, always ahead of her time, on TV in 1937. As Kay saw it, she had been thanklessly upstaged by an electronic device.

On a happier note, DiMaggio's presence created a photo opportunity of which Thompson took full advantage. One of the press pictures was staged in the makeup room where Joe was getting powdered, combed, and manicured by Kay and a "bevy of beauties" from her chorus. Days later, the shot turned up in major newspapers across the country, including the *New York World-Telegram*, where Joe was quoted saying, "This is hotter'n a ballpark."

Manhattan Merry-Go-Round had its world premiere in San Francisco at the Paramount Theater on November 17, 1937, with a first week gross of $13,000—a smash hit by Republic's modest standards. Local reviews were good, too. *The San Francisco Examiner* proclaimed, "Republic Studios jumped into the grade 'A' feature program category yesterday [with a movie that is] more entertaining than some widely heralded, highly financed films with music."

However, when the film was launched the following month in Manhattan at the Criterion Theatre, Bosley Crowther's review in *The New York Times* was less upbeat. He mentioned that "Kay Thompson and her radio choir" were among "assorted personalities paraded into camera range," none of which caught his fancy.

Nevertheless, publicity generated by the movie drummed up Hollywood interest in Kay. Long before the picture even opened, she was approached for a second movie appearance, this time for RKO, a studio considerably higher on the food chain. *Radio City Revels* would feature appearances by Ann Miller, Milton Berle, and the Vass Sisters (formerly of Kay's Rhythm Singers). Hal Kemp and His Orchestra was also on board and it had been hoped that Alice Faye, currently teamed with Kemp on *Chesterfield's Music from Hollywood*, would sing "Take a Tip from the Tulip" and "Speak Your Heart" with the band. Faye was under exclusive contract to Twentieth Century-Fox, however, and her bosses would not agree to a loan-out. That's when Kay got the call. Not only would Thompson's reunion with Kemp be something of a vindication, she relished the idea of snatching anything away from Alice Faye.

"Kay was completely scornful whenever Alice Faye came up in conversation," recalled *Eloise* illustrator Hilary Knight. "She would say things like, 'Alice has the biggest cold cream jars I've ever seen in my life.' I guess she didn't think someone like her should need cold cream, but Kay was jealous of anyone who was pretty." Especially a pretty girl who had stolen her radio gig.

Just before Kay signed the contract for *Radio City Revels*, however, she demurred. A much more intriguing opportunity had come her way: Vincente Minnelli wanted Kay to be a leading lady in his new Broadway musical, *Hooray for What!*

The genesis of *Hooray for What!* began when Broadway impresarios Lee and Jake Shubert were in search of a vehicle for the popular comic Ed Wynn. Upon hearing this, E. Y. "Yip" Harburg dusted off an unproduced story outline and the Shuberts went for it. Harburg and Harold Arlen were commissioned to compose the songs, Howard Lindsay and Russel Crouse were hired to flesh out the libretto, and Vincente Minnelli was engaged to direct the show and design the sets.

Ed Wynn would play Chuckles, a horticulturist and inventor who, as Harburg described it, "had an apple orchard, and he was trying to invent an insecticide that wouldn't kill [his beloved] worms."

A manufacturer of poison gas for the military is convinced that Chuckles has developed "a gas so terrible that whoever had it could conquer the world." European superpowers get wind of the discovery, then trip over each other trying to acquire the formula first.

Leading the arms race is Stephania Stephanovich, a modern-day Mata Hari with a thick Eastern European accent—think Natasha Fatale, Boris Badenov's vamp from *Rocky and Bullwinkle*. In a tight black dress, oozing duplicity, the dragon lady seduces Chuckles while using a hand mirror to catch sight of his formula. After writing it down, she escapes to Switzerland.

There, at Le Grande Hôtel de l'Espionage, the walls have eyes and ears—literally—with every oil portrait hiding a spy (a device Kay would later adapt for her book *Eloise in Moscow*). Secret agents steal the formula from Stephania, then from each other, but in the end, they discover it is nothing more than laughing gas. Why? Stephania's notations were backward due to the mirror's reflection.

Vivian Vance, who later immortalized Ethel Mertz in TV's *I Love Lucy*, campaigned tenaciously for the role of Stephania. Back then, however, Vivian was just an anonymous chorus girl who, because of her similar size and features, had understudied for Ethel Merman in *Anything Goes!* and *Red, Hot and Blue!*

Crouse and Lindsay had written the librettos for both Merman productions and had seen Vivian step into Ethel's shoes on the exceedingly rare occasions when the star allowed hell to freeze over. They liked her, and Vivian had begged them to write a part for her in their next project.

"We didn't think of [Vivian] for the part of 'Stephania,'" Russel later recalled, "because we knew a 'name' was wanted. 'All right,' she said, when she heard the bad news. 'I'll go into the chorus again.'"

The Shuberts thought Beatrice Lillie would be ideal for Stephania, but after agreeing to pay Ed Wynn a fortune, they were not about to part with another star's ransom. When the door opened for lesser known performers to be considered, Russel proposed Vivian. He had his heart set on her—in more ways than one. Despite her marriage and his own rekindled relationship with his ex-wife, Vance and Crouse carried on an affair that was anything but clandestine. As a result, Russel's casting preference was written off as hopelessly biased.

Meanwhile, the same week that Thompson and Joe DiMaggio were pictured in all the papers, Minnelli invited Kay to audition for the role of Stephania. Minnelli thought that Thompson's natural comedic impulses, her love of silly dialects, her lanky appearance, and her red-nailed talons made her a delicious choice to play the femme fatale. He also felt her arranging talents and choral direction could be used to great advantage. Her audition impressed everyone—with the exception of Russel, who continued his one-man crusade for Vivian.

The final decision was made public on August 14 when columnist Larry Wolters broke the story in the *Chicago Daily Tribune*: "Kay Thompson and her Rhythm Singers have been engaged for the new Ed Wynn musical, *Hooray for What!*"

As a consolation, Vance would be hired as Thompson's understudy. Outwardly, Vivian kept a stiff upper lip, but privately she was furious. It was one thing to understudy Merman, a bona fide star, but Thompson had never set foot on a Broadway stage. Vivian had paid her dues—in the wings and under the sheets. If Russel couldn't deliver, she'd find someone who could.

The next thing everybody knew, Vance attached herself to Yip Harburg. "I thought she might be having an affair with Yip Harburg because they were dating a lot, pretending it was platonic," Hugh Martin recalled. Of course, Russel was jealous and both men began vying for Vivian's affections.

At a rehearsal space in Manhattan on East Fifty-fourth Street, Kay practiced her part in the show while pulling together her largest chorus yet—eight men and eleven women—including Hugh Martin, Ralph Blane, and Meg Mundy (who later played matriarchs in *The Doctors* and *All My Children*).

To Kay's utter disgust, however, the Shuberts' business manager, Harry Kaufman, spiced up both the chorus and the ranks of the dancers with an assortment of floozies to appease his bosses and certain investors.

"I had to take them," choreographer Agnes De Mille chafed, "and I couldn't fire them, not if they fell down dead drunk at my feet, not if they were three hours late. They wore fine furs over their bathing suits, and diamonds, and platinum slave bracelets. Great limousines with liveried chauffeurs fetched them at the stage door."

Thompson did everything in her power to thwart the moll invasion but that only intensified inappropriate advances on her proper ladies. Nevertheless, she soldiered on.

With Her Singing Spies doing backup harmonies, Kay's solos would be "Moanin' in the Mornin'," "The Night of the Embassy Ball," "I'm Hangin' On to You," and the musical's first act finale showstopper, "Down with Love."

On their own, the Kay Thompson Singers would perform "Viva for Geneva," "Click Ze Heel," and "Hooray for What!" Ralph Blane, the best male voice in the chorus, would sing the lead vocal on "A Fashion Girl."

"In the Shade of the New Apple Tree" would be sung by ingenue Hannah Williams (wife of prizefighter Jack Dempsey) and her love interest, Roy Roberts, with a male quartet from Kay's chorus (Martin, Blane, Harold Cook, and Johnny Smedburg); "God's Country" would be sung by Roy and the chorus; "I've Gone Romantic on You" and "Napoleon's a Pastry" were duets for Hannah and Roy; "Buds Won't Bud" would be sung by Hannah; and featured dancer Paul Haakon would perform two spotlights, "Life's a Dance" and "Hero Ballet."

Astonishingly, there were no numbers for the star of the show. Because

Wynn couldn't sing or dance, he was to stick to what he did best: delivering one-liners. At first, he didn't have a problem with that until he began to feel like an extra lost in a pageant of vocalizing and dancing. As time went on, his mood progressively soured. That's when Vivian Vance suddenly "became friendly with Ed Wynn," and soon she had *three* men chasing after her.

Meanwhile, the show was in serious trouble. With a two-week out-of-town tryout set to open in Boston on October 28, *Hooray for What!* was nowhere near ready for public consumption. Three days before the opening, *The New York Times* reported that a second choreographer had been hired to stage additional dances: Bob Alton—the dance instructor Kay had met years earlier in St. Louis—now a top Broadway choreographer.

The stress took its toll on Arlen and Harburg, who both fell ill with stomach ulcers. Then, at the recommendation of a friend, Minnelli began popping uppers and downers to keep up with the frantic pace.

"We were all treated to the spectacle of our chiefs screaming and reviling one another across the theater," De Mille reported. "Harburg, who had just gotten out of a hospital, denounced Minnelli; Minnelli, his eyes bulging from his head with fixed fury, turned on Wynn; Wynn took his time; [Kaufman] harassed and chivied Crouse and Lindsay. Hannah Williams was in tears; Jack Dempsey wanted to poke someone but did not rightly know whom; Kay Thompson was grim-lipped and sardonic."

"The dress rehearsal lasted, without break, three days and two nights," De Mille recounted. "We went into the theater on a Tuesday and came out on Thursday at noon." Incredibly, the show had never been performed straight through. No one had a clue how long it was, nor if it had any pace or coherence. And yet the curtain was scheduled to go up at eight o'clock that night.

"Then with no warning, this super human collapsed," Minnelli confessed. "My system couldn't absorb such drugs."

"Vincente Minnelli took to his bed," De Mille explained. "The Shuberts' lawyers flew around like bats near a burning belfry . . . there was no one to take charge."

With Minnelli, Arlen, and Harburg out of commission, it was unthinkable to open that night, yet somehow they had to. Known for getting sick before shows, Kay puked more guts out than ever before. Everyone did. Staggeringly, the performance lasted *six* excruciating hours. Elinor Hughes' review in the *Boston Herald* was surprisingly charitable, singling out Thompson as "a striking blonde girl with a husky voice and an original style." However, the general consensus among other critics was that the show would never make it to Broadway.

"The next morning I was fired," said Agnes De Mille. She returned to New York, licking her wounds, and Bob Alton took over the show.

When performances on Friday and Saturday showed little improvement, the producers insisted on a midnight rehearsal in the wee hours of Sunday—the morning of Halloween—at which time Harry Kaufman's bad karma came back to haunt him.

Dead asleep in Manhattan, Agnes De Mille was awakened at 2:30 a.m. by a telephone call. It was Thompson.

"I have good news for you," Kay sneered. Savoring every detail, she explained that Kaufman had lost his balance and plunged from the stage into the orchestra pit, sustaining a serious back injury for which he had been rushed to the hospital.

"This isn't true," Agnes gasped. "You're just trying to make me feel better." But no one could have dreamt up such poetic justice.

With Minnelli still feeling sick, the Shuberts assigned Bob Alton to direct the musical numbers, and Howard Lindsay to direct the dialogue sequences.

To lighten the load, one of Kay's songs, "I'm Hangin' On to You," and one of her chorus's numbers, "Click Ze Heel," were thrown overboard; Hannah Williams' only solo, "Buds Won't Bud," was nipped in the you know where, and verses from other numbers were slashed.

Crouse and Lindsay had no choice but to truncate their book, de-emphasizing story in favor of Wynn's slapstick. Looking out for himself, Wynn hired joke writers to punch up his lines.

On a daily basis, Kay had to memorize revised dialogue, learn new dance routines, change vocal arrangements, rehearse her chorus, and guard her belles from molestation. She never dreamt that putting on a show could be more gnarly than her experience on *Low and Behold!* yet it was, by far.

On Friday night, November 5, after nine days of performances in Boston, Thompson was heading toward her dressing room when the stage manager, Archie Thomson, tapped her on the shoulder.

"That will be your last performance, Miss T."

It took a moment for the information to sink in. Was the show closing? No. The news was worse. Starting with the next day's matinee, her understudy, Vivian Vance, would take over the role of Stephania until another star could be hired. There was no gentle way of putting it: Thompson had been fired.

"An absolute *scandal*," Hugh Martin declared, still fuming seventy years later. "To fire that marvelous woman was unforgivable. We all knew Kay was great. Star quality! She could have been another Ethel Merman. Nobody could understand it."

Unable to breathe, Kay proceeded to her dressing room, shut the door, and fell apart.

"It was the worst thing I have ever, *ever* heard." Hugh shuddered, pained by the memory. "The screaming and the sobbing were something you can't imagine out of Kay—she went to pieces in such a spectacular way. Kay is so cool, so sophisticated, and so in command of herself that to picture her going to pieces is almost incredible. And yet I heard it. I heard her sobbing in the most ghastly, pitiful, heartbreaking way. I never got over it. It haunts me to this day."

The Shuberts claimed in the press that "Thompson had throat trouble and withdrew from the cast." The lie did little to ease the pain.

"We all said, 'Kay, we want to leave out of loyalty to you,'" Hugh recalled. "And she said, 'No, you'll protect my work if you stay and besides, you need the jobs. I don't want you all to be out of work because of me.' She made us all promise to stay, which was very generous and sweet of her."

Kay saw no dignity in trying to incite an uprising among her loyal troops, so she took the high road and got the hell out of town.

"If you're going to be a target, be a moving one," she later philosophized. "It's not as easy to be hit. If you stand still and allow yourself to be hit from various angles—emotionally, psychologically—you might not get where you're going. But if you have a goal, particularly a career, you can't let these things get on you like mosquitoes. You gotta just go on and go. Go to the next thing, and go with a joyous heart."

Who was responsible for the crime? Some believed it was Harry Kaufman's order. But a decision of such magnitude would had to have come from the very top, from the Shuberts themselves.

While the producers tried and failed to lure such replacements as torch singer Libby Holman and cabaret chanteuse Ethel Shutta, Vivian Vance sank her fangs into the role and, with every ounce of her feminine wiles, campaigned relentlessly to keep it. Eventually, with time and money running short, the Shuberts gave in.

But why was Thompson dumped in the first place? Hugh said, "The switch was made partly because Kay was not what the Shuberts considered sexy in the 1930s. Vivian was very much like a Joan Blondell type, blonde and plumpish, but in an attractive way. She was curvaceous and vivacious."

Exactly. So, how could anyone imagine Vance in the role of the prickly spider woman? On the other hand, perhaps it was typecasting after all. Eve Harrington à la Ethel Mertz. Even though the Shuberts were legendary for capricious changes, it appears that the growing membership of Vance's fan club—Yip Harburg, Russel Crouse, and Ed Wynn—had blood on their hands, too.

"When I asked Yip why they fired Kay," recalled Hugh, "he said, 'Because she was rotten.' I really hated him for it because I thought she was marvelous, and I felt it was disloyal of both Yip and Harold not to stand up to the stupid Shuberts and say, 'We want this woman. We found her. That's who we want and we will not allow you to replace her.' That's what they should have done, in my opinion. But they didn't."

Minnelli had always been Kay's strongest ally, but after his illness and his falling-out with Wynn, his power had eroded. When the additional credit "Book Staged by Howard Lindsay" suddenly appeared in the program, it was clear Vincente's opinion no longer carried much weight—which automatically gave Vivian another leg up in her divide-and-conquer strategy.

Disingenuously, she went to Kay and offered to quit. "You must do the show," Thompson replied. "It won't help me if you refuse. They'll just get someone else and you need the break. You're a gifted person."

Gracious speech, but Kay knew full well that Vivian had the upper hand—and there was nothing to be gained by getting into a catfight. Game over.

Nine years later, it was still hot gossip among Kay's confidantes at MGM, as evidenced by some no-holds-barred lyrics in "The Passion According to St. Kate, Opus 19, #46," the satirical cantata composed by Roger Edens in honor of Kay's birthday. Performed at a private party by Judy Garland and two *Hooray for What!* alumni, Ralph Blane and orchestrator Conrad Salinger, the song attributed Kay's dismissal to "the Shuberts' fornicality and Vivian Vance's sexuality."

Though Kay had left the show, the Forrest Theatre program for the subsequent Philadelphia tryout credited "The Kay Thompson Singers" and noted: "Soloists Coached by Miss Kay Thompson." Those "soloists," however, were dropping like flies—including Hannah Williams and Roy Roberts, both fired in Philly.

By now, all the dirty laundry from *Hooray for What!* had been worked up into a lather of bad press. With the official Broadway opening now set for December 1, something had to be done to quell the negativity. So, Russel Crouse wrote an article entitled "So You Heard a Rumor?" and hoodwinked *The New York Times* into publishing it on the Sunday prior to opening.

According to Russel's fabricated version of events, all the people who left *Hooray for What!* did so of their own volition. "It all started when Kay Thompson decided that she preferred her native radio to musical comedy," Crouse alleged. "We hated to lose her but there was nothing we could do about it." Apparently trying to be funny, he sarcastically listed potential replacements for Kay, including "Greta Garbo, Sophie Tucker, Eleanor Roosevelt, and, if she were still alive, Sarah Bernhardt . . . This kept up until Vivian Vance went into the part—and very nice, too." Anything but spin control, Crouse's article merely drew attention to the show's colossal fallout of talent.

Although reviews were mixed, critics generally agreed that Ed Wynn was a hoot, which, box office–wise, was all that really mattered. Even so, just imagine the satisfaction Kay must have felt when she read in *The New York Times* that Vivian's singing was "nothing remarkable." In several other reviews, Vance received the absolute worst indictment imaginable: no mention whatsoever.

Despite the turmoil, *Hooray for What!* became a modest hit, chalking up two hundred performances over the next six months. Throughout the run, Thompson continued to receive credit in the *Playbill* program for coaching the chorus, and took personal pride in the fact that her vocal arrangements were heard nightly on the Great White Way.

Although Wynn was the primary reason for the show's longevity, the musical's score and arrangements would be far more influential in the greater scheme of things. Upon seeing the show, MGM producer Arthur Freed signed Arlen and Harburg to compose the songs for *The Wizard of Oz,* and the connection did not end there. "I'm Hangin' On to You," one of Kay's solos cut in Boston, was resuscitated for *Oz* with new lyrics and a new title: "If I Only Had a Brain." Freed was well aware of Thompson's contributions as a vocal arranger, too, and in the years to come he would draw upon that talent.

Just when Kay thought it was safe to forget about *Hooray for What!* she was in for a surprise. For his NBC show, *The Royal Gelatin Hour,* Rudy Vallee wanted to feature selections from *Hooray for What!* performed by the musical's cast. However, the radio program went on the air at the same time the play was being performed at the Winter Garden. Someone proposed the unthinkable: Would Kay consider salting her wounds for one more night? If it meant that millions of people would hear her proudly sing her own arrangements of "Down with Love" and "Moanin' in the Mornin'," rather than Vivian Vance, then hell yeah.

The blissful exuberance of Kay's "Down with Love" arrangement was the perfect complement to the irreverent lyrics, and for good measure, the backup trio tossed in her idiosyncratic "Simone Simon" riff. In contrast, for the blues ballad "Moanin' in the Mornin'," Kay reached deep down into her gut and delivered an aching performance, pleading in a way that, when heard today, brings to mind Judy Garland. Of course, this was a full year before another Arlen-Harburg ballad brought out the gut-wrench in Judy, in a land you may have heard of, once in a lullaby.

Still not done with *Hooray for What!* Kay pulled some strings with Chappell and Company, Arlen and Harburg's music publisher, for Jack Jenney and His Orchestra to be granted "first recording rights" for two songs from the show—enabling her husband to land his debut recording contract with Vocalion Records, a subsidiary of Brunswick. And so, on January 14, 1938, two months after his wife had been fired from *Hooray for What!* Jenney found himself in the surreal position of recording "In the Shade of the New Apple Tree" and "I've Gone Romantic on You."

Kay had hoped to be the guest vocalist on the tracks, but Eli Oberstein, her boss at Victor Records, would not agree to a loan-out. Instead, Jack hired Adelaide Moffett, the scandalous, twenty-one-year-old heiress to the Moffett Newspaper millions. Thompson was not amused.

It is not known if Adelaide was one of Jack's extramarital conquests, but he had a reputation as a philanderer. Jealous and suspicious by nature, Kay apparently decided two could play that game.

It was around this time that she connected with Dave Garroway, who later became the founding host of NBC-TV's *The Today Show* (from 1952 to 1961). Born in Schenectady, New York, Garroway moved to St. Louis in 1927 at the age of fourteen and attended Washington University beginning in 1931, overlapping Kay's final year there. An avid music buff, he became a fan of Thompson when he heard her sing on KMOX and, since then, he had followed her career with keen interest. With a wife and baby daughter, Dave moved in 1937 to New York, where he "won an entry level position at NBC as a page" and "enrolled in the network's training school for announcers." Knocking around Radio Row, he made a point of meeting Kay, and their friendship progressed to an extramarital affair—which only simmered down when Dave moved away in 1939 for radio gigs in Pittsburgh and Chicago.

Sadly, infidelity was not the only marital woe brewing between the Jenneys. "Jack was a heavy drinker," Bea Wain confirmed. "He was smashed a lot. Kay drank pretty good back then, too, but Jack was worse."

Hughie McFarland, Jack's band boy, regaled acquaintances with stories about the couple's "legendary consumption of alcohol." Ted Straeter told friends, "In her early days, Kay was a drunk." And Paul Hemmer, director of the annual Jack Jenney Music Festival, recalled, "A woman from Jack's hometown in Iowa told me that the locals weren't impressed with Kay because 'she smoked that weed and had Jack smoking it, too.'"

Hearsay should not be taken as gospel, of course, but Kay did later tell playwright Mart Crowley, "Wherever there are musicians, there are drugs." Considering Kay and Jack's reputation as boozers, it is not hard to imagine them indulging in marijuana or perhaps even harder recreational substances. But, by all accounts, it was Jack who really let it get out of hand—especially in 1938 when, during a gig at the Onyx Club on "Swing Street" (West Fifty-second Street between Fifth and Sixth avenues), he got fired for showing up "drunk as a skunk."

Thompson's career was on shaky ground, too. She'd been dropped from several major radio series; her bid for Broadway had been a bust; her movie debut had been only a blip; and she was being held captive by a record label that no longer wanted her. Unemployed and demoralized, Kay was running low on money and self-esteem. It seemed like only yesterday she'd been making headlines, but those newspapers had gone to the bottom of the birdcage. Welcome to showbiz.

At that time, the star of the family was Jack. Although he wanted to tour with an orchestra of his own, he was too much in demand on the freelance circuit, where his reputation as a top trombonist kept him booked full-time. "He was besieged with so many offers that he had to hire a secretary to remind him of his numerous engagements," noted an article in *Song Hits*.

In early 1938, one of Jenney's gigs was in the orchestra for *The Kate Smith Hour* on CBS. One day when Kay was visiting, Kate Smith asked if she would be interested in forming a chorus to perform as backup singers on the series. Thompson did not want to toil strictly as a choral director, so she suggested her old pal from St. Louis, Ted Straeter, for the job.

Kay and Ted had formed a very tight bond in New York, though strictly platonic; he was one of her many gay friends. In putting together his choir for Smith, Straeter relied heavily on Thompson's former backup singers to fill the ranks, including Bea Wain.

"One night on *The Kate Smith Hour* I had a four-bar solo," Bea recalled. "After we got off the air, I got a phone call from bandleader Larry Clinton, who wanted me to audition for him." Bea had some doubts about her own abilities to be a solo vocalist, so she called Kay for advice.

"Meet me down at The Plaza," Kay told her. "In the Persian Room."

"It was during the day so nobody was there," Bea remembered. "Kay sat down at the piano and said, 'Okay, let me hear you sing 'The Best Things in Life Are Free.' Well, it's a rangy song. It goes from way down here to way up there. I mean, she was feeling me out, you know? And I did it. And she said, 'If you can do that, *okay*!'"

Who else but Kay would crash The Plaza and commandeer the Persian Room as her own private rehearsal studio? Of course, she thought nothing of it, striding through the hotel as if she owned the place. With her matter-of-fact bravado, some of the employees probably thought she did. Thompson had a piano in her apartment, but that just would not do. Singing in someone's living room was nothing compared to a real, honest-to-God stage.

"Kay just put me out on the right road," Bea marveled. "I really adore her."

Clinton liked Bea so much, he asked her to become his regularly featured vocalist, and from there she became a singing star in her own right.

Kay was also mentoring Ralph Blane and Hugh Martin. In 1938, she helped Ralph land his own Monday afternoon radio show on NBC, for which she served as a creative consultant. At the same time, Thompson put in a good word for Hugh with composers Richard Rodgers and Lorenz Hart that helped him land his first job as an arranger, on their Broadway musical *The Boys from Syracuse*. When Martin and Blane teamed up professionally, Thompson was like a proud parent. As *Family Circle* reported, "Kay encouraged them in their first songwriting ventures by making suggestions and helping to work out arrangements."

Many of her colleagues noted, however, that just below the surface of Kay's generosity was a fragile ego ready to erupt with anger and jealousy whenever a minion's success threatened to eclipse her own.

To reconfirm her standing as queen bee, Kay needed a job and, luckily, one was about to fall in her lap. In February 1938, bandleader Richard Himber, known for his theme song "Monday in Manhattan," was hired to conduct a twenty-piece orchestra—including Jack Jenney on trombone—for a new CBS variety series, *The Monday Night Show*, to be emceed by veteran vaudevillian Lou Holtz, set to debut on March 7.

Holtz would be accompanied in comedy sketches by the versatile thespian Agnes Moorehead, a fixture on Bill Spier's *The March of Time*.

Rounding out the regular cast on *The Monday Night Show* would be vocalist Connie Boswell—or so it was announced. Suffering from a start-up cashflow crunch, producer Freddie Mayer asked everyone to take a cut in pay "until the show got rolling." All agreed except for Boswell, who quit. At Jenney's suggestion, Thompson was hired as a last-minute replacement.

Mayer promised Kay she could have her large chorus of Rhythm Singers when money started rolling in, but for now, she'd have to sing solo. For the premiere broadcast, Kay performed "Exactly Like You," one of the songs she had recorded for Victor. Never satisfied with leaving well enough alone, she tinkered with the arrangement, slowed down the middle section, and kicked it into an even bigger climax—with Himber's lush orchestration puffing it up even further.

"Richard Himber gave a party for Kay Thompson, Lou Holtz, and the rest of his co-workers on his radio program," wrote columnist Virginia Vale, "and ever since the CBS studios have looked like a meeting of the Society of Amateur Magicians. Himber did card tricks at his party. Not to be outdone, Lou Holtz learned to pick watches out of the air. Kay Thompson is specializing in those old scarf tricks where one small handkerchief torn into bits turns into yards and yards of vari-colored scarves."

Though the musical aspects of the program were generally deemed magical, *The Monday Night Show* was one rabbit short of a hat trick. "Lou Holtz," according to *Radio Guide*, "was a big disappointment to many."

"The zing of Miss Thompson," noted *Variety*, "simply finger-pointed the unprofessionalism of the humor department."

New comedy writers were brought in to make improvements, but the cash-flow problem only worsened. After a month, the regular cast members were still collecting only a fraction of their contracted fees. Then, the paychecks started showing up late. Faced with uncertainty and stonewalling, Kay lost her patience and bailed after the sixth broadcast.

Upset that her manager, Mark Hanna, had not done more to protect her, she fired him and signed with the William Morris Agency, where her agent would be Marc Daniels (later a prolific television director on such series as *I Love Lucy* and *Star Trek*).

Trolling around CBS for job opportunities, Kay sought out her old friend Bill Spier, whom she'd gotten to know in 1934 on *Pontiac Surprise Party*. They'd already reconnected in 1936 when Kay sauntered by his *March of Time* studio at CBS, where he'd introduced her to his stable of actors, including Agnes Moorehead, Joseph Cotten, and the baby of the group, twenty-one-year-old Orson Welles (who'd made his radio debut on March 22, 1935, under Spier's direction).

As Bill had gotten to know Kay over the years, he realized they had an awful lot in common. They were both highly skilled, classically trained pianists and they loved playing double pianos together, jamming on all kinds of music, especially swing. They were also dedicated social climbers and, like Thompson, Spier had spent much of his life covering up his father's Jewish heritage in order to join high-society clubs where Jews were often not allowed. At parties and niteries, they both independently cultivated friendships with the rich and famous, always working the room with an eye toward upward mobility.

The palpable electricity between them, however, had been kept at arm's length in deference to Thompson's matrimony with Jenney and Spier's marriage to BBDO ad agency colleague Mary Scanlan (with whom he had two small children). The restraint, however, was not going to last forever—especially as both of their marriages were showing signs of wear. So, when Kay came to Bill's office in the summer of 1938, she was ostensibly looking for work, but her eyes betrayed the possibility of a whole lot more.

Still creating radio shows for clients of BBDO, Bill proposed a reunion of his all-time favorite musical conglomerate: André Kostelanetz and His Orchestra featuring Kay Thompson and Her Rhythm Singers. Kay and Kosty loved the idea and so, with vaudevillian Walter O'Keefe attached as host, Bill shopped the package to potential sponsors until Ethyl Gasoline agreed to underwrite the series.

Written, directed, and produced by Bill Spier, the program would be called *Tune-Up Time* and was set to premiere January 12, 1939, broadcast in front of a live audience of two thousand inside CBS Radio Theater 1, at 242 West Forty-fifth Street. Kay would earn $750 per week, her largest radio salary to date. With wage minimums now set by the newly organized American Federation of Radio Artists (AFRA), each of Kay's chorus members (nine women, three men) would take home around $62 per week. All would be Thompson alumni, including her sister Marian, who was back in New York singing again. (Under the stage name Mary Thompson, Marian had briefly headlined at New York's Hotel Commodore, where one review called her the "young and pretty sister of kilocyclin' Kay." Ultimately, however, Marian was too shy to make a career of it alone.)

Between musical numbers, comedy sketches were performed by O'Keefe and an ensemble including Agnes Moorehead, who gamely lampooned herself in a regular feature called "Waste of Time," a burlesque of *The March of Time*.

A major "name" guest star would join the regulars each week, and, depending on the magnitude of the celebrity, the sponsor was willing to cough up as much as $3,500 a pop. Among those who appeared were Douglas Fairbanks Jr., Beatrice Lillie, Dick Powell, Joan Blondell, Gene Autry, Lily Pons, Edward Everett Horton, and composers George M. Cohan, Richard Rodgers, and Lorenz Hart.

The most significant guest, however, was sixteen-year-old Judy Garland, who appeared on the April 6, 1939, broadcast. Judy had just finished principal photography for *The Wizard of Oz* in mid-March and was on a five-week personal appearance tour under the watchful eye of her vocal coach and accompanist Roger Edens. Roger had written a new number for Judy called "Sweet

Sixteen" and he had prepared an arrangement of "F. D. R. Jones." Kostelanetz shunned the use of outside arrangements, always insisting on original treatments by his own team. "Sweet Sixteen" was not changed much, but Kosty and Kay had already collaborated on a more elaborate arrangement for "F. D. R. Jones" that was used instead—performed by Judy with Kay's Rhythm Singers.

It was a fateful occasion marking Kay's introduction not only to Judy but also to Roger, who happened to share Thompson's November 9 birthday. It was no secret that Roger was born in 1905, but he was still trying to pinpoint Kay's birth year when he produced *Funny Face* with her in 1956.

Thompson got right down to business. Dressed in her trademark slacks, she breezed into the no-nonsense dress rehearsal in full makeup yet wearing a red bandanna over her damp, freshly washed hair (to be styled later for the night's program). According to chorus member Elizabeth Newburger Rinker, Kay demonstrated the special arrangements to Judy and Roger, playing piano and singing for them. After that, Roger took over at the piano as Kay coached Judy and the chorus until her shoulders tingled.

"Judy and Roger loved Kay from the get-go," Elizabeth recalled. "I remember they laughed at lot."

While in town, Judy performed five live shows daily at the Loew's State in Times Square, between screenings of *The Adventures of Huckleberry Finn*. According to Elizabeth, Kay and several of the Rhythm Singers went to see Judy during that engagement and caught her show again in August when she performed at the Capitol between showings of *The Wizard of Oz*.

During the latter engagement, Judy was being looked after by *Oz* producer Mervyn LeRoy's young assistant, Barron Polan, who would later become Thompson's agent. And, keeping it all in the family, the revue also featured Thompson's protégés Hugh Martin and Ralph Blane, who by then had formed a quartet known as the Martins, with sisters Jo-Jean and Phyllis Rogers.

"There were two pianos onstage," recalled Phyllis Rogers Whitworth, "and I remember Roger Edens playing one while Hugh played the other when we weren't singing. Kay was around all the time, helpin' us."

Of course, no one had a clue then just how significant all these connections would eventually become.

Tune-Up Time was beloved by critics, but struggled in the ratings because of two dreaded words: Bing Crosby. Bing hosted *Kraft Music Hall* during the same time slot on NBC, and routinely decimated the competition.

Fighting a no-win situation, the sponsor axed guest stars from the budget after the May 25 broadcast. With only five shows left (out of the original commitment of twenty-six weeks), CBS finally moved *Tune-Up Time* to Monday night, starting June 5, up against the less formidable *Eddy Duchin and His Orchestra* on NBC. But the change was easier said than done.

It turned out that CBS Radio Theater 1 was not available on Mondays, so *Tune-Up Time* moved to Theater 3 (now known as the Ed Sullivan Theater), where Kay and Kosty had done *The Chesterfield Radio Show*. The shift also meant cutting the show to a half hour. Spier slashed all the comedy routines and diminished O'Keefe's presence to little more than announcer. The spotlight would now be squarely on the music of Kay, chorus, and Kosty—which is what Spier had wanted in the first place.

The changes were worth it. The series slaughtered NBC, motivating Ethyl Gasoline to renew its sponsorship in August after a six-week summer hiatus. On the last show before the break, the closing number was Kay and Her Rhythm Singers performing Noël Coward's "I'll See You Again."

While all this was happening, Kay had decided to try to salvage what was left of her marriage to Jack, using songwriting as therapy. The result was the aptly titled "What More Can I Give You?" a blues number composed jointly by the couple, which was recorded by Jenney and his orchestra for Vocalion Records on April 11, 1939. A review in *Metronome* called it "a grand combination of a pretty tune played just as prettily on trombone by Jenney."

With Jack's drinking somewhat under control, Kay encouraged him to form a permanent orchestra and mount a tour. *Down Beat* wrote that MCA fronted Jack a loan of fifteen thousand dollars to get the band up and running. Jenney unwisely borrowed another fifteen grand from trumpet player Ruby Weinstein, who would collect an onerous percentage of Jenney's gross "up to 1949 in return for the loan."

The Jenneys had personal expenses to worry about, too, not the least of which was Jack's obligation to pay his ex-wife a hundred dollars per month for child support—which, according to his son, was often late or did not arrive at all.

Kay loaned Jack quite a bit of her own money, too. In a moment of clarity, she admitted to a reporter, "I'm the dumb cluck who is always getting drunks out of scrapes and lending them money that I never get back."

Singer Louise Tobin saw a pattern in Kay's behavior: "When you think about how close she later became with Judy Garland, who shared Jack's addiction problems, I think Kay had an affinity for the helpless—a mothering complex or something."

A fixer by trade, Thompson thought she could tame people's demons with the ease of rearranging a song, but all too often, their excesses would prove to be more than she could handle.

With initial gigs in Cincinnati, Boston, and Atlantic City that June, Jenney's touring orchestra got off on the right foot. *Down Beat* raved that Jack's new outfit "sounds like a million, plays like a million, and will probably make a million."

During a Boston radio interview, host Ruth Moss asked Jenney, "Does Kay ever sing with your band?"

"I wish she would," Jack lamented, "but she can't."

Moss wondered aloud, "I don't know if it would be good for two musicians in the same family to be working together, conflict of temperament and so on."

"Well, no, there's no temperament," Jack responded, keeping his cool. "We're very seldom together, you see, so it is all right."

Publicly, the Jenneys kept up pretenses of harmony. "I [used to think] that marriage and a career can't mix," Kay told a reporter that same year. "Well, Jack Jenney, the orchestra leader, and I have been married for two and a half years, and I admit I was all wrong. Today, I feel that most business women make a mistake when they try to make their marriages conform to exactly the same pattern as the marriages of women who stay home. It's not the actual details that decide whether or not a marriage is a success, but the spirit behind it."

One of those unimportant "details" was a singer traveling with Jack's band named Lucille Matthews, described by *Down Beat* as "a brunette Carole Lombard . . . who will knock you out." If this didn't raise Kay's eyebrow, widespread reports of Jack's falling off the wagon certainly did.

While fretting over her husband's relapse, Kay received word on July 12, 1939, that her sixty-five-year-old father had died of a heart attack. She dropped everything and flew to St. Louis to attend the funeral. Thompson's mother, Hattie, a homemaker all these years, was now faced with running Leo's pawnshop to make ends meet. While the rest of the family remained paralyzed with grief, Kay sprang into action, organizing everything, helping out at the store, making sure that her father's affairs were put in proper order. It was her way of dealing with loss—by refusing to let it get her down.

Compassionately, Jack rearranged his touring schedule and arrived in St. Louis to start a gig at the Chase Hotel—where Kay could keep closer tabs on his drinking.

Not long after the Jenneys returned to New York, Jack recorded his most celebrated record, "Stardust," during which he hit a high E-flat that was earth-shattering.

"No trombone player had ever done that," recalled his son, John Jenney. "That was a great, *great* moment."

John was not alone in his opinion. In 1946, *Down Beat* magazine declared, "Jack Jenney's solo on 'Stardust' (Vocalion label, his own band) is generally acclaimed as the greatest trombone record of all time."

Meanwhile, Kay's agent at William Morris, Marc Daniels, was packaging a new Broadway musical, *Ladies and Gents*, with libretto and lyrics by William Engvick and a score by the progressive jazz musician Alec Wilder. "It was a biography in the form of a revue about a man and a woman named Peter and Helen," Engvick explained. "It began when they met as children, and then there are various scenes of their meetings throughout their lives. They get married, then get divorced—that sort of thing."

Kay was attached to star in the show and there was talk of Bob Hope or Tony Martin for the male lead. In August, Audrey Wood and William Liebling, who represented Tennessee Williams, organized a backers' audition. Accompanied by pianist Walter Gross, Kay blazed through such scorchers as "I Wanna Dance," "Got On My White Pants," and the irresistibly titled "The Vamp of the Auto Camp."

"Kay did a superb job with our songs," recalled Engvick. "They were so beautifully rehearsed and laid out. It was just really exciting to see Kay do those songs in her own inimitable way."

The only missing ingredient was money. In search of some traction, Kay pressed her husband to add one of the show's tunes, "Lullaby," to his band's repertoire. Revisionists at heart, Kay and Jack could not help but play around with the arrangement and, in collaboration with Wilder and Engvick, they modified the lyrics and renamed the song "City Night." Taking it to the next level, Jack adopted "City Night" as his orchestra's theme song and recorded it for Vocalion Records.

Unfortunately, Jenney's support was not enough to help *Ladies and Gents*; the money just never came together. "It was a little abstract," Engvick lamented. "Maybe too abstract. The songs were pretty good, though, and if Kay Thompson had gotten to do them on Broadway, we really would have had something."

A few years down the road, in the summer of '42, Wilder and Engvick approached Kay again, this time to star with Jimmy Durante in an entirely new musical, *Sweet Danger* (aka *Brace Yourself, Brother*), a frothy mystery-comedy aimed straight at the masses. "The story revolves around a bevy of beautiful models," read an account in *The New York Times*, "who go to the home of a society matron to display some costumes and there become involved in a spy plot." But alas, once again, the financing never materialized.

On August 21, 1939, a more musically focused *Tune-Up Time* resumed broadcasting on Monday nights with singing heartthrob Tony Martin replacing Walter O'Keefe as host. Kay had known Tony since 1932, when they were wannabes with Tom Coakley's band. Since then, Tony had become a star in movies and radio, bolstered considerably by his marriage to Alice Faye, which was all the rage in fan magazines. In stark contrast, Thompson had only achieved recognition in radio and had not yet mastered the art of celebrity. Her emotions were mixed about Tony; though she was intensely jealous of his success, she liked him and seemed to realize that riding his coattails might not be such a bad thing.

Ratings for *Tune-Up Time* started off big until *The Adventures of Sherlock Holmes* (with Basil Rathbone and Nigel Bruce) was launched at the same time on NBC, becoming as much of a threat as Crosby had been on Thursdays.

As if that weren't enough, Tony Martin was suddenly hired by producer Irving Starr to top-line Columbia Pictures' *Music in My Heart* opposite the young Rita Hayworth. Much as *Hit Parade* had moved to Hollywood for Fred Astaire, *Tune-Up Time* now had to relocate itself in Hollywood for the five-week production schedule.

In exchange, Columbia Pictures agreed to plug *Tune-Up Time* in the movie itself. It made perfect sense because Tony's fictional character, Robert Gregory, was the star of a radio show that now, in a case of art imitating life, would be called *Tune-Up Time*. Kostelanetz would play himself as the conductor and it was assumed that Thompson and her chorus would appear as well.

To curb costs, Kosty would use local musicians from the orchestra at KNX, the new CBS affiliate. However, there was no Los Angeles equivalent of the Rhythm Singers, so Kay had to assemble a new choir from scratch. During the first Hollywood broadcast of *Tune-Up Time* on October 2, Kay performed two hot new Arlen-Harburg songs, "Ding-Dong, the Witch Is Dead" (with her West Coast Rhythm Singers) and "Over the Rainbow" (a duet with Tony)—both, of course, from *The Wizard of Oz,* which had just been released in August.

Meanwhile, prerecordings got under way for *Music in My Heart.* According to Tony Martin, Thompson was involved as an uncredited vocal arranger and choral director on some of the numbers. These most likely included "Punchinello," sung by Martin and the Brian Sisters, which was loaded with Thompsonian tempo shifts and harmonics. Kay also likely provided the choral arrangement and direction of the large mixed choir for "I've Got Music in My Heart," sung by Martin, which was subsequently performed on the November 6 edition of *Tune-Up Time* by Tony and Kay's Rhythm Singers.

However, when Kay realized she would only get to sing one duet with Tony in the movie, and that the rest of her screen time would be spent in the background directing the choir, she balked. If she couldn't "look like a star in this movie," she would rather not do it. And so, she didn't.

"If you have no confidence in yourself," Kay told a reporter, "who's to have confidence in you? You've got to carry your nerve in your pocketbook, along with your powder-puff and make-up. Otherwise you'll never get anywhere."

A tad less nerve might have gotten her farther. The executives at Ethyl Gasoline felt Kay had blown a huge opportunity to promote their show, and despite Bill Spier's valiant defense of her point of view, they decided to let her go when her contract expired at the end of the year.

Her artistry was never in question. Reviewing the October 30 install-ment of *Tune-Up Time*, *Variety* reported, "Musical ingredients were topflight Monday, especially Kay Thompson's whammo version of 'I Didn't Know What Time It Was' from [George] Abbott's *Too Many Girls*."

And in November, it was reported that Cole Porter was so impressed by Thompson's rip-roaring version of "Katie Went to Haiti" from his upcoming Broadway musical, *Du Barry Was a Lady*, he adopted certain riffs during the last week of tryouts.

Nonetheless, her days were numbered. "Kay Thompson and her choir de-part from the show after the broadcast of December 25," a columnist lamented in *Radio Guide*. "An unwelcome Xmas present, I'd say."

Even more depressing was the situation with her husband. A slave to his alcohol addiction, Jack had become frightfully emaciated, his weight falling below 140 pounds. The robust five-eleven buck who married Kay in 1937 had aged twenty years in less than three.

"He wasn't the poster boy for marriage," recalled Gary Stevens, Kay's publi-cist around that time. "And Kay wasn't the marrying type really. They were hardly ever together. She was running around with her entourage, song pluggers and singers. He used to hang out at Charlie's Tavern with a lot of musicians. His big pal was Bunny Berigan, who was an unforgivable drinker. Jack seemed to be just involved with his drinking and playing his instrument, working with the guys."

The most damning account, though, was the claim by Jenney's band boy that various items of jewelry were being "hocked to supply booze money." If that jewelry belonged to Kay, the betrayal would have been irreparable.

"Hughie McFarland was Jack Jenney's band boy and great friend," Robert Wagner recalled. "They were drunks together. They hung out together. Hughie told me that on at least one occasion, Kay had thrown Jack out of her apart-ment."

"As far as I'm concerned, a less likely couple never married," Alec Wilder wrote in an unpublished memoir. "They both loved swinging music and were talented musicians but there, outside of probable sexual attraction, the similarity of taste stopped. He loved to drink and she went with him to the bars, but I never remember seeing her the worse for it."

Walter Winchell was onto something when he wrote in his October 12, 1939, column: "Kay Thompson, the thrush, and her groom are talking Renonsense." As in Reno, Nevada, the land of the quickie divorce.

The December 1, 1939, issue of *Radio Guide* reported, "They say all is not well between Kay Thompson and her bandleader husband, Jack Jenney, and a visit to the divorce courts is on their schedule."

At the same time, Kay's relationship with Bill Spier was becoming more serious. Spier's daughter, Greta, recalled that her parents' marriage was dissolving during that period. "Once my sister, Margaret, was born in September of '39, their marriage didn't last much after that."

The romance between Thompson and Spier intensified in October when they spent five weeks at the same hotel in Hollywood for *Tune-Up Time*. "Kay and Bill were very friendly," confirmed Tony Martin, "and we could see it developing."

In the autumn of her life, Kay admitted to Liza Minnelli that, although Jack's alcohol consumption was crippling their marriage, it was his womanizing that broke the camel's back. In a 2008 interview for this book, Liza said, "Kay told me that, in those days, filing for divorce wasn't easy. There had to be a specific reason and you had to prove it."

"Will these do?" Kay deadpanned to the police as she dangled a pair of women's panties that did not belong to her. To Thompson's dismay, however, harder evidence was required.

To bolster her case, Thompson had to engage a private detective to photograph Jenney in the act—an indignity that Kay found "highly unattractive."

The divorce petition was filed in late 1939, and Kay and Jack went their separate ways. Jack wasn't just losing a wife; in March 1940, MCA dropped him as a client and his orchestra bookings dried up. Unable to keep his ensemble afloat, Jack turned up a few months later blowing trombone for Artie Shaw and His Orchestra. That same year, columnist Dorothy Kilgallen scooped, "Jack Jenney, the bandleader, will marry Bonnie Lake, Ann Sothern's sister, as soon as his divorce from Kay Thompson, the singer, is sealed."

On October 10, 1940, Jack and Bonnie made it official in a quickie Reno ceremony. Shortly thereafter, his new bride joined Shaw's band as a vocalist.

"Jack was a helluva musician," recalled trombonist Ray Conniff, who sat next to Jack in Shaw's band. "But gosh, he just ruined his life with that booze. Kay used to try to help him the best she could. Artie did. We *all* did. But he couldn't control it."

When things were not going well, Kay was drawn to the light—but not in the heavenly sense. Her idea of spiritual healing was being blinded by a spotlight while performing in front of an adoring crowd. Having just lost her father, her husband, her youth (she'd just hit the big 3-0), and the best radio job she ever had, she needed a round of applause. So, she created an act and, on February 6, 1940, she headlined the Famous Door nightclub on Swing Street.

"She did a twenty-five-minute set with a pianist and a bass player," recalled her publicist Gary Stevens. "She did some of the show standing up and occasionally she just slid in at the piano and played a few numbers on her own. Kay had a very sophisticated act, far and above what Fifty-second Street required—interpretations of songs, special material, she did the arrangements, she wrote special lyrics, she did everything. She was writing it herself and changing it every three or four days—adding stuff, taking it out."

Kay performed her set twice a night at eleven and twelve-thirty. Incredibly, she also ran through a condensed eight-minute version of the act four times daily at the Loew's State in Times Square, between showings of *Balalaika*, with her last performance ending around nine-thirty. Unlike the hipster-cool atmosphere of an intimate jazz club, the Loew's State was strictly old-school vaudeville, with square-jawed action star Chester Morris among the acts.

"Kay Thompson comes into vaude with quite a national radio rep," read the review in *Variety*, "but the latter has been built up via her singing in front of a choral group. On the stage here, however, she's appearing solo and the chorus is missed by the audience."

Like it or not, Kay's choir had become her claim to fame as well as her ball and chain. The *Variety* critic conceded that "as a singer and in stage deportment in front of a mike, Miss Thompson is A-1," but found fault in her decision to open with a blues number, "The Answer Is Love," which was deemed "much too slow to tee-off." Heeding the advice, Kay switched to a jazz-hot swing makeover of "How Deep Is the Ocean" that got the house rocking and became one of her most beloved arrangements.

"Kay was just using those engagements as a test for herself," Stevens concluded. "She wanted to know if she was serious about doing a nightclub act. In the end she wasn't too happy with how it turned out. She just said, 'Oh, the hell with it.'"

In search of a new direction, she nixed radio appearances and visited friends in Hollywood, hoping another movie role might come her way. When it didn't, she earned money by coaching singers and freelancing as a vocal arranger. According to pianist Skitch Henderson, Kay collaborated with Conrad "Connie" Salinger on the arrangements for a couple of Judy Garland numbers in *Ziegfeld Girl* and *Andy Hardy Meets Debutante*—Thompson's first brush with MGM.

"Kay, of course, was a big friend of Connie's because they worked together a lot," recalled orchestrator Alexander Courage in an interview with Leonard Maltin. "They were known for all those long impossible endings they put on all those numbers at MGM that went on forever. André [Previn] and I used to imitate them on the road when we were driving along."

For *Andy Hardy Meets Debutante*, Kay and Connie arranged "Buds Won't Bud," a song originally written for *Hooray for What!* that, like Thompson, had been axed during the Boston tryout. By the time *Andy Hardy Meets Debutante* hit theaters, however, "Buds Won't Bud" had died on the vine again, left on the cutting room floor. The third try was the charm when Ethel Waters sang "Buds Won't Bud" in *Cairo* (MGM, 1942).

"That was the mafia, Connie and Kay," Skitch Henderson fondly recalled. "And they joked that our conductor, Georgie Stoll, knew *nothing*, which was the first time I'd heard anybody put down conductors."

Still, Thompson was feeling restless and unfulfilled. Shortly thereafter, she returned to New York to form a new backup chorus that she named the Okays; together, they recorded several songs for Viking Records, including a cover version of "Dolores," the Oscar-nominated song from *Las Vegas Nights*. The results, however, seemed uninspired and sales were limp.

It was Bill Spier who snapped Kay out of her rut. Finally leaving his wife (and all but abandoning his three children), he and Thompson became a couple, carrying on publicly like high school sweethearts. They were known to play double pianos for hours on end, which resulted in a song they composed together called "More Wonderful Than These." True romance was the only excuse for such mushy lyrics as "The dreaming clouds above the seas, you are more wonderful than these."

After years of navigating from the passenger seat, what Kay really wanted was to drive her own radio show. Whether by serendipity or grand design, it just so happened that Bill Spier had become head of development at CBS and was in charge of *Forecast*, a summer series that presented pilots of proposed radio programs to test audience reaction and fish for sponsors. Eager to create a vehicle for Kay, Bill assigned writers Leonardo Bercovici and Robert Sloane to collaborate with her on a farcical backstage melodrama entitled "51 East 51," set in a mythical Manhattan supper club of the same name (the real-life address of Spier's apartment). Kay would play a fictionalized version of herself, working at the nitery as a singer, with songs interspersed throughout the story.

The plot of "51 East 51" revolved around a succession of telegrams that repeatedly interrupt Kay's nightclub act. These communiqués were supposedly from her Hollywood boyfriend but turn out to be the dirty work of two practical jokers (played by Everett Sloane and craggy-voiced Lionel Stander). Erik Rhodes, the dimwitted continental playboy from *The Gay Divorcee* and *Top Hat*, played the similar part of Ramone, "a charmingly wacky Latin man about town" who can't get enough of Miss Thompson. After being thrown out of the club several times, Ramone finally decides to just buy the place.

The conductor for the show was Archie Bleyer, thirty-two, a staff arranger at CBS who would later form Cadence Records, an unstoppable hit factory in the 1950s for such artists as the Everly Brothers, Andy Williams, and, not coincidentally, Kay Thompson's Eloise.

Kay got to sing four numbers, including a fun duet with Rhodes called "Daddy" (from the movie *Two Latins from Manhattan*), with special lyrics by Thompson—including a shameless plug that "51 East 51" was available for sponsorship "at very reasonable dough."

Reaction was upbeat. In *Variety's* words: "This program has the good sense to discover Kay Thompson in a bigger and better way than this first-rate artist has heretofore been discovered. Both as a song stylist, where she is among the best, and as a leading lady in featherweight gaiety (oh, blessed breeze in a heavy world!) Miss Thompson is about the most plausible candidate in her class for general discovery hereabouts."

Being recognized as an actress and comedienne must have sent Kay over the moon, but more important, reviews like this gave Spier ammunition to press for a series commitment.

CBS chairman William S. Paley adored Kay but felt a continuing story-line set in a nightclub was too limiting. He preferred another pilot presented on *Forecast* that summer called "Class of '41," a sketch comedy revue featuring an ensemble of fresh comics. Shrewdly, Spier suggested taking the obvious strengths of both shows and combining them. As luck would have it, a Wednesday night series, *Meet Mr. Meek,* would be going on hiatus for five weeks beginning September 3, 1941, creating a void that had to be filled with *something*. Slam-dunk. *The Kay Thompson Festival* was born.

The only carryover from "51 East 51" was Kay. From "Class of '41" came ready-for-prime-time newcomer Jim Backus, his writing partner, Larry Berns, and the twenty-three-year-old whiz-kid director, Perry Lafferty, who would be closely monitored by Spier.

"51 East 51" conductor Archie Bleyer was no longer available, thanks to Kay. "When we did *Best Foot Forward,*" recalled Hugh Martin, "Ralph [Blane] and I were stuck for a music director since we had never done a Broadway show of our own before. We called Kay, she recommended Archie Bleyer, and we took him."

In place of Bleyer, CBS house conductor and pianist Walter Gross was assigned to *The Kay Thompson Festival.* He was so pleased to be working with Thompson, he "borrowed a string section from the symphony orchestra" to augment his regular band. For her part, Kay arranged and conducted the Okays, her backup chorus.

The first show included an amusing sketch spoofing soap operas entitled "Life Can Be Life," starring Kay as Margo, a heroine so distraught over *something,* she fails to reveal just what it is—for the duration of the entire sketch.

"I'd *rawther* you didn't repeat it," Margo pleads to her lover, John (Jim Backus).

"Don't worry, I won't," he replies, keeping the audience mystified.

Dry and sophisticated, the humor was not everyone's cup of tea. *Variety* preferred the singing of "the stylistic Miss Thompson" over sketches "decidedly on the weakish side."

More accessible was Thompson's closing number at the end of the first program, "More Wonderful Than These," the love song she had composed with Spier. The following week, a telegram arrived: DON'T LET KAY GET OFF THE AIR TONIGHT WITHOUT SINGING THAT GRAND SONG SHE HAS JUST WRITTEN— MORE WONDERFUL THAN THESE. It was signed: TONY MARTIN, KATE SMITH, AND ANDRÉ KOSTELANETZ. From then on, the tune closed every show, becoming Kay's signature sign-off (like Bob Hope's "Thanks for the Memory").

As the weeks ticked by, however, no sponsor turned up with an open checkbook, forcing CBS to continue footing the bill. When *Meet Mr. Meek* returned after its five-week hiatus, *The Kay Thompson Festival* lost its time slot and appeared to be doomed.

"We didn't, any of us, know what we were doing," Kay told a reporter. "But despite the fact that we were an instantaneous flop, we all learned a lot from it. It was my first chance at coordinating a whole project, and it enthralled me."

With the show on the verge of cancellation, Spier finessed a move to Saturday mornings beginning October 11, under the new title *Kay Thompson and Company.* In her opening monologue, Kay made light of the less than desirable time slot: "It appears now that the really big, up-and-coming, new favorite time for listening is Saturday mornings."

But the sarcastic style of humor that had not gone over very well with the Wednesday night cocktail crowd fell even flatter with the Saturday morning coffee klatch. Nonetheless, Kay enjoyed herself immensely and developed a solid chemistry with her partner in crime, Jim Backus—so much so, it occasionally made waves with his fiancée, Henny Kaye. During the run of the show, Jim married Henny but delayed their honeymoon because of Thompson.

"We can leave for our honeymoon tomorrow right after the party," Jim told his blushing bride.

"What party?" Henny asked.

"The party I persuaded Kay Thompson to give to celebrate our marriage," stated Jim matter-of-factly.

The bride's mood went black. "You asked Kay to give us a party?"

Jim replied, "Well, we're doing the radio show together every week. It's the least she can do."

Henny later admitted to moments of jealousy: "Jim feels that working closely with someone he likes creates a mystic bond. If he had his own way, he would go through the complete Indian rite of blood brotherhood. I didn't understand it at the time, but a party was a party, and who was I to complain."

The last show of the thirteen-episode commitment was broadcast on November 29, 1941. With no sponsor and only moderate listenership, Kay and the others were certain they'd be unemployed by month's end. To everyone's amazement, however, Spier persuaded Paley to renew the series for a second round of thirteen. The first show of season two was broadcast on Saturday morning, December 6. The new beginning reinvigorated everyone and hopes were high, but within twenty-four hours, all that changed.

On Sunday morning, December 7, America awoke to the news of the bombing of Pearl Harbor. The mood of the entire country turned grim as tens of thousands of men were mobilized into military action. Kay's brother, Bud, enlisted in the United States Coast Guard. Dozens of her radio colleagues followed suit in all branches of the military—including her director, Perry Lafferty, one of her Okays, Andy Love, and several musicians in the orchestra.

In light of the situation, *Kay Thompson and Company* dropped its supercilious attitude and became patriotic. Kay opened with a pitch for United States Defense Bonds and introduced a new "Kiss the Boys Hello" segment dedicated to soldiers, with performances of flag-waving songs like "Of Thee I Sing." As scores of women bade farewell to servicemen, the sentimentality of Kay's signature song, "More Wonderful Than These," hit home. No longer aloof, the show was suddenly dealing with real, raw emotions.

Empowered by this, Spier got CBS to move the show back to prime time on Wednesday nights starting January 28, 1942. But with only five weeks left in the season commitment, there was precious little time to reestablish a foothold.

In a last-ditch effort to attract listeners and a sponsor, Bill and Kay called in favors from friends like Vincent Price, who performed a vignette from his new Broadway smash, *Angel Street*. (The thriller was later adapted into the movie *Gaslight*.)

For added oomph, Kay brought in the Martins quartet to join her singing "Buckle Down, Buck Private," a militarized makeover of "Buckle Down, Winsocki" from Hugh Martin and Ralph Blane's *Best Foot Forward*, still running on Broadway.

On the air, Kay asked Martin and Blane, "Who writes the titles of your songs?"

"I do," Hugh and Ralph blurted out simultaneously.

Fast on her feet, Kay ad-libbed, "I now pronounce you man and wife."

The show had found its footing and Thompson had really hit her stride as a confident mistress of ceremonies, singer, and comedienne. All the effort and good intentions, however, still did not attract a sponsor—hardly surprising during the uncertainties of war, yet essential nonetheless. Unwilling to pay the tab any longer, CBS decided against renewing the program. After twenty-six weeks of giving it their best shot, Kay and her gang were retired.

"After this show I came to a serious decision," Kay recalled. "I had to be an actress and I had to be alone. So I went to Hollywood, where I was neither."

Part Two

THE MGM YEARS

Chapter Four

MGM'S SECRET WEAPON

Kay Goes to Hollywood
(1942–44)

Kay was the best vocal coach in the world.
—*Lena Horne*

As 1942 got under way, there was an exodus of entertainers and musicians from New York, leaving either for military service or for greener pastures in Hollywood. In April, Kay's protégés Hugh Martin and Ralph Blane got hired by MGM as staff composer-arrangers. Just before leaving for the West Coast, they met with Thompson.

"We all had a cup of tea," Kay recalled, "and I said, 'You have to send for me.'"

Sweet on the surface. But in truth, Thompson was intensely jealous of the boys' good fortune—though her own goal was to star on the silver screen, not work behind the scenes. Shortly thereafter, she enlisted the aid of their manager, Fred Steele, to see if she could follow suit.

Around that time, Kay told writer Larry Carr that she would be perfectly happy to have a career like character actress Charlotte Greenwood, who specialized in middle-aged kooks. Making light of the obvious, Kay confessed that her mug was "a young face made up of old materials."

Self-deprecation from Thompson, however, usually meant just the opposite. Deep down, she dreamed of becoming the next Joan Crawford or Greta Garbo. This desire was certainly evident when she asked her publicist, Gary Stevens, to set up a photo shoot with a top glamour photographer.

"Murray Korman was a good friend," Stevens recalled, "so I went up there with Kay and she said to me, 'Don't let him get any profile shots because, Christ, I look like Basil Rathbone.'"

Meanwhile, Kay formed a new vocal quartet featuring Phyllis and Jo-Jean Rogers (of the Martins, which was now defunct), Pat Haywood (Jo-Jean's husband and Hugh Martin's understudy), and George "Cookie" Richmond (of Broadway's *Banjo Eyes*; later replaced by Jimmy Engler). Even though all of the members were in their twenties, Kay christened them the Four Teens and she got jitterbug bandleader Johnny Long to add the group to his ensemble for a May gig at the New Yorker Hotel.

"Kay came down there all the time, three or four nights a week," Stevens recalled. "After midnight, she would rehearse the Four Teens."

"With Kay, we never got to bed before dawn," Phyllis Rogers Whitworth confirmed. "It was really dynamic. You know, Kay had such *fire*. I remember her saying, 'That's just right as rain!' That was her favorite phrase. She'd sit out at the tables at night and listen to us, and even when we were on the road sometimes, she'd be out there and she'd come back and tell us if we were just a little bit off pitch."

"The Four Teens recorded a song called 'Can't Get Out of This Mood' by Frank Loesser and Jimmy McHugh," Stevens remembered, "and Kay knocked off the arrangement in about an hour."

Released by Decca Records, the song shot to No. 20 on the *Billboard* chart and was subsequently performed by the quartet in *RKO Jamboree: Johnny Long and His Orchestra*, an eight-minute musical featurette.

"Kay was thrilled for us," Phyllis recalled, "but I think she kind of wished she'd recorded the song herself."

"Kay wrote special lyrics for the Four Teens that were very clever," Stevens added. "For the song 'I Can't Get Started with You,' she wrote the line, 'And Joe DiMaggio's bats over me,' and for some other song she came up with, 'Smokio over Tokyo,' describing a bombing raid or something. She created as she spoke. She never edited anything. It was an emotional outburst, superseded by superior talent."

On the acting front, Kay was summoned to California to audition for a supporting part in Republic Pictures' *Hit Parade of 1943* starring Susan Hayward. Kay read for the role of Belinda Wright, Hayward's wisecracking older sister, a character that was ultimately awarded to Eve Arden, who, ever since her splash in *Stage Door*, had all but cornered the market on sardonic female sidekicks.

Though she didn't get the job, Thompson still managed to be involved in the film. Her friend and fan Jule Styne had composed six new songs for the musical, and when he heard that Kay was pounding Hollywood pavement, he convinced Republic's music director, Walter Scharf, to bring Thompson on during the prerecordings to beef up the vocal arrangements. She received no credit, which was typical of the often unsung art of vocal arranging.

On that picture, Kay met the Music Maids and began coaching and creating vocal arrangements for them. The quartet's leader, Alice Ludes, recalled that they were paired with the Three Cheers to sing "Do These Old Eyes Deceive Me," for which they were all coached by Thompson. Kay also chose Music Maid Jeanne Darrell to dub Susan Hayward's singing voice on several numbers, including "A Change of Heart," which received an Academy Award nomination for Best Song.

But, all things considered, Kay really did not want to work for a Poverty Row studio like Republic Pictures; she had her heart set on Metro-Goldwyn-Mayer. Not only had she freelanced as a vocal arranger for two MGM movies (*Ziegfeld Girl* and *Andy Hardy Meets Debutante*), she also had a growing number of friends who worked there—Hugh Martin, Ralph Blane, Lennie Hayton, Vincente Minnelli, Charles Walters, and Conrad Salinger among them. Even if she had to freelance behind the scenes in the music department, Thompson figured that once she got her foot in the door, the opportunity would arise for her to star in one of MGM's pictures.

Accordingly, in October 1942, Kay got herself hired at MGM to beef up the finale of *Presenting Lily Mars* (produced by Joe Pasternak). From a vocal arrangement by Hugh Martin—though Thompsonian in style—"Paging Mr. Greenback" (Sammy Fain–Yip Harburg) was a spectacular five-minute number sung by Judy Garland, with patriotic lyrics promoting war bonds. It was hoped that Kay's coaching and choral direction would add extra oomph.

While Kay was earning greenbacks in Los Angeles, her boyfriend was doing just fine in New York. Bill Spier had successfully championed a *Forecast* pilot called *Suspense* into a smash anthology series on CBS, distinguished by big-name guest stars each week—including Orson Welles, who had transformed himself from Spier's protégé to the Hollywood wunderkind of *Citizen Kane*.

A bigger mystery than any story ever presented on *Suspense*, however, is why Thompson never appeared on the show, particularly given her desire to advance her career as an actress. On the October 25 episode of another Spier series, *Radio Reader's Digest*, Kay's acting skills were put to the test as daredevil reporter Nellie Bly in "The Front Page Girl." (Promoting *Casablanca*, Claude Rains also appeared.) But Bill's main interest in Kay remained personal.

Two weeks later, on November 11, 1942, Kay and Bill were married—though the circumstances remain shrouded in mystery. Margaret Spier Angeli, Bill's daughter from his first marriage, disclosed, "My mother got a New York State separation but there was never an official divorce decree. She told me that my father had gone to Mexico and gotten a 'quickie' divorce but I don't think it was considered legal in New York or New Jersey. That's why I think Kay and my father were married in either Mexico or California, where the divorce was recognized."

From then on, Bill's children—Peter, eleven, Greta, nine, and Margaret, three—rarely saw their dad, and they never met Kay. He paid child support for a while but eventually stopped. Clearly, neither Bill nor Kay was cut out to raise children; they were far too career-driven and self-absorbed.

Just days after her wedding, Kay received word that the Four Teens had been offered an on-screen appearance in Universal's *Hit the Ice*, starring Bud Abbott and Lou Costello, the No. 1 Box Office Stars of 1942. In the film, the Four Teens would team up with ingenue Ginny Simms to sing "I'm Like a Fish Out of Water," accompanied by Johnny Long and His Orchestra. And, while at Universal, the quartet was also assigned to sing "Penny Arcade" in a musical featurette entitled *Swing Time*.

So they could prepare for the West Coast prerecording sessions in late November, the sheet music for both songs had been sent to the Four Teens in Philadelphia, where they were playing a gig. "Kay came to Philly and worked out the arrangements," Phyllis recalled. "Then she came with us to Hollywood to coach us."

"Penny Arcade" was so well liked, the Four Teens' rendition was recycled in Universal's *See My Lawyer*, produced and cowritten by Edmund L. Hartmann, Kay's former colleague from Washington University.

While in Hollywood that December, Kay got hired again at MGM to do some freelance vocal arranging for Judy Garland in *Girl Crazy*. Though her work went uncredited, it marked Thompson's first official involvement on a picture made by the "Freed Unit"—the crème de la crème musical factory-within-the-factory at Metro, led by producer Arthur Freed and his associate producer, Roger Edens.

There was a palpable competition among the various producer "camps" on the lot, particularly in the musical genre, with Joe Pasternak, Jack Cummings,

Irving Starr, and others vying for the best properties and stars. The leader of the pack, however, was Freed.

Strategically, Kay made herself useful to Judy Garland, the studio's golden girl. In addition to coaching her singing on *Girl Crazy*, Thompson gave her pointers on posture and gestures, in collaboration with Roger Edens and the film's choreographer, Charles Walters, whom Kay had known since 1933 (when they both appeared in *Low and Behold!*).

"[Garland's] best early film was *Girl Crazy*," noted film historian Albert Johnson, "largely because of Kay Thompson who taught Judy Garland how to be a younger, more dynamic version of Kay Thompson in such brilliantly designed numbers as 'Bidin' My Time' . . . and 'I Got Rhythm.'"

Kay also wowed her colleagues as a choral director on "I Got Rhythm" and "Bronco Busters," for which she assembled a swinging choir that included the Music Maids, Six Hits and a Miss, and Hal Hopper (formerly of Kay's Three Rhythm Kings).

Back on the East Coast, a new star was about to be born. After three years and a string of Top 10 hits with Tommy Dorsey and the Pied Pipers, twenty-seven-year-old Frank Sinatra made his solo debut at the Paramount on December 30, 1942. When he took the stage, scores of teenage girls began screaming hysterically. Sinatra's PR man, George Evans, admitted that "certain things were done" to get things started but the frenzy spread like wildfire and Sinatra mania took on a life of its own. It was the birth of the teen idol—the kind of fan worship that would later besiege Elvis, the Beatles, and Michael Jackson.

After record-breaking grosses, Sinatra agreed to extend his booking at the Paramount from January 27 to February 20, 1943. Prior commitments prevented his backup band, Benny Goodman and His Orchestra, from continuing, so plans were made to replace the outfit with Johnny Long and His Orchestra featuring the Four Teens, just back from Hollywood.

At the request of Phyllis Rogers, Thompson returned to New York to work with them during the day and after hours at the Paramount, at which time Kay met Frank and they became fast friends. He was so taken with her musicianship, he spent a lot of time observing her in action.

"We'd be working with Kay at three o'clock in the morning," recalled Phyllis, "and there'd be the orange glow of a cigarette out in the dark, empty theater. He didn't think we could see him but we knew it was Frank—just watchin' us."

Surrounded by success, Thompson and Spier grew anxious about their own careers. Bill envied Orson Welles' remarkable transition from radio to the movies. Similarly, Kay was turning green over her own growing list of protégés who had struck gold in Tinseltown. Hollywood beckoned. It would be easier for Bill to populate *Suspense* with stars there than it was in New York, and the movie capital was the place to be if Kay really wanted to be in the game. But relocating to California was easier said than done, especially given Bill's executive position at CBS. The newlyweds were pretty much resigned to stay put when the phone rang. It was for Kay.

Panic at Metro. *Presenting Lily Mars* tested poorly. The "Paging Mr. Greenback" number was out. A whole new finale had been ordered for Judy Garland.

Before Kay finished packing her bags, Bill announced he was coming, too. Spier had convinced his bosses to let him bring *Suspense* to California for a trial run, while Thompson would be doing CPR at MGM.

Insert montage: Takeoff. Landing. The Hollywoodland sign.

They checked into a bungalow at the Garden of Allah, the legendary residence hotel nestled halfway between Hollywood and Beverly Hills, on Sunset Boulevard at Crescent Heights.

Bill set up shop at Columbia Square, the KNX/CBS Studios at Sunset and Gower, two and a half miles down the road from the hotel. There, several weeks of *Suspense* episodes were churned out with West Coast guests like Fredric March, Mary Astor, Bela Lugosi, and Sydney Greenstreet—enough to convince CBS that a permanent move to Hollywood was in order.

Kay's commute to MGM in Culver City was seven miles—and she was put right to work. In place of the discarded "Paging Mr. Greenback" number, a mammoth ten-minute medley called "Where There's Music" would be performed by Garland for the new finale of *Presenting Lily Mars*.

Kay expanded and refined the arrangement that Roger Edens, Hugh Martin, and Conrad Salinger had been preparing for Judy's next window of availability on March 4 and 5, when the marathon two-day recording session was scheduled to take place.

Meanwhile, Thompson got sucked into helping out on Metro's *Swing Fever*, for which she arranged and conducted the choir on "Mississippi Dreamboat," sung by Marilyn Maxwell.

"You can hear Kay's voice really clearly singing with the chorus," noted MGM authority George Feltenstein.

"Kay occasionally did sing with us," confirmed Music Maid Alice Ludes, "but mostly she would just direct the chorus because her voice was deeper and stronger and did not blend in well with a group."

Despite the variety of undertakings, Thompson's main focus was on Judy Garland. In the four years since Kay had first met her on *Tune-Up Time*, the young star had gone from sweet sixteen to Mrs. David Rose, wife of the famous composer-conductor. But marital bliss had come to a screeching halt when Rose had been inducted into military service in the fall of 1942.

"Judy was alone, save for his two weekend visits a month," wrote Gerold Frank in *Judy.* "When he came home . . . he would walk into his house in his fatigues and heavy army boots to find a party in progress, with people he hardly knew or had never met. There was Kay Thompson, one of the wittiest of women, and her husband, Bill Spier . . . Roger Edens . . . Conrad Salinger . . . Charles (Chuck) Walters . . . June Allyson, Van Johnson, June Havoc, all brought from the East to Hollywood by MGM—all new people, exciting people. They played intricate word games and charades, everyone dealt in wit, satire and put-downs, and he felt out of it." By summer, David and Judy would be officially separated.

Having worked professionally since the age of three and with more than a dozen movies to her credit, Judy had never had time to mature emotionally. Studio doctors had her on a merry-go-round of addictive medication, uppers for work, downers for sleep, and diet pills to keep her weight in check. Somehow, through this medicated haze, she developed an insatiable need for constant love and approval. To that end, Judy could make a perfect stranger feel as if they had known each other their entire lives.

Kay was naturally enthralled, if not a bit smitten, by this "laser beam of pure emotion." As intensely as Judy was addicted to pills, Thompson became mesmerized by Garland and her blossoming career. If this was any indication of what life was like working for MGM, Kay wanted to join the club.

However, no sooner had she made herself indispensable at MGM than the Great White Way beckoned. On March 8, 1943, *The New York Times* reported that Thompson had been offered the lead role in a Broadway musical called *Early to Bed*, featuring thirteen new songs by Fats Waller to be conducted by Archie Bleyer (Kay's maestro from *Forecast:* "51 East 51") and choreographed by Bob Alton (*Hooray for What!*).

The bawdy comedy would have Kay playing Rowena, the madam of a bordello that gets mistaken for a hotel. All the ingredients were there for a hit, including some hilariously suggestive songs like "A Girl Doesn't Ripple When She Bends," "When the Nylons Bloom Again," and "This Is So Nice (It Must Be Illegal)." This was the offer Kay had been waiting for all her life—to be a leading lady on Broadway.

At the very same moment, however, MGM offered Kay an exclusive, longterm contract to be their in-house vocal doyenne. To the surprise of many, she accepted.

Kay would now be a member of the MGM boys' club—no small feat in that era. The press noted that Thompson was the "first and only woman arranger in American music."

On March 16, 1943, Kay scrawled her John Hancock on an agreement with MGM that would commence on Monday, April 5, with options up to seven years (someone's wishful thinking). A contract memo was officially drawn up between Loew's Incorporated (the parent company of MGM) and "Mrs. Catherine F. Spier, professionally known as Kay Thompson (Arranger)." At a starting salary of $500 per week (to be raised by $100 each year), her job was described as follows: "Exclusively for us as a vocal arranger, vocal coach and other duties in the Music Department as we require and she capable of performing (other than composing complete songs)."

When arranging vocals, Kay never wrote anything down, so accommodations were made for her unusual way of working: "She [is] not required to do actual 'physical scoring' of her arrangements, and we [are] to furnish musical steno or assistant as required by her to transcribe arrangements into manuscript form."

The MGM publicity department would control Kay's public image, so she was expressly forbidden to hire her own publicist.

The agreement allowed her to "render services for herself or others" on one radio broadcast per week during off-hours. Regarding possible "loan-out" offers for Kay's services from competing studios, Metro would consider these on a case-by-case basis.

Kay was given two weeks to close up shop in New York and make the permanent move to Los Angeles. Bill went east with her and did a couple of *Suspense* shows from New York while they packed and vacated their Manhattan apartment.

"Kay tried to get me to go to California and assist her," Phyllis Rogers Whitworth of the Four Teens recalled, "but somethin' had happened to me by then. I was finished with showbiz. I just had to get out of it. I said good-bye to her and our group disbanded not long after that."

In an interview with writer Hugh Fordin, Kay recalled the date when she and Bill returned to Los Angeles: "It was April the 1st, if you believe in omen."

Wasting no time getting into the swing of the glamorous life, the Spiers attended a private preview of *Cabin in the Sky*, a new MGM musical starring Lena Horne. "We had just come from New York," Kay recalled, "and the two of us fell sound asleep during it."

The following Monday, her first official day on the job at MGM, Kay ran into her *Hooray for What!* director, Vincente Minnelli.

"Oh hi, honey," Vincente said. "Did you see the picture? Did you see *Cabin?*"

"I didn't see much of it because I fell asleep," Thompson replied, not realizing that Minnelli had directed it.

Despite that embarrassment, Vincente immediately requested her vocal arranging services for his latest picture, *I Dood It.* The movie was all but completed, save one isolated number for Lena Horne that, when necessary, could be cut out of prints exhibited in racist Southern theaters.

"I did 'Jericho,' and Vincente directed it," Kay later recalled. "Down I go to the [rehearsal studio], hiring the sixty singers, and I have them for five days, and then Lena came in."

The coming together of Horne and Thompson was auspicious for both of them. "[Kay] taught me how to open up and let the music out," Horne was quoted as saying in the *Philadelphia Daily News.* "I had a little voice and couldn't carry a tune. I was afraid to sing."

"Even though my mother had worked a number of nightclub gigs without a microphone, she had never, ever learned about singing *out* before," recalled Horne's daughter, Gail Jones Lumet Buckley. "Kay got her to just open her mouth and let it rip. Belting, I guess you'd call it."

Thompson took an immediate liking to Horne. "As naturally friendly as a puppy," Kay recalled, "[Lena] sends out a liking for others and is eager to be liked in return. All in all, she is one of the few completely *real* people in Hollywood."

Similarly, Horne was impressed with Thompson right off the bat. "The most important thing [Kay] taught me was breath control," she later elaborated. "We were working on her arrangement of 'Jericho' and it really extended me and I was hitting the notes I didn't know I could."

Something special was combusting in that rehearsal hall and the buzz reached the producer, Jack Cummings (nephew of studio head Louis B. Mayer).

"Jack came down," Kay remembered, "and we knocked him over with great joy. It was after that I was called by him to say, 'Make something for Hazel.'"

Hazel Scott was another African-American performer being groomed by the studio—a darker, earthier singer and piano player. She was to prelude "Jericho" with a jazzy keyboard solo of "Taking a Chance on Love" and reappear in the middle of "Jericho" for an improvised piano break.

Movieland magazine reported that Lena and Hazel came face-to-face for the very first time "in the office of Kay Thompson."

According to Gail Lumet Buckley, "Lena turned up, California style, in pigtails, slacks and loafers. Hazel, fresh from New York, was dripping in silver fox."

"Hazel was always known for her fabulous clothes and jewels and furs," Lena wrote in her memoir. "[The next] day I was determined to outshine her and I came to work in my best dress and wearing my mink and my few little pieces of jewelry. Of course, that was the day Hazel decided to go California. She came to work in slacks and a blouse."

Hazel took one look at Lena and cracked up laughing.

"It was a laugh all around," Lena recalled, "with Kay Thompson leading the chorus."

The Dreamers, an African-American quartet, was a key ingredient in Kay Thompson's large, racially mixed choir, which brought together a number of preexisting singing groups, including the Music Maids, the Three Cheers, and Six Hits and a Miss.

"Kay was color-blind compared to a lot of folks in those days," recalled Dreamers member Leonard Bluett (whose mother was a cook for Humphrey Bogart for thirty years). "She'd mix us right in with white singers, which just wasn't done in Hollywood back then. Our experience had mostly been singing Negro spirituals in Jester Hairston's all-black choirs on movies like *Gone With the Wind*. So all of us black kids thought Kay was on 'our side,' you know. She was very open-minded and she was very tight with Lena."

Bluett described what it was like to work in Kay's chorus: "When we got on the lot, the music would be handed to us. We would go over it with Kay and learn our parts, like an actor would learn his lines. The singers were on risers, like at a basketball game. We would first be in a rehearsal hall and then we'd go to the recording studio when we were ready. Kay was definitely a perfectionist. She would really tell you exactly what she wanted and it had to be just right. After breaks, she'd say, 'Everybody up! Let's go! Function! Function! Function!' Firm but very upbeat, like Lauren Bacall. Everybody liked her."

Conrad "Connie" Salinger was assigned to create the orchestration to match Thompson's complicated vocal arrangement. "Connie always used to say that he couldn't do jazz," Kay recalled, "but on 'Jericho,' he did it. He was so adorable when we started that patter. I said I wanted a 'badoobadeep, badoobadeep, badoobadeep' underneath it going all the way through. He said, 'Well, would you like it in the celli?' And I said, 'Yeah, I think it'd be great in the celli! Let's put it there.' *God*, the patience he had!"

Everyone needed patience when it came time to record the thing. Conductor Georgie Stoll was faced with one of the more difficult arrangements of his career. Lena recalled, "During the course of the long, wearing evening, conducted by a gentleman that I never did enjoy working with—too Prussian in attitude, with everybody—Kay and I began to gripe. 'What a drag,' Kay said. 'If Lennie were doing this we'd have been finished eight hours ago.'"

Kay was referring to her beloved *Bing Crosby–Woodbury Show* and *Lucky*

Strike Hit Parade maestro Lennie Hayton, but Lena liked him even less than Georgie.

Not long before, Vincente Minnelli had taken Lena to a private party where Hayton was among the guests. One of Hayton's cronies, comedian "Rags" Ragland, was telling racist jokes that Lena overheard. By association, Horne assumed Hayton was a racist, too.

The more Lena grumbled how much she disliked the guy, the more steadfastly Kay defended him. Lena recalled, "Toward the end of the evening Kay said, very firmly, as if making up her mind about everything: 'He's very much the kind of man I think you'd like.' You know how your girl friend can plant something in your mind? I admitted I'd never really had a chance to know what Lennie was really like and Kay had managed to pique my interest."

Thanks to Matchmaker Kay, a romance did indeed develop between Lennie and Lena, which wasn't easy in those days.

"Very few restaurants would serve Lena," recalled Peggy Rea, who was then working as a secretary for Arthur Freed. "There was one place on Sunset just east of Gardner—I forget the name of it—but I was there many times with Lena and Lennie, Kay and Bill, just the five of us."

At that time, the laws of California prohibited marriage between races, but even if it had been legal, MGM would never have allowed it. So, Lena and Lennie kept things discreet.

From her previous marriage to Louis Jones, Lena had two young children, Teddy, three, and Gail, who, like Eloise, was six years old when she met Kay.

"Many of my best childhood friends were grown-ups," wrote Gail in *The Hornes: An American Family*. "Roger Edens, Kay Thompson, Conrad Salinger of the Freed Unit." Having traveled with her mother on tours, Gail always had *rawther* sophisticated stories to tell her bemused older pals. "I took to hotel life like a duck to water," Gail recalled. "All kids do. Hotels represent luxury, magic, and freedom—all those corridors, elevators, and opportunities for solo missions. My life was excitingly similar to that of Eloise . . . 'This is me, charge it please!'"

When the time finally came to shoot the "Jericho" number, director Vincente Minnelli summoned Kay for help.

"Vincente Minnelli was always busy fixing Lena's gown," Leonard Bluett chuckled, "so he had Kay there to make sure the sound was going right and that we were mouthing the words right."

Some of the on-screen singers were new and didn't know the words to the prerecorded track, so Thompson stopped the shooting and ordered a quick rehearsal. "I said, 'Come to the piano!' with all the authority of Queen Mary," Kay recalled. "And I go 'tada tada *ta da*' on the piano, but it is one of those dummy pianos and not a sound came out of it. And this whole group fell out—just *roared* with laughter. And I fell out and said, 'Just go back to where you were.'"

Next on her docket was *Meet the People*, starring Lucille Ball, Dick Powell, and June Allyson. It would be lyricist Yip Harburg's debut as a producer, a career move loaded with more drama than the film itself. Harburg's entrée into producing only happened because of Arthur Freed's endorsement and yet, on every level, Harburg blew the opportunity, requiring Freed to cover for his mistakes and clean up the mess.

Kay had loathed Yip ever since *Hooray for What!* when his affair with Vivian Vance had led to the one of the more serious crimes of the century. Somehow, for the good of *Meet the People*, she managed to bury the hatchet, but it was a shallow grave on the edge of a slippery slope.

Later, in 1950, Harburg would be among many entertainment figures named as "suspected Communists" in *Red Channels*, the newsletter that prompted blacklisting during the heinous McCarthy era. Consequently, whenever Yip's name came up in conversation, Kay always venomously snapped, "That pinko!" The cold war between them never thawed.

The person who made the production of *Meet the People* tolerable for Kay was Lennie Hayton, the Freed Unit's preferred music director. It was this picture that professionally reunited them for the first time since founding *Hit Parade* in 1935. And, unlike prior movies for which her contributions were limited, *Meet the People* afforded Kay her first complete menu of songs from which to cook—and her first full-fledged Freed Unit assignment.

Thompson created yet another superchoir for the production and would soon be adding new groups to the mix like Mel Tormé and the Mel-Tones (aka the Skylarks), whose members included Ginny O'Connor (later Mrs. Henry Mancini). But the ones she loved the most were four bumpkins from Iowa, the Williams Brothers—Bob, Don, Dick, and sixteen-year-old Andy. The boys were signed by MGM to appear in *Anchors Aweigh* and *Ziegfeld Follies* but had to bow out of both when Bob was drafted into the Army. In the meantime, Kay kept Don, Dick, and Andy steadily employed in her chorus.

Thompson's choral work was most outstanding on "I Like to Recognize the Tune" (based on a Hugh Martin arrangement originally intended for RKO's *Too Many Girls*, but never used). Historian Will Friedwald pointed out that the song was "embellished and updated by MGM's resident wit Kay Thompson, who borrowed liberally from Gershwin's 'By Strauss,' threw in a reference to

Rodgers & Hart themselves, and switched the line, 'A guy named Krupa plays the drums like thunder' to 'When Tommy Dorsey tears a tune asunder.'"

"I was just handed a song for yet another cameo role and told to learn it and be ready to sing it," June Allyson recalled in her autobiography. "It was called 'I'd Like to Recognize This Tune,' [*sic*] and I remember telling Lucille Ball, 'I'd like to recognize where I'm going. I think it's *nowhere*. That's where.'"

Kay did not warm up to June, nor vice versa. "Never trust a woman who wears a Peter Pan collar," was Kay's curt indictment. Playwright Mart Crowley recalled that even in later life, Thompson was still mocking Allyson by imitating her "in that high, whiny voice."

Lucille Ball's tonality was just the opposite—low and scratchy. Kay was responsible for replacing it in the prerecordings with the more mellifluous singing voice of Gloria Grafton. Thompson worked closely with Ball on the set, making sure that her lip-synching was credible.

"Lucy was on one side of the camera and I was on the other side," Kay explained during a joint appearance with Ball on *The Tonight Show Starring Jack Paar* in 1960. "That's when we first became acquainted and became very good friends."

Lucille dreamed of one day warbling her own songs in a musical—a goal Kay would later help her achieve. Ball admired Thompson tremendously and Kay not only loved Lucy, she also liked her husband, Cuban bandleader Desi Arnaz. Soon, the Spiers and the Arnazes were frequently spotted together at hot spots all over town.

While the Freed Unit kept Kay occupied on *Meet the People* from May through August, producer Jack Cummings arranged for her to work on *Broadway Rhythm*, with an overlapping recording schedule of June through September. Although producers were highly possessive of their own pools of talent, it was financially beneficial to share because, on overlapping weeks, for instance, Kay's salary of $500 was split between the two movies' budgets.

In some ways, *Broadway Rhythm* was an extension of the work Kay had been doing on *I Dood It*; it was for the same producer and it again featured numbers by Lena Horne and Hazel Scott. But the most Thompsonian song in the film was "Milkman Keep Those Bottles Quiet" sung by the diminutive and feisty Nancy Walker, backed by Tommy Dorsey and His Orchestra (dressed as milkmen on-screen). Calling it a "rhythm novelty classic" and a "wartime favorite," historian Will Friedwald declared, "Walker and Tommy Dorsey walk off with top musical honors."

The ingenue in the film was played by Gloria DeHaven. "I never had a singing lesson in my life," recalled DeHaven, "but I can sing and it's because of

Kay Thompson. Kay Thompson was a vocal *coach*. There's a big difference . . .
[Kay] gave you style, how to sell a song, how to move your body, how to stand.
'Not on every word,' she would say, 'do you use a gesture.' She was phenomenal,
just phenomenal."

Although Kay mingled with a multitude of celebrities at work, there were
plenty more when she went home to the Garden of Allah. Once the home of
silent screen star Alla Nazimova, the Spanish-style house had been converted
to accommodate a reception area, administrative offices, eight guest rooms, a
restaurant, and a bar. Twenty-five villas, each subdivided into multiple bunga-
lows, had been added throughout the three-and-a-half-acre estate, surrounded
by tropical trees, fountains, and goldfish ponds. In the center of the property
was a large swimming pool in the shape of the Black Sea.

But nobody came for the amenities. The attraction was all about star wattage. When the Spiers arrived, residents included actors Humphrey Bogart
(soon to be joined by Lauren Bacall), Errol Flynn, Charles Laughton and Elsa
Lanchester, Edward G. Robinson, Fredric March, John Garfield, John Carradine, and Nazimova (reclusively peering from behind drawn curtains); writers
Robert Benchley, Elliott Nugent, and Clifford Odets; musicians Paul White-
man, Xavier Cugat, José Iturbi, Artie Shaw, Benny Goodman, and Woody
Herman; and singer Perry Como.

Kids were an endangered species. Walter O'Keefe had two bratty sons
whom Kay called Leopold and Loeb, inspired by convicted murderers Nathan
Leopold and Richard Loeb. And six-year-old David Carradine ran around in
a cowboy hat shooting at everybody with his toy pistol.

One of the rare little girls on the premises was Sylvia Sheekman, daughter
of screenwriter Arthur Sheekman and actress Gloria Stuart of *Titanic* fame,
known back then for starring in the James Whale classics *The Old Dark House*
and *The Invisible Man*.

"Kay was my best friend," confirmed Sylvia Sheekman Thompson (no relation) in 2002. "I was eight and I was a lot like Eloise. I wasn't living at The
Plaza, but I was a little girl at the Garden of Allah surrounded by adults. I was
inquisitive and I loved everybody. I'd see Kay all the time at the pool and I
would visit her place. I remember the upright piano, Kay and I, sitting side by
side on the stool playing 'Chopsticks.'"

Thompson enjoyed the girl's visits and spoiled her with treats and gifts.
"When I had my tonsils out," Sylvia remembered, "Kay actually made a record,
a song she wrote for me called 'Sylvia Having Her Tonsils Out.' It was so

incredible . . . a 78 disc, one-sided. The fact that anyone would do this during the war for a little girl having her tonsils out was amazing. All I remember is it started with distant calling, 'Sylvia . . . ? Sylvia . . . ?' as if I were coming out of the anesthetic. Can you imagine doing that for a child?"

Kay's generosity did not stop there. "She also gave me two orange kittens," Sylvia added. "I remember coming home from school and they were there in a box. My mother said Miss Thompson had left them for me. Kay had named them Roger and Wilco, like they say in the Air Force over the radio."

It was no accident that Kay and Bill had chosen a bungalow in the inner circle, a prime location on the ground floor of a villa located diagonally across the pool from Bogart and Errol Flynn.

Both were on a mission. Kay longed to be a movie star, and the Garden enabled her to mingle among them and live like one. Bill was on the prowl for big-name actors to bolster his radio series, so the Garden was a natural casting depot—with Kay as his willing accomplice. In a matter of weeks, they had rounded up such neighbors as Charles Laughton and Elsa Lanchester to appear on *Suspense*, spiking the ratings further upward, thus setting the stage for Bill's most monumental accomplishment in radio—and a scream heard coast to coast.

On the May 25, 1943, installment of *Suspense*, Agnes Moorehead starred in "Sorry, Wrong Number," the story of an invalid woman who, in the process of trying to place a phone call, gets a wrong connection and overhears a man plotting a murder. The climax culminates in the horrifying discovery that the murderer is making the calls from inside the woman's home and that she herself is the targeted victim.

In the original script, written by Lucille Fletcher (wife of *Suspense* composer Bernard Herrmann), the assassin enters the bedroom to kill the woman, but the police break in just in time to save her life. When Thompson read it, she felt the happy ending was a yawn and jokingly suggested a more grisly denouement. Spier didn't think the idea was funny at all but rather a stroke of genius. He immediately rewrote the climax so that the murderer would finish the deed, concluding the episode with nothing but the bloodcurdling scream of the helpless victim. Little did Kay or Bill know that this sadistic shock ending would knock the wind out of millions of listeners coast to coast, resulting in one of the most talked-about radio milestones of all time—second only to the hysteria caused by Orson Welles' *The War of the Worlds*. In fact, Welles himself called "Sorry, Wrong Number" "the greatest single radio script ever written." The phenomenon exploded further when Decca licensed the broadcast for commercial release, with sales so brisk it ended up as the third-highest-selling record of the year. Then *Life* published a pictorial of Bill coaching Agnes.

Right in the midst of this career high, however, Bill suffered a massive heart attack in mid-July. For a workaholic like Spier, being laid up in the hospital, then confined to his bungalow at the Garden for convalescence, was downright depressing. And for someone as hyper as Kay, being a nursemaid was sheer torture.

During the sabbatical, she tried shaving her husband every morning. "But it was too much for me," Bill said, "Kay coming at me with a razor." So a beard took root and became his trademark for life. Sheilah Graham dubbed him "the first hippie of Hollywood"; June Havoc described him as "tall, dark and woolly"; and Robert Montgomery called him "King George." Judy Garland remarked to *Modern Screen*, "Those high Hooper ratings Bill Spier always gets on his radio shows are not because Bill looks like a genius. Whiskers won't register on the air, but talent does."

Kay liked the beard as well as the rest of the package. "To look less like an invalid," she explained, "Bill decided that he would not wear pajamas. He was an exciting man in the nude."

Kay wasn't the only one who got to see Bill in his birthday suit. One night, the Spiers woke up to the heart-pounding discovery that an intruder was standing at the foot of their bed.

"Bill quite forgetting his heart attack got up and chased him to the patio," Kay said. "He was about to call for help when he realized he was stark naked . . . Bill, to make it more interesting, told [the police], 'They took my gold cuff links.' I don't believe they did, but he always had a sense of the dramatic." As if she didn't.

When Bill was back on his feet in September 1943, he not only resumed his position as producer and story editor on *Suspense*, he took over directing chores as well. And to help him get back into the swing of things, Orson Welles agreed to star in not one, but four consecutive installments of the series.

Welles had just married Rita Hayworth, whom Kay had befriended in 1939 on the set of *Music in My Heart*. So it was only natural that the Welles and the Spiers socialized. Between Bill's star-studded radio triumphs and Kay's splash at MGM, they sashayed onto Tinseltown's high-society A-list. And, just as young Kitty Fink had made herself the life of every party, Kay breezed into every gathering, made a beeline to the piano, and got everyone singing till dawn.

Seemingly inexhaustible, Kay often volunteered for the war effort, too. "Every week," she recalled, "I went to a hospital or a ward at some veterans' hospital to sing and play the piano. Some of the wards were depressing and it was emotional to go there. One got caught up in the horror of the damage to the young guys who . . . didn't know who they were, walking around in those bathrobes, hanging around the piano and listening with eyes somewhere else. It was always difficult to go back to the studio after one of those."

A year earlier, President Roosevelt had ordered the Special Services Division of the War Department to provide entertainment for soldiers via radio; and thus, the Armed Forces Radio Service (AFRS) was formed. Uplifting variety shows were produced and transcribed on records, then shipped to hundreds of portable front-line transmitters to help boost morale among the troops.

Headed by Colonel Tom Lewis, a former radio producer, AFRS was run by a unit of privates that included the aspiring actor Howard Duff (who served as announcer), Kay's old pal Pat Weaver (who wrote and/or directed), and Barron Polan (who headed the "talent-procurement department"). Thompson had met Barron in New York in 1939 when he was shepherding Judy Garland on her promotional tour for *The Wizard of Oz*. Since then, he had dated Judy and become her agent.

Through his tight associations with Garland and MGM, Barron had become friendly with Kay and was eager to book her on AFRS programs. Thompson was only too happy to oblige. In May, she appeared on *Personal Album* (accompanied by Hugh Martin); in September, she did an installment of *Mail Call*, hosted by Ingrid Bergman, for which she sang her jazzed-up arrangement of Irving Berlin's "Louisiana Purchase" (with Ralph Blane in the chorus); and in November, she did another *Mail Call*, hosted by Lucille Ball, for which she performed a brassy version of Cole Porter's "I'm in Love with a Soldier Boy."

At a birthday party for Judy in June 1943, Kay ran into Broadway star Danny Kaye, who had just arrived in Hollywood to begin shooting his first motion picture, *Up in Arms*, produced by Samuel Goldwyn for RKO. Danny was a big fan of Kay's work and he convinced her to do the choral arrangements, a moonlighting job that would have to be done under the radar because of her exclusivity to MGM.

Getting away with one outside job encouraged Thompson to test the boundaries of her contract further. Over the next several years, she worked clandestinely with Danny again on *Wonder Man* (Samuel Goldwyn/RKO, 1945); with her Garden of Allah neighbor Perry Como for his debut in Irving Starr's *Something for the Boys* (Twentieth Century-Fox, 1944); with the Williams Brothers on *Something in the Wind* (Universal, 1947); and with the Music Maids on several films.

• • •

Her most daring extracurricular activity occurred at the behest of a certain blue-eyed crooner she'd befriended earlier that year in New York. When RKO brought Frank Sinatra to Hollywood on August 12, 1943, to star in his first movie, *Higher and Higher*, it was no accident that he took up residence at the Garden of Allah in a bungalow right next door to the Spiers. Frank wanted Kay to be his coach and advisor and she threw caution to the wind when he came calling.

"Frankie led a quiet life at the Garden," wrote Sheilah Graham, "preferring to stay home in the evenings rather than test Hollywood night life."

Many of those evenings were spent singing in the Spiers' living room, with Kay accompanying him on piano. These neighborly jams served as coaching sessions, and there is no doubt that Sinatra came away with adjustments to his repertoire based on their melodic canoodling. Thompson's services were rewarded with "big bowls of Italian spaghetti" delivered to her door every night by Sinatra's cook.

Kay helped Frank rehearse his Hollywood Bowl engagement on August 14 and, that same month, helped him prepare his five numbers in *Higher and Higher*, including "I Couldn't Sleep a Wink Last Night," which earned an Oscar nomination for Best Song.

On weekends, Frank and Kay often hung out together by the pool and seemed mighty chummy to those who observed them—though there seems to have been more laughing than stolen glances.

"A picture no artist could paint," was how columnist Edith Gwynn described one poolside scene in late September when Frank and Kay were joined by three smashed stooges: Charlie Butterworth, Ed Gardiner, and, most conspicuous, Robert Benchley, "with gay Hawaiian trunks about his avoirdupois." Thompson encouraged Benchley to greater heights of public humiliation by giving him "lessons in swing singing." Before long, an audience of dozens had gathered to witness the buffoonery. In the *Los Angeles Times*, columnist Hedda Hopper dubbed the lesson Kay's all-time "funniest assignment." And Sinatra had never laughed harder.

Frank adored spending time with Kay and, before long, the camaraderie evolved into something more. Thompson later regaled family and friends about the night that Sinatra made a pass at her—but she insisted that she remained faithful to her husband.

After the filming of *Higher and Higher* was completed, Frank headed to New York for a two-month gig at the Waldorf. Halfway through that engagement, Hopper noted, "Frank Sinatra still telephones Kay Thompson about song arrangements and asks for advice."

Up until then, few were aware that Kay had become Frank's "vocal guru," least of all her employer. MGM apparently turned a blind eye because, by then, Sinatra was being sought to star in one of the studio's pictures.

To that end, for Frank's second RKO movie, *Step Lively* (with songs by Jule Styne and Sammy Cahn), MGM agreed to loan out Gloria DeHaven and the services of Kay Thompson—to coach both Frank and Gloria—in exchange for RKO allowing Frank to star in Metro's *Anchors Aweigh*.

For *Anchors Aweigh*, Kay collaborated with Jule Styne and Sammy Cahn to create "special arrangements" and "revised lyrics" for several numbers, including the Frank Sinatra–Gene Kelly duet, "If You Knew Susie Like I Know Susie" (Joseph Meyer–Buddy G. DeSylva). For the film's leading lady, Pamela Britton, Thompson spent several weeks teaching her to sing "good and loud," but by the time the movie started shooting, her proposed numbers had been dropped.

Though Sinatra tried his best to monopolize Thompson, she still devoted quality time to MGM's favorite daughter. "I like the title of the song Judy Garland has written with Kay Thompson, her gal arranger," mused columnist Louella Parsons in September. "It is 'If I Fell and Broke My Heart.'"

Nothing came of it, however. Countless Garland endeavors were stalled because of her legendary substance abuse, enabled for years by MGM's studio-sanctioned doctors. "When Judy sometimes disappeared from MGM and they couldn't find her," wrote Sheilah Graham, "she was usually with Kay and Bill in their spare bedroom."

Recognizing Thompson's positive influence over Garland, Arthur Freed inquired about her availability for Judy's next picture, *Meet Me in St. Louis* (directed by Vincente Minnelli). To his dismay, he would have to share Kay with rival producer Joe Pasternak, who had already secured her priority services for *Two Girls and a Sailor*.

Because Kay was not available to work full-time on *Meet Me in St. Louis*, Freed used Hugh Martin to do much of the vocal arranging for the songs Hugh had composed with Ralph Blane, including "Have Yourself a Merry Little Christmas" and "The Trolley Song."

Thompson's contributions to the picture are less obvious, yet ubiquitous. When six-year-old Margaret O'Brien was cast to play Garland's little sister, Tootie, she had never sung or danced in a movie. On November 8, 1943, columnist Harrison Carroll reported that "little Margaret O'Brien is being coached by Kay Thompson" for her songs, including her charming duet with Judy, "Under the Bamboo Tree."

On the first day of rehearsal, Kay inquired, "Margaret, how do you like the idea of singing?"

"Fine," the precocious youngster replied. "But, please don't try to make another Shirley Temple out of me."

Kay didn't. By the time she was done with her, Margaret's persona in the picture was something more akin to Eloise—with a morbid curiosity and an impish way with words.

When contacted for this book, the adult Margaret O'Brien remembered her teacher well. "Aside from being a great vocal coach," Margaret recalled, "Kay was a great choreographer. My mother, being a dancer, did a lot of my choreography, but I remember that Kay and my mother talked dance a lot and Kay offered advice on some of my moves."

After the film came out, Margaret was honored with a special Academy Award for Outstanding Juvenile Performer.

Another beneficiary of Thompson's guidance was Dorothy Gilmore Raye, a contract dancer who appeared in the movie. "The first time I ever met [Kay]," Raye recalled, "she came swinging in a stage door and my eyes bugged right out of my head because here she was, with this full-length mink coat, dragging it across the floor. She swung it out in front of us and said, 'I'm here. I'm ready.'"

Kay's other duties on *Meet Me in St. Louis* were directing the choir, coaching Judy during the recording sessions, and supervising the lip-synching during filming. She even promoted the picture on radio by singing "The Trolley Song" five months before its release.

Next to the lavish and colorful *Meet Me in St. Louis,* the black-and-white production of *Two Girls and a Sailor* pales by comparison, though it does have its modest charms. The cast included Van Johnson, Jimmy Durante, June Allyson, Gloria DeHaven, Lena Horne, Don Loper, Frank Jenks (Kay's 1933 radio partner), and Thompson's newest assignment, Ava Gardner (who appeared as a canteen hostess).

Thompson created the vocal arrangements for nearly all of the twenty numbers performed in the film—most notably "My Mother Told Me There Would Be Moments Like This," sung by Gloria DeHaven and a jazzy twelve-boy harmony chorus; "Paper Doll," sung by Lena Horne; and "Young Man with a Horn," sung by June Allyson with Harry James and His Orchestra.

"There's a story about June Allyson," related Michael Feinstein. "June's hair was all done, so she didn't want to put on earphones to hear the music. Losing patience, Kay said, 'Darling, put your earphones on and forget about the *hair*! We've got work to do!'"

Kay got along much better with Jimmy Durante, who was so impressed, he hired her to write songs and create special arrangements for his new CBS radio series, *The Jimmy Durante–Garry Moore Show*, which premiered October 8, 1943.

Thompson was also exerting her prerogative on her husband's radio shows. She convinced Bill to cast up-and-coming MGM star Gene Kelly on the November 16 installment of *Suspense* to coincide with the release of his first nonmusical gig, the war drama *The Cross of Lorraine*.

Gene and Kay shared an intense fondness for playing charades, aka The Game. At his home on Alta Drive, Gene and his wife, Betsy, were known for hosting charades parties and Kay became an instant regular. Songwriter and musical director Saul Chaplin remembered one such party: "We arrived at 10:30 and rang the doorbell. No one answered. We tried the door. It was open, so we walked in. We were in a room packed with a lot of noisy people."

The guest list included Thompson, Sinatra, Garland, Horne, Tyrone Power, Mickey Rooney, David O. Selznick, Betty Comden, and Adolph Green, among others. A high school teacher had been hired to umpire, and it was clear that Gene took The Game very seriously.

"It was scary watching our easygoing hosts turn into veritable storm troopers right before our eyes," Chaplin related. "The time between games was taken up with postmortem recriminations. Gene would yell, 'If it weren't for *you*,' naming the unfortunate who was slow coming up with the answer. It could be a movie star like Tyrone Power or a quick-witted comedienne and writer like Kay Thompson; Kelly didn't care."

Kay's idea to put musical stars like Gene Kelly and Lucille Ball on *Suspense* helped establish one of the hallmarks of the series: casting against type. "We had people like Cary Grant, Jimmy Stewart, Olivia de Havilland, Bette Davis, and everyone," recalled Bill Spier. "They would do it because they got to play things that they could not do any other way. Jimmy Stewart would be a murderer, or Jack Benny, a murderer. Or Edward G. Robinson would be totally innocent. Boris Karloff would turn out to be completely wronged."

*B*etween work at MGM, moonlighting for Durante's radio show, and her volunteer casting chores for *Suspense*, Kay was burning the candle at both ends. In early December, the pace took its toll.

"Kay Thompson, the ace arranger, collapsed on a Metro set the other day," announced columnist Dorothy Kilgallen, "and was rushed to the hospital for an emergency operation. At the time she was working on a Jimmy Durante song called 'I'm Completely Floored.'"

On December 10, 1943, *Daily Variety* reported that she was "in Good Samaritan Hospital recuperating from [a] major operation."

The exact nature of the surgery was left to the imagination—a highly unusual circumstance because, in those days, ailments of everyone in Hollywood were routinely reported in breathtaking detail. But, for some reason, MGM felt it necessary to downplay the situation. Metro's first official statement was issued by Nat Finston, head of the music department. Dated December 9, 1943, it claimed that Kay "went home ill" and would continue being paid during her convalescence. This did not jibe with press reports of hospitalization. Later, the studio contended that Thompson was suffering from "a bout of the flu."

There was, in fact, a flu epidemic that winter—even President Roosevelt had fallen ill—but if Kay had actually been suffering from influenza, MGM would have seen to it that she was properly quarantined from its most valuable assets. Evidence abounds, however, that no one seemed concerned about contagion.

"Judy Garland and Lana Turner sent the male patients' temperatures sky high when they walked into Good Samaritan Hospital together," noted Louella Parsons in her column on December 14, 1943. "They were visiting Kay Thompson, MGM's vocal coach." As did many others, including Gene Kelly, Lucille Ball, Orson Welles, Rita Hayworth, Johnny Green, and Ava Gardner.

So why the subterfuge? Insiders began to speculate that perhaps some "female problem" was being covered up. Had Kay been pregnant? If so, was Bill the father? Or, had Thompson's flirtation with a certain blue-eyed crooner gone farther than she would ever admit? Whatever happened, it clearly was something the studio decided to quash—and Howard Strickling, Metro's resident spin doctor, was well versed in suppressing any potential scandal.

By the end of December, Kay must have been feeling better. She returned home to the Garden and began secretly moonlighting—though the cat did not stay in the bag for long.

"Kay Thompson is coaching Alan Curtis in singing," tattled Hedda Hopper on January 4, 1944, in the *Los Angeles Times*.

Because Curtis was exclusive to Universal, Kay was in serious breach of her contract, especially since she was playing hooky while doing it. In a terse memo, Nat Finston instructed the MGM payroll department to suspend Thompson's sick pay, effective January 10.

The suspension apparently motivated a miraculous recovery. Three days later, Kay wrote this conciliatory letter to Finston: "My dear Nat, Time heals everything I'm happy to say and here I am once again my happy and dying-to-get going self . . . Happy Metro-Goldwyn-Mayer and thanks again, Nat. As ever, Kay Thompson."

On January 14, she optimistically strolled through the gates at Metro, confident that nothing more needed to be said. Or so she thought. Finston greeted her with a piece of paper that explained she would have to make up for her sick leave by extending her obligation to the studio by an equal number of days. She had little choice but to sign the contract addendum.

For months, Kay had been floating ideas for the Freed Unit's upcoming production, *Ziegfeld Follies*, a pastiche of musical numbers and comedy vignettes that would feature many of MGM's top stars.

"There was a lot of talk about what numbers there would be," Kay explained.

Since the summer of 1943, dozens of submissions had been developed by various personnel on the lot and Kay was central among them. Collaborating with Lemuel Ayers (production designer of Broadway's *Oklahoma!*) and Don Loper (the future clothing designer), Thompson spent much of her free time writing a treatment for "Frankie and Johnnie," a "dramatic ballet" set in 1890, with Lena Horne in mind as Frankie.

On weekends, Kay had Lemuel and Don over to the Garden of Allah, where they brainstormed by the pool. They were often joined by Kay's old pal Tennessee Williams, who had just given up a $17-a-week job as a theater usher in New York to earn his first big payday of $250 per week as a screenwriter for MGM. He was concurrently collaborating with Lemuel and Eugene Loring (Kay's future choreographer on *Funny Face*) on a "folk-opera" treatment for *Billy the Kid* (a Freed Unit project that ultimately never came to fruition).

There were distractions, however, that hampered progress on both fronts. During those poolside gatherings Tennessee openly lusted after Lemuel's "darkly gleaming curls" and "perfectly formed body," and soon the young men were paying more attention to each other than to the work at hand.

Nevertheless, a treatment for "Frankie and Johnnie" somehow managed to get finished and it was submitted on August 27, 1943. Freed liked it and was very close to giving it a green light until the material was flatly rejected by the Breen Office (the censorship bureau run by the Hollywood Producers Association) due to the "flavor of prostitution and excessive sex suggestiveness."

Undaunted, Kay shed her distracted collaborators and, by herself, wrote up another treatment for Lena called "Pistol Packin' Mama," submitting it on January 31, 1944. Freed's associate producer, Roger Edens, met with Kay in mid-February to deliver the discouraging news that it had been turned down. But, as a consolation, he suggested, "Let's write a number for Greer Garson."

"So Roger came up to my office," Thompson recalled, "and we got down to it. I don't know who said what, [but we settled on] doing an interview with a star."

Kay and Roger decided to spoof Garson's image as a serious actress who frequently starred in melodramatic biographies, specifically her most recent MGM vehicle, *Madame Curie,* about the scientist who discovered radium. In their musical send-up, Garson would announce to the gentlemen of the press the subject of her next biographical characterization.

"So we began to improvise," Kay continued. "I thought of the name 'Madame Crematante.'"

The name was an amalgam of "crème de la crème" and "dilettante"—meaning übersuperficial—a biting indictment that would sail right over Garson's head . . . or would it? They'd take their chances.

"And what did Madame Crematante invent?" Kay added. "The safety pin." This absurdity became the basis for Kay and Roger's satiric gem, "A Great Lady Has an Interview," or, as it is more commonly referred to, "Madame Crematante."

"When we finished it," Kay explained, "I acted it out in the office. Roger played piano and Ralph [Blane] was a reporter."

Obviously, it would require a certain amount of self-deprecation and a sturdy sense of humor on Garson's part. But the timing could not have been worse. Greer had just received an Academy Award nomination for Best Actress in *Madame Curie.* Being up for an Oscar was—and still is—an emotionally charged period for any nominee, especially those prone to delusions of grandeur.

Just days before the March 2, 1944, Oscar ceremony, Roger arranged for a presentation of "Madame Crematante" at Arthur Freed's house, attended by Garson, her mother, her husband, Richard Ney, Vincente Minnelli (under consideration to direct), and Charles Walters (under consideration to direct and/or choreograph). With Edens on piano and Blane as a reporter, Thompson demonstrated the number, hamming it up to the hilt.

"As Kay and Roger got deeper into the satiric piece," Vincente Minnelli recalled, "and the music became more challenging, it became obvious that a singing performer would have to play 'Madame Crematante.'"

When it was over, there was no reaction. "Absolute dead silence," Kay remembered. "Vincente pursing his lips. And finally Richard Ney said, 'Your house is beautifully appointed, Arthur.' Nobody moved. Then, Greer said, 'Well . . . I was thinking more of doing . . . a number about, oh, a red beard and a bicycle.' Vincente didn't say a word, not a goddamn word. Neither did

Arthur . . . The mother said, of course, nothing. And I got up and went over to Roger and said, 'Don't you think we have to go?' And Ralph said, 'Geez, we gotta go.' Then the three of us just left."

In retrospect, Kay still pondered the rejection with amazement and anger. "Isn't Greer Garson an ass?!" she snarled. "I mean anybody who would not like this—aaarrrrgh! It was *great*."

"Oh, it would have been fun, wouldn't it?" Garson later reflected to *The Hollywood Reporter*. "But at the time I didn't think it was appropriate to be making fun of the hand that was feeding me, so to speak."

Thompson did not give up. If Garson didn't want to do it, maybe Garland would. "Kay suggested Judy," Minnelli recalled. "It was a singing tour de force preceded by devastating commentary, the sort of number Kay did herself with such great high style. Judy was capable of the biting lines, if her way with a story was any indication. Yes, I agreed, Judy would be perfect."

"So the next day," Thompson remembered, "we called Judy and said, 'Come up to Kay's office.'"

On a break from shooting *Meet Me in St. Louis*, Garland sat down and watched Thompson do the routine, from start to finish. "So I did it," Kay recalled. "I flounced all over the thing. When it was over, Roger said, 'Do it again.'"

This time, however, he made Judy stand beside Kay. "Do it exactly like she does it," Edens instructed Garland. Judy began emulating Kay, as if they were synchronized images, side by side.

"I'm saying, 'Now go over here,'" Kay explained, "and she got up on the desk and I'm saying, 'Put your hand on your hip like that.'"

Suddenly, all that mattered in the entire world to Garland was this fascinating new kind of character she was being asked to play.

"Judy was just captivated," Kay said. "Just electrified. She was just in her little girl period, you know, of innocence, whatever it was. But she hadn't made her departure yet, and this was certainly it. You never saw such an infusion of vitality, but she got it in pretty good shape. And then we quickly went down to Rehearsal Hall C and had that *long* table built and Ralph put all the props there and went over it with her, just drumming it. And I'm doing it like wild, and placing her arms and her hands, you know, just really going to work on her. And then, Chuck [Walters] came in to see it, and he became one of the reporters, so we had Chuck and Ralph as the reporters."

When they got it in presentable shape, Roger brought Arthur Freed over to see it. "Just before we started," Kay recalled, "I was gonna give Les, the pianist, the downbeat and I lifted my hand and hit Arthur right in the crotch. He really jumped a few feet, and I turned—I just said right to his crotch, 'Oh

Arthur!' And Ralph turned and patted him on the leg. It was an awful way to impress anybody. And Roger said, 'Come on, Katie, let's *go!*' So, we tried not to laugh too hard [as we] acted the whole thing out. We get to the end—and Judy really did do it great, you know, for having learned it in a half-hour—and we all are, 'Hola, hola, hola, *holaaaaa* [singing the finale of the song]!'"

To the astonishment of all, Arthur said nothing about the performance and began making small talk, predicting winners for the upcoming Oscars. "We'd had this poor treatment from Greer a couple of nights before, so we didn't give a shit by then," Kay cursed, the memory still blistering.

Later in private, Arthur told Roger that the idea of casting Judy in such a sophisticated role was in direct conflict with the wholesome image that had been cultivated for the twenty-one-year-old star. Before proceeding, they would have to get the blessing of studio management. Since the number one chief, Louis B. Mayer, still viewed Judy as a child, Roger hoped that the number two boss, Sam Katz, might be more open-minded.

"So we went to Sam Katz's office," Kay recalled. "It was at 9 o'clock in the morning, and the upright piano faced the wall and Roger played and I did it right by the piano. Sam was dictating a letter or on the phone and he said, 'Yeah, yeah,' when we finished. He didn't say anything. I left and Roger carried on babbling. It was a matter of minutes and . . . Roger called me and said, 'Let's get started. It's in.'"

Columnist Hedda Hopper visited the rehearsal hall and reported, "The corkscrew knots Judy ties herself into while getting her picture taken will have you rolling. Bet she gets a touch of Hepburn's 'Rally, rally, I do' and Garbo's 'I tank I go home' in her impersonations."

Lennie Hayton conducted the prerecording sessions with Kay's chorus of seventeen men, including Andy Williams, Don Williams, Ralph Blane, and a fifteen-year-old kid named Earl Brown.

"She loved tenors squealing out there," Earl Brown recalled. "Sometimes she'd make the chord even higher than it had been written. One time, the tenors were really too much, and she said, 'My God, darling, it sounds like a pit of hissing snakes.' She was just great and so talented. I was really listening to every word she said. I had a feeling I might use it and I did."

Earl went on to become a member of the Skylarks and later, he would become a top vocal arranger for television and movies (including *New York, New York*), frequently crossing paths with Kay along the way.

Though Judy's performance was Kay's creation from beginning to end, Charles Walters choreographed the gaggle of reporters. He wanted to direct the sequence as well, and spent weeks planning every aspect of the production. To his dismay, however, the directing reins were handed over to Vincente Minnelli. Vincente must have been in sync with what Charles had so carefully prepared because, according to Walters' biographer, Brent Phillips, "Chuck always insisted that every shot in 'The Interview' was his." Nevertheless, Minnelli got the "Directed by" credit while Walters had to live with a "Dance Direction" attribution.

The person who *really* got gypped was Kay. Though Thompson received a cowriting credit with Edens, her contribution went far beyond ink on a sheet of paper. But Kay thought it was undignified to beg for credit. She opted for false modesty, later claiming, "I don't think I ever gave Judy anything."

With "Madame Crematante," however, Thompson not only reinvented Judy, she pioneered a whole new genre of music: rap. "Kay introduced the first rap song, 40 years before Harlem did," marveled critic Rex Reed in 1998.

"Shooting the number was great fun," Minnelli wrote in his autobiography. "Judy came off extremely well. Her singing was as vibrant as ever, and she revealed a satirical style which owed a great deal to her terrific version of Kay's performance."

Newsweek enthused that Garland "displays an unexpected flair for occupational satire," and *The New York Times* raved that Judy possessed "a talent approaching Beatrice Lillie or Gertrude Lawrence."

"But you see that's the marvelous thing about invention," Kay proudly declared, having just viewed the sequence on television in 1972. "As I saw it [again] last night, it's right *now*. And you know, I liked it better on television than I've ever liked it before. That's the wonderful thing that God gave me, if he ever gave me anything, which was a sense of no time . . . That's what you call style. And that's what this thing had."

Aside from "Crematante," Kay worked on many other segments for *Ziegfeld Follies* as a vocal arranger, vocal coach, and choral director—including Lena Horne's powerful rendition of "Love" (Hugh Martin–Ralph Blane), conducted by Lennie Hayton.

One day during rehearsal, Lena "protested she could not reach high C in a certain passage."

"My voice isn't that good," Lena insisted. "Better put it down at least one key."

On the next run-through, Horne hit the note pitch-perfect.

"You see?" Lena said. "B-flat is my limit."

"I see." Kay nodded knowingly. "For your information, I didn't change the key, and you can hit high C right on the nose as long as you think it's B-flat!'"

Horne's appreciation ran deep. Years later, she always declared, "Kay was the best vocal coach in the world."

Hugh Martin begged to differ. "Sometimes Kay overworked people," he said. "I know that when Lena Horne recorded my song 'Love' for *Ziegfeld Follies*, she had a tired voice because Kay worked her too hard just before the recording. Kay had a real strong voice and she didn't have to worry about getting tired, but she sometimes forgot that other people had more fragile voices."

Martin actually preferred Thompson's own rendition of "Love," performed on *Philco Radio Hall of Fame* in January 1945, fifteen months before *Ziegfeld Follies* was released. "I was nervous about whether Kay could bring that last note off, but she did with flying colors."

Few people knew that Kay's singing voice made it into *Ziegfeld Follies*. During Fred Astaire's "Limehouse Blues" sequence, she can be heard on a Victrola warbling "'E Pinched Me," a bawdy British pub song, which she comically screeches in an unrecognizable, high-pitched Cockney accent.

Whenever Kay wasn't needed on *Ziegfeld Follies*, other producers on the lot commandeered her services for various assignments on *Lost in a Harem, Thrill of a Romance, Music for Millions, Week-End at the Waldorf, Her Highness and the Bellboy, The Clock, Yolanda and the Thief*, and three *Tom & Jerry* cartoons.

While juggling all of this, Thompson had a crisis at home. On May 18, 1944, while eating Italian food at Preston Sturges's Players Club (on Sunset Boulevard opposite the Garden of Allah), Bill Spier suffered a *second* heart attack. He had just finished directing Orson Welles in the first half of "Donovan's Brain," an ambitious two-part *Suspense* special that was being presented on May 18 and 25. Spier was laid up in the hospital for six weeks and was then ordered to convalesce at home for three months.

A professional nurse had been hired to keep Bill resting in bed, but not a moment was lost as he feverishly interrogated the poor girl on unusual medical means of homicide, collecting "insidious ideas for new stories." The unsettling truth was that there may have been a darker purpose behind Bill's curiosity.

"If I have one more night in this bed in this room," Bill told Kay, "I'll blow my brains out."

Even when he wasn't bedridden, Bill suffered from severe bouts of depression, with talk of suicide a common occurrence.

"Spier was always threatening to kill himself," said Dick Williams of the Williams Brothers. "Of course, he would never do it. He was the sort of person who was crying out for help. So one day at the house, a package arrived from the sporting goods store. It was a gun. Kay took the gun back and for the money that he'd spent on the gun, she got a big box full of baseballs and had it sent to the house. She included a note that said, 'Bats to DiMaggio. Balls to you.'"

When Bill was back on his feet, he and Kay decided to give up their bungalow at the Garden of Allah and buy a sprawling, $39,000 Georgian farmhouse at 11580 Bellagio Road in the tony neighborhood of Bel Air. It had more privacy, more rooms, and most important, more space for entertaining. And it wasn't long before corks were popped.

Less than two weeks after moving to Bel Air, Kay inaugurated the First Annual Kay Thompson–Roger Edens Birthday Bash on November 9, 1944 (her thirty-fifth, his thirty-ninth), which would also serve as a listening party for Lena Horne's star turn on *Suspense,* broadcast live that same evening.

"Oh God, what a night," Kay gleefully recalled. "It was *so* exciting. We did the first birthday at my house with no furniture except the two pianos and a rented 'Abbey Rents' bed. We glutted [the house with] everything—hurricane lamps and the tables and the food—and I got a Mexican girl to come and sing and lean on the piano."

Lena arrived fashionably late. "I figured by this time the broadcast would be forgotten," Horne explained, "and no one would feel obliged to say 'You were wonderful!' just to be polite."

But no one had forgotten. Cheers exploded and the party escalated further as Lena prompted the mob to sing "Happy Birthday" to Kay and Roger.

"And then," Kay reminisced, "just when everybody was at the height of going mad, we just said, 'Shut up, *we've* got a song! A birthday song for Roger.'"

Thompson and Ralph Blane had composed a song called "Roger de Coverley," Kay's nickname for Roger Edens. It was a reference to Sir Roger de Coverley, an eighteenth-century columnist for the British newspaper *The Spectator,* but historical significance was hardly the point. Kay just liked the way the name rolled off her tongue.

"Judy Garland and Peter Lawford secretly rented these outlandish getups from the studio costume department," Kay remembered, "and we performed this number in my living room. And Roger just sat there listening, crying . . . And if we did it once, we did it a hundred thousand times. The crowd kept begging for more. '*Again!*' So we just kept singing it over and over and over."

The annual tradition was born, with Kay and Roger trying to one-up the other. "Kay would have no clue what Roger was doing, and Roger would have no clue what Kay was doing," *Funny Face* screenwriter Leonard Gershe told *Vanity Fair* journalist Marie Brenner. "People would die to be invited!"

"We had the most elegant food," Kay explained. "Mexican with tacos and tamale pies, and salad was a favorite, then always Wil Wright Ice Cream, several kinds like fresh mint pale green ice with chocolate burnt almond served together . . . We began to outdo each other. The best decorated table, something special in flowers shipped in from Honolulu. Steak from Paris. Candied apples from Alabama."

"Every once in a while," Peggy Rea recalled, "Kay would make corned beef hash and she did it right." Thompson was such a connoisseur of the delicacy that, in 1951, she would become the spokeswoman for canned Broadway Corned Beef Hash, appearing in a newspaper ad campaign.

"*All* the parties were great," Kay declared. "Arthur [Freed] gave some marvelous ones. Jerry Kern and Tallulah [Bankhead] and Irving [Berlin] and Harold Arlen. There was music from start to finish. When Roger got up from the piano, Lennie [Hayton] sat down, and when he got up, I sat down and all of us sang, including Arthur. We were moved by the moment, stirred by the affection of that moment and anybody who didn't participate wasn't there."

Another event on the A-list calendar was July Fourth at Villa Tramonto, the Pacific Palisades home of Joseph Cotten and his wife, Lenore Kipp (a former associate fashion editor under Diana Vreeland at *Harper's Bazaar*).

"We had the Rams football team band one year," Cotten recalled, amazed by his own extravagance. "Then there was the time Ethel Merman sang 'The Star-Spangled Banner,' and Kay Thompson once did 'Columbia, Gem of the Ocean.' Everybody had a good time and there were no bras in the bushes the next morning."

"I would sing with Kay at all the parties," Margaret Whiting recalled, "and we used to hang out with Judy sometimes up at the Café Gala, the bar we found in Hollywood. It was the first club where everybody sang all the songs from New York, Cole Porter songs, all the great Broadway show tunes. Lana Turner and all the people that were bright and fun used to go there every night." (It later became Spago, home of Swifty Lazar's Oscar parties.)

Cabaret singer-pianist Bobby Short recalled, "We would just close down the place and keep the bar kind of secretly going. And we'd have a good time. I mean when you've got Roger Edens, Conrad Salinger, and Kay Thompson and Lena Horne and God knows what else sitting out there, all drinking their heads off, and the place closes. And there are two grand pianos. A lot of wonderful things happened."

Skitch Henderson said, "You know where I'd sometimes see Kay, too? There was a café society group that would go to Rocky Cooper's house on Saturday nights. Rocky was Gary Cooper's wife—a Connecticut Yankee type.

Kay was very close to Cole Porter and a couple of times they performed some special material they'd prepared."

Another favorite watering hole was Frances Edwards' Bar and Grill, nick-named "the Hangout," across the alley from the Metro lot. "Judy Garland, Donald O'Connor, Kay Thompson, Mickey Rooney, June Allyson, Jane Powell, and others, would gather around the piano for a singing session," wrote colum-nist Bob Thomas. The establishment also had a tiny dance floor frequently used by Gene Kelly to rehearse routines.

Beneath all the merriment, however, Thompson envied the stars around her. Determined to boost her profile as an actress, she and her husband con-cocted a musical-mystery radio pilot entitled *Kay Thompson's Club Midnight*, a hybrid of the Thompson *Forecast* pilot, "51 East 51," and the Lena Horne episode of *Suspense*, "You Were Wonderful," both set in nightclubs. The idea was for Kay to play a cabaret star who solves crimes on the side—with big-name guest stars dropping by each week. Spier's golden imprimatur as director and producer made the project even more enticing. Nonetheless, no sponsors signed on, so the series never got on the air.

Thompson felt unappreciated and underutilized, and her mounting resent-ment was not always kept in check. In his unpublished memoir, jazz composer Alec Wilder observed that after Kay had been in Hollywood for a while, "a tougher, harsher, more cynical person" emerged. She had reason to be cyni-cal. Bolstering the careers of others was a bittersweet endeavor for someone who craved the spotlight so intently. But, stuck in a dead-end job, Kay had no choice but to submerge those feelings and bide her time.

Chapter Five

FRIEND OF DOROTHY

Somewhere Over at Metro
(1945–47)

Kay is my best critic and severest friend.
—*Judy Garland*

O ne of the most triumphant sequences in screen-musical history" was how
The New Yorker film critic Pauline Kael described Judy Garland's "On
the Atchison, Topeka and the Santa Fe" in the Freed Unit production of *The
Harvey Girls*. It was just one of a multitude of kudos lavished on this classic
sequence—but few recognized Kay Thompson's contribution: she had entirely
transformed a three-minute ditty into this nine-minute tour de force.

Harry Warren and Johnny Mercer had written the song for the film, but
Kay had been assigned to embellish it with her vocal arrangement and choral
direction. In her hands, "Atchison Topeka" became the showstopper to end all
showstoppers. Kay told writer Stephen M. Silverman that the reaction to the
number at the premiere was so euphoric, the crowd was "screaming."

"It is absolutely wonderful," declared Michael Feinstein. "I think probably
'Atchison Topeka' is Kay's greatest film achievement."

Neither composer agreed. Years later, Feinstein asked Harry Warren why
he and Mercer had not embellished "Atchison Topeka" on their own. Warren's

response: "Well, in those days at MGM, we'd write the song and they would take it. We'd turn it in and it was good-bye. We could have written that special material if they'd given us the chance, but then Kay Thompson reared her ugly head!"

Johnny Mercer was equally incensed. "They're going to make me look like an idiot," he fumed. "Everybody's going to think I wrote that junk." He lodged a formal complaint with Arthur Freed, but Freed dismissed it out of hand: "What are you talking about? It's wonderful."

Unassuaged, Mercer and Warren boycotted the Academy Award ceremony. When "Atchison Topeka" was named Best Song, presenter Van Johnson had to accept the Oscar on their behalf.

No matter. The song became a Top 10 hit, selling over a million records and a half million pieces of sheet music. Thompson proudly proclaimed, "That number was just a peach."

It helped to have Garland at the mike. "On *Harvey Girls*, Judy was fun," Kay remembered. "Her brain . . . was a little vacuum cleaner, which just picked up all this stuff . . . She was at ease. She was in love with Vincente [Minnelli] and everything was so calm."

In fact, Judy was in such a blissful state, she married Vincente on June 15, 1945, with Kay and Bill among the well-wishers.

For *The Harvey Girls*, Kay assembled one of her largest choruses ever, forty strong, featuring two future singing stars, Andy Williams and Frankie Laine.

"I learned that MGM was holding auditions," explained Laine, "so I went over to Culver City and tried out for a lady named Kay Thompson. I did a jazz tune for her and she liked what she heard." Kay booked him for the chorus and also "to dub in the voice for a dancer—a great big guy—in 'March of the Doagies.'"

Another new chorus recruit on *The Harvey Girls* was Kay's younger sister, Marian Fink, who had changed her name to Marion (with an *o*) Doenges (pronounced "DAWN-jeez"). Marion had recently married a career Air Force pilot named Robert Doenges, and while he was serving in the war, Kay persuaded her to take a job at MGM as the secretary to George Schneider, "the librarian in the Music Department in charge of copyright clearances and accounting." Once Marion was in close proximity to her sister, Kay couldn't help but put her voice to good use. When it was decided that Cyd Charisse's chirping wasn't good enough for her songs in *The Harvey Girls*, Kay hired Marion for $100 per session to be Cyd's voice double.

Angela Lansbury's singing voice was also replaced in *The Harvey Girls*. "As far as I remember, I don't think Kay or Roger [Edens] ever had me in to try me out singing the songs," Lansbury recalled. "They just assumed that my voice was pitched very high and that I didn't have the chest tones to play that earthy lady of the night."

For Lansbury's vocal, Kay hired Virginia Rees, who had prior experience dubbing Marlene Dietrich and Eleanor Powell. "[There was no] publicity," Rees recalled. "It was all rather hush-hush that a star had to have someone sing for them."

Lansbury was also scheduled to perform "The Continental Polka" (Johnny Green–Ralph Blane) in the upcoming production *Easy to Wed*, so Thompson had Rees bank that vocal at the same time. However, when "The Continental Polka" went before the cameras, Lansbury had been replaced by Lucille Ball, resulting in a rather unusual twist of fate: Lucille Ball lip-synching to Virginia Rees channeling Angela Lansbury.

Lansbury recalled her earliest memories of Thompson: "When I first arrived at MGM in 1943, I remember seeing this extraordinary, marvelously glamorous woman who used to come into the commissary with her blond hair and usually in a very long mink coat that kind of dragged on the floor. She always had a coterie of males with her. She talked in this very strong voice and you couldn't *not* notice Kay Thompson in those days."

"Lunch was divine in the commissary," Kay remembered. "At our table it was an event. Creative spirits breathing in the same air and helping to get it on film."

But all was not equal. "It was very caste conscious," Skitch Henderson observed. "Kay was a czar. She would eat with her own gang—with Roger [Edens] and Connie [Salinger] and those people."

Kay admitted, "The clannishness of us drove people to remark that, 'There goes that snob Freed Unit.' Snobs we were, but *good* snobs . . . We bounced off of each other with violent enthusiasm."

The clique also had a mascot named Eloise. "Kay used that voice quite a lot," Angela Lansbury recalled. "I don't think she had narrowed it down to the character living at The Plaza at that point. But yes, she would go into her Eloise voice. Quite often."

While Kay was busy with prerecordings for *The Harvey Girls*, she convinced her husband to find a juicy role for Frank Sinatra on his *Suspense* radio series. And so, on January 18, 1945, Frank played opposite Agnes Moorehead in "To Find Help," the story of a hired hand who turns out to be a psychopathic killer.

"Until Bill gave Sinatra his first dramatic role in a *Suspense* episode, no one thought he could act," wrote Sheilah Graham. "Frank was excellent, and this led indirectly to *From Here to Eternity*. They might never have allowed him to test for it if [Columbia Pictures' chief] Harry Cohn had not heard him on *Suspense*."

Other *Suspense* guest stars taking cues from Spier during 1945 included Humphrey Bogart, Lana Turner, Henry Fonda, Lucille Ball, Edward G. Robinson, Myrna Loy, Boris Karloff, Peter Lorre, Ronald Colman, John Garfield, Joseph Cotten, and Clifton Webb.

As the premier radio director-producer in the business, Bill Spier decided the time was right to branch into movies. Supportively, Kay got him a movie agent, Barron Polan, and suggested that he pitch film versions of the best *Suspense* installments to her associates at Metro. As a result, it was announced that Spier had been hired by MGM to produce several film noir thrillers—including *The Beast Must Die* (to star Edward Arnold), *The Men Who Couldn't Lose* (to star John Hodiak), and *Desire* (to star Robert Young)—but not one was ever made. Like Kay's, Bill's motion picture ambitions remained frustratingly stymied.

Meanwhile, Thompson's first husband reappeared on the scene. Jack Jenney had been "honorably discharged" from the Navy due to health problems obviously related to his alcoholism. Having declared bankruptcy, he was desperate to find work, and so, with Kay's blessing, Lennie Hayton hired him to play trombone on Garland's Decca Record sessions for songs from *The Harvey Girls*, featuring Thompson's chorus.

Trumpet player Uan Rasey, who sat next to Jenney in Hayton's orchestra, recalled, "Jack got along just fine with Kay. They had fun working together. You could tell they still liked each other. But Jack was still drinking very heavily and there was nothing anyone could do to stop him. He was probably into drugs, too, because there was plenty of that going around. I remember Lennie Hayton experimenting with an LSD-like drug he'd gotten from France."

By early December, Jack was hospitalized with kidney failure—then appendicitis. On December 16, 1945, he died in Hollywood Hospital of "peritonitis after complications resulting from an appendectomy." He was only thirty-five.

While working on *The Harvey Girls* in the spring of 1945, Thompson was also juggling duties on *Easy to Wed*, *Twice Blessed*, and *Abbott and Costello in Hollywood*, which featured her delirious choral arrangement for "Fun on the Wonderful Midway" during the frenzied climax. But in May, her slate of projects suddenly dried up, allowing her to officially consider outside productions.

"Get me Kay Spier!" ordered independent producer Samuel Goldwyn.

"Because Goldwyn kind of slurred his words," Don Williams recalled, "they brought him a case of beer."

Despite the mix-up, a deal was struck on May 11, 1945, for Kay to be loaned out to Goldwyn for *The Kid from Brooklyn* (RKO, 1946), a Jule Styne–Sammy Cahn musical directed by Norman Z. McLeod, starring Danny Kaye as a milkman-turned-prizefighter. Her $700 weekly salary from MGM would cease while Goldwyn was paying her $1,050 per week.

Also appearing in the picture would be the Goldwyn Girls, a bevy of eighteen "glamazons," cast as a wholesome group of milkmaids who tend the cows for the Sunflower Dairy, which provides the milk Danny Kaye delivers.

Defying all logic, the same girls would also appear in a "fashion parade" prelude to the song "Josie" (Styne-Cahn, with additional music and lyrics by Thompson), performed in a music hall. Because they were just models with little acting or singing training, it was Kay's job to find eighteen distinctive voices to match each face. To accomplish this economically, she called in a versatile performer, Peg La Centra, who in the 1930s had provided dozens of voices for Bill Spier on *The March of Time* and, with Kay's coaching, would go on to dub the singing voices of such stars as Susan Hayward and Ida Lupino.

Peg later told the *Los Angeles Times* that of all her jobs, the task of replacing the voices of the Goldwyn Girls in *The Kid from Brooklyn* was her "prize stint."

"Each of them recited a little verse of music," Peg explained. "Kay Thompson, who was staging the number, sent for me and asked me to speak for them all. I suddenly found myself before an orchestra parroting—in rapid succession—a Southern girl, a Stork Club type, a sweet, nice girl, a prissy one, a sexy one and so on."

There was one exception. In the movie, Kay's own voice is heard coming out of the lips of the fourth Goldwyn Girl, saying, "You all may be her beaus, but I taught Josie all she knows."

Styne and Cahn also wrote "The Sunflower Song" for the young ladies to chirp in a promotional film-within-the-film. Kay expanded the introduction to the number, adding a brief appearance by a new character she called the Matron of the Sunflower Milkmaids, a disciplinarian who keeps the girls in line—much like Marjorie Main's den mother in *The Harvey Girls*. When Thompson demonstrated the bit part, Goldwyn asked, "Do you want to be the Matron?"

"I thought this man is so sweet to have just asked me," Kay recalled, "so I just said, 'Yes.'" Feigned innocence aside, this was the outcome Thompson had been passive-aggressively plotting since her arrival in Hollywood in 1943. It was about time someone took the bait. (MGM screen tested Kay for the music teacher in *Bathing Beauty* but jazz organist Ethel Smith got the part.)

The segment was filmed on September 7, 1945. The script supervisor's notes read, "BOOM SHOT—on doors. MATRON enters. DRAWS back to Full Shot, PANNING with Matron as she inspects GIRLS."

"Good morning, girls," says the Matron in a no-nonsense tone of voice. "At ease."

Like an Army drill sergeant, she walks the lineup, scrutinizing each maiden for any imperfections. When she stumbles upon a stray camisole, her eyes narrow and she picks it up, dangling the offending evidence from her index finger. "Whose underthings are these?" she bellows, as a guilty milkmaid lowers her head in shame. "For that you inherit the usual demerit."

Next, one of the girls is caught chewing gum and the Matron orders her to swallow it. When the inspection is finally over, she proclaims, "For some very special duties, we have chosen all you beauties . . . Heigh Ya Ta Ho, Heigh Ya Ta Ho . . . it's off to work you go."

And that was it. Eight takes to get it perfect. Kay was released by one o'clock in the afternoon, her big break over in the blink of an eye. Shortly afterward, press releases and photographs were sent to the media touting her cameo appearance in the movie.

In the meantime, however, test screenings of the two-and-a-half-hour film were not going well. As a result, editors made mincemeat of it right up to its premiere in New York on March 21, 1946.

Butchered to 113 minutes, Kay's entire role got cut (along with all but one of Danny Kaye's musical numbers). Adding insult to injury, her elimination was so last-minute, they didn't bother to remove her name from the on-screen cast list, perpetuating false expectations that continue today. Her long-awaited, highly publicized movie acting debut ended up an embarrassing no-show. "The whole thing was weird," Thompson concluded.

There is one footnote of interest before closing the file on *The Kid from Brooklyn*: one of those eighteen Goldwyn Girls happened to be Donna Hamilton, who, in the summer of 1946, was brought to Twentieth Century-Fox by talent scout Ben Lyon, along with her friend, model Norma Jeane Dougherty. The two were signed exclusively to the studio for $125 per week. Donna was allowed to keep her name, but Norma Jeane was rechristened Marilyn Monroe.

"Both girls were groomed for stardom," noted columnist Maxine Cheshire in *The Washington Post*, "with dancing lessons by Leonide Massine and singing lessons by Kay Thompson and acting lessons by Elia Kazan." However, in August 1947, after a year of intensive training, the know-it-alls at Twentieth

Century-Fox decided that Hamilton showed the most promise. As Cheshire drily observed, "She's the one they kept on salary the day they let a girl named Marilyn Monroe go because they couldn't afford them both."

By 1950, however, the tables had turned for Thompson's alumni; Monroe was well on her way to superstardom while Hamilton had quit the business.

In July 1945, Thompson got a call from Metro executive Sam Katz, who said, "I want to send over one of our loveliest girls."

From experience, Thompson knew exactly what this meant. "Mr. Katz was always having affairs with actresses," Kay explained, "which was no big surprise since MGM was the biggest whorehouse in the world."

Katz told Thompson that Ilona Massey, the "Budapest bombshell," had been put on contract with the studio and that she needed coaching to sing "You, So It's You" in *Holiday in Mexico*.

A man of few words, Katz said to Kay, "I want you to give her sex." End of discussion. Massey was sent to Thompson's office.

"She came with her Hungarian song teacher and her red hair—Lucille Ball colored hair," Kay recalled, "and she was absolutely outraged."

"Why am I here?!" Ilona fumed. "What am I doing here?! *What?!*"

"Well frankly," Kay replied, "Mr. Katz asked me to give you sex."

"We just stared at each other," Kay later recalled. "She wondered what in heaven I knew about sex that she didn't know—and I wondered the same."

After a long, incredulous silence, the girl turned to her Hungarian song teacher and signaled the meeting was over. "So with that," Kay continued, "the two of them left."

Thompson exacted her revenge. Although Massey was billed as "the singing Garbo," Kay replaced her warbling with Rece Saxon.

Around that same period, Kay was also assigned to coach Pat Kirkwood, a British musical star making her Hollywood debut in *No Leave, No Love* with Van Johnson and Keenan Wynn.

From the moment Kirkwood landed on American soil, she was stalked for sexual favors by the producer, Joe Pasternak, and the director, Charles Martin, while studio doctors loaded her up with pills for every occasion. Her only happy memories at MGM were her sessions with Thompson.

"Kay Thompson was certainly the best thing to happen to me," she recalled in her memoir. "She was a tall, gangling blonde with an intelligent and witty personality. After I sang a couple of songs while she played the piano accompaniment, she sat back, gave me a grin and said, 'Gee, honey, you don't need to come to me for lessons, so forget it—just come and talk to me when you feel like it . . .' She was a great girl and we had some laughs together, which made everything seem easier. I had found a friend."

For *No Leave, No Love,* Thompson did the vocal arrangements for fourteen songs, four of which she wrote or cowrote. The most outstanding was a snappy, upbeat ditty called "Love on a Greyhound Bus" (Kay Thompson–Ralph Blane–Georgie Stoll), sung by Kirkwood with Guy Lombardo and His Orchestra and a male quartet that included the voices of Ralph Blane and Andy Williams. Covered by a slew of artists, the song ranked No. 1 on the Top Jukebox Request chart and it was used as a jingle for Greyhound Bus commercials—one of Kay's most successful songwriting ventures ever.

The movie itself, however, was nearly overshadowed by two public relations nightmares. Disillusioned, Pat Kirkwood refused to attend the premiere, abandoned Hollywood for her native England, and "suffered a nervous breakdown, spending eight months in a sanatorium."

But the studio was far more concerned with covering up the fact that the two male stars of the film, Van Johnson and Keenan Wynn, were having an affair—resulting in Wynn's wife, Evie, being pressured into a highly unusual arrangement.

"[Louis B.] Mayer decided that unless I married Van Johnson, he wouldn't renew Keenan's contract," Evie Wynn Johnson recalled. "I was young and stupid enough to let Mayer manipulate me. I divorced Keenan, married Van Johnson, and thus became another of L.B.'s little victims. They needed their 'Big Star' to be married to quell rumors about his sexual preferences, and unfortunately I was 'It!'—the only woman he would marry."

Thompson would soon learn that her own private affairs were the studio's business, too.

Meanwhile, she contributed vocal arrangements and choral direction for a few numbers in *Two Sisters from Boston* and *A Letter for Evie*—the latter most notable for Kay's new swing arrangement of "The Trolley Song" heard playing on a radio—sung by the Mel-Tones with Kay's rehearsal pianist, Joe Karnes, replacing Mel Tormé, who was serving in the military.

To mark the end of the war in August 1945, Kay staged and starred in a one-hour variety show honoring returning fliers at an Air Force base in Santa Ana, California. She sang "On the Atchison, Topeka and the Santa Fe" and, with actors Keenan Wynn and Peter Lawford, performed comedy skits.

She also attended a celebration at the home of conductor Johnny Green and his wife, Bunny Waters, honoring Navy hero John F. Kennedy, twenty-seven, who had been awarded the Purple Heart. None of the partygoers could have imagined that Kennedy would one day be the President of the United States and that Thompson would direct his Inaugural Gala.

During this same busy period, Kay was secretly moonlighting as a vocal coach to Rita Hayworth for *Gilda* (Columbia, 1946). "I wanted to study singing," Hayworth told biographer John Kobal, "but Harry Cohn kept saying, 'Who needs it?' and the studio wouldn't pay for it." So, Rita took matters into her own hands and took private voice lessons from Kay.

"I once made and intercut eighty-four takes of a song with Rita singing," recalled music arranger Fred Karger, referring to "Amado Mio," a number performed in *Gilda*. "The effort was certainly made and Rita worked hard. She was going to Kay Thompson at the time."

"Kay told me that she went with Rita into the music studio at Columbia," Hilary Knight recalled, "and while she was there, Harry Cohn came by, saw them working, and just broke it up. He lashed out at Kay, 'You are *not* getting involved with this. Rita is going to be dubbed!'"

"Although Anita Ellis dubbed most of Hayworth's singing in the film," noted the *AFI Catalog of Feature Films*, "Hayworth actually sang the acoustic guitar version of 'Put the Blame on Mame.'" So, Kay's vocal training was not entirely for naught.

On September 9, 1945, Kay threw a surprise fifty-first birthday party for Arthur Freed. "All of us, the clique, the Freed Unit, chipped in I think $50," Kay recalled, "and it was decided by somebody that the party would be at my house. And it cost a *fortune*."

Hell-bent on making an impression, Thompson hired World's Fair designer George Hyam to create a spectacular "vertical garden and waterfall," dressed up the badminton court with several twenty-eight-foot rococo statues that had been sculpted by Tony Duquette for *Ziegfeld Follies*, and recruited one of MGM's top lighting designers to bathe the outdoor wonderland in a dramatic glow.

Her extravagance did not sit well with her husband. "I was running around and Bill would not help," Kay recalled, so she threw him out of the house. The friction was not an isolated occurrence.

"Everything had been so fun, so *soigné*, so terribly grand," recalled Peggy Rea, who had given up her job with Arthur Freed to become Spier's assistant. "And then it got old. You could see there was a vacuum, that their marriage was disintegrating."

But on this occasion, Kay reveled in the revelry. "Oscar Levant was playing at the piano," recalled Tony Duquette. "Judy said, 'Oh, Kay, let's just sing real loud!' And it became one of our 'family' statements when we really wanted to have a good time, we'd say, 'Oh, let's sing real loud!'"

"I sing loud, and Judy sings loud," Kay told a reporter. "Once Judy, Ethel Merman and myself sang together at a Hollywood party and you could hear us in Hawaii."

*O*n *September 22, 1945,* Kay began work on the Freed Unit's *Till the Clouds Roll By,* a colorful tribute to the music of Jerome Kern, featuring performances by Garland, Sinatra, Horne, and many others. Thompson created the vocal arrangements for all twenty-two numbers in the picture and, in October, she sang them in a rehearsal hall for a delighted Jerome Kern.

Highlights of the film include Sinatra's rendition of "Ol' Man River" (from *Show Boat*); "The Last Time I Saw Paris" sung by Dinah Shore; "All the Things You Are" sung by Tony Martin; and "Leave It to Jane / Cleopatterer" sung by June Allyson (with Andy, Dick, and Don Williams in the off-screen chorus).

During the "Show Boat Medley," Lena Horne sang "Can't Help Lovin' Dat Man" and Kay can be heard on the soundtrack calling "Magnooooolia!" with an exaggerated Southern drawl.

Angela Lansbury was assigned "How'd You Like to Spoon with Me?" and was finally allowed to use her own singing voice. "Kay and Roger seemed to take it for granted I could pull that one off," Lansbury recalled, "but, in all honesty, I didn't have the expertise that I learned in my later professional life to really sell that song. I was too demure."

Another first was Van Johnson singing "I Won't Dance" with Lucille Bremer (dubbed by Music Maid Trudy Erwin). Van was panic-stricken, so he summoned Kay to calm his nerves. "She came in wearing a lynx coat and just sat there and smiled, and I sang to her," Johnson recalled. "That was it. I got over my fright."

Garland's participation in *Till the Clouds Roll By* had to be rushed through as a top priority because she was pregnant. She prerecorded and filmed her songs in October and early November with Thompson by her side. Judy's baby bump was concealed behind stacks of dirty dishes in a kitchen as she sang "Look for the Silver Lining." While filming the number "Who?" Judy joked to Kay, "What a song to sing in my present condition."

They completed Garland's numbers on November 7, 1945, and two days later celebrated the Second Annual Kay Thompson–Roger Edens Birthday Bash, this year held at Edens' residence. Still suffering from hangovers on

November 11, the partygoers received the sobering news that Jerome Kern had suddenly died of a cerebral hemorrhage, adding poignancy and purpose to the entire production of *Till the Clouds Roll By* as a heartfelt, posthumous tribute.

As 1945 drew to a close, Kay organized a charity Christmas concert for kids at the Hollywood Bowl on December 22. Sharing the bill with Santa Claus, Roy Rogers, and Trigger, Kay performed her hot new arrangement of "Kay Thompson's Jingle Bells" that stopped the show. It was a revisionist's delight, with rip-roaring harmonics dashing all the way.

The next evening, she wowed the nation by performing it on *Request Performance* (CBS-Radio). "Kay's own arrangement of 'Jingle Bells' as they've never been jingled before" was how the announcer introduced the number, and it hasn't stopped jinglin' since. Subsequently recorded by many artists, the most popular version of "Kay Thompson's Jingle Bells" appeared on the classic No. 1 *Andy Williams Christmas Album* in 1963. Before Liza Minnelli sang it in concert in 2002, she warned the audience, "Hang on to your hair!"

The holiday spirit at MGM in 1945, however, was dampened by salacious rumors of a lesbian romance between Thompson and Garland.

"I think Kay and my mom were closest friends," said Lorna Luft, the second of Garland's three children. "I won't say that there wasn't a relationship of having Kay put her arms around my mom, and hold her when she was crying or whatever. I would definitely say there was a closeness like that. But as far as a sexual relationship? No. Not between my mom and Kay."

Nevertheless, by 1946, the gossip had taken on a life of its own and was starting to get out of hand.

"I remember Kay was married to Bill Spier," recalled Leonard Bluett of the Dreamers. "But she was never with him. She was *always* with Judy, so we always thought she was a lesbian. We all talked about it."

"Everyone back then believed the rumor," recalled *West Side Story* writer-director Arthur Laurents. "But what's that worth?"

Indeed, the rumor does not prove that Thompson was lesbian or bisexual, but it does establish that the *supposition* was very much alive among her colleagues in the 1940s. Several Garland biographies have recklessly reported the Kay-Judy affair as if it were a proven fact, and yet in the more than seventy years since Thompson first met Garland, nothing but flimsy circumstantial conjecture has ever surfaced. After a decade of delving into the substantiated sexual habits of both women and gathering testimony on the matter from more than one hundred insiders, the only reasonable conclusion this author can reach is that both women were, first and foremost, attracted to men.

It is, however, easy to understand how the rumor got started—and it had very little to do with Garland. Clearly, stereotypical assumptions were made about Thompson because she did not fit the mold of traditional femininity. "I remember her always in pants," Sylvia Sheekman Thompson recalled. "Her style indicates in a way she might have been lesbian, too. I mean she was so mannish." Or, as the defense-attorney-turned-mystery-writer Carolyn Wheat once put it, "the elegantly butch Kay Thompson."

"She wasn't going to wear flowing dresses like Loretta Young," Lorna Luft reasoned, "because she'd have looked ridiculous and she knew it. I guess you can say she was a bit masculine, but that doesn't make you gay."

"I know there was a lot of speculation about her being a lesbian and I could certainly understand why," stated actor Robert Wagner. "But I never had any evidence of that. I never saw her with a female companion or a partner or anything like that."

Thompson's masculine aura was more than just skin deep. "Kay was the kind of girl that all the other girls in camp would have crushes on," surmised Elizabeth Newburger Rinker, Kay's chorus member throughout the 1930s. "She had that kind of strength. Mannish strength."

"I think if Kay had leaned that way," Marion Marshall Donen Wagner responded, "she would have made a pass at me because we were very close friends. But she never, not even sideways, did that."

"Strident and masculine as Kay would seem, she was not a lesbian," insisted Peggy Rea. "Employees are privy to private matters more than the closest of friends. I witnessed plenty of discord between Kay and Bill that no one else knew about, but I never saw any evidence of hanky panky between Kay and Judy or any other woman. Kay had her eye firmly planted on men like Howard Duff and Andy Williams. She couldn't stop talking about how sexy they were."

"I knew Kay *very* well," stated Andy Williams, "and I never, *ever* knew of any gay relationship that she had with anybody."

"It would be my very, very firm opinion that she did not swing both ways," declared Leonard Grainger, Thompson's business manager, "because she so much needed a man's love. And wanted it. From 1946, I was very close to Kay in all senses and her desire to have a male lover was always there."

"Kay's interest in men was *serious*," observed Hilary Knight. "You could tell from her comments about men. She liked them *a lot*. And her husbands were very sexy guys. I just don't believe she swung both ways because I was around her too much. I would have sensed something if it was there."

On the other hand, Thompson occasionally made comments that implied her tastes were varied. At one point, she confessed to Rex Reed, "I'm stimulated by whoever is around—queens, dukes, dishwashers. If the tailor is attractive, it's him for a week."

"A fan named Bobby Cook used to speak to Kay on the phone on a regular basis," recalled Michael Feinstein. "He believed that she was a lesbian. Bobby said at one point he asked her about being gay and she said, 'Well, darling, we are what we are.'"

But remarks such as these should not be taken too seriously, since Thompson was notorious for making provocative statements, just to keep people guessing.

One thing is for certain: she was remarkably inquisitive about the subject. "Through the years, I had many, *many* discussions with Kay about homosexuality," noted Leonard Grainger, "and she always, *always* treated it with the greatest respect and gentility."

"Kay was *very* curious about homosexuality," recalled Richard Grossman, Kay's *Eloise* editor at Simon & Schuster. "Almost morbidly curious—or she would affect to be very curious about it. She would ask me how guys hit on guys and stuff like that. Isn't that funny? And yet that must have been a put-on because this was a sophisticated dame who'd been around the corner, right? She must have known."

"Around the time she was making *Funny Face*," recalled Hilary Knight, "Kay told me in a hushed tone that [producer] Roger Edens and [screenwriter] Lennie Gershe were 'sweethearts.' It was such a corny way of putting it. But her comments and thinking on the subject were always so corny. That's one of the main reasons why I just don't believe Kay was a lesbian."

Nonetheless, anything is possible. Aside from the Garland speculation, wildly unsubstantiated rumors have circulated for years that Thompson also had affairs with Marlene Dietrich, Lena Horne, and Ethel Merman—none of which seems likely. But if Kay really did harbor an attraction to women, it was a closely guarded secret—as conscientiously suppressed as her Jewish heritage.

To the powers that be at MGM, the validity of the gossip was not what really mattered. Perception was the threat. After the Van Johnson–Keenan Wynn cover-up, there was a renewed determination to protect the studio's most valued assets from damaging hearsay.

"Somebody kept spying on Judy," Kay later recalled. "[The studio] had real ways and means of the FBI on another level."

Howard Strickling, the studio's resident spin doctor, aka "the Fixer," routinely quelled unsavory notions about its stars. And so, as 1946 got under way, it appears to have been no accident that newspapers and fan magazines were suddenly rife with stories of marital bliss about the Spiers and the Minnellis.

"The William Spiers . . . are rated Hollywood's happiest wedded couple," gushed Walter Winchell in his January 17, 1946, column. "They go for picnics by themselves every Sabbath."

"Oh, brother," Peggy Rea laughed when the item was read to her. "That's a load of you-know-what."

At the same time, Garland's pregnancy was played up as the ultimate consummation of a happy marriage.

When confronted with questions about the unusual closeness she shared with Kay, Judy told a reporter, "You teeter along the edge of all sorts of moods and complexes when you are expecting, and that's how the camaraderie began to spring up between Kay and me. She's so full of interests, that I never had time while waiting for Liza May's arrival to get blue or giddy or listless."

Though it was downplayed in the press, Garland suffered from terrible mood swings during the pregnancy. Kay told a friend that when Judy was expecting, she had sworn to stop taking pills. When she caught Garland red-handed breaking that vow, Thompson confiscated them.

"Kay, I swear on the eyes of my unborn child that I will never take pills again," Judy pleaded.

Kay's eyebrow rose in disbelief. That did it. Judy grabbed the bottle out of her hands and defiantly swallowed a handful of pills.

"Kay was one of the people who wouldn't take any of the nonsense of my mom," Lorna Luft observed. "She knew my mom was sick but she didn't know what to do about it. Nobody did. If my mother did something—even if it was something *awful*—Kay wasn't mean. Kay was a duchess. She could act like a bitch—but she wasn't mean, and there's a big difference. Kay was her only real friend that *knew* my mother. Kay would raise her eyebrow and my mother didn't like that at all. That's when my mother would yell at her. Kay wouldn't stand for it."

Whenever things got ugly, Thompson had the ultimate exit line: "The drapes are on fire!"

"Kay would always say that and leave," Lorna concurred. "People would go, 'What?' But by then, she'd already be gone."

"I was frustrated in not knowing where [Judy] was getting [pills]," Vincente Minnelli admitted in his autobiography. "Yet, with the unspoken terror engulfing us, Judy and I continued outwardly functioning as happily married husband and wife."

And as new parents. On March 12, 1946, Judy gave birth to Liza May Minnelli. Just prior to the baby's arrival, Judy and Vincente had selected godparents for their new bundle of joy: "They would be Kay Thompson, who'd been my friend for ten years, and who was now also very close to Judy," wrote Vincente in his autobiography, "and her husband, Bill Spear [*sic*]."

"That clinched the friendship [between Garland and Thompson]," *Modern Screen* reported.

Liza was christened in June. "I knew she'd be sprinkled with a few drops of water," Garland recalled, "but she looked like a baby duck taking her first bath."

"The photographers took her picture," Kay added, "and from the word goo, Miss Liza May Minnelli knew where she was going."

"Liza is always cheerful and seldom cries except for a real reason," Judy told a reporter eight months after the birth. "Just let me sing Brahms' 'Lullaby' or 'Over the Rainbow,' though, and she yells a mile. Then Kay walks in, um-de-ums something simple and Liza brightens up like a marquee after dark."

Kay chimed in, "Maybe Liza plans to grow up to be a music critic!"

Judy laughed. "Touché, my friend. Touché!"

Garland adored Thompson's sarcastic sense of humor, which was honestly depicted in the Emmy Award–winning television movie *Life with Judy Garland: Me and My Shadows* (ABC-TV, 2001). During one dressing room scene before a concert, Garland (played by Judy Davis) frets, "They're all waiting for me to fall on my ass."

"I know I am," Thompson (played by Sonja Smits) remarks sardonically, putting a smile on Judy's face.

"Only Kay could get away with saying something like that to my mother," Lorna Luft confirmed. "If anyone else had said that, their ass would be out of there. But Kay could say that and get her to laugh."

"Judy and Vincente and Kay and Bill saw each other several times a week," wrote Gerold Frank in *Judy*. "There was a panache, a swash—sophistication is too limited, too worn a word." In fact, vocabulary was a group obsession. "Their games, many of them intricate word games, were talked about everywhere," Frank added. "Fractured French was to stem from these later. Bill Spier invented idiomatic French witticisms: *Honoré de Balzac: no hitting below the belt. La meme chose: your fly's open.*"

"They had these little languages between them," Peggy Rea confirmed, "like 'I'm Gloria be-Holden to you,' using the names of movie stars."

Following the studio's edict, Judy, Vincente, Kay, and Bill seemed happy as clams to the outside world. But, as with most fairy tales, it was too good to be true.

"It was a miracle to me that Kay and Bill were married," Angela Lansbury confessed. "Their temperaments were so different. She was a woman who was consumed with energy and he was the opposite. He was terribly laid back."

"They certainly had their differences," recalled Peggy Rea. "Kay had a bunk bed in one of the spare rooms. She just loved to tuck back in that and get away from Bill."

Separate bedrooms didn't stop Thompson from butting her nose into her husband's work. As the self-proclaimed "First Lady" behind *Suspense,* she voraciously read every script, offering her opinions whether "President Bill" wanted them or not. One that she rescued from the trash heap was "Dead Ernest," about a cataleptic man who the authorities mistakenly believe is dead. When the episode won the 1946 Peabody Award for Best Drama of the Year, Thompson gloated for weeks.

Around the same time, Kay helped launch the career of the celebrated science-fiction author Ray Bradbury. "I was in *love* with the *Suspense* program," Bradbury recalled. "I was publishing stories in *Weird Tales* and various other pulp magazines, which gave me the courage to make up a package of short stories and mail them to Bill Spier." In April 1946, Bradbury got a call to come for a meeting at the Spiers' home in Bel Air.

"When I rang the doorbell," Bradbury explained, "the person who answered the door was an explosion named Kay Thompson. She welcomed me like an old friend because she had read my short stories, too, and she thought they were terrific. I was in love *instantly.* She dragged me into the living room, sat me down, and brought me a glass of wine, so we were off to a great start."

Before Bill arrived, Kay and Ray had time for a little chitchat. "I knew that she was occasionally doing choreography for Judy Garland [in *Ziegfeld Follies,* which had just opened that month]. We discussed that just a little bit but she mainly wanted to know about me, which was very nice. She made me feel like I'd been established for a lifetime. That was part of her character. She was always outsized—the grand gesture, the overstatement—but sincere. It was not fake. Her enthusiasm was so wonderful and it certainly didn't hurt because when Bill finally joined us, he ended up buying one story at that first meeting."

The acquisition was Kay's favorite, "And So Died Riabouchinska," a chilling murder mystery about a vaudeville ventriloquist and his dummy, and it proved to be the lucky break that launched Bradbury's prolific career in movies, television, and books.

Flush with popular and critical success, Spier was the most sought-after radio director-producer in the business. "Larry White, who had been Dashiell Hammett's agent for a great many years, had always wanted me to do *Sam Spade*," Bill recalled, "[and] after I was well launched into *Suspense* for many years . . . I said, 'Sure, let's do it.'"

Not only was Bill a huge Hammett fan, but he and Kay had been friends of Humphrey Bogart—who, of course, played Spade in *The Maltese Falcon* (Warner Brothers, 1941)—ever since they lived across the pool from one another at the Garden of Allah. While everyone else called him Bogie, Kay came up with her very own nickname—Humpty Bogus—which she never failed to use in his presence.

"The original plan [was to] use Humphrey Bogart," Bill explained, "[but] he would have cost us, at that time, $20,000 a week. I said, 'No. It would be better for us to find an unknown . . . than be saddled to a star, great as he is, who's going to be going into movies . . . who's going to want to leave for Africa when you need him for next week's show.'"

And so, in late April 1946, Lloyd Nolan, Elliott Lewis, and several other solid radio actors were invited to sit around a conference table and take turns reading scenes as Sam Spade.

"[Kay Thompson] was and is a woman of infallible taste," recalled *Sam Spade* writer Robert Tallman, "with an unerring ear for the sound of success. Howard Duff, a young and unknown actor, was one of those auditioning. To everyone's astonishment, Kay said that Howard Duff was *it* and no one else would do."

According to Tallman, Kay was simply "mad for Howard's voice" and made an impassioned pitch in his favor. "She said he sounded real ballsy."

The others in the room were not so convinced. "Bill took exception and I had my doubts about Duff," Tallman admitted, "but not about Kay, who had never, to my knowledge, taken a strong stand that was a wrong one. [Cowriter] Jo Eisinger absented himself from the whole conflict and Kay prevailed."

Thompson was not only responsible for the casting of Howard Duff, she set the tongue-in-cheek tone of the series. "Our first script was influenced by the Bogart performance," Tallman explained. "Somehow we had overlooked the first Hammett short story about Spade, in which he was described as 'a blond Satan' with a diabolical sense of humor. Kay pointed, or *screamed* this out, and that is how *Adventures of Sam Spade* became the first of all send-ups of the fictional private eye."

Premiering July 12, 1946, the series became a smash hit, running until 1950, when, to the great disappointment of fans, it was canceled due to the blacklisting of Duff and Hammett by the House Un-American Activities Committee during the rabid anti-communist fervor of the McCarthy era.

Back in the innocent days of 1946, however, Kay would come home from her MGM day job to participate in brainstorming sessions with *Suspense* and *Sam Spade* writers into all hours of the night. One of the most beloved *Spade* adventures was "The Kandy Tooth Caper," a direct sequel to *The Maltese Falcon*, presented in two parts on November 24 and December 1, 1946. The term "gunsel" became a topic of bemused discussion. In *The Maltese Falcon*, Hammett used the obscure word to describe Wilmer (played by Elisha Cook Jr., in the movie), the unimposing and rather inept "bodyguard" of Casper "the Fat Man" Gutman (Sydney Greenstreet in the movie). It turned out that "gunsel," derived from the Yiddish word *gendzl*, was a dictionary-coy euphemism for a homosexual.

In keeping with that sly tradition, a new "gunsel" was introduced in "The Kandy Tooth Caper" named Lawrence Laverne, an effeminate dentist who has hidden the sacred tooth of Buddha in the bridgework of one of his patients. Before the Fat Man can get his hands on the priceless fang, however, Laverne is found dead in Sam Spade's apartment, resulting in Spade being arrested for murder.

Unexpectedly, Laverne was portrayed on the broadcast by none other than MGM's beloved orchestrator, Conrad Salinger. *Sam Spade*'s composer-conductor, Alexander Courage, told historian Leonard Maltin, "They hired Connie for his one and only radio role as a queer dentist . . . And he cries, he does everything." To the great amusement of his peers, Salinger's "nervous Nellie" turn at the mike stole the show—even if it wasn't much of a stretch.

"Kay was the one who cajoled Connie into doing it," Peggy Rea said with a chuckle. "They were extremely close friends and it was just the sort of inside joke she lived for."

Thompson's fingerprints were also detectable in the matchmaking department. When Ava Gardner was having an affair with Orson Welles—while he was still married to Rita Hayworth—Kay was determined to re-orchestrate her friends into happier duets. So, she introduced Ava to Howard Duff and that took care of that.

Meanwhile, at MGM, Thompson was assigned to do the vocal arrangements for the Freed Unit's *Summer Holiday* until composer Harry Warren threw a hissy fit, insisting on hiring someone who would be more faithful to his original compositions. Caught in the middle, lyricist Ralph Blane tried to put a positive spin on the betrayal: "Kay is very flamboyant, showy and original. I knew a fabulously talented fan, Bobby Tucker, working at CBS in New York. His style of vocal arranging was quite different from Kay's. Tucker sticks right with the original material."

Though Thompson wanted Warren to take his score and shove it, Blane prevailed upon her to direct the choir for such numbers as "The Stanley Steamer," a copycat ode to locomotion "from the transportation fellas who gave you 'The Trolley Song,' 'Chattanooga Choo-Choo,' and 'On the Atchison, Topeka and the Santa Fe.'"

Despite Warren's tenacious campaign to protect his score, the picture tested poorly and was drastically truncated. "When [Harry and I] met in 1979," Michael Feinstein recalled, "it was all fresh in his memory, and he still resented the MGM 'brass' for cutting his score to shreds."

Warren's grudge toward Thompson never abated either, as evidenced by the crude anecdotes he told about her. "Harry said that Kay always used to wear this big round watch," Feinstein related, "on a long chain around her neck, hanging way down below her waist, and he said that when she'd walk, it would bounce against her 'cous.' He said, 'She got big thrills from that.'"

Next, Thompson was recruited to work with Sinatra again for Jack Cummings' production of *It Happened in Brooklyn*. With Ted Duncan, she created the vocal arrangement for Mozart's "Là ci darem la mano" from *Don Giovanni*, performed by Sinatra and Kathryn Grayson, and conducted by Johnny Green (featuring a piano solo by seventeen-year-old André Previn). She also created vocal arrangements for several new pop songs composed by her old pals Jule Styne and Sammy Cahn, the most Thompsonian being the delightful "It's the Same Old Dream," sung by Sinatra with the Starlighters (including Andy Williams).

In August, Cummings lassoed Kay to coach Van Johnson for six songs in *The Romance of Rosy Ridge*. The film's ingenue, Janet Leigh, had no numbers, but long before her iconic shower scene in *Psycho*, she had an unexpected lavatory encounter with Thompson at MGM.

"I seem to have a lot of incidents that happen in bathrooms, don't I?" Janet joked in 2002. "One day I was in this bathroom on the lot, just singing away. All of a sudden, the door busts open, and this woman said, 'That sounds lovely! You have to do a musical!' And then she went out again without saying anything else. I was like, 'What happened?' *Bombastic* is the word. I later learned who she was."

Thompson provided several vocal arrangements for Joe Pasternak's *This Time for Keeps*, with Esther Williams, and when the fall of 1946 rolled around, conductor Johnny Green got her to do some choral work on *Cynthia*, starring a fourteen-year-old Elizabeth Taylor.

Then came *Living in a Big Way*, starring Gene Kelly in his comeback role after eighteen months in the Navy. For his opening dance sequence, Thompson created the vocal arrangement for "It Had to Be You," sung by the Starlighters (again featuring Andy Williams), with Lennie Hayton conducting the orchestra. She also coached Gene and the Maury Rubens' Children's Choir for "Children's Dance," a nine-minute medley of nursery rhymes.

After that, Thompson did quite a bit of work on Pasternak's *Three Daring Daughters*, starring Jeanette MacDonald as a fashion magazine editor (pre–*Funny Face* inspiration?) raising three young girls played by Jane Powell, seventeen, Ann E. Todd, fifteen, and Elinor Donahue (who later became famous as Robert Young's daughter on TV's *Father Knows Best*), nine. A divorcée, MacDonald is being courted in the picture by pianist-conductor José Iturbi (as himself).

Kay soloed as pianist on the prerecordings of "Happy Birthday," Mozart's "Turkish March," and three versions of "The Dickey-Bird Song" (Sammy Fain–Howard Dietz), which rose to No. 2 on *Your Hit Parade*.

José Iturbi actually finger-synched to Thompson's piano playing for "The Dickey-Bird Song"—a surprising cheat for a pianist of his stature. In 2008, Elinor Donahue remembered that "Kay Thompson played the piano with her fingers straight out, but Mr. Iturbi played with his fingers bent in the proper way." Because Thompson maintained long, manicured red fingernails, she always played the ivories with her talons outstretched, to prevent breakage.

To dub for Elinor Donahue, Thompson plucked an eleven-year-old girl from Maury Rubens' Children's Choir, Beverly Jean Garbo. Against normal policy, Kay invited Elinor to the prerecordings as an observer.

"She wanted me there at the recording sessions," Elinor said, "so that I was familiar with what I was going to sound like, before she gave me the disc to practice with at home. Then, whenever a song was being lip-synched in front of the cameras, she was always on the set to make sure that everybody's mouth was moving the way they were supposed to."

Kay also arranged and conducted a large choir for the sublime concerto "Ritual Fire Dance" (from Manuel de Falla's *El Amor Brujo*). For filming, it was staged at an open-air amphitheater with an eighty-piece symphony orchestra. On risers behind the musicians stood Kay's forty-eight-member choir. Though she is only microscopically discernible in wide shots, eagle eyes can spot Thompson standing among her ensemble—taller and blonder than anyone else, dressed in a floor-length white gown. While this celluloid speck hardly counts as "an appearance," it does represent the one and only time Kay was allowed to stand in front of the cameras for an MGM movie.

Kay turned thirty-seven on November 9, 1946. For the Third Annual Kay Thompson–Roger Edens Birthday Bash, Roger wrote the "The Passion According to St. Kate, Opus 19, #46, a birthday cantata for baritone, contralto, coloratura soprano and choir." The ten-minute roast was lovingly sung by Judy Garland, Ralph Blane, Conrad Salinger, and chorus, accompanied by Edens on piano.

But there was more than just one number performed at that historic party. "That's when I did 'Jubilee Time' for [Roger]," Kay recalled. With music and lyrics by Kay, "Jubilee Time" was a take-no-prisoners swing blowout, sung and danced by Thompson while Judy Garland, Cyd Charisse, Peter Lawford, and Ralph Blane provided powerhouse backup harmonies, syncopated hand claps, and synchronized steps—choreographed by Bob Alton.

"We certainly prepared ['Jubilee Time'] like we were never gonna get to prepare another thing," Kay reminisced. "And Bob [Alton]—oh God!—rehearsing every night! Great fun!"

"It was the first time I saw Kay perform," Adolph Green recalled. "She was spectacular that night. It was thrilling. *Thrilling!* It obviously evolved into her later nightclub act with the Williams Brothers."

At parties like these, Bill Spier and Vincente Minnelli were bystanders, keeping each other company while the girls did their thing. With so much in common, the foursome was often a better match than the couples themselves.

"Friendship of two couples for each other doesn't happen every day," Judy marveled about the rare affinity she and her husband shared with Kay and Bill. "If the wives get along, the husbands don't, or it's a reverse of that . . . We're lucky."

Modern Screen devoted an entire spread to "the Boresome Foursome," subtitled "That's what Judy Garland calls the Minnellis and the Spiers. But when a laughing jag hits 'em, who wants to go home?"

The article described in great detail a November 1946 weekend the two couples spent "among the artists, crackpots, and plain honest citizens" at the Coast Inn in Laguna Beach. To the casual reader, it seemed fairly innocuous. But for those in the know, the Coast Inn was the home of the South Seas Bar (later renamed the Boom Boom Room), which, according to the *Los Angeles Times*, was "frequented by sailors and became notoriously known as a clandestine meeting ground for homosexuals."

Given the extraordinarily high percentage of gay men that populated the social circle of the Spiers and Minnellis, it seems unlikely that they were oblivious to the destination's lurid reputation. And, after a yearlong campaign touting the wholesome harmony among the Boresome Foursome, the Coast Inn had to be the very last place on earth where MGM's spin doctor wanted them to be seen. But, luckily, the activities delineated in the report seemed perfectly harmless. When they decided to eat in their room, for instance, the men went grocery shopping and, with a portable Sterno stove, Kay became their short-order cook for the evening.

"It's a miracle," Judy marveled. "Oscar of the Waldorf never served a finer banquet."

The next day, Kay got out her camera and handed it to the "experts in camera angles and direction." As Vincente and Bill took turns behind the lens, "Judy and Kay posed like fashion models, on the high stairway which leads to the ocean, sitting on the rocks, looking out halfway to Honolulu."

"Get this one," Judy called, striking a pose. "I'm looking out longingly."

"Some actress," Kay retorted. "You look like a mermaid standing in a row-boat that isn't there."

Shortly after they returned to Los Angeles, Garland guest-starred as a terrorized car-hop waitress in "Drive-In," the November 21 episode of *Suspense* that gripped listeners coast-to-coast. Reviews were ecstatic, and, in conjunction with her first nonsinging movie role in *The Clock*, it helped establish her as a serious actress.

On the night of the broadcast, Bill directed Judy while Kay and Vincente provided coaching and moral support. The occasion was immortalized in a series of behind-the-scenes snapshots that were dispensed to the media with alacrity and purpose—reinforcing notions that the foursome was right as rain.

Half of that grand illusion crumbled when Kay and Bill separated in mid-December.

"They'd had a series of spats," recalled a friend, "and you know she was very volatile. It came to a head when Bill said, 'After all, who the hell are you but a voice coach for Judy Garland?' She said, 'To hell with you.'"

While still sharing the same home with Bill—though they were sleeping in separate bedrooms—Thompson focused on work, which included the Freed Unit production of *The Pirate*, Garland's comeback movie with Gene Kelly, directed by Minnelli, featuring songs by Cole Porter. The studio and Vincente relied heavily on Kay to be not only Judy's vocal arranger and coach, but also her motivational therapist. While prepping, Garland described Thompson as "my best critic and severest friend."

Kay had reason to be tough on Judy, who was acting out in all the wrong ways. Of *The Pirate*'s 135 shooting days, Garland missed 99 due to "illness." Tension on the set and at home proved unbearable for Vincente, who vowed never to direct Judy again. Not long afterward, their marriage would be kaput, too.

In the wake of weak test screenings, *The Pirate* went through a number of changes. Kay's manic, six-minute "Mack the Black" opus was replaced by a shorter, blander arrangement without Thompson's involvement. Louis B. Mayer hated the "Voodoo" number so much, he purportedly bellowed, "Burn the negative!" Cole Porter thought the movie was "unspeakably wretched." The public agreed. It was the one and only Garland vehicle at MGM that lost money.

Years later, Mart Crowley asked Kay, "What the hell went wrong on *The Pirate*?" Thompson's eyebrow went up and she responded with one word: "Drugaroonies."

While at work on *The Pirate*, Kay briefly contributed to the breezy whodunit *Song of the Thin Man* (MGM, 1947), starring William Powell and Myrna Loy as Dashiell Hammett's Nick and Nora Charles, the lovably boozy husband-wife detective team. Kay provided the vocal arrangement and coaching for a prerecording of "You're Not So Easy to Forget," by the Williams Brothers, who were scheduled to perform the song on-screen. Ultimately, however, sullen starlet Gloria Grahame, portraying a nightclub chanteuse, performed all versions of the song (dubbed by Carol Arden under Thompson's direction).

That same winter of 1947, Kay also worked on *The Hucksters*, starring Clark Gable as an advertising agency/radio producer strikingly similar to Bill Spier when he was at BBDO in the 1930s. The fictional ad agency's main client was Beautee Soap, owned by a gruff and eccentric tycoon (played by Sydney Greenstreet)—a biting send-up of real-life tobacco magnate George Washington Hill, who had fired Thompson and Lennie Hayton from *The Lucky Strike Hit Parade* in 1935. With considerable irony—and a poetic dose of payback—Hayton was the music conductor on *The Hucksters*, and he enlisted Thompson to create several faux advertising jingles for Beautee Soap.

Also featured in the film was Ava Gardner, who performed "Don't Tell Me" in a nightclub sequence. After Kay coached her for weeks, Ava prerecorded her own vocal on January 21, 1947. But the studio disliked the result. Consequently, Thompson replaced Ava's voice with that of Eileen Wilson, one of her former Rhythm Singers.

In February, Kay was assigned to the Freed Unit's *Good News*, based on the 1927 Broadway musical. "Much of the original DeSylva-Brown-Henderson score was retained for the screen," wrote George Feltenstein, "but given a new, dynamic harmonic sense by vocal arranger Kay Thompson. Thompson used her genius to dramatically alter several of the songs with her complex, wonderful arrangements."

Starring Peter Lawford, June Allyson, and Joan McCracken, *Good News* marked the directorial debut of choreographer Charles Walters, with Bob Alton on board to choreograph—a collaboration of like-minded specialists that resulted in what critic Norman Frizzle hailed as "some of the most zestful dance sequences ever conceived for movies."

"[Thompson] changed 'He's A Ladies' Man' by rewriting the lyrics to 'Be A Ladies' Man,'" noted Feltenstein, "and developed a magnificent vocal routine with Peter Lawford and Ray McDonald, who were ably supported by Mel Tormé and (on the soundtrack only) The Williams Brothers (Andy, Bob, Dick, and Don)."

In a 1997 phone interview with writer Lisa Jo Sagolla, Thompson commented, "They just loved singing [it]. Peter Lawford . . . ah! He was *so* happy. He didn't want to do the picture and there he was smiling and singing."

"In the breaks between takes on 'Varsity Drag,'" Feltenstein added, "you hear Kay singing along with Peter Lawford, to try to get him on key. That's why they had him shouting, 'Down on your heels, up on your toes,' in a speaking voice because he just couldn't sing."

It worked like a charm. "Most surprising of all is Peter Lawford as the juvenile lead," read one review, "belting out numbers with 100% charm and commitment."

Several compositions were added to the score, including a *Ziegfeld Follies* reject, "Pass That Peace Pipe" (Roger Edens–Hugh Martin–Ralph Blane), sung by Joan McCracken and Thompson's choir, which went on to be Oscar-nominated for Best Song. Critic Norman Frizzle wrote that it "ranks amongst the greatest production numbers ever devised for the camera."

Recalling McCracken, Thompson told Sagolla, "She came up to my office . . . and I asked her what she was supposed to be doing in my office. Nobody told me. She said, 'Well . . .' and she took off her bra."

When Sagolla asked *why* McCracken had exposed herself, Thompson replied, "I didn't ask her . . . and she wasn't the least bit interested in whom I was or what I was gonna do for her. Just *oomph.*" End of story.

What happened after that is anyone's guess—and Thompson obviously enjoyed the head-scratching it induced.

Although Kay put forth an aura of invincibility, things were not always as they seemed. In the mid-1940s, what began as occasional headaches escalated into migraines and other ailments.

"Kay was rather delicate and it was common knowledge," noted actress June Havoc. "She had all this energy when she was *on*, you know? Enormous energy. But, she wasn't that strong. She lost a lot of weight and was very, very slim. She ate baby food at one point. It was an intestinal something or other and everyone was very, very worried."

Kay's disorders went undiagnosed. By choice. It was during this time that she took an interest in Christian Science, a religion that believes true healing comes from the mind, not from modern medicine.

"Don't you think that's interesting that that's why Kay became a Christian Scientist?" pondered Lorna Luft. "She found a religion so that she could put doctors off. It's a great excuse. 'It's against my religion.'"

However, Thompson had no problem relying on the medical profession for cosmetic alterations. "I took Kay to the doctor when she got a nose job done," revealed Andy Williams, referring to her *third* rhinoplasty. "It was in the spring of 1947 before we went out on the road with the act. I know she had already split with Bill, which is why he did not take her instead of me."

The positive-thinking aspect of Christian Science was well-suited to her own philosophy. "I've discovered the secret of life," Kay once said. "A lot of hard work, a lot of sense of humor, a lot of joy and a whole lot of tra-la-la!"

"Kay was really visual," Lorna Luft explained, "and she would say things like, 'Let's pretend. Just picture yourself floating on a cloud. It's a pink cloud and it's just the most beautiful thing and you can just lie there and put your head on it and just pull part of that cloud up over you like covers.' Next thing you knew, you were feeling better."

Armed with pink clouds and a new nose, Kay asked to be released from her MGM contract. "I had had a headache for two years," she told writer Stephen M. Silverman. "I thought, 'I gotta get out of this place. It's just too much.'"

"Ooooh, that MGM," Kay later railed in the *Los Angeles Times*. "I was using about 5% of my potential. How I wanted to get away from there. I used to tell my husband, 'I'm going to quit . . . even if I have to scrub floors in General Hospital and bring my own scrub bucket.'" She complained to another writer, "I used to audition songs for the big producers. They'd say, 'Gee, that's great, Kay. Now, who'll we get to sing it in the movie?'" Dick Williams thought "she'd had enough of making all these other people sound great—Judy, Lena Horne. I think she just wanted to show that she could do it herself."

MGM had options on her services that could extend her exclusivity through May 15, 1950, but when her annual renewal came up on May 15, 1947, she appealed to Louis B. Mayer himself for her freedom. He agreed to let her go on the condition that she sign a sixty-day extension, through July 14, "for completion of services" on *Good News* and *The Pirate*.

Things had come to a crossroads in her personal life, too. Garland's emotional state was worse than ever, leaving Thompson wracked with guilt and frustration that she could not seem to help her. According to Garland chronologist Scott Schechter, "With Judy's work finished on *The Pirate*, she made a quiet, unpublicized suicide attempt and was admitted to Las Campanas, a California sanitarium, followed by a few weeks stay at Austen Riggs Center in Stockbridge, Massachusetts."

As Garland hit rock bottom, so did Thompson's marriage. Spier was dating other women. "I knew Bill quite well," Angela Lansbury explained, "and after he left Kay, he used to take me out a lot." Not coincidentally, Angela guest-starred on *Suspense* on May 29, 1947, in a tale aptly titled "A Thing of Beauty."

Then along came Havoc. "I was kind of on a double date with my agent, Barron Polan, and Bill and Angela Lansbury," June Havoc recalled. "And we went to a restaurant. The first thing I did was squirt grapefruit into Bill's eyes. From then on, he was mine."

Despite his still-legal marriage to Thompson and his involvement with Lansbury, Spier made no secret of his new romantic interest in Havoc, which got reported in all the papers. He hired Havoc to guest star in the June 12 installment of *Suspense* and then, with her voice disguised in a variety of character parts, she appeared under the pseudonym Armana Fargey in several installments of *The Adventures of Sam Spade*.

When asked her perspective on the breakup of Kay and Bill, June said, "Well, you know, it was just one of those drifting apart things. It was very romantic while it lasted but I think it was more of a love affair than a marriage. Bill eventually came and moved in with me. I lived in Malibu."

"Kay got the house on Bellagio Road," recalled Leonard Grainger. "Other than that, there was no division of anything."

In the early 1970s, Kay told Rex Reed, "I love love and I believe in divorce. Two great things. I've lived with quite a few men and alone is better. That doesn't mean I'm a loner; I just don't like to ask permission."

Impatient, Thompson insisted on a "quickie divorce" from Nevada but, in order to get one, she'd have to become a resident of the state for six straight weeks. So, in early August, she relocated to Las Vegas.

"To pass the time I put together this little act and tried it out," Thompson explained. The "little act" turned out to be Kay Thompson and the Williams Brothers. And show business would never be the same.

Part Three
THE NIGHTCLUB ERA

Chapter Six

ATOMIC ART

Kay Thompson and the Williams Brothers
(1947–49)

The greatest thing since bubble gum.
—*Marlene Dietrich*

*A*fter wiping her slate clean at home and at work, Kay was ready to take on the world. "Bob [Alton] and I had a talk," Thompson recalled, "and he said, 'Katie, what are you gonna do?' I said, 'I don't know, Bob. I can always sing in a saloon.'"

Imagining herself surrounded by dancers like Judy Garland in "Madame Crematante," Thompson decided she needed reinforcements.

"Why don't you use those Williams kids?" Alton suggested.

"I'm too tall and they're too short," Kay replied.

"Fine," Alton countered. "It will be funny."

Having reunited after World War II, the Williams Brothers (Andy, Dick, Don, and Bob) were finding it hard to jump-start their career at MGM.

"Let's get out," Kay suggested. "Let's go form an act."

"She loved how we sang," noted Dick Williams, "but she didn't know what we were going to do exactly."

Standing idly around a microphone, Kay and the Williams Brothers sang together publicly for the first time in May 1947 for some all-star volunteer shows at veterans hospitals. Then, they made their radio debut performing "Louisiana Purchase" on *Personal Album,* presented by the Armed Forces Radio Service. Recognizing their potential, agent Barron Polan (currently repping Bill Spier, June Havoc, Howard Duff, and Ethel Merman) took them on as clients.

"Roger Edens and Kay would hold these elaborate joint birthday parties and perform at them," recalled Don Williams. "Kay wrote 'Jubilee Time' for that and one day she decided to teach it to us."

"It sounded so great," Kay recalled, "so I called Bob [Alton] and . . . he said, 'Come on over to the house at about 8 o'clock.'"

"After Bob heard us sing 'Jubilee Time,'" Don added, "he said, 'Learn this step.'"

"We had never danced before, *ever,*" Dick Williams said, laughing. "We didn't know our left foot from our right."

"Oh my God, Kay," Alton lamented. "They're not dancers. What am I going to do?"

"Just get them to dance a little bit if you can, Bob," Thompson replied. "They don't need to be Fred Astaire."

"And it just expanded from there," Don said. "Kay would write the thing— and then we'd go to Bob at night and he would stage it. We'd rehearse until midnight or even later. He'd go to work the next day at MGM [choreograph- ing *The Pirate*] and come home in the evening and work with us again."

They needed a rehearsal pianist. Enter Joe Marino, thirty-one, who grew up in Chicago and, at the age of fourteen, had worked as a pianist for Al Ca- pone at the Paddock Club in Cicero, Illinois. Now serving time as a pianist for MGM, Marino was appropriated by Thompson for her cause. She also stole Bill Spier's girl Friday, Peggy Rea, to become her personal assistant.

"We rehearsed for at least six weeks without anyone asking what we were rehearsing for," Kay stated.

And nobody was getting paid. "It was a labor of love for all of us," said Don, "because we didn't know what was going to happen."

"When we began rehearsing," Dick recalled, "we'd do the opening number and would be absolutely exhausted. We'd say, 'We can't do an act. We can't *move* after just one number!' Kay would say, 'Oh, yes you can. Just try harder.' Little by little, we built our stamina to thirty-five minutes."

"We all looked exactly alike," Don explained, "and when we did a hand move, we all did it exactly alike, *bam,* in perfect sync."

"I am only five-feet, five-and-a-half," Kay Thompson recalled, "but [next to the boys] I look like ten-feet tall with my arm up in the air."

"It was like four penguins and a giraffe," Peggy Rea chuckled.

"I remember one time we were trying to learn a new song," Dick recalled, "and we just got all screwed up, lost our places, and Kay said, 'Keep rowing, boys! Keep rowing!'"

Bursting with confidence, Thompson tried to hire Sinatra's press agent, George Evans—the man who created Frankie's screaming bobby-soxers—but because the act was still gestating, Evans "couldn't see her for dust." Instead, she ended up hiring Maury Foladare, "the most rotund press agent in the world," who had represented such giants as Bing Crosby and *King Kong*. He convinced *Vogue* magazine to do a spread on his new client.

The session with *Vogue* photographer George Platt Lynes went longer than expected, and Kay was running late for rehearsal at Alton's house in Bel Air.

"So I drove the car across the golf course," Kay explained. "This wonderful, gorgeous, millions of yards of green grass. Just heaven."

Alton greeted her by asking, "Who do you think you are, coming here five minutes late?"

Kay answered in a high-pitched voice, "I am Eloise, I am six."

So there it was. The official anecdote told a thousand times—in a thousand variations—to describe the supposedly extemporaneous 1947 "birth" of Eloise, even though it was a bald-faced lie. Kay had been talking in the voice of Eloise for decades.

"The boys loved Eloise and they gave themselves names," Thompson elaborated. "Andy, for instance, gave himself two names. He was Junior *and* he was Melvin. The good and the bad. One helped his mother; the other smoked marijuana."

Alton became Nicholas Aubrey Carstairs; Barron Polan became Stinky; Polan's sister, Connie Wald, became Sarah Jane; and her husband, Warner Brothers producer Jerry Wald, became Pee Wee.

Despite the distraction of Eloise chatter, "Kay Thompson and the Williams Brothers" managed to evolve into an act. "I think you can go to Las Vegas," Alton proclaimed. They were ready. Not only that, it was just the excuse Kay needed to establish six weeks of Nevada residency to get her "quickie divorce" from Bill Spier.

Back then, the Las Vegas Strip was no great shakes—just a small oasis of three hotel-casinos—the Last Frontier, the El Rancho, and the brand-new Flamingo—the last two controlled by mobsters Meyer Lansky and Lucky Luciano. Their associate Bugsy Siegel had just been gunned down on June 20, 1947, for failing to control construction cost overruns at the Flamingo.

After Siegel's death the operation of the Flamingo and the El Rancho was taken over by Sanford Adler, "a gambler with a long record of arrests" who was a front man for Meyer Lansky. Adler was convinced that the survival of Vegas hinged on luring big stars to its stages. Lansky's friend Frank Sinatra would have been first in line, but at that time, he was keeping a low profile due to intense scrutiny by the press and the FBI regarding his ties to the Mob.

On July 25, 1947, large advertisements appeared in *Daily Variety* and *The Hollywood Reporter* announcing three daily chartered plane flights, free of charge, for anyone coming to Las Vegas from Los Angeles, "inaugurated by Sanford Adler, the owner of The Hotel El Rancho Vegas and the Flamingo Hotel." To enhance the publicity stunt, Adler hired the object of Sinatra's unbridled flirtations, Ava Gardner, to christen the first flight. In keeping with the hard-boiled cast of characters, Ava brought along her current beau, Howard "Sam Spade" Duff.

According to Jerry Lewis, "*every* important nightclub of the 1940s [was] owned by the Mob. I'll maintain till the end of my days . . . that in the 1940s and '50s, before the Mob lost its hold on nightclubs and Vegas, it was literally impossible for an entertainer, any entertainer, not to deal with them."

Realizing this, Barron Polan organized a private preview of Thompson's act for Meyer Lansky, Sanford Adler, and other shady characters from the nightclub underworld. The secret summit took place in Bob Alton's living room.

Don Williams remembered, "It knocked them all out because it was something nobody'd ever seen before."

It didn't hurt that Thompson had Sinatra's enthusiastic stamp of approval. As a result, Lansky and Adler booked the unproven act at the El Rancho for a two-week engagement starting August 6, 1947, at a rate of $2,000 per week.

Kay was now faced with the daunting task of making sure an audience would show up, twice nightly, for two solid weeks. On Sunday, August 3—just three nerve-racking days before their debut—Polan organized a press preview for Hedda Hopper, Louella Parsons, and all the other major columnists. Florabel Muir of *Daily Variety* hailed it "the greatest nightclub act that I've ever seen or hope to see," and the rest of her colleagues agreed.

"We had *enormous* support," Kay later recalled, still astounded by the snowball effect of the preopening buzz.

Everything seemed to be falling into place just perfectly except that no contract had been drawn up between Kay and the boys. The Williams Brothers' career had always been managed by their father, Jay Williams, so Kay and Barron would have to strike a deal with him. Fast.

"The Williams Brothers featuring Kay Thompson" was how Jay Williams wanted the act to be billed, but Kay scoffed at that notion. As far as she was concerned, the Williams Brothers were nothing more than her backup group. While Jay Williams tried to stand his ground, the boys—particularly Andy—seemed content to do whatever Kay wanted. In the end, they agreed to be billed as "Kay Thompson and the Williams Brothers."

"The split was fifty-fifty," recalled Dick Williams. "Fifty percent to Kay and fifty percent that we had to split up among the four of us."

Polan's 10 percent agent commission would come off the top, but Kay was forced to assume all other costs out of her share, including salaries for the pianist, publicist, and secretary, plus wardrobe expenses, etc.

"You know, every obstacle was there," she later remarked. "And I just kept saying, 'We're going forward.'"

Another unanticipated kink was how to amplify the voices of five whirling dervishes. Back then, hand microphones were tethered by long electrical cords that would have become hopelessly tangled amid five pairs of eggbeater legs. Inspired by overhead boom mikes on film sets, Thompson declared, "The microphones have to be hung from the ceiling."

"We hung those mikes ourselves," Andy recalled. "It was the first time that had ever been done." And it has been copied and refined ever since—even Broadway theaters adapted the idea—but it all traces back to the mother of invention.

"There'd never been an act like it," Andy concluded, "because it employed the movie technique of singing and acting and dancing and everything, but all live."

The learning curve was fast and furious—both for the performers and their audience. "We didn't know the facts of nightclub life," Andy explained in *The Saturday Evening Post*. "On our second night at El Rancho, my brother Dick jumped off-stage and belted a guy who kept talking while we were on. The truth is people didn't know what hit them on our opening night . . . [but] they stood up and cheered when we were through."

In Kay's humble opinion, they were simply "the greatest group that ever hit humanity."

On August 15, *Daily Variety* reported, "Kay Thompson and the four Williams Brothers have proved such a click at the El Rancho Vegas that they've been booked to play the Flamingo Sept. 11, with other offers swamping them from niteries all over the country."

With a two-week break before opening at the Flamingo, they took a booking in the Tahoe Village Casino at Lake Tahoe.

"Two thugs named Russian Louie Strauss and Sir Abe Chapman ran the place," Andy recalled. "One time, Kay invited these guys for tea. It was a hot August day, and they asked if they could take off their jackets; Kay said yes, so they did, and they each had two guns strapped over their shoulders! Right after our two-week booking, Russian Louie and Sir Abe drove Kay to the airport, then went back and shot their other partner dead right there in the lobby. I think Russian Louie Strauss is buried somewhere out in the desert. It was a rough group."

Afraid to look back, Kay and her boys hightailed it to Vegas for their gig at the Flamingo—with Sinatra, Peter Lawford, and many others flown in to cheer them on.

The *St. Louis Post-Dispatch* reported, "Kay and the Williams Brothers were an instantaneous hit with everyone except the dealers in the gambling casino . . . Kay knicked them for $18,000 winnings by the end of her engagement."

The money was a godsend because the heavy start-up expenses had consumed her entire six-week earnings for the act in Nevada. Three days after her divorce was decreed on September 22, 1947, she sold her Bel Air mansion for $50,000, which eased the financial stress.

Kay and the boys next played San Francisco's Mark Hopkins Hotel, collecting $2,000 per week for a fortnight beginning October 26. It was reported in *Daily Variety* that the act was the "town's newest rave." However, after a splashy opening the act did not sustain big crowds. As word spread, interest from other clubs suddenly dried up.

"We have no bookings," Kay lamented to columnist Florabel Muir.

"Let me talk to Herman Hover," Muir suggested. "He could sure use this act at Ciro's."

Located at 8433 Sunset Boulevard in West Hollywood (now the Comedy Store), Ciro's was, according to Jerry Lewis, "the ritziest nightclub on Sunset Strip and Herman was quite a power in the Hollywood of the late forties. Short, gruff, always impeccably tailored, he was the same height and build as Edward G. Robinson."

"Whoever heard of these people?" was Hover's initial response to Muir's recommendation.

"Right now, nobody, but give 'em time," Florabel urged.

Begrudgingly, Hover decided to give them a shot for two weeks starting October 14, 1947, at $3,000 a week.

To cut expenses, Kay persuaded MGM producer Jack Cummings to let her reside rent-free in the pool house behind his Beverly Hills mansion at 603 N. Canon Drive (later bought by Robert Wagner and Natalie Wood).

Then, with a complete lack of modesty, she sent letters to everybody she'd ever met: "We have found a sound which is greater than Thomas Edison ever dreamed of . . . The act is the greatest that has ever hit show business . . . This is your chance to see the one and only Kay Thompson—singer, actress, dancer, arranger, and comedienne. See you at Ciro's."

It worked. Big-league reservations began pouring in and soon there wasn't a seat to be had. "Their opening . . . will, no doubt, break every existing record," predicted *The Hollywood Reporter*.

"You should have been here opening night," Kay marveled. "Everybody else was."

The pantheon of stars that showed up rivaled Oscar night: Judy Garland and Vincente Minnelli, Angela Lansbury, Orson Welles, Dinah Shore, Jackie Cooper, Ava Gardner and Howard Duff, Ronald Reagan and Jane Wyman, and scores of other famous folk.

"It was like a bombshell," recalled Connie Wald, "the most exciting night I've ever witnessed in my entire life."

"It was unbelievable," Angela Lansbury rhapsodized. "I'll never forget Kay coming out in those shoes and that outfit, those pants and everything. I'm telling you, it was some event. It really was."

"It wasn't an act," recalled another eyewitness. "It was a scrimmage. Tumbles, pratfalls, leapfrogs, and zany songs filled the air with flying figures and frantic music. It was the most frenetic act in nightclub history."

Kay later parsed the recipe for lightning in a bottle: "My *enormous* sophistication, my thinness, my angular *thing*, and the lovely innocence, purity, and simplicity of the Williams Brothers and their dear little eager eight eyes."

Thompson's shoulder-tingling was off the chart. But, several nights into the engagement, the sensation stopped cold when she spotted Walter Winchell in the audience—the columnist who had crucified her in the 1930s for spoiling "lovely hits by re-writing them." However, by the end of the first number, Walter was cheering along with the rest of the crowd. After the show, he proclaimed himself Kay's "top fan," religiously devoted to her "atomic art." He nicknamed her "Kay Thompsonsational."

"He couldn't stop writing about us," marveled Andy Williams.

Winchell explained his about-face to *Variety* by admitting, "I didn't appreciate [her style in the 1930s]. What she was doing then with her arrangements is what I'm so nuts about now."

"I have always been twenty years ahead of myself," Kay reflected philosophically.

Money couldn't buy notices like the ones they got—and if an unfavorable review exists, it has yet to be found.

On subsequent nights, tables continued to be jammed by the likes of Sinatra, Bogie and Bacall, Dietrich, Gable, Crosby, Astaire—to name just a smattering. No one had ever seen audiences so starry.

Each forty-minute show would consist of about eight numbers. They always opened with "Hello, Hello," which playfully introduced Kay and the boys by name to the audience. This segued into rip-roaring workouts like "Jubilee Time," "I Love a Violin," and "On the Caribbean." Between high-energy songs, they would do comedic odes such as "Myrtle (of Sheepshead Bay)," with Thompson as a Brooklynese floozy, and satiric sophistication like "Broadway (Street of Dreams)," which *Life* described as "a typical Noël Coward–Gertrude Lawrence tête-à-tête."

But, hands down, the audience favorite was "Poor Suzette (with Her Restoration Bosom and Four Lovers)," aka "L'Histoire de la Pauvre Suzette," because every night, Kay cleverly inserted four names of real celebrities as Suzette's lovers, and tailored bawdy new lyrics to each. Thompson did not dare to ambush her "Suzette" victims without warning, so she wrote witty telegrams like this one to Orson Welles: DEAR DARLING ADORABLE ORSON: I'M TAKING THE LIBERTY OF USING YOUR NAME IN A NUMBER CALLED SUZETTE UNLESS I HEAR FROM YOU TO THE CONTRARY. NEEDLESS TO SAY, IT IS USED WITH CHARM AND AFFECTION AND IF YOU ARE NOT HERE BY 11:30 I WILL REFUSE TO GO ON YOUR LOVER. KAY THOMPSON.

Though celebrities' names were assigned to Suzette's suitors, it was the Williams Brothers who actually portrayed them: "The Man She Loved," "The Man She Didn't Love," "The Man She Loved Too Much," and "The Man She Loved Too Often." The routine was loaded with slapstick, mugging, and acrobatics.

"Andy was the one that she loved too much," Kay recalled, "and [he] fell dead on the floor."

"Bob Alton taught him this fall and taught him how to break it with his hands before he fell," Don explained, "but . . . one night, he missed and he didn't catch himself, hit himself in the head and knocked himself out cold."

Another night, he miscalculated and slid under a ringside table. "The man at the table said, 'Get away from my wife's ankles,'" Andy recalled, "and kicked me right in the ear."

"By the time our shows were over," said Dick, "you could hear the sweat sloshing in our feet. Our suits were dripping wet." Peggy Rea noted that

Bob Williams perspired so profusely, "they had to cut his necktie off every night."

Subtlety was out. "We ram it down their throats," Thompson put it bluntly. "I always wanted to be a big fat ham."

But she knew when enough was enough. "Kay refused to do encores," Dick remembered. "She'd say, 'Leave 'em wanting. Never give 'em too much.'"

"We never mingled with the crowd," Don added. "It was Kay's philosophy: 'Don't become commonplace.' And she was right. We'd go to Kay's dressing room, have champagne, whiskey, or whatever, and wait to see who'd come."

"She was always extremely charming to anyone visiting in the dressing room," Dick Williams confirmed, "but often when a person would leave, she would turn around and say, 'Oh, what an asshole.' It made me wonder what she would say about me when I left the room." Many others echoed the same fear.

*W*ith *Thompson suddenly the* talk of the town, *Daily Variety* posed the question on everyone's mind: "How could MGM hide her all this time?"

"They're knocking their heads against the walls out there [now]," Thompson gloated to a reporter. "Serves 'em right. I beat my brains out for them long enough."

And—no surprise—suddenly the studio wanted her back. On October 15, 1947, the *Los Angeles Times* reported, "Kay Thompson . . . recently contributed a musical comedy scenario, along with her partners, the Williams Brothers, which Metro is reportedly considering for production along *The Harvey Girls* line." The project would be entitled *Happily Ever After*, with Bob Alton attached to choreograph and direct.

Not only was MGM feeling remorse, Thompson's ex-husband became a groupie. When confronted by the press, Bill Spier described his attendance as a damned-if-you-do, damned-if-you-don't situation: "If I stay away from Ciro's I'm jealous. And if I go in and look sad—I'm taunting her." One night, he brazenly brought June Havoc, whom he would soon marry on January 25, 1948.

In the wake of Thompson's popularity, other clubs in town found themselves virtually empty. The Mocambo, Ciro's top competitor, took out serio-comic ads in *The Hollywood Reporter* and erected a billboard on Sunset Strip begging Kay to mercifully "get the heck outta town."

But her holdovers just kept multiplying. The act's weekly guarantee doubled to $6,000, and they demanded and got a percentage of the gross. At first, "The Incomparable Hildegarde" graciously agreed to postpone her scheduled

Ciro's opening, but after the third postponement, she pitched a fit and canceled altogether.

Another unanticipated phenomenon was the unusually high number of repeat customers. "Kay Thompson's 'I've Seen Her 12 Times' club growing apace," wrote Florabel Muir in *Daily Variety*. Judy Garland, Peter Lawford, and Margaret Whiting were among the most obsessed.

"Nobody yells and screams louder than Judy Garland for Kaytee at Ciro's," reported Muir. "She was doing it again Monday night."

"I would always say to Peter Lawford, 'What are you gonna wear tomorrow night?'" Margaret Whiting recalled, "because we'd been there twenty-nine nights in a row."

Ads in the trades included testimonials from dozens of major stars, including Garland ("Kay Thompson is a brilliant performer!") and Orson Welles ("Greatest act I've ever seen!").

One of Kay's biggest fans was Bing Crosby, who booked the act on his current series, *Philco Radio Time* (ABC, November 12, 1947), during which she performed in a comedy sketch with Peter Lorre. After appearing on other shows with the likes of Danny Kaye and Perry Como, Thompson was suddenly hot again on the airwaves. The Milton Biow advertising agency, which represented *Suspense*, offered to provide a sponsor for a proposed *Kay Thompson and the Williams Brothers* radio series "wherever, however and whenever they would like." Pass. The last thing Kay wanted to do was regress back to radio on a regular basis.

Broadway offers were raining like confetti: Irving Berlin's *Miss Liberty*, a revival of George M. Cohan's *45 Minutes from Broadway*, Arthur Schwartz's *Inside U.S.A.*, and an untitled revue from producer Leland Hayward. But Kay turned them all down.

Next, a blitz of magazine spreads in *Life, Look, Time,* and *Vogue* elevated her national profile.

On the cover of its December 17, 1947, issue, *Daily Variety* headlined: "KAY THOMPSON, INC.," with a report that the "nitery star" had formed a company "to handle radio, motion pictures, recordings, night clubs, theatres and the manufacturing of Kaytee Slacks."

And then she signed a book deal with Little, Brown and Company to write *Beds I Have Slept In*, a collection of amusing ruminations "about people who live in hotels. The pulpwood people."

When asked how much of it got written, Peggy Rea laughed, "Not word one. I was assigned to hang around and take notes, but I was too busy getting shoes sewn and scarves fixed." Of course, Kay did retain one germ of the idea by making Eloise a hotel dweller.

• • •

Decca Records decided to cash in on Thompson's heat by unearthing long-forgotten recordings she had made in 1944 as a guest vocalist for Johnny Green's orchestra, including "The Steam Is on the Beam," "You're Mine, You," and "Coquette." This "fresh" Johnny Green album was promoted in the press for featuring "new nightclub sensation Kay Thompson," and Green took out a congratulatory ad in *The Hollywood Reporter* stating, "Your new act is just a big NEON LIGHT shining in a wilderness of doldrums."

A bidding war erupted among Decca and its competitors for exclusive rights to future Thompson recordings; Columbia Records emerged victorious. In December, before a strike by the American Federation of Musicians went into effect, Kay quickly recorded four sides, only two of which featured the Williams Brothers—that way, she could command considerably more than the fifty-fifty split she reluctantly shared with them for her nightclub act. Unfortunately, when the records were released the following spring, sales were tepid.

"Class material has never been given more gloss nor spirit than the Thompson turn evokes," noted *Daily Variety*, "but the ceiling on pop-platter tastes has never been high. What rocks 'em in niteries just doesn't seem to panic the platter public."

Clearly, Thompson needed to expand her fan base to more cities. So, after eight record-breaking weeks at Ciro's, she moved on to Miami's Copacabana beginning Christmas Eve 1947 for $6,500 per week, plus 40 percent of the gross over $30,000. "They should walk out with at least $10,000 each week," calculated *The Hollywood Reporter*.

But would Kaytee mania translate to a place like Miami, where she would have to rely on attendance by mere mortals? The answer came swiftly. "450 were squeezed into the ordinarily 300 seating space on opening night," reported Walter Winchell, "and 1200 were turned away." And when the pace didn't let up, her two-week engagement was extended to three.

"One night in Miami, Milton Berle came into Kay's dressing room," Peggy Rea recalled, "and she had her Christian Science books on the table and he said, 'Well, Kaysie, I see you've been over at Mary Baker & Eddie's.' I have treasured that joke all my life, because, you see, Mary Baker Eddy founded Christian Science, and Leon & Eddie's was a famous comedy club in New York."

When a reporter for the *New York World-Telegram* noticed an open Bible in her dressing room, Kay responded, "That's the side of me nobody knows.

You see, I adore children. I'm making a special arrangement of the 23rd Psalm ["The Lord Is My Shepherd"] to be sung by a large group of children on records, without musical accompaniment. The record label will say 'Just Children and a Young Man's Voice.'"

The "young man" in question was intended to be Andy Williams, but nothing came of it—at least not right away.

When asked how religious Thompson really was, Peggy Rea said, "Kay got into Christian Science for about twenty minutes. Then she started healing people. When pianist Joe Marino's little boy and little girl got sick, Kay started healing them. I mean, this was a woman who was a dynamo, but nutty, too."

After Miami, Kay and the boys accepted an offer of $7,500 per week, plus percentage, to play Chicago at the Mayfair Room in the Blackstone Hotel (January 20–February 13, 1948). The Blackstone was owned by Arnold Kirkeby, the wealthy hotelier whose properties included the Beverly-Wilshire in Beverly Hills and the St. Regis in Manhattan. A Chicago native, Kirkeby had many business connections with Meyer Lansky and Lucky Luciano.

"'Ho-la! Ho-la! It's Jubilee time!' chortles Kay Thompson in a telegram from Chicago, where she and the Williams Boys played to a total sockeroo on their opening night," reported Florabel Muir in *Daily Variety*. "'All records smashed.' Well, there's a tornado that won't blow itself out soon."

Chicago Daily Tribune critic Will Davidson wrote that until Thompson's act came along, show business had been suffering from a bad case of "pernicious anemia—lack of Vitamin Kay."

Reservations were not easy to come by. *Daily Variety* reported that even Broadway's beloved Mary Martin was refused at the door. Although she outwardly took the disappointment in stride, Martin harbored a lifelong belief that Thompson had purposefully blackballed her. Like she did with June "Peter Pan Collar" Allyson, Kay categorized Mary as "hopelessly square," a dismissal that apparently Thompson wore on her sleeve, because two years later, Martin was still holding a grudge and would exact her revenge when the moment was right.

With all the orgasmic hosannas being heaped upon the altar of Thompson in major cities, it was easy to forget that she was barely known in Middle America—where zebra-print pants and Noël Coward parodies were not the norm. To regular Joes, Kay was a fringe showbiz kook. But that did not matter to her.

"I don't think she craved recognition by the public," observed Lorna Luft. "She craved recognition among her peers in show business."

Though Kay resisted repeat engagements because of her "leave 'em wanting more" motto, she could not turn down $10,000 a week, plus 10 percent, to encore in Miami.

"We shared a house with Dean Martin and Jerry Lewis," Peggy recalled. "They had a duplex and we had a duplex."

Martin and Lewis would soon be giving Thompson a run for her money. But in February 1948, the comedy duo was still an opening act for more established stars.

"Kay was a brilliant performer, an incredible choreographer, and a great singer, and she utilized the four boys brilliantly," Jerry Lewis recalled. "A *great* act."

Shattering her own attendance record, Thompson ended her Miami gig on March 15, 1948, and then disappeared for several days without letting anyone know where she was. Was it a publicity stunt? After a flurry of rumors concerning her whereabouts, *The Hollywood Reporter* scooped on March 23 that she had been located in Cuba, where she was "resting prior to her New York opening."

The story got better. Kay was holed up at the notorious Hotel Nacional in Havana, where Meyer Lansky and Lucky Luciano were fixtures. In fact, Frank Sinatra was currently under investigation by the FBI for meeting with these gangsters at that hotel during the December 1946 "Havana Conference"; it was then that the hit on Bugsy Siegel allegedly had been ordered. Suspected of delivering a briefcase full of cash to Luciano, Sinatra was spending a lot of his own money defending himself against the charges—though many, including Jerry Lewis, had witnessed Frank's shady dealings with the Mob on countless occasions.

It seems ludicrous to suggest that Kay was in cahoots with the Mob, but in an era marked by media suspicion and government-sanctioned witch hunts, did she really think she was immune to guilt by association? This was brazen, attention-grabbing mischief of Eloisian proportions.

Meanwhile, Barron Polan closed a deal for the act to play New York at Café Society Uptown, 128 East Fifty-eighth Street, which had recently been acquired by Herbert Jacoby and Max Gordon, owners of the Blue Angel.

"Kay called Jacoby 'the Prince of Darkness,'" said Bill Harbach, composer Otto Harbach's son, whom Thompson had just hired as her New York aide-de-camp. "He scared the shit out of Kay. He had a thick European accent and he looked like Dracula."

Jacoby and Gordon wanted to "set this town on its ear" by reopening Café Society Uptown under a new name, Le Directoire, with a new look by celebrated interior designer William Pahlmann, and "the greatest act in nightclub history." To conduct, Kay insisted they hire her old pal Ted Straeter and his orchestra, heralded by *The New Yorker* magazine as "the best dance band in these parts."

Opening on April Fool's Day, Thompson would earn an unprecedented $10,000 a week, plus 15 percent of the gross. Refusing to perform on a ground-level dance floor, Kay demanded a special hydraulic performance platform. At a cost of $4,000, "[Pahlmann] built a stage, eighteen inches high," recalled Gordon, "and had it wired so that at the push of a button, it could move and come to rest on the dance floor."

As one problem got solved, however, another blew up. "On the afternoon of the opening," wrote historian James Gavin, "Jacoby and Gordon discovered that they had inadvertently reduced the seating capacity from 300 to 212." This was a cataclysmic disaster since every night had been sold out weeks in advance.

Like the riot scene out of Nathanael West's *The Day of the Locust*, the furor that erupted over denied reservations only added to the "must-see" mystique of it all. Those who managed to survive the stampede on opening night included Marlene Dietrich, Maurice Chevalier, and William Randolph Hearst.

When it was time to start the show, the band stopped playing, the dance floor was cleared, and the hydraulic stage was ready to make its dramatic de-scent. Peggy Rea howled as she described what transpired next: "The Prince of Darkness went to the wall and pushed the button but nothing happened. That damn stage didn't budge one inch. They frantically put in a call to the engineer in Jersey and he had to drive through the tunnel, so it was going to be a while. Milton Berle got up and ad-libbed, treating it all as a horse race. 'All right, now the engineer is at the corner of such-and-such.' He got Dean Martin and Jerry Lewis up there, he got Ethel Merman, he got every star in the house to come up and do a turn. It was unbelievable. By the time the engineer finally got there and that damn floor came down and the boys came on with Kay, everybody went bananas."

Radie Harris proclaimed in *Daily Variety*, "[The opening] goes down in the records as one of the greatest nights in the memory of supper club habitués. For Kay and the 4 Williams Brothers not only lived up to expectations—they surpassed it."

"Ethel Merman came every night," said Peggy Rea, "and knew every joke and every line and started to laugh beforehand. Kay would send me down to speak to her: 'Excuse me, ma'am. You're bothering the rest of us because we haven't heard the joke yet.' Couldn't have cared less."

There was stiff competition to be Thompson's new best friend. Columnist Erskine Johnson reported that Marlene Dietrich was regularly "haunting Le

Directoire [and] convulsed everyone by telling Kay, 'You're the greatest thing since bubble gum.'" Then Joan Crawford started showing up every night.

When she wasn't being wined and dined at the Stork Club by every star in the galaxy, Kay would slum it with her boys. Winchell noted, "Kay Thompson and the Williams IV taking out their final Broadway citizenship papers by dining at Hanson's drug-store counter in the middle-of-the-night."

The Williams brethren were privy to a side of Kay Thompson that was all but extinct—the less pretentious woman who had pounded the pavement of Tin Pan Alley during the 1930s and hung out on Swing Street with musicians like Alec Wilder. "[By the time] her extraordinary act with the Williams Brothers hit Hollywood and then New York," observed Wilder, "she was a completely fabricated personality as far as I was concerned."

Like it or not, the fast lane bred superficiality. There was no time for real emotions. Hell, there was hardly time to go to the loo.

Forgoing respites between shows, they made themselves available for nearby private parties such as the one they played honoring the Duke and Duchess of Windsor, for which they pocketed a cool $5,000. Edward and Mrs. Simpson loved the performance, and became instant friends of Kay's. In the years to come, they would socialize often on both sides of the Atlantic. Of cultural significance was the Duke and Duchess's passion for pug dogs that rubbed off on Kay—and, by extension, on Eloise, whose pet pug, Weenie, later caused a spike in pug adoptions across America.

Another memorable night at Le Directoire was the time Kay finally came face-to-face with Noël Coward. When Thompson heard he was in the audience, she turned to her lieutenant and said, "Billy, dah-ling, while I'm onstage, I want you to go get seven million candles for my dressing room."

"There was a little joint called the Sazerac on Lexington Avenue around Fifty-sixth Street," Bill Harbach recalled, "so I ran in there and asked, 'Can I have all the candles in this building?' And the owner said, 'Why?' I said, 'Noël Coward is coming to see Kay Thompson and she wants to be impressive.' And he said, 'Well, sure, for Noël and for Kay, you got it.' I got about ten cardboard boxes filled with these little candles in glass jars and I put them all over that fucking dressing room. It took me twenty minutes just to light them. It was *wild.*"

Coward was not only enchanted by the wonderland of twinkling flames, he was particularly taken by Thompson's unusual bow after her last number.

"Kay would kneel on one knee, spread her arms out with a bow, and almost have her head on the floor," Harbach remembered. "She'd give one of these bows at the end of the show, and then she would walk off. There would be screaming and screaming and screaming, but she would never come out again. No second or third bow, no encores, that was it. Well, when I brought Noël Coward up to the dressing room, he said to her in that marvelous crisp accent, 'Dear girl, you were absolutely magnificent. And when you did that beautiful bow and left the stage, I screamed for you to come out again and have a second bow, and if you had, I would have killed you.'"

To thank Walter Winchell for his relentless drumbeating, Kay decided to stage a benefit for the Damon Runyon Cancer Fund, established by Winchell in memory of his mentor, who had died of throat cancer in 1946. Radie Harris reported in *Daily Variety*: "Kay not only conceived the whole idea, but wrote all the new lyrics and arrangements, did all her own contacting and personally sent out every wired invite . . . To see Ethel Merman in a blonde wig and slacks, the exact duplicate of Kay's, and hear her sing 'Jubilee' was worth the $50 admission price alone . . . Nancy Walker said, 'Look Ma, I'm Dancin'' in her famous ballet satire—Henry Fonda played Noël Coward to Kay's Gertie Lawrence—and the Nicholas Bros. tore down the house with their 'Harlem' routine. All this, in addition to Kay and the Williams Bros.' regular show."

Kay and her boys headlined in other charity shows, too, including ones held at the Winter Garden Theatre with Martin and Lewis, Carnegie Hall with the Katherine Dunham Dance Company, and the Waldorf-Astoria Hotel with Ethel Merman.

"We were the No. 1 act in the world," Andy Williams recalled, shaking his head in amazement.

On June 2, 1948, after nine weeks of taking Manhattan, Kay and her boys bid adieu to Le Directoire and to two members of their entourage. Peggy Rea had decided to pursue a career as a character actress and later became known for playing Lulu Hogg on TV's *The Dukes of Hazzard*.

Bill Harbach aspired to find work behind the scenes in television. "Kay was a great friend of Pat Weaver, the president of NBC," Harbach recalled. "She told me, 'Go see Pat, say I sent you, and you gotta call him Weaver Feathers.'" Armed with those magic words, Harbach became a fixture at the network and later launched and produced a promising new program called *The Tonight Show*.

Next up, Thompson and company did a return engagement at the Blackstone in Chicago starting June 18, earning a whopping $12,000 per week, plus percentage. It was, according to the *Los Angeles Examiner*, "the biggest salary ever paid an entertainer."

To break away from the 24/7 hubbub at the Blackstone, Kay checked herself into the nearby Edgewater Beach Hotel, where she met a ten-year-old resident named Marilou Hedlund, another of the many inspirations for Eloise.

"The Edgewater was a wonderful playground," Baroness Marilou Hedlund von Ferstel remembered in 2007, "with lots of ballrooms, restaurants, and stores—all of which piqued the interest of a child. I was gregarious about meeting people. My standard opening line was always, 'I am Marilou. My mother is 4'11" and wears a 3½ shoe, and my father is 6'2" and weighs 200 pounds.' It was my marketing slogan."

On meeting Kay, Marilou recalled, "She thought I was amusing and she tried to give me singing lessons, but it was not a success, because still to this day, I cannot carry a tune in a bucket."

Years later, Marilou bought a copy of *Eloise* to read to her daughter. "When I saw 'My mother wears a 3½ shoe,'" she explained, "that's when I discovered that Kay must have based some of her lines on my patter."

On the promotional front, Thompson appeared on several radio shows hosted by her former paramour Dave Garroway, now one of the top radio personalities on WMAQ, Chicago's NBC affiliate. Like Kay, he was divorced and available. Circumstantial evidence suggests their romance may have been rekindled: not only were they spotted dining together on several occasions, Dave waged a personal crusade that summer to turn Kay's swing recording with Johnny Green's orchestra, "The Steam Is on the Beam," into a local hit.

Another Chicago radio personality had his sights set on her, too: Mike Wallace, who later coanchored *60 Minutes* on CBS-TV for thirty-eight years.

"In 1948, I was hosting an afternoon interview show called *For the Luvva Mike*," recalled Mike Wallace in 2007, "and I remember interviewing Kay Thompson when she was in Chicago with the Williams Brothers. In those days, I was fairly square. I was a little taken by, and enchanted by, and *puzzled* by show business people, especially someone as extraordinary as Kay Thompson. We became fast friends because she was an adorable individual and she was willing to help educate this young 'Myron' Wallace. What I remember most about Kay was her terrific performances with the Williams Brothers at the Blackstone, and at the time, she was already involved in that Eloise business. She'd speak to me often in the voice of Eloise."

That summer, Kay was also stepping up her strategy to conquer Broadway. *Happily Ever After*, a stage adaptation of her unproduced screen treatment, was to be directed by Bob Alton—who was negotiating a leave of absence from his MGM contract. According to *The New York Times*, Thompson and Alton were devising ways to "introduce movie effects, like the 'dissolve,' with skits merging into musical numbers and vice versa," an innovation that would "soft-pedal the blackout and curtain devices traditional to the form."

Unfortunately, President Truman's newly instituted military draft got in the way. Three of the Williams Brothers—Andy, twenty, Dick, twenty-two, and Don, twenty-five—were eligible to be called up for duty. Because of the uncertainty, *Happily Ever After* was put on hold and Alton stayed at MGM to choreograph *The Barkleys of Broadway*, with Fred Astaire and Judy Garland. On July 15, 1948, *Daily Variety* reported that Kay Thompson and the Williams Brothers would make an appearance in the movie, but four days later, Garland was suddenly dropped from the project due to "chronic illness," and replaced by Ginger Rogers. Out of loyalty to Judy, Kay withdrew.

That very same month, Thompson got another movie offer to appear in Samuel Goldwyn's *Billion Dollar Baby* with Betty Hutton. In the role that Mitzi Green had originated on Broadway, Kay was to play Georgia Motley, a fictionalized depiction of Texas Guinan, the colorful speakeasy hostess. Sadly, the film never got made.

From the start of their collaboration, Thompson appointed herself tutor to the Williams Brothers. "Kay taught us everything while we were on the road," Andy recalled, "not only about show business, but about the arts." She knew the trick was to make lessons entertaining. "When we were learning about Impressionist painters," Andy elaborated, "she wrote a song that went like this . . . 'Toulouse-Lautrec, Renoir, Bonnard; Manet, Monet, and Degas; van Gogh, Goya, Gauguin; Sisley, Cézanne, Matisse; Mary Cassatt, et aussi; Georges Seurat, et aussi,' and so on. She also wrote one called 'The New York Public Library,' rattling off names of famous authors. This was our education."

"The Impressionists" had a simple singsong melody but much of "The New York Public Library" was spoken rhythmically—her second honest-to-God rap song, expanding on the innovation she and Roger Edens had started with "Madame Crematante" in 1944.

"She was the first rapper," Liza Minnelli marveled to *New York* magazine in 2007.

"I call her L. L. Cool Kay," added entertainer Jim Caruso.

While the Godmutha of Rap tried very hard not to show any outward favoritism among her Boyz, it was impossible not to notice that Andy got preferential treatment. For instance, when she wrote a number for their act spoofing Gertrude Lawrence and Noël Coward, it was Andy who got to play Noël opposite her Gertie.

Soon, rumors of a love affair were flying. In those days, May-December romances were still considered scandalous, especially when it was the woman on the winter end of the calendar. So, it was no wonder that the sight of a thirty-eight-year-old woman and a twenty-year-old boy hanging out together raised eyebrows and made the papers. (The eighteen-year gap exceeded the fourteen years between her parents—plus Kay was now the father figure.)

"Sensational Kay Thompson's big romance is Andy Williams," insisted Dorothy Kilgallen in her April 12, 1948, gossip column, setting off a blaze of press reports. Both parties denied it (even to Andy's own brothers).

But in his 2009 memoir, *Moon River and Me*, Andy Williams finally confessed: "I couldn't help letting my feelings show. To my surprise and delight, [Kay] admitted that she felt the same. We made up for lost time over the next couple of years, but even though we were now lovers, it remained a completely private affair."

It was not a well-kept secret. "They lived together for a while," Bill Harbach confirmed. "As a matter of fact, they went to Nantucket for the summer [of 1948] on a little *vacances*—just the two of them—and they had a little bed-and-breakfast place they lived in. They were having a marvelous time. They'd say, 'We're staying there for the summer. Give us a call.' They didn't talk about it but they presented themselves as a couple. They were *always* together."

After what some referred to as "their Nantucket honeymoon," Kay and Andy reunited with Dick, Don, and Bob and resumed touring on August 2, 1948, for two weeks at the Piping Rock, an elegant spa and casino resort near the horse-race tracks of Saratoga Springs, New York, controlled by Thompson's favorite mobster, Meyer Lansky. Earning $10,000 per week, plus a percentage, they broke the house record, grossing $25,000 per week.

What a difference a year had made. Since they debuted at the El Rancho Vegas on August 6, 1947, *Daily Variety* tallied that with just ten engagements in twelve months, their act had earned an eye-popping $436,000.

Then came the announcement, on September 15, 1948, that Thompson had just signed a "three-year $1,000,000 deal with the Kirkeby hotel chain." Eleven years before Elizabeth Taylor broke the seven-digit threshold for an actor's salary in a single movie (for *Cleopatra*), Thompson was the million-dollar baby of cabaret. Even more astonishing was the fact that the contract required only half of her time, "a total of 26 weeks annually for the Kirkeby chain." Because of the tenuous nature of the Williams Brothers' availability, the agreement was drawn up with Kay alone, allowing her the flexibility to reconfigure the backup singers if circumstances dictated it. Using the military draft as an excuse, Thompson had artfully wrested complete control over her act, with or without the Williams Brothers.

As part of her deal with Kirkeby, she negotiated three years' free use of a suite at the Beverly-Wilshire—a perk to which she rapidly grew accustomed.

This was a defining moment for Thompson, whose potential had been dismissed by so many for so long. Now a self-made star, she was her own boss, calling the shots. After all the setbacks and humiliations, it was a triumph and vindication of everything she'd strived to achieve. Revenge was sweet but it wasn't long before it went to her head. No longer flexible to negotiate or collaborate or compromise on future projects, she had to be in charge. If not, she didn't give a damn—she'd rather not work at all.

Just as Le Directoire had been transformed especially for Kay, she demanded that the Florentine Room at the Beverly-Wilshire undergo a serious makeover. So, while a costly overhaul got under way, she and the boys accepted interim tour dates, starting with the Oval Room of the Copley Plaza Hotel in Boston.

Oddly, their reception in Boston was considerably cooler than it had been in other cities. *Daily Variety* reasoned that Thompson's excessive "weekly stipend necessitated doubling the couvert—a matter resulting in the Cod City dwellers folding their pocketbooks and staying home." The act's four-week booking was quietly shortened to three.

This humbling experience was followed by a whole new challenge. The Roxy Theatre, at 153 W. Fiftieth Street (at Seventh Avenue) in New York, was a cavernous 5,920-seat vaudeville palace that presented live acts as a warm-up for motion picture presentations. Thompson and her boys had been booked for two weeks, starting October 15, at $15,000 per week plus a fifty-fifty split over a weekly gross of $120,000, "the highest fee ever paid on the vaudeville circuit."

Four times daily, the quintet would be the lead-in to *Apartment for Peggy*, the heartwarming story of a young couple (Jeanne Crain and William Holden) who give their suicidal landlord (Edmund Gwenn) a new lease on life. The glitz of Kay's act was a cockeyed mismatch, yet reviews were glowing.

"It is the first time in this writer's knowledge that you have been able to see a top-flight musical comedy for the price of a movie ticket," proclaimed the *New York Herald Tribune*.

Lines stretched for blocks and attendance records were broken. The two-week run was extended for ten days, the maximum availability before Kay and the boys were due back in Los Angeles to begin their gig at the Beverly-Wilshire.

One person who saw Kay's act at the Roxy was twenty-two-year-old comic Mel Brooks, one year before landing his first job writing jokes for Sid Caesar. "I *loved* her," Mel recalled in a 2006 interview. He would later write for Thompson and use her act as inspiration.

Another impressionable spectator at the Roxy was twenty-two-year-old illustrator Hilary Knight—his very first exposure to Kay in the flesh, though only from afar. "The audience was not sophisticated," Knight recalled, "and they didn't quite know what to think of it."

"It wasn't fun," Dick Williams reflected, "because we were a very intimate act and we needed a small room. It was the best money we ever made, but that was the only time we played a theater. None of us liked it, Kay included."

While Thompson was anchored in the East, she was being lampooned in the West. On October 14, 1948, the Annual Hollywood Press Photographer's Costume Ball was held at Ciro's. It featured what *The Hollywood Reporter* called "probably the greatest bit of showmanship ever to hit a night club floor— Danny Kaye as Kay Thompson, with Jack Benny, Jack Carson, Van Johnson and George Burns as the Williams Brothers! There's never been anything like it! Danny was done up with a K.T. hairdo, complete unto bun, nail polish and Kay's working wardrobe. You couldn't tell Kaye from Kay, it was so brilliantly handled. Whole stunt was Benny's idea, but the major credit goes to Bob Alton, who rehearsed the lads for two weeks at Benny's home."

"[Danny's] resemblance was so striking, his mimicry so uncanny, that some in the audience actually believed it *was* Kay Thompson," wrote historian Martin Gottfried. "Since there already was a mannish quality about her, it was an esoteric moment in the history of sexual ambiguity."

"Kay Thompson telephoned me from New York," Florabel Muir reported in *Daily Variety.* "She said she wept at the high compliment . . . Kay sent huge bunches of flowers to Danny and the other guys and congratulatory telegrams . . . She said. 'There is nothing that can happen from now on that will give me such a thrill.'"

The gag proved so popular, two repeat performances were given at Friar's Club Frolics in L.A. and San Francisco. Then, at a party thrown by Betty Hutton, Danny did his "absolutely final farewell impersonation of Kay Thompson" for a crowd of cheering friends. The last song of his set was so strikingly realistic, Van Heflin sputtered, "Why that's better than Kay herself!" Turned out, it *was* Kay who had prearranged the encore switcheroo as a prank. Consequently, when reporters spotted Danny and Kay dining together at The Stork Club in Manhattan, it became an irresistible photo op that made all the papers.

Then, Warner Brothers producer Jerry Wald arrived in New York to talk to Kay and the Williams Brothers about appearing in his next Joan Crawford movie, *The Broadway Story,* written by Phoebe and Henry Ephron, about "the attempts of an old-time actress to stage a comeback." Unfortunately, the project was still "in development" in June 1950 when Wald parted ways with the studio, effectively nixing its future.

While Kay was breaking attendance records at the Roxy, several second-run movie houses began showing "KAY THOMPSON in MANHATTAN MERRY-GO-ROUND," though her appearance in the 1937 oldie was only brief.

To celebrate her return to Los Angeles and her upcoming opening at the Beverly-Wilshire—also her birthday (she turned thirty-nine on November 9)—Kay was the guest of honor at an opulent soirée thrown by Arnold Kirkeby on November 13, 1948, at his palatial Bel Air estate. Built by architect Lin Atkinson of Hoover Dam fame, the twenty-thousand-square-foot mansion was later used for establishing shots in *The Beverly Hillbillies* (CBS-TV, 1962–71).

"I asked Kay Thompson how you get from a Culver City soundstage to a palace in one short leap," wrote Hedda Hopper. "She said, 'You've got to have long legs, a face like mine, the Williams brothers and Bob Alton.'" Escorted by Jack Benny, Kay was toasted by three hundred of Hollywood's brightest lights.

For Thompson's run at the Beverly-Wilshire, the Florentine Room had not only been redecorated, it had been renamed the Mayfair Room. Kay and her boys christened the new venue on November 17 to an SRO crowd of nothing but glitterati. Louella Parsons joked, "When Kay got up to sing at her opening—we all thought it was Danny Kaye."

Danny couldn't make it, but all four of his faux Williams Brothers—Jack Benny, George Burns, Jack Carson, and Van Johnson—did. Thompson promptly cast them as the lovers in "Poor Suzette," reprising the routine they had learned the month before, only now with the real lady in question.

From Clark Gable to Bette Davis, the assemblage of stars was so spectacular that *Silver Screen* published ten pages of pictures commemorating the event, which *The Hollywood Reporter* declared broke all records "with a Kay-O wallop."

"What a story Kay's sensational rise to fame is—much more thrilling than fiction," marveled Louella Parsons. "Someday somebody's going to write it—it would make a fascinating story." Ya think?

During the run, Kay and the boys guest starred on *Louella Parsons' Woodbury Journal* (ABC Radio, December 26, 1948), for which Thompson and Alton cowrote a hilarious new song, "Don't Tell Louella," satirizing the columnist's inability to keep a secret. The group not only performed it on the radio program, they added it to their nightclub repertoire, too.

Meanwhile, interest was heating up again at MGM to bring Kay Thompson and the Williams Brothers to the big screen in *three* Freed Unit musicals: *Annie Get Your Gun* with Judy Garland; *On the Town* with Gene Kelly and

Frank Sinatra; and an untitled starring vehicle of their own being scripted by Sidney Sheldon for Bob Alton to direct.

With all three projects in mind, the studio ordered a screen test. On January 26, 1949, Hedda Hopper reported, "Arthur Freed, Bob Alton and all of us are pulling for the Technicolor test Kay Thompson and the Williams Brothers made at Metro."

While the studio mulled things over, Kay and the boys headed east for their third gig in Miami, this time at the brand-new Copa City. Their warm-up act was Jack Cole and His Dancers—including future star Gwen Verdon and two young men who would later dance for Thompson: George Martin and Buzz Miller. There was one small problem, however. Cole's troupe was getting as much applause as Thompson—and she was none too pleased.

"Miami is buzzing about the feud between Kay Thompson and Jack Cole," dished *The Hollywood Reporter*. "[When] Kay found it tough to follow Cole's dynamic act (the applause) she ordered the management to have him eliminate his jazz number because 'it wasn't part of his East Indian routine.'"

Noël Coward came to see her en route to his newly constructed Jamaica pied-à-terre, Blue Harbour. He insisted that Thompson join him there the moment her gig was over—and she did, becoming the first famous visitor to christen Noël's new vacation hideaway. Though Kay pretended to enjoy the tropical setting, she later admitted to Rex Reed that "heat, Caribbean islands, suntans, flies, mosquitoes and wasps (living or dead)" were high on the list of things she "detests." She much preferred frolicking with Noël behind screened doors.

"Noël adored her," noted Paul Methuen, friend of Coward and future cabaret partner of Thompson. "Whenever she stayed with him in Jamaica, their great fun was to play two pianos together."

All was not well, however. Kay had become rail thin, having dropped to barely a hundred pounds. "I only eat when I'm hungry," Thompson said in defense of her stick figure. Optimists wanted to believe that she was simply born with ants in her pants and that the Olympian rigors of her nightclub act would make anyone lose weight.

"I don't know what Kay took for energy," remarked her former publicist Gary Stevens, "but *she* should have been given out as a vitamin herself. She was ever dancing, running, and humming against the wind. She arranged her songs that way and she disarranged her life that way, too."

But Thompson's legendary vigor did not always come naturally. Most people were thrown off the scent because she drank so little alcohol. Friends would comment that Kay was "sober as a judge" and when others became inebriated around her, she was the first to raise an eyebrow. However, as it turns out, she was in no position to cast aspersions. Accompanist Joe Marino, conductor Ted Straeter, and orchestrator Ralph Burns independently told friends that Thompson was "the queen of cocaine."

"I never, *ever* saw her do any coke," Andy Williams insisted, "but she definitely got hooked on Dr. Max Jacobson's injections." Jacobson was famously known in showbiz and high society circles as the original "Dr. Feelgood."

"Kay Thompson was a patient of my father and friend for many years," related Jill Jacobson, the doctor's daughter. "They went back a long time. My father was very friendly and obliging to her. But then he was that way with most of his patients."

The obliging doctor was administering "vitamin cocktails" to Kay and a slew of other devoted clients—many of whom were Thompson's associates.

"Dr. Max Jacobson was injecting all of the show business people in New York," Hugh Martin explained. Initiated in 1950, Hugh was so enthralled by the revitalizing effects of Jacobson's injections, he recommended the doctor to anyone who needed a pick-me-up, including a hoarse Eddie Fisher during a New York engagement at the Paramount in 1953.

"Max looked like a mad scientist," wrote Eddie Fisher in his memoir. "What I did not know was that Max's 'vitamin cocktail' was a mix of vitamins, calcium, and methamphetamine, mixed in whatever dose Max thought was appropriate. Speed."

"Instant euphoria" was how Truman Capote described the injections he received from Jacobson. "You feel like Superman. You're flying. Ideas come at the speed of light. You go 72 hours straight without so much as a coffee break . . . Then you crash . . . [Next] you're running back to [his office at 155] East 72nd Street . . . looking for the German mosquito, the insect with the magic pin-prick. He stings you, and all at once you're soaring again."

"In those days that stuff was not only legal, but nobody really knew what it was," Fisher added.

"He told me they were liquid vitamins," said Hugh Martin. "I never knew I was on heavy drugs for ten years, but I was. It nearly killed me. I fell apart in London in 1960, and ended up in a mental hospital. I'm lucky to be alive."

Likewise, *Time* magazine reported that Tennessee Williams "spent three months in a mental hospital after Jacobson's treatments." It took Eddie Fisher thirty-seven years to kick the habit. Others never got over it and, allegedly, some may have died as a result.

"Amphetamine is not an addictive drug," Jacobson swore defiantly in an interview with *The New York Times* in 1972. When observant patients noticed the label on Methedrine vials, he would insist, "It's not for kicks. Only for people who have work to do."

But most patients never asked any questions, taking it on blind faith that he was looking after their well-being. His golden rule was admonishing patients in a fatherly tone that they were "forbidden to drink liquor." So, while Thompson played the part of the obedient teetotaler, she was getting hooked on something far more potent.

Surely, Jacobson's patients must have suspected something wasn't quite right. "There were broken hypodermic needles on the counter and on the floor," observed Doris Shapiro, assistant to Alan Jay Lerner (*My Fair Lady*). "The wastebasket was overflowing with their wrappers" and it was common to see "blood on his polo shirt and sneakers."

But the only thing stronger than the drug itself was the collective denial among Dr. Feelgood's faithful flock.

"He did say they were vitamins, but you couldn't 'not know,'" recalled singer-actress Marti Stevens. "Everybody who went to Max Jacobson—and everybody did—knew better than that. Especially with Kay's mind, for God's sake. I went with a friend to Max Jacobson and tried him once—and *only* once. What a dirty, filthy surgery. His sleeves were rolled up to his elbows and the needles looked like they'd been used for 10 or 15 people. I wound up on the ceiling and I didn't get down for three days. I have never been so frightened in my life. I never, *ever* went back. But everybody went there. Jack Kennedy, Jackie, Dietrich, the whole bunch. The ones I knew who went there used to go there at midnight, 1:00 in the morning, any time they liked, to get a bunch of shots so they could stay up. Marlene would go on Sundays or late at night at 1:00 in the morning because she didn't want to be seen. He got everybody hooked."

"He'd pull up our arms and stick us," Hugh Martin recounted. "My arms looked like a battle-scarred veteran of the war because he stuck me so many times."

In cases of public speakers and singers, Jacobson often aimed his needles directly toward their vocal cords. "Kay got methamphetamines shot right into her neck," recalled one source who wished to remain anonymous. "She was injected when she sang."

According to Jacobson's widow, Ruth, every time Kay came to see Max, she presented him with a rose, so they nicknamed her "the Lady with the Rose." And, although Thompson continued to preach that she never saw doctors because of her Christian Science beliefs, she admitted to friends and colleagues that she routinely received "B-12 injections."

"That's what Jacobson told people they were getting," Hugh Martin confirmed. " 'B-12 injections.' But he was a big liar. They were amphetamines, believe me. He never gave a shot to anybody that wasn't."

In addition, to help his patients rest, Jacobson prescribed potent prescription tranquilizers, and to counteract a variety of other side effects, he gave them steroids and antibiotics.

How could Thompson have kept up a regimen of injections and pills on the road? According to the New York State Board of Regents, "Dr. Jacobson mailed out vials of his solution to addresses throughout the world each day." Jacobson taught Eddie Fisher how to inject himself by sticking needles into a grapefruit.

Because meth is an appetite suppressant, it is no wonder that Kay became dangerously anorexic, dropping to barely 100 pounds—a far cry from the 121 pounds she boasted during her radio days of the 1930s.

Doris Shapiro called it "the spooky look of a Charles Addams lady," and *Who's Who in Hollywood* described Thompson as "cadaverous."

"I've never known a woman as thin as Kay, *ever*," arranger Buddy Bregman recalled. "I've never seen a human being as thin except in pictures of Dachau and other extermination camps. I just remember seeing bone with some skin."

The media began to take notice. Kay's coverage shifted dramatically from accolades about her dazzling performances to a morbid preoccupation with her weight and well-being.

*W*hen Kay's Jamaican holiday was over, she rushed back to Los Angeles and announced she was going to whip up an entirely new act.

Bob Alton, who was spending long hours every day choreographing Judy Garland in *Annie Get Your Gun*, would race home from MGM to moonlight with Kay and the Williams Brothers until the wee hours of the morning. Unfortunately, Garland was in such bad shape, shooting was soon suspended and she entered Peter Brent Brigham Hospital in Boston "to cure her dependency on prescription medications." Any notion of shoehorning Thompson and the Williams Brothers into the movie evaporated after that. But, because shooting would not resume until the fall (with Betty Hutton instead of Garland), Alton suddenly had a free schedule to devote to Kay—and she was bursting with ideas.

The Williams Brothers were not so gung-ho. Kay's insistence on a completely new repertoire meant weeks of hard labor with no immediate compensation to motivate the troops. It did not help that they hadn't had a paying gig since February. When she signed a new contract with Decca Records in June as a "solo artist" and recorded two new songs without them, was it any wonder that the boys' morale sank to an all-time low?

On July 22, 1949, Louella Parsons announced the inevitable: "Kay Thompson has definitely broken with the Williams Brothers."

"The act glowed so hot it had to turn to ash," concluded one reporter, "flaming out like a comet."

Dick Williams said the four boys had been "joined at the hip" since they were kids. "We had no social skills because we mostly just sort of hung out with each other. So we just decided that we should get away from each other."

Though the split was made out to be "amicable," a later interview with Thompson in the *Los Angeles Examiner* revealed there had been a "feud," and that "the breakup was caused by too many bosses and a lot of temperament and came suddenly." There also may have been a rough patch in the secret relationship between Kay and Andy that factored into the dissolution.

Angry that Thompson had allowed the group to break up for any reason other than the military draft, Arnold Kirkeby demanded renegotiation of Kay's $1 million contract. She responded by moving out of her free suite at the Beverly-Wilshire and renting a second-floor apartment at 1364 Beverly Glen in Westwood (directly above Marti Stevens), where she stayed up to all hours of the night indulging in outlandish decorating flourishes.

"She papered her apartment on Beverly Glen with tiny clusters of flowers; the walls and ceiling were completely covered," wrote Marie Brenner in *Vanity Fair*. And, even though the living room was modest in size, she installed an enormous, thousand-dollar chandelier. *Funny Face* screenwriter Leonard Gershe remarked, "The overall impression was like being inside a candy box."

Now, Kay was free to do anything she pleased—though she was becoming harder to please by the minute.

First, she considered, then turned down the lead in the London production of Hugh Martin's *Look Ma, I'm Dancin'* in the role made famous by Nancy Walker on Broadway.

Then she toyed with the idea of playing Madame Arcati, the eccentric clairvoyant, in Mel Ferrer's summer stock revival of Noël Coward's *Blithe Spirit* at the La Jolla Playhouse (south of Los Angeles), but ultimately decided against it. Six years later, Kay was asked again to play Madame Arcati in a television production of *Blithe Spirit* for *Ford Star Jubilee* (CBS-TV, January 14, 1956), with Noël Coward, Lauren Bacall, and Claudette Colbert, but, again, she turned it down. In *both* cases, Mildred Natwick, who had portrayed the character on Broadway, filled in.

On the movie front, Twentieth Century-Fox announced in July 1949 that Thompson would play "Mamie," the sardonic housekeeper, in *Love That Brute*, a remake of the 1941 gangster comedy *Tall, Dark and Handsome*, in which Charlotte Greenwood had originated the character. However, by the time it went into production that November, Kay had decided it wasn't right for her, so they rushed Joan Davis into service.

Then, according to Sheilah Graham, Thompson and Bing Crosby were "hatching a plot for Kay to appear in Bing's next picture, *Mr. Music*." But Paramount nixed Thompson in favor of Nancy Olson, a studio contract player who was getting a big push on the heels of her supporting part in *Sunset Blvd*. "Which was kind of crazy because Nancy was still at UCLA," scoffed dancer Marge Champion, who costarred in *Mr. Music* with her husband, Gower. "Kay would have been so much better for it, not only because she was so brilliant, but also because Nancy made Bing look like an old man."

Even if Paramount had offered Thompson the role, many wonder if she would have gone through with it. Some colleagues believe that the trauma of being fired from *Hooray for What!* shattered her confidence, rendering her forever gun-shy. But there is also much to suggest that, after her ego-inflating, self-made success on the nightclub circuit, coupled with delusions of grandeur routinely associated with methamphetamine use, Kay had morphed into a monstrous control freak, spurning anything of which she was not fully in charge. Whatever the explanation, the outcome was the same: deadlock.

Disturbingly, however, she made it worse than it needed to be. Kay thrived on feeling wanted, so when offers came her way, she would express initial interest, string everyone along with enthusiastic creative discussions, and instigate rewrites based on her suggestions. But, in the end, she'd invariably get cold feet. She'd start making unreasonable demands that could never be met until the parties reached an impasse. She turned playing hard-to-get into a sadistic exercise in futility.

This serial syndrome of botching opportunities and burning bridges was why Kay's magnificent potential was so rarely realized.

As weeks of unemployment passed the six-month mark, people began to wonder if she had lost her marbles. "I am shocked," Louella Parsons commented. "It seems to make no sense." Was Thompson on the brink of a self-destruction?

Chapter Seven

LIFE IS A CABARET

Living out of a Suitcase
(1949–55)

Kay Thompson [is] the youngest 176-year-old Iroquois squaw
in captivity, and the livest, wittiest,
fireman-save-my-childest lady on earth.
—*Kenneth Tynan*

*I*n the fall of 1949, Kay Thompson finally ended months of unemployment and bad press by forming a new trio to replace the departed Williams Brothers quartet. First, she chose George Martin and Buzz Miller (future companion of Jerome Robbins), whom she had admired as members of Jack Cole's dance troupe. Lee Scott, who had just finished hoofing for Bob Alton in *Annie Get Your Gun* (MGM, 1950), would be the third member.

"When I started with the Williams Brothers, they were all singers and I had to teach them to dance," Thompson observed. "This time the situation is reversed."

So was the money. Instead of forking over 50 percent, Kay would pay each of her three new boys a flat $250 per week.

"We used to drive out to the Pacific Palisades to Bob Alton's new house," George Martin recalled. "For two solid months, we would rehearse at night after he got home from the studio. Bob and Kay came up with the idea of having two black rectangular boxes as interactive set pieces. We sat on them, jumped on them, moved them around in all sorts of configurations. It was very chic and brought a whole new dimension to the act."

On October 20, 1949, Kay got back into business with mobster Meyer Lansky when she and her trio made their public debut at his Beverly Club Casino located just outside the city limits of New Orleans—attended by Andy Williams, who stayed for several days. According to Walter Winchell, she had to accept "$5,000 per week for the new act unseen," just to get things started.

Kay's forty-minute routine was entirely new, including "Gotta Rejoice," with Thompson as "a Holy Roller, arm-flailing revivalist"; "Get Away from Me, Boys, You Bother Me," during which Kay tells her trio "to return to their paper routes"; and "The Lives and Loves of Madelaine d'Esprit," described as "a murderous burlesque" of Bette Davis, Tallulah Bankhead, and Katharine Hepburn, about a sadistic society dame "who tramples over three men."

And, for fans who like their comedy pitch-black, there was "Rubyocco from Morocco," "the horrible adventures of an Arabian miss adrift in the cosmopolitan world," whose life comes to an abrupt end when she dives into a mirage that turns out to be an empty swimming pool.

What did the Louisiana crowd think? "Well, either you fell in love with Kay," George Martin said, "or you thought she was maybe the strangest lady in the world."

Winchell was among the amorous, declaring her show "better than the old act." That endorsement was enough for Arnold Kirkeby to let bygones be bygones and book the foursome at the Blackstone in Chicago, where business was "socko" and reviews were sublime.

Dave Garroway was front and center on opening night. By then, he had parlayed his radio success into the new medium of television with WNBQ's *Garroway at Large,* broadcast nationally by NBC-TV. Kay made her television debut on the program—chatting, not performing.

"When Dave was doing *Garroway at Large,*" recalled Mike Wallace, "I was doing the eleven o'clock news on the same station. Dave and his writer, Charlie Andrews, and Hugh Downs—we were all there together in the Merchandise Mart in Chicago, on the eleventh floor. We had a big Webster's dictionary on wheels and, for a buck a word, we'd spend our time testing the literacy of each other. When Kay came to see Dave, she would hang out with us and I remember that she loved playing that game, too. I would entertain her with words."

For the last night of her Chicago engagement on December 8, Kay wanted to stage a charity spoof of Mary Martin's new Broadway hit, *South Pacific.*

"Kay and company, with able assistance from Julie Wilson of *Kiss Me, Kate*, Chester Morris of *Detective Story*, Myron [Mike] Wallace of the radio, and Dave Garroway of practically everything, will put on a *South Pacific* show," reported the *Chicago Daily Tribune*. "Recordings of Mary Martin and Ezio Pinza's voices will be used, with Kay and Wallace pantomiming the parts."

In the wee hours of Sunday morning, December 4, however, the *Tribune* stopped the presses to include a late-breaking news flash: "Last minute complications over rights to the use of certain material has forced Kay Thompson to cancel her plans for a benefit performance Thursday night."

The Scrooge who put the kibosh on the enterprise was none other than Mary Martin. For nearly two years, she had been lying in wait to exact her revenge for being refused at the door of Thompson's act at the very same Chicago venue—and now was her day of reckoning. What started as a minor faux pas escalated into a world-class diva feud of Aaron Spelling proportions. Now the ball was in Thompson's court—and, yes, in due time, there would be payback.

During this period, Kay had several chances to go to Broadway. Columnist Dorothy Kilgallen reported that she was being wooed to star in Irving Berlin's *Call Me Madam* as Sally Adams, a Perle Mesta–like society "hostess with the mostes." True to form, however, Kay eventually turned her nose up and the role instead went to Ethel Merman—who went on to win a Tony.

Not long after that, Winchell reported that Thompson was the "top candidate for Cole Porter's new musical comedy, *Out of This World*." Kay would play the Greek goddess Juno, who dons earthly disguises to catch her husband cheating with a mortal. At first, Kay seemed genuinely interested, but by the time they ironed out her many libretto concerns, she had decided against it. Charlotte Greenwood took her place for a robust eighteen-month run.

Thompson's career as a recording artist was only slightly more productive. Ankling Columbia Records, she signed with Decca and recorded four songs—including her own chirpy composition, "(The Birds Are Talkin') 'Bout You 'n' Me"—an obvious nod to the rumors floating around about her relationship with Andy Williams. When two singles were released in 1949 and 1950, sophisticates ate them up, but Thompson was still an acquired taste among the hoi polloi. Consequently, her contract with the label was allowed to quietly expire. In 1953, she would record "Old Fashioned Hammock" (Kay Thompson) and "On the Caribbean" (Kay Thompson–Bob Alton) for Allied Records, but again, sales figures were just so-so.

As a nightclub headliner, however, Thompson was hard to beat. After

Chicago, Kay and her trio opened at La Boheme in Broward County, eighteen miles up the Florida coast from Miami, owned by Meyer Lansky and his brother Jack.

There was a problem with Kay's accompanist that needed correcting, however. "Joe Marino was an alcoholic and he slipped," George Martin confirmed. "In fact, one night Joe was so bombed out that Buzz had to put him in the bathtub to try to sober him up."

So Kay got another Joe, Joe Karnes, her former accompanist from MGM. They honed the act further in Boston and Providence, Rhode Island, before braving Manhattan for a run at Versailles, a swank supper club at 151 East Fiftieth Street, where Desi Arnaz had gotten his start as a bandleader. Taking diva demands to new heights, Kay insisted that "a sliding platform be built for her at a cost of $12,000."

With a lot at stake, a major publicity stunt was staged at Grand Central Terminal on January 29, 1950, that turned Miss Thompson's New York arrival into a cause célèbre. Dressed in a smart skirt suit with a mink coat draped around her shoulders, Kay perched herself atop a mountain of luggage on an enormous forklift that paraded her through the rotunda.

"Excuse me," she blithely asked stunned passersby. "Could you tell me the directions to Versailles?"

Eloise could not have done it better.

Her opening turned heads, too, with critic Bill Smith declaring the act to be "better and sharper than ever."

She was also a hit on the new medium of television. Although she had made a few appearances on chat shows, her *performing* debut was singing "Gotta Rejoice" on *Ed Sullivan's Toast of the Town* (CBS-TV, April 30, 1950), which *Variety* testified was "dynamite."

*W*hen *Thompson told her* trio that the tour would soon be headed to Paris, Lee Scott decided to drop out—ostensibly because he was "homesick." In truth, his excessive drinking had caused one rift too many. To replace him, Kay hired Jimmy Thompson (no relation), a contract dancer at MGM, who came to Minneapolis to study the show before Scott departed.

On the way to Paris, Kay stopped off in New York to substitute-host for *The Walter Winchell Show* (ABC Radio), guest star on *Irving Mansfield's This Is Show Business* (CBS-TV), and to pose for a Jergens Dryad deodorant print campaign. Then, Barron Polan threw her a bon voyage party with such well-wishers as the super-rich industrialist Bror Dahlberg and his wife, Gilda.

A former Ziegfeld showgirl from Pittsburgh, Gilda told Kay to look up her twenty-one-year-old nephew, Peter Matz, a virtuoso pianist who was studying music theory in the City of Lights. Kay would later give Peter his first break as an arranger and mentor his rise to the top.

"Kay Thompson and Company will make their Paris debut at Les Ambassadeurs June 12," announced *The Hollywood Reporter,* "for a three-month engagement . . . Barron Polan set the deal with the new management, Pierre-Louis Guérin and Rene Fraday, who also manage the Lido and are considered the smartest commercial showmen in Paris today." Winchell reported that Thompson would earn "the tallest wages ever paid an American in Paris."

Ringsiders included Rita Hayworth and Prince Aly Khan, with whom Thompson socialized often during her time abroad.

"Kay told me she went on Aly Khan's yacht in the south of France," recalled Deanna Wenble, Liza Minnelli's manager in the 1970s. "He'd just been married to Rita Hayworth for a very short time. Kay said he made a pass at her but she didn't accept his advances."

Though critiques were generally positive, they were somewhat restrained. "Nobody said it was *not* going well," recalled George Martin, "but you could feel it. The locals didn't go for her."

Several newspaper accounts complained about the excessive cover charge and a sizable language barrier. So, after the first week, prices were reduced and Kay performed several numbers *en français.* The diplomacy did little to thaw the French *résistance,* but Thompson continued to be a magnet for famous faces, including Eleanor Roosevelt, Edith Piaf, and Tennessee Williams.

Columnists were agog when the Duke and Duchess of Windsor showed up several nights in a row with their constant companions, Jimmy Donahue and his mother, Jessie Woolworth Donahue (heir to the Woolworth fortune).

"Dave Garroway was visiting Paris that summer," recalled Art Buchwald, "and he took me to see Kay's show several times." Curiously, Kay and Dave were staying at the same hotel, the Relais Bisson, a small Left Bank establishment located on the Quai des Grands Augustins, later immortalized as Eloise's home away from home in *Eloise in Paris.* Had things temporarily cooled with Andy?

Barbara Stanwyck's passion for Kay's act was so intense, people wondered aloud if the legendary actress might be a trifle smitten. If so, the infatuation was one-sided. Thompson bristled with disdain when she recounted how "Barbara Stanwyck came running back after one performance and said, 'Oh, Kay . . . after last night, I went out to dinner and I did the whole 'Suzette' number.' She believed that she had done it. It was just pitiful."

One fan whom Kay truly appreciated was Lena Horne, who was concurrently appearing in Paris at Club Baccarat, accompanied by her conductor-husband, Lennie Hayton. Their secret three-year marriage was revealed in the press that summer, as was the appearance of Lena's name in *Red Channels* as a "suspected Communist." They were residing at the Hôtel Raphaël with Lena's twelve-year-old daughter, Gail, who was "teased about being adept at room service." Like a doting aunt, Kay dropped by often that summer, collecting mental notes that eventually turned up in the pages of *Eloise.*

Both Lena and Kay would be out of a job sooner than they anticipated. First, it was announced that Club Baccarat was closing, and then, just five weeks into Thompson's three-month booking, Les Ambassadeurs folded, too. Kay had to sue the owners for her guarantee and she never accepted another nightclub booking in Paris again. *Fin.*

Thompson and her trio moved on to London to reopen the Café de Paris (off London's Piccadilly Circus) on August 28, 1950. "Besides being the first cabaret artiste at the Café de Paris after the war," wrote historian Charles Graves, "Kay Thompson was the first to be labeled as receiving a salary of one thousand pounds a week [$2,800]."

The money was low, but so was the workload—just six midnight shows per week, Sundays off. In addition to the usual parade of stars, members of the royal family showed up, including Princess Elizabeth and Princess Margaret.

"The reception in London was *very* big," recalled George Martin. "Big, big, *big*! They *loved* Kay. And business was terrific. Complete opposite of Paris."

Walter Winchell called her "The Toast of Piccadilly," noting that "Kay Thompson's London notices were practically love-letters." The duration of the run expanded from three weeks to six.

Cecil Beaton, one of the world's most celebrated designers and photographers, was assigned by *British Vogue* to capture Thompson's elusive mystique for a spread in its November issue. "One of the misfortunes about being a card manipulator is that nobody can ever write about you," Beaton recalled. "I feel much the same way about Kay Thompson, whose magic is similarly incommunicable . . . The facts about her are that she sings and prances in cabaret between Los Angeles and Istanbul; that she is skeletal, hatchet-faced, blonde and American; that she wears tight, tapering slacks, and moves like a mountain goat . . . The proper language in which to review her is not English at all but Esperanto. Or possibly Morse code."

While in London, Kay rented a place near Noël Coward's 17 Gerald Road apartment and took an immediate liking to his local entourage, led by his thirty-two-year-old lover, Graham Payn, and his confidant-biographer, Cole Lesley.

"She had a flat round the corner at Chesham Place," noted Cole Lesley, "came at weekends to White Cliffs [Coward's seaside home at the White Cliffs of Dover] and as good as lived with us at Gerald Road where she flew to the piano to improvise and compose and ate nothing except very thin slices of bread burnt black, piled thick with Tiptree jam."

After she'd had her fill, Kay left Merry Old England for Old Blue Eyes in the Big Apple, where she guest starred on *The Frank Sinatra Show* (CBS-TV, October 28, 1950). The variety series had debuted earlier that month to downbeat reviews and limp ratings, so producer Irving Mansfield (husband of *Valley of the Dolls* author Jacqueline Susann) had been brought in to help turn things around. Because he barely knew Sinatra, Irving signed Thompson, not only as a guest but also as an ongoing "creative consultant."

As a guest, Thompson sang her two Decca singles, "That Old Feeling" and "(The Birds Are Talkin') 'Bout You 'n' Me"—the latter performed as a duet with Sinatra, with backup vocals by the Whippoorwills.

Kay and Frank also performed in a comedy sketch entitled "Hot Closet," set in the boudoir of a British manor where the lady of the house, Cynthia (Thompson), is carrying on an illicit affair with Sir Guy (Sinatra). When her husband, Lord Humphrey (Ben Blue), returns home unexpectedly, Sir Guy hides in the closet. Breaking character, Sinatra comes out of the closet, complaining that it is too hot inside. Blue suggests they switch roles. But he can't handle the heat either. Frustrated, Kay calls them both "cream puffs" and insists *she'll* play Sir Guy, forcing Frank to portray Cynthia in drag.

Unfortunately, Sinatra was in terrible shape—emotionally and physically. His records were not selling and MGM had fired him in April 1950. Then, in May, while performing at New York's Copacabana, he had suffered a vocal cord hemorrhage. By the time work began on his television series that fall, his voice had barely recovered and his mood was grim. One of Sinatra's "three Manhattan throat specialists" was apparently Dr. Max Jacobson, who routinely administered his "magic elixir" throat injections. The mood swings associated with methamphetamine abuse—particularly when mixed with alcohol and other medications—would certainly account for Frank's "impatience, irritability, and grandiosity," and his "exaggerated sense of personal power."

Kay was privy to disturbing displays of obsessive-compulsive behavior, such as Frank constantly washing his hands and changing his underwear every twenty minutes—in full view of the entire television crew. She was around Frank during off-hours, too. They both were residing at the Hampshire House at Fifty-ninth and Sixth, where Frank had sublet a love nest for himself and Ava Gardner, though he was irrationally paranoid that Gardner was cheating on him.

"I know she's with that goddamn Artie Shaw," Frank barked like a rabid dog. "I know she's with that bastard. I'll kill her. I'll kill her. I'll kill her."

After only four shows, Irving Mansfield threw in the towel and Thompson gracefully bowed out to resume touring, first at El Rancho Vegas, then at the Mocambo in L.A. on the Sunset Strip—Ciro's top competitor. Ringsiders included two new couplings making news: Judy Garland and Sid Luft; and Ronald Reagan and Nancy Davis.

"The competition on the Strip was deeeelighted yesterday when the Mocambo banner for Kay Thompson was torn down and replaced by one for Vic Damone," noted Herb Stein in *The Hollywood Reporter*. "F'get it, lads—it was simply for a film sequence needed by MGM for *The Strip* and Kay went right back up after it."

A murder mystery set amid the Sunset Boulevard nightclub scene, *The Strip* (MGM, 1951) was a Joe Pasternak production starring Mickey Rooney, Louis Armstrong, and others. There was talk of Thompson performing a song in the film but, naturally, they couldn't meet her demands.

Even so, Kay did not shy away from visiting the Metro lot to catch up with old pals. Gene Kelly solicited her opinion about the young actress who had been cast in his next picture, *Singin' in the Rain*. As they quietly observed Debbie Reynolds working on a routine for the movie, Kay told Gene, "This girl's gonna be big, and she's gonna stay around—look how much she sweats."

It was during this same visit that Kay recommended her own dancer, Jimmy Thompson, for the "Beautiful Girl" number.

"The next thing we knew," said George Martin, "Jimmy had left to do *Singin' in the Rain* and Jonathan Lucas, of *Touch and Go*, replaced him in our trio—but the chemistry never quite gelled. Don't ask me why but Kay warmed up to Buzz and me more than the various third members."

"Kay told me the difference between working with the Williams Brothers and the three dancers," said Liza Minnelli with a giggle. "After a show with the Williams Brothers, the boys would say, 'Do you wanna grab something to eat?' But after a show with the three dancers, they'd say, 'Kay, we're rinsing out our underwear. Do you want us to do your panties?' That was the difference."

After a Chicago gig, Kay agreed to a return engagement in London for six weeks, at the Café de Paris starting April 9, 1951. Conveniently, Judy Garland had been booked for a month at the London Palladium starting on the exact same date.

Arriving on April 5, Judy checked into the Dorchester Hotel while Kay moved into the Chesham Place flat she had occupied the previous fall. Then, it was down to business, rehearsing Judy day and night.

"Judy just had a big voice," noted Rex Reed. "Kay softened the tones and made her hold certain notes longer. She is the one who put the sob in her voice. Judy was always running out of steam on notes and she would have to catch her breath. She'd say, 'Oh, God, I ruined it.' And Kay would say, 'You didn't ruin it—use it!'"

Kay also gave Judy lessons on what to do with her hands and how to move about the stage. "There was the hand on the hip," noted *Vanity Fair* writer-at-large Marie Brenner, "a gesture Liza Minnelli later adopted as well. Thompson had a distinct bow—one arm perpendicular, the other behind her back—which Garland used."

"They stole from each other," concluded Lorna Luft. "They were the presidents of each other's fan club."

On opening night, Garland made Thompson stand in the wings for moral support. "I've got the order of the songs," Judy told her before going on. "I know the words and so long as I don't fall down I shall be all right."

Famous last words. "Just after the fourth number," wrote Gerald Clarke, "she tripped and fell—landing smack on her backside."

"Get back up!" Kay screamed from the wings. "They love you!"

After the pianist helped her to her feet, Judy shrugged her shoulders and said with a grin, "That's probably one of the most ungraceful exits ever made."

The crowd exploded, and by the time she climaxed with "Over the Rainbow," London was over the moon for Judy Garland.

But the night was young and Judy had a favor to return. Just before midnight, she sashayed into the Café de Paris to a standing ovation and took her ringside seat. Now it was Kay's turn to shine—and boy, did she. The crowd was so pumped up, the place nearly went berserk.

"The success of Kay Thompson's return engagement here has eclipsed her earlier triumph," raved *Variety*, "a performance rich in artistry, graceful in rhythm and reaching its peak in sophistication and polish."

Thompson's six-week booking turned into nine—plus two more days beyond that—until the next scheduled performer, Beatrice Lillie, could be politely bumped no further. It went down in the history books as the longest engagement of any Café headliner.

Barron Polan came to see the show with his fiancée, Julie Wilson, currently in the London production of *Kiss Me, Kate*. However, Barron's devotion to Julie, in addition to his ever-expanding list of other female clients, was a bit too much competition for Kay. So, she decided it was time for a change in management.

"Barron recommended my name to her," recalled Lou Weiss, a young agent at William Morris—and the nephew of George Burns. Lou advised her that if she were to reunite with the Williams Brothers, the sky would be the limit.

Andy's solo career had floundered, so he was more than eager to earn some serious dough (not to mention the potential "fringe benefits"). Don could use the money, too. Dick was singing with Harry James and His Orchestra, but was willing to quit for the reunion. The main holdout was Bob Williams.

"Bob was a milkman with a family in the San Fernando Valley," Weiss recalled, "so it was my chore in those days to convince him it was worth it."

Eventually, Bob caved. On July 10, 1951, *Daily Variety* announced: "Kay Thompson and the Williams Brothers are re-teaming." At first, William Morris pitched a *Kay Thompson and the Williams Brothers* variety series for television.

"The story line must be the thing," Kay insisted, "and so the show will be musical comedy on television. It will be an intimate sort of revue. After all, television is intimate, right in the living room, and sweeping staircases just won't fit in. Good music, good stories and, we hope, a good show."

TV networks were not so sure Middle America was ready for a steady diet of Miss Thompson, so Kay and her boys packed their bags for the supper club circuit, where the appetite for them remained insatiable.

They reunited at Ciro's on July 27, 1951, with an audience of all-stars, including a twenty-one-year-old actor named Robert Wagner, who became pals with the entire quintet.

"Triumphant," wrote critic David Hanna in *The Hollywood Reporter*. "The zany, irrepressible five, played the performance of their careers."

"One of the funniest numbers was 'Mad about the Ballet,'" recalled record store owner Randall Wallace. "The lyrics went something like, 'Spencer Tracy wanted her. Cary Grant wanted her. Even Clifton Webb wanted her.' And the Williams boys shouted back, 'Clifton Webb?!' Insiders knew that Clifton was gay, so everyone *howled*. The innuendos were absolutely outrageous."

The media made a few innuendos of their own, fixating on regular female clientele such as Dietrich, Crawford, Moorehead, and Stanwyck, describing their devotion with suggestive phraseology.

"Barbara Stanwyck and Kay Thompson have formed a mutual admiration society," winked *The Hollywood Reporter*. "Barbara's on the front line at Ciro's most every nite."

These teasing column items needed little decoding, though there was absolutely zilch to back up any Sapphic insinuations. And yet the perception persisted.

Next, Thompson and the Williams Brothers headed for New York, where they were booked as guest stars for the debut broadcast of NBC-TV's *The Kate Smith Evening Hour* on September 19, 1951. They performed "Jubilee Time," and if the surviving twenty-five-second clip of the climax is any indication, it was a razor-sharp *wow*. At one point, Kay is lifted off the ground into a rigid horizontal position above the boys' heads, then tossed to a perfect, featherweight landing of Olympian grace. Smith adored them so much, she invited them back for three more shows before the year was out.

While in Manhattan, the quintet opened a four-week engagement in the Persian Room at The Plaza. "The charade here is show business with its best foot forward," declared *The New Yorker*.

While Kay was setting off fireworks at The Plaza, *I Love Lucy* (CBS-TV) made its smash debut on October 15, 1951. With a growing number of "must-see" TV shows every week, café society was turning into a bunch of couch potatoes. *Look* magazine concluded that Thompson was among "only a handful of well-known stars left in night clubs who are guaranteed money-makers."

The night after Lucy ignited, Judy Garland opened at the Palace Theatre in New York. Once again, Kay coached her during rehearsals—along with her old pals Roger Edens (who wrote the act), Charles Walters (who staged and choreographed), and Hugh Martin (who provided piano accompaniment).

Kay and Hugh were still receiving regular "vitamin cocktail" injections from Dr. Max Jacobson, and at some point, Judy tried his "magic elixir," too. But not for long. "Jacobson stopped treating Judy," noted historian Rick Lertzman, "because she was doing everything else in the world and the interaction was too dangerous."

Nevertheless, Garland needed every ounce of energy to keep up with the Thompsonesque choreography. Like a double dose of Williams Brothers, Garland was backed by "Judy's Eight Boyfriends," a gaggle of chorus boys reminiscent of the ones who performed with her in "Madame Crematante" for *Ziegfeld Follies*. In fact, "Crematante" was to be part of the show, but for reasons unknown, it was dropped during rehearsals.

"The demand for tickets was so great," wrote Garland chronologist Scott Schechter, "that the scheduled four-week run would ultimately be extended to a record nineteen weeks." And then it won a special Tony Award.

While Garland was doing the Palace, Thompson got to spend some quality time with her goddaughter. "I remember once we were walking around in New York," Liza Minnelli told *New York* magazine in 2008. "I was about 4, and she had a big wolf coat, gray, just heavenly looking—she was so tall and thin. She stopped by the Stork Club. This very nice black gentleman opened the door, and she asked for Mr. So-and-So [owner Sherman Billingsley], and the man wasn't in. And she said, 'Yeah, well, just tell him that Miss Thompson and Miss Minnelli stopped by.' And my world changed! I was Miss Minnelli."

Meanwhile, the usual suspects horded Persian Room tables throughout Kay's run—along with Audrey Hepburn, who was in rehearsals for her Broadway debut in *Gigi*.

The tour next took them to Dallas at the Hotel Adolphus, where Kay rekindled her friendship with Billie Cantrell, the high school sorority sister who had married Stanley Marcus of Neiman-Marcus.

"I was about fifteen or sixteen years old—still at a very impressionable age—when I first met Kay Thompson," recalled Jerrie Marcus Smith, Billie and Stanley's daughter. "I remember the time that Kay came over to our house for dinner and following her in the door were four handsome boys—the Williams Brothers. Kay played the piano and they sang. I was sitting on the couch, openmouthed. It is a vivid memory and I was mightily impressed."

Then the regiment conquered Las Vegas, Washington, D.C., and Miami before setting their sights on London for an engagement at Café de Paris beginning February 11, 1952—marking the Williams boys' very first trip abroad. However, on February 6, the day they were set to cross the pond, the world awoke to the news that King George VI had died.

Kay and company boarded that plane anyway, figuring the show must go on. But when they arrived in England, they found an entire country in bereavement. "It was a no-no to be seen out on the town during the mourning period," recalled Dick Williams, "so we had to postpone. Instead, we went to Paris and stayed there a few days, with Kay as our guide."

"At Le Louvre," Andy recalled, "I watched this little girl with just one roller skate. Years later, after I married Claudine [Longet], I was telling her about it and she said, 'That was me! I used to go over there every day and I only had one skate!'"

They also took a side trip to Rome, where Kay visited *another* Williams chap who had taken up residence there, Tennessee Williams, who took her on joy rides in his shiny new Jaguar XK120 Roadster. With Mr. Toad eyes spinning with envy, Kay had to have a sports car like his, and sure enough, by

September of the following year, she did—a new and improved 1953 Jaguar XK125 Convertible, silver with red leather upholstery. Never one to miss an opportunity, she appeared in ads for her dealer, International Motors of Hollywood, in exchange for a deep discount on the sticker price.

When they finally opened in London on February 18, critic Kenneth Tynan wrote to Cecil Beaton, "Kay Thompson came back to the Café de Paris, the youngest 176-year-old Iroquois squaw in captivity, and the livest, wittiest, fireman-save-my-childest lady on earth: do you love her, too, as I do?"

"We would go to Kay's apartment after the show and play charades," Don Williams reminisced. "One night, Bob had had too many beers when it was his turn. She held up four fingers: 'Four syllables!' She set something down, and Bob said, 'Set!' Next she held up ten fingers and he said, 'Ten!' Then she acted all cold and Bob said, 'Brrrr!' And finally she pointed to some music and Bob said, 'Song!' He got all the syllables right, 'Set-ten-brrrr-song!' But he was so loaded, he couldn't get that it was 'September Song.' He just kept saying 'Set-ten-brrrr-song!' and everybody was just dying laughing!"

The next stops on Tour Thompson were Chicago (at Conrad Hilton's Palmer House) and Philadelphia (at the Latin Casino). But the *big* Thompson buzz that month had nothing to do with her act.

"[Kay] thinks quite highly of Frenchman Georges Champigny," reported Hedda Hopper. "Says Kay: 'He's really divine, and answers my particular requirements. Since my divorce in '47, I've met an awful lot of dull guys. Now instead of listening to suspense stories on dark and rainy nights, I'm listening to French love songs.'"

The melody did not linger on. Thompson later alluded to the affair in an interview with columnist Sheilah Graham: "I only know a few attractive Frenchmen. They are rather mysterious for my American taste. You don't know if they like you only because they think you have money." Were these the words of a woman scorned by a Gallic gold digger?

Though short-lived, the Champigny fling apparently put a crimp in the status quo with Andy and his siblings. Within a month Hopper announced, "Kay Thompson and the Williams Brothers again have broken up their act."

With her nightclub tour grounded, Thompson entertained stage offers to play the part of Charlotte Diensen in Noël Coward's *Quadrille*, costarring Alfred Lunt and Lynn Fontanne, and the juicy role of Laura Carew, the no-nonsense editor of *Everywhere* magazine, in Jule Styne's *Hazel Flagg*. After protracted deliberations, however, Kay declined both.

In Los Angeles, Kay attended the July 19, 1952, party thrown by Judy Garland to celebrate her recent marriage to Sid Luft and her just-announced pregnancy (Lorna would make her debut on November 21).

And then, as if nothing had ever happened, Kay and the Williams Brothers were back on track. After a Dallas warm-up, they headed to New York for six weeks at The Plaza's Persian Room, beginning September 18, 1952.

The return engagement was promoted in that month's *Harper's Bazaar* with a Diana Vreeland–assigned spread featuring photos by Richard Avedon. This proved to be quite prophetic; in *Funny Face*, Kay would impersonate Vreeland opposite Fred Astaire's impression of Avedon.

One of the most unusual ringsiders on opening night was an eccentric Plaza resident named Clara Belle Walsh. Even though she "had more money than God," Clara insisted on getting her hair done economically in the men-only barbershop located off the lobby, a ritual Kay later used in *Eloise*. Clara also amused high society with stunts like painting fake eyes on her eyelids—another quirk Thompson would co-opt.

Hilary Knight recalled that when Kay met fashion designer Norman Norell, she adorned her eyelids with two red dots, producing a "subliminal flash-of-red effect."

During this Persian Room gig, Kay received word that her forty-one-year-old brother, Bud, had suffered a fatal heart attack on October 6, 1952. Bud had been helping their mother, Hattie, run the family pawnshop, L. G. Fink, Inc. Now, with his passing, she would be left to handle the business on her own. By then, Kay's sister Blanche Hurd was busy raising two kids, Julie and John, in Alexandria, Virginia, while moonlighting as Blanche Alexander, a diva with the Washington Opera Guild. Kay's other sister, Marion Doenges, had given up dubbing singing voices at MGM and had moved to Alexandria, too, not far from Blanche, because both of their husbands were career military men, based in the D.C. area. As soon as Kay finished gigs in Cleveland and Boston, she went to St. Louis to spend the Christmas holidays with her mother.

Kay rang in 1953 by visiting Denver, Colorado—Ethel Merman's new stomping ground. Ethel had fallen hard for the charm and vast fortune of Denver's Bob Six, CEO of Continental Airlines, and had moved into his baronial mansion in the highfalutin suburb known as Cherry Hills.

"About the only things I miss in Denver are the entertainment they have back East," lamented Merman. "But we do have the Emerald Room in the

Brown Palace Hotel where they have outstanding big-time entertainment, particularly Kay Thompson." Kay and the Williams boys played there January 1–10, with Ethel ringsiding every single night.

Then it was on to San Francisco for a two-week gig in the Venetian Room at the Fairmont, where her most ardent local fan was Lynne Carter, a white man known for impersonating black women.

"There was a dive in the gay district called the Beige Room," recalled Randall Wallace, retired owner of San Francisco's Gramophone record stores. "Lynne Carter was the headliner, famous for doing Pearl Bailey and Josephine Baker—both of whom had donated dresses from their own wardrobe."

One week after Lynne attended Kay's opening, *San Francisco Chronicle* columnist Dean Jennings remarked that "Beige Room mimic" Lynne Carter was a look-alike of "Venetian Room bonanza" Kay Thompson, "especially if you squint a bit." Tossing his Pearl Bailey and Josephine Baker frocks to the wind, Lynne slipped into a pair of slacks, grabbed a long scarf, hired four hunky dancers, and, by February, had debuted Lynne Carter and the Four Cartiers, an uncanny re-creation of the Thompson–Williams Brothers act.

When Kay heard about it, she was not amused. But when she learned that her own compositions were being performed without authorization or compensation, she flipped her lid.

Chinkie Naditz and Al Burgess, owners of the Beige Room, immediately launched an ad campaign in the *San Francisco Chronicle* and *The San Francisco Examiner* touting the "Spectacular Satirical Impression of Kay Thompson & the Williams Bros."

On the very same page in the *Examiner*, columnist Ivan Paul wrote, "Kay Thompson is *maaad* at the Beige Room's Lynne Carter for imitating her act. Maybe he does it too well?" The one-two punch resulted in lines around the block.

"You've seen pictures of Danny Kaye doing Kay?" Randall Wallace asked. "Well, Lynne looked even *more* like her. Kay felt Lynne was infringing on her copyright and he really didn't have a leg to stand on because he was lifting her material exactly."

But Thompson also objected to Carter's mimicry on the basis that it was defamatory—a legal challenge that was far more difficult to prove.

On April 27, 1953, *Daily Variety* reported, "Frank L. Ippolito, attorney for Miss Thompson, has demanded that Carter stop performing in 'slacks, costume, facial makeup and other device that imitates Miss Thompson.'"

The irony of demanding that a female impersonator stop wearing pants was apparently lost on both Thompson and her attorney.

"Carter had his own lawyer [Jake Ehrlich] counter-propose that both he and Thompson do their acts before a court," reported *Gay News*, "who could then decide whether he was defaming her. Not wanting to give her 'rival' any more publicity, Thompson declined, but it was too late to stop the noise. The brouhaha had already made Carter a 'hot commodity.'"

Slumming at the Beige was suddenly the shabby chic thing to do, with an A-list stampede that included George Burns, Sammy Davis Jr., and Audrey Hepburn (appearing locally in the road company of *Gigi*).

In short order, Lynne Carter and the Four Cartiers were getting offers from top-tier venues across the country. Incredibly, Kay was a star-maker even when she tried not to be.

Having learned that the wrath of Thompson could be profitable, Carter used every trick in the book to bait another hissy-fit. When he arrived in Los Angeles for an engagement at Charlie Foy's Supper Club, it was announced that the owner was "building a special stage for Lynne Carter and his troupe." This stunt smacked of parody because Kay had famously demanded the construction of custom stages at Le Directoire, Versailles, and elsewhere.

Next thing she knew, Carter and the Cartiers were entertaining disabled veterans at Southern California hospitals, a charitable tradition that Kay and the Williams boys had forged in 1948.

Then, columnist Army Archerd claimed that Carter had become a patient of Kay's dentist. Creepy stalker behavior? Hardly. Lynne was pulling everyone's leg over the fact that Kay was a practicing Christian Scientist and did not see dentists as a matter of faith.

"Kay *never* went to the dentist," Mart Crowley chuckled. "She'd put chewing gum into a cavity."

Carter knew how to get Kay's goat. And, even though her objections had considerable merit, she inevitably came off as the Wicked Witch of the West.

Meanwhile, the authentic quintet discarded *all* clothing for the erection of a billboard to promote their opening at the Mocambo on Hollywood's Sunset Strip. The depiction of Thompson and the Williams boys in their birthday suits gave new meaning to "doing the Strip." Predictably, crowds were huge, but *The Hollywood Reporter* observed that Kay's "double-barreled glitter" was "all surface sheen" with "no heart." The criticism didn't faze Thompson. If anything, she continued to move farther left of center—which seemed to suit her loyal followers just fine.

The next stop on the Thompson-Williams tour was the Ramona Room at the Last Frontier in Las Vegas beginning March 2, 1953. Though Kay had rehired Joe Marino as her pianist, his drinking was just as bad as before. Consequently, twenty-four-year-old Peter Matz, nephew of Kay's friend Gilda Dahlberg, was drafted into service.

"I was probably thirty-fifth on the list," Matz joked, "but they called me and I went to Vegas. Joe Marino said, 'There'll be no problem. There are two pianos. I'll be there playing with you.'"

"Peter was just starting then," confirmed choral arranger Ray Charles (not to be confused with the African-American blues singer). "He was very nervous but he got through the first show and it was fine. And he comes back for the second show and he looks over and there was nobody at the other piano. He looked out into the audience and there was Joe Marino giving a thumbs-up. From that point on, Peter played it by himself and conducted it."

"Peter always credited Kay for giving him his first break," recalled his widow, singer Marilynn Lovell. "He was just staggered by her musical ability. It stuck with him for the rest of his career." And quite a career it became, conducting for Barbra Streisand and nearly every other big name in show business.

"Kay was the only performer I ever worked with who sent me notes after every show," Peter told friends. "She was a genius in her musical talent and her sense of humor."

After Vegas, they played the Latin Casino in Philadelphia, then bounced back west for a two-week stint in the Cal-Neva Lodge at Lake Tahoe. When the engagement ended on July 23, 1953, no one realized that this would be the final public performance of Kay Thompson and the Williams Brothers.

After a planned hiatus, they were supposed to kick off a whole new touring season beginning September 17 in the Persian Room at The Plaza. However, Bob Williams was having second thoughts about continuing. As hemming and hawing mounted, it was clear that the act had gone from fun to drudgery. On September 4, Dorothy Kilgallen revealed, "Kay Thompson has cancelled all her bookings. She just decided, once again, that it simply isn't worth the effort."

Was that really the end? On November 10, 1953, word leaked that Thompson and the Williams Brothers were together again, secretly developing a new act, using the Mocambo during the day for rehearsal space. But on December 9, the unthinkable happened.

"Kay Thompson and the Williams Brothers completed a rehearsal at the Mocambo minutes before the sign went up announcing Lynne Carter and His

Four Cartiers opening Tuesday [December 15]," reported Army Archerd in *Daily Variety.* "Wonder if Kay'll attend?"

Thompson was apoplectic. She called for a boycott of the Mocambo, and her attorney threatened to file an injunction if Carter warbled a single note of a Thompson composition, or if her name appeared in any advertisements.

When Lynne opened four days later, his repertoire consisted of original songs hastily composed by his accompanist, David Morton, and all references to Kay Thompson had vanished. Nevertheless, everyone knew exactly who the act was lampooning and throngs of people came to see it.

In one last petulant act of defiance, Kay decided to cancel her reunion with the Williams Brothers altogether. If her lawyers couldn't suck the wind out of Lynne Carter's sails, perhaps the death of her act would. Besides, by going solo, she could finally collect all the glory and the spoils.

*O*n January 7, 1954, Kay opened *toute seule* in the Persian Room at The Plaza. There were only three tunes woven into the forty-minute routine—"I Love a Violin," "Madelaine d'Esprit," and "Rubyocco from Morocco." A satirical monologue was the main event—a one-act, one-woman playlet entitled *Cocktail Party*, cowritten by Thompson and Bob Alton.

"As soon as she stepped onstage," explained *Time* magazine, "she peopled it with imaginary cocktail guests. She became an outrageously blasé hostess greeting newcomers with explosive 'Dahlings!' and whipping out quips behind their backs."

The opening night audience included Ethel Merman, Carol Channing, and Gloria Swanson, who, according to columnist Earl Wilson, "was suh-WOONING over Kay Thompson's single act . . . 'And you know, I've seen *everything,*' Gloria reminded us."

But, despite mostly glowing notices, Kay fixated on the review in *The New Yorker*, which stated, "One keeps wishing that she'd asked her old sidekicks, the Williams Brothers, around for a drink."

By February, gossip columns were rife with talk of yet *another* Kay Thompson and the Williams Brothers reunion tour, with dates in Chicago and San Francisco booked and announced. It did not take long, however, before negotiations broke down. "The Williams Brothers are making so much moo in real estate," noted *The Hollywood Reporter*, "they don't care if they never see Kay Thompson again." Ouch.

With something to prove, Kay got herself on TV and showed America that she could shine on her own. On February 23, she sang "I Love a Violin" on *The Buick-Berle Show* (NBC-TV), surrounded by an anonymous army of sixteen dancers choreographed by Herbert Ross—and it was a doozy. Nearly a half century later, it served as inspiration for Mel Brooks' Broadway smash *The Producers*.

"There's a big number in the second act called 'Springtime for Hitler' that stops the show," recalled Mel Brooks. "There is a break in the middle of the song that is 'a Kay Thompson moment' with forties bongos and things. It's very Kay."

"I had a set of DVDs of old Milton Berle shows and Kay was the guest on one of them," confirmed *The Producers* music arranger Glen Kelly. "She sang 'I Love a Violin' and she's being carried around by these guys and, you know, being bounced around *a lot*. Anyway, I just thought, 'It would be so funny if this was Hitler doing the number instead of Kay.' I showed it to Mel and he thought it was very funny so we worked together on that section, 'The Führer Is Causing a Furor.' It was Hitler doing Kay Thompson doing 'I Love a Violin' on Berle."

Within days of the Berle broadcast, Kay bagged her biggest recording deal ever, this time with MGM Records for her first LP, the relatively new twelve-inch vinyl format, to feature a dozen tracks—a remarkable improvement over her scattershot output of only twenty-eight songs in twenty years.

"Kay knew exactly what she wanted," recalled Joe Lipman, the album's arranger-conductor. "Very precise. I would make notes and then I'd go and complete the orchestration."

The album featured Thompson's interpretations of such standards as "How Deep Is the Ocean," "It's All Right with Me," and "Basin Street Blues." There were several of her own compositions, too, including "I Love a Violin," "Poor Suzette," and "Myrtle (of Sheepshead Bay)." For those three tracks, a quartet of backup singers was assembled: Andy Williams, Lyn Duddy, Steve Steck, and Ray Charles, who, since 1950, had been conducting the Ray Charles Singers for both *Your Hit Parade* and *The Perry Como Show*.

Titled *Kay Thompson Sings*, the album was released on November 19, 1954, featuring a cover caricature drawn by the renowned Broadway poster artist Don Freeman. And it was well-received. *The New York Times* noted, "Kay Thompson, whose usual métier is the supper club, proves herself a potent performer on discs, too."

To promote the release, Kay returned to *The Buick-Berle Show* on December 28 to perform two cuts. Yet, with everything stacked in its favor, record sales were just moderate.

"Really, it was only for people who knew Kay Thompson," Ray Charles reflected, "and she wasn't everybody's cup of tea. She was too smart. There's a certain sophistication that eludes the great unwashed."

Though Kay may not have fit the mold of a 1950s American idol, her composition of "I Love a Violin" developed an extraordinary cult following. Through the years, it has been covered by Petula Clark, Teresa Brewer, Dinah Shore, Dorothy Collins, Michael Feinstein, and Liza Minnelli.

Starting March 11, 1954, Kay began a four-week solo gig in Chicago at the Palmer House but, much to her chagrin, reviews were bleak. And when she brought the show to Ciro's in Los Angeles the following month, *Daily Variety* called it "a dud" with too much "interminable yakkity-yak."

Then she took her yakfest to San Francisco to play the Fairmont Hotel, beginning May 18. Taking advantage of Kay's return to the Golden Gate city, her archenemy, Lynne Carter, was simultaneously booked to appear at Ann's 440 Club, setting the stage for a showdown. Though he carefully abided by her cease-and-desist order, his ad campaign featured a photograph of Lynne Carter and the Four Cartiers that duplicated a famous Thompson–Williams Brothers publicity shot pose. And, determined to press *all* of Kay's buttons, Lynne brazenly showed up for one of her performances in full Thompson drag with his Cartiers in tow.

Having learned her lesson, Kay took the high road. As a result, the expected catfight never materialized, rendering an anticlimax to a matter that was already so last year. By summer, Lynne stopped doing Thompson altogether and, instead, took on Mary Martin as Peter Pan. With the Thompson-Martin feud still brewing, Kay must have relished the news. Some wondered if she had instigated it.

Then, Kay went to London for a monthlong gig at the Café de Paris starting September 20, 1954. After seeing the show several times, Noël Coward introduced her to a British gentleman named Paul Methuen, a Louis Jourdan doppelgänger who gardened for Cecil Beaton and decorated for Beatrice Lillie.

"I think it was all planned," Methuen reflected. "We went to her dressing room *first,* which I thought was really strange. We chatted a bit and then she turned to me and said, 'Would you like to come and do a show with me in New York?' I mean, she didn't even know if I was on the stage, which I wasn't. But anyway, she said, 'Go and see the show and when you come back, tell me if you'd like to come.' I saw her show and she was the best cabaret performer I'd ever seen. So, I came back afterwards and said, 'Yes, I would.'"

Noël convinced Kay that Paul should portray a beleaguered British butler as a "straight man" to her incessant chatter. Hence, in a burst of creative collaboration, Noël and Kay turned the one-woman script for *Cocktail Party* into a two-character commedia dell'arte.

"We rehearsed the new material in Kay's dreadful little flat on Chesham Place," Methuen recalled. "There were holes in the carpet, which made us laugh because she always wore six-inch pin heels and they never stopped getting caught in the carpet."

Paul was particularly struck by Kay's diet: "She hardly ate anything. 'I don't eat like other people,' she said. 'You must try Fig Newtons.' In fact, I can't recall her ever eating anything else *but* Fig Newtons! And I said, 'Well, Kay, I think they're delicious, but you can't live on Fig Newtons. What else do you do?' Her response was, 'Oh, well I have B-12 injections at least twice a week.'"

It seemed so innocent at the time.

After her solo engagement was over, she extended her stay in London to tinker with the new act—and her appearance. As a forty-fifth birthday gift to herself, Kay got her *fourth* rhinoplasty, along with a complete face-lift. No matter how she reconciled her Christian Science beliefs, she treated her mug like all her creative endeavors—as a work in progress. And critics had a field day reviewing nips and tucks beyond "the severance of the Williams Brothers."

In a mood for change, she also canned her agent at William Morris and went back to Barron Polan. He began by booking the debut of her two-person act at The Plaza's Persian Room starting November 18, 1954—for which she would earn $6,000 a week, plus a percentage of the gross. Out of that, Kay would pay Methuen a flat $200 weekly salary and require him to provide his own wardrobe.

"On opening night," recalled business manager Leonard Grainger, "Andy Williams and I were standing with Paul in the wings, waiting for his cue to go on, which was about ten minutes into the show. He was dumbfounded, consumed with stage fright. When it came time for him to go on, Andy and I literally had to shove him out onto the stage. Fortunately, he came to life."

"Look what I found in London!" Kay exclaimed to the audience. "A real dragoon, if I ever saw one."

"With these words," noted *The New Yorker*, "out steps the dragoon himself, wearing an inconspicuous brown suit and a black bowler, and carrying an umbrella and a bunch of posies . . . He remains a bit aloof but admiring as she leads him through a cozy specialty number about a music lesson. It's an engaging routine, and Paul makes an excellent foil for the mercurial Miss Thompson . . . [in] the best show of her long career."

"Paul gave an impeccable performance and was just charming," said Leonard Grainger. "As a matter of fact, from Kay's point of view, too charming."

It did not help when *Variety* called her a "blonde widow-spider" whose "malice needs sharpening," while raving that Methuen was "an astonishingly competent stooge."

Buttressed by the buzz and his good looks, Paul became the darling du jour among wealthy admirers of both sexes.

"Kay was very jealous of him," observed Grainger, "because he was being wined and dined and taken on boats for weekends and all that kind of stuff."

"I had a lot of very social friends in New York," Methuen explained, "particularly at The Plaza. And Kay didn't really approve of them. She said, 'They're all a waste of time. If you want to be in the theater, give all that lot up.'"

Clearly, Methuen rubbed her the wrong way, but there were other disturbing matters weighing on her mind. Unbeknownst to most of her friends, Kay's sixty-six-year-old mother, Hattie "Flavia" Fink, had suddenly become seriously ill.

"Kay cared very deeply for her mother and she called her regularly in St. Louis," recalled Leonard Grainger. "But around that time, Kay started noticing that her mother was acting very strange, not herself, like she was losing her mind. Then all of a sudden, she could barely walk. Kay was busy in New York performing, so she arranged for her sister, Marion, and I to go to St. Louis to get her. Marion and I literally carried her mother onto a plane. I had a private ambulance waiting for her in New York at the airport and a lawyer arranged for her to go into a hospital in New Jersey. And then we found out she had a tumor of the brain. There was nothing they could do."

Rather than let their mother die in a New Jersey hospital, the sisters decided to move her to Marion's home outside Washington, D.C.

"As soon as Kay finished her engagement at The Plaza [on December 22, 1954]," Grainger explained, "she went to see her mother in Washington, loaded with all these Christmas gifts from Saks Fifth Avenue—lingerie and stuff to wear in bed."

The day after Christmas, Hattie passed away.

"Kay came back to New York with all the lingerie because her mother never got to wear it," Grainger added. "I took the stuff back to Saks Fifth Avenue because Kay just couldn't face it."

In early January 1955, the Thompson-Methuen act opened at the Balmoral Hotel in Miami Beach, Florida. As if she had planned it, Andy Williams and Dave Garroway happened to be there at the same time because NBC had sent both its *Today* and *Tonight* shows on location for the week of January 10–14, 1955.

Kay's protégé Peter Matz was also there accompanying Mae West at a local gig. "It was terrifying," Methuen exclaimed. "Mae West looked like a thing from outer space. I said to Kay, 'Thank you for taking me because now I can say I've seen Mae West.' Kay said, 'Well, it's not worth talking about, dahling, now is it? One has got to go *on*.'"

Methuen tested Thompson's patience when he pulled his back out while taking surfboard lessons. Not long afterward, when they played Montreal, he came down with a terrible cold and nearly lost his voice. Apparently, the last straw was when he dropped her during a performance.

"Our next engagement was to have been Las Vegas," Paul noted, "but first we were going back to New York for an interval where I was supposed to go and have some more singing and dancing lessons."

"That's when Kay had me get rid of Paul," Grainger recalled. "I gave him some story that there was a problem with his immigration and he would have to go back to England. Kay locked herself up in The Plaza Hotel while I took him to the airport and when I came back, she said, 'Are you sure he's gone?' I said, 'Yes.' But then she called the airline to be sure the plane left."

"I felt very lucky to appear with such a remarkably talented lady," Methuen reflected. "But I was just very distressed at the end that she didn't have the manners to say good-bye. It was beastly."

"Everything about Paul got on Kay's nerves," Grainger said, "but mainly it just drove her crazy that he was so well received."

On January 19, 1955, Mocambo owner Charlie Morrison suffered a heart attack, and while he was recuperating, his business nearly went bankrupt. To help out, Lucille Ball and Desi Arnaz filmed an episode of *I Love Lucy* at the club. Then showbiz friends including Danny Kaye, Dinah Shore, and Jack Benny organized a dozen star-studded benefits to save the beloved nitery.

Everyone assumed that Kay, who still held the boîte's all-time record, would take a night, but she was not on speaking terms with Charlie because of the Lynne Carter incident. The pressure got laid on thick: Don Loper volunteered to design her wardrobe; then Bob Hope offered to be her warm-up act; and, finally, Frank Sinatra called and said, "Come on, Kaysie. Bury the hatchet." Reluctantly, Thompson agreed to headline two shows on March 8, but swore they would be her last—not just at the Mocambo, but *anywhere*.

Kay's announced retirement sent shock waves through the industry, causing a near-riot for seats. Ringsiders included Sinatra, a very pregnant Garland (who would give birth to Joe Luft on March 29), and Howard Hughes.

During that same busy spring of 1955, Kay became a founding member of the Rat Pack. It all began during late-night social gatherings at the home of Humphrey Bogart and Lauren Bacall at 232 S. Mapleton Drive, a stone's throw from Judy Garland's house in the exclusive neighborhood known as Holmby Hills. As Bacall later wrote in her memoir: "If the light over the front door was on, we were home and awake and a chosen very few could ring the bell."

The "chosen few" included Kay, Garland and Luft, Sinatra, David Niven, restaurateur Mike Romanoff, literary agent Irving "Swifty" Lazar, songwriters Jimmy Van Heusen and Sammy Cahn, Noël Coward, and a bunch of semi-regulars.

During the summer of 1955, the group became known as the Holmby Hills Rat Pack (with several conflicting legends as to how the moniker was coined). "Bogie ran with the idea," noted writer Scott Duhamel in *The Boston Phoenix*, "inventing a coat of arms (a rat gnawing on a human hand), calling together a tongue-in-cheek press conference, and conferring official titles to [key members]."

As Kay remembered it: "We were all terribly young and terribly witty and terribly rich and old Humpty Bogus was the head of it." And if an official mascot had ever been designated, Eloise surely would have been it, because Thompson often kept the group in stitches by conversing in the voice of her alter ego.

Despite her announced retirement, Kay soon realized that she truly missed the spotlight—and the money that went along with it—so she quietly accepted an offer to bring her solo act to the Shamrock Hotel in Houston, Texas, for a week in late June 1955.

Fired up for another fresh start, Kay gave Barron Polan the boot (again) and enlisted agent Wynn Rocamora, whose client roster included Gloria Swanson and Dorothy Lamour. Thompson knew in her gut that if she really wanted to hit the trail with guns blazing, her act would have to resemble the one that she was most known for: Kay Thompson and the Williams Brothers. Inconveniently, Andy had landed a regular gig on *The Tonight Show;* Dick was a member of the Cheerleaders; and Bob was just flat-out disinterested. But Don Williams was available, so Kay grabbed him. One Williams Brother was better than none.

Then she added three Williams clones: Gordon Thorin of the Whippoor-wills, Bill Norvas of the Upstarts, and Jack Mattis, who had danced for Bob Alton in *I Love Melvin* (MGM, 1953).

Because Alton was busy in New York choreographing *The Vamp* with Carol Channing, Mattis ended up choreographing most of the new routines.

"Kay said I'd get equal billing with her," Jack Mattis recalled, "and that I would get paid a thousand dollars per week, double what the other three boys would get."

Thompson staged a preview of the new act to drum up word of mouth and bookings. "All the people from MGM came," noted Mattis, "and we just wowed them."

But all was not rosy. "The next day, I got a call from Kay's agent," Mattis continued. "He told me that Kay did not want me to have *any* billing at all and that I would not be paid double what the other boys would get. I explained that promises had been made, but none of that seemed to matter. I *loved* working with her but, in light of the situation, I was left no choice but to sue—and I won the case."

As a result, Kay had to scrap the choreography and hire a new dancer, Paul Burton, to replace Mattis in the lineup.

"Strangely enough, I worked with her a week after that on *The Milton Berle Show*," Mattis marveled, "and we were friendly again. You know, things happen in this business. I have nothing but love and admiration for her."

On that same *Milton Berle Show* (NBC-TV, November 8, 1955), Kay launched the next salvo in her ongoing feud with Mary Martin by suggesting that she and Milton do "a wicked takeoff" of the Noël Coward–Mary Martin *Ford Star Jubilee* special, "Together with Music," which had just aired on October 22.

Berle jumped at the idea and assigned the sketch to an up-and-coming staff writer named Gore Vidal. It was titled "The Amorous Percolations of Passionate Penelope."

On the broadcast, Kay wondered aloud, "Do you think the audience will understand it?"

"Who cares?" Berle replied. "We will."

Dressed in a leopard-print smoking jacket, Berle warbled with an operatic vibrato that was more Cowardly Lion than Coward—and Kay interjected with high-pitched, incongruous verses of "My Heart Belongs to Daddy," "It's De-lovely," and "Barney Google"—with his "goo-goo-googly eyes."

When sought for reactions, Noël thought it was "highly amusing," but Mary Martin was nowhere to be found.

Back to the business of putting together her new act, Kay got a booking at Ciro's beginning November 17, 1955. "Kay Thompson was so impressed with Bob Wells' lyrics in the current Ciro's show," *Daily Variety* noted, "she's asked him to write material for her Thursday opener." Ten years earlier, Wells had collaborated with Mel Tormé on the enduring classic "The Christmas Song

(Chestnuts Roasting on an Open Fire)," but Kay also knew him socially as the husband of *Kiss Me, Kate* sensation Lisa Kirk.

With Wells' help, Thompson chose a Southern minstrel theme for the act, utilizing several old standards such as "I Wish I Was In Dixie" and "By the Light of the Silvery Moon." *Daily Variety,* however, felt the choice of material fell flat, complaining that "an act of this kind needs satire, not straight stuff."

Rattled by the criticism, Kay restored "Hello, Hello," "Jubilee Time," and other sure-fire favorites from her heyday.

She also collaborated with Wells on a novelty song called "Eloise," to help promote her new book of the same name, which had just been published. Notes and lyric sheets from Wells' estate, acquired by Joan Denise Hill, reveal that, originally, the "Eloise" song took the form of a satirical saga along the lines of "Madame Cremantante," "Poor Suzette," and "Myrtle (of Sheepshead Bay)." Thompson was the narrator and enacted the main characters of Eloise and Nanny while her four backups portrayed naughty neighborhood kids named Junior, Stinky, Melvin, and Fenwick. At the climax, there was a rap that went like this: "That's how it was with Eloise. No birds and bees. For Eloise. So young, so bright, and so shy, and so shy, and so delightful, so frightful, she really had a house that was a home. The Persian Room, diversion room, perversion room. So on your knees for Eloise. The beautiful queen called Eloise."

"Toward the end of her run at Ciro's," recalled Bob Baker, of the Bob Baker Marionettes, "Kay performed the 'Eloise' song, which was brand-new at the time. After the show, Kay told me, 'You know, I'm going to do an Eloise record. As soon as they're hot off the press, you've got one.'"

Herman Hover tried to get Kay to extend her engagement through Christmas and New Year's, but she had a book to publicize, so she declined and let the act close on December 1, 1955. Neither she nor anyone else realized that it would be the last time Kay would ever perform on a nightclub stage.

Part Four

THE *ELOISE* AND *FUNNY FACE* REVOLUTION

Chapter Eight

A STAR IS BORN

Eloise Explodes
(1955–57)

The *Alice in Wonderland* of the Atomic Age.
—Los Angeles Times

I was shoved into it," Kay Thompson conceded.

"*Eloise* never would have happened as a book had it not been for D. D. Ryan badgering Kay and putting us together," Hilary Knight explained.

After years of carrying on phone conversations with Eloise as if she were a real person, D. D. finally blurted out, "Look Kay, Eloise is a book."

"There's nothing to write about," Thompson replied. "It's just fun."

Since childhood, Kay had been assuming the persona of her alter ego to entertain friends, but that's as far as she had taken it. D. D. Ryan, a junior fashion editor under Diana Vreeland at *Harper's Bazaar,* passionately believed that Eloise was a book just waiting to happen—especially if the right illustrator could be found.

D. D. lived in a brownstone on Swing Street, above the hotbed of jazz clubs lining West Fifty-second Street, between Fifth and Sixth avenues (including the Famous Door, where Thompson performed in 1940). Across the hall lived a man named Hilary Knight, an artist of many mediums.

In 1951, Hilary had created an elaborate fan of white feathers and rhinestones that caught D. D.'s eye. She immediately grasped its potential as an outré prop for a photo shoot she was setting up in Los Angeles. Hilary gladly loaned it for the occasion, which turned out to be a Richard Avedon session for Kay Thompson. Kay posed with the fan but, for reasons unknown, the shots were never published. Nevertheless, it represented the first fusion of Thompson and Knight—presaging better things to come.

"[Hilary] used to make little drawings and shove them under my door," D. D. explained. "One morning he made a drawing of a fat little prissy pretty girl with frizzy blonde corkscrews. She had a satin ribbon in her hair and a bulging belly, and she was facing a little girl who looked just like Eloise. I said, 'I have a drawing of Eloise.' And Kay got enormously interested."

"Around December 1954, D. D. and I went to the Persian Room and saw her new act," Hilary Knight recalled. "After the show, D. D. introduced me to Kay and we sat down in The Plaza and had a long conversation."

"He seemed terribly impressed with me," Thompson remembered, "which naturally impressed me terribly with him. I noticed his hands, which were slim and artistic, and thought that was a step in the right direction."

They discussed his background. Born November 1, 1926, Hilary had spent his early youth in Roslyn, Long Island; and then, in 1932, he and his family had moved into Manhattan. "I attribute any abilities I possess to the fact that both my parents are artists and writers," Knight explained. "My father, Clayton Knight, is well-known for his aviation paintings and books. My mother, Katharine Sturges, has done fashion drawings, fabric designs as well as many children's books."

Notably, his parents had collaborated on the cover art for the April 17, 1926, issue of *The New Yorker*, a portrait of a thoroughly modern flapper in pink, black, and white. The color scheme would be resurrected for *Eloise*.

Hilary had attended the Art Students League under the tutelage of Reginald Marsh (who taught him "how to make a figure move"), and since the early 1950s, he had been selling humorous illustrations to magazines like *Mademoiselle, House and Garden,* and *Family Circle.*

When Kay saw Hilary's drawing of the two little girls, she was intrigued. "The prissy one Kay would call Dorothy Darling," Hilary explained. "The other suggested the wicked schoolgirls of Ronald Searle."

Kay envisioned her brainchild as something in between—not too frilly and not too demonic. "So I wrote twelve lines on a piece of paper and handed it to him," Thompson explained. " 'I'm going to write this book,' I said. 'I'll leave this with you. If you're interested, get in touch with me.'"

From there, the visualization of Eloise began to percolate. "Physically, Eloise is a composite of a lot of things," Hilary noted. "About 1930, my mother did one small painting of a little girl in Victorian costume—but not quite a Victorian air—and when it came time to develop a character for Eloise, unconsciously, I used this as a model."

Other seminal works included Ernest Shepard's drawings for *Winnie the Pooh* and *The Wind in the Willows;* Edmund Dulac's exotic depictions in *Stories from the Arabian Nights;* and, most especially, the illustrations of Louis-Maurice Boutet de Monvel in the 1887 book of manners, *La Civilité.* "[Boutet de Monvel's] drawings of naughty children using damask curtains for handkerchiefs and forks as combs planted the seed that became Eloise," said Knight.

There were more roots as well. "In the 1940s, I discovered *Punch* and *Lilliput,*" Hilary elaborated, "famous British satirical magazines that featured black-and-white pen-and-ink drawings, including the wicked little St. Trinian's girls by Ronald Searle."

A real-life Eloise was part of the recipe, too. "A relative of my brother's wife, named Eloise Davison, was a food writer for the defunct *Herald Tribune,*" Hilary explained. "She was a roly-poly little woman with this very bizarre hair that went straight out in various uncontrolled angles. She was in her fifties when I knew her, but I thought, 'What would this woman have looked like when she was a little girl?'"

Distilling these ideas to paper, Hilary used pen and ink to come up with his version of a six-year-old Eloise.

"That Christmas [of 1954] I received a card from Knight," Kay explained. "It was an interesting, beautifully executed and highly stylized picture of an angel and Santa Claus, streaking through the sky on a Christmas tree. On the end of the tree, grinning a lovely grin, her wild hair standing on end, was Eloise. It was immediate recognition on my part. There she was. In person. I knew at once Hilary Knight had to illustrate the book."

"We started working on the book right away," Hilary confirmed. "Exclamations of 'Go!' or 'Get cracking!' were typical Thompson orders to work. But 'work' it never was—just exhilarating, all-out fun."

Because Eloise was drawn in black ink, her hair color was up for interpretation. Knight initially envisioned her as a brunette but Thompson thought of her as a blonde, as a tribute to her own bleached locks. That's why the dust jacket of the book, and other color representations, would have a wash of yellow applied to Eloise's flyaway mop.

Regarding her silhouette, Thompson originally imagined Eloise as "thin" and "wiry," much like herself. But, at Knight's suggestion, Eloise was given, as Kay called it, "a *rawther* large stomach." Thompson embraced the idea that Eloise was entirely guilt-free: " 'Oooooooooo I absolutely love meringue glace,' Eloise says, with some delight and with no shame whatever."

While on tour with her nightclub act in early 1955, Kay spent off-hours jotting down Eloise chitchat. "Ideas popped out of my head like grapes," Thompson marveled. "I used to go to bed with a notepad on my chest. Fifty brainstorms would come and I would whisk them down. You ought to see the material we threw away."

Some of those discarded bon mots included: "Nanny eats a cucumber like an apple." "I have a fleet of elevator cars that zoom me from the lobby all the way to Mars." "When I go to sleep, hallways have to wear don't disturb signs."

Subliminally or otherwise, Kay drew inspiration from the many precocious young girls she'd known over the years, including Liza Minnelli, Lorna Luft, Gail Jones (daughter of Lena Horne), Lucie Arnaz (daughter of Lucille Ball and Desi Arnaz), Rebecca Welles (daughter of Rita Hayworth and Orson Welles), Princess Yasmin Khan (daughter of Rita Hayworth and Prince Aly Khan), Sigourney Weaver (daughter of Pat), Dena Kaye (daughter of Danny), Portland Mason (daughter of James), Sylvia Sheekman (daughter of Gloria Stuart), Margaret O'Brien, Elinor Donahue, and many others. There were a few mischievous boys in the mix, too, like David Carradine (whom she'd met at the Garden of Allah), John Jenney (son of her first husband, Jack), and Stephen Bogart (son of Lauren Bacall and Humphrey Bogart).

Cue the grave spinning. When Kay was alive, she'd go ballistic when anyone claimed to be an inspiration for *her* alter ego. "Eloise is *me*," Kay once declared to fashion publicist Eleanor Lambert. "All me!"

In less possessive moods, she would flip-flop to the other extreme. "Understand me, she's completely imaginary," Kay insisted in a 1956 interview for the *Los Angeles Times*. "I never knew any little girl like Eloise. I didn't live in hotels as a little girl. I invented her years and years ago."

The truth, of course, lies somewhere in between. Fleshing out the bible of Eloise's world, Thompson chose The Plaza for the child's home because it was her own New York residence and had been one of her most familiar and beloved stomping grounds since the 1930s. "Write what you know," the sage advice goes. Well, Kay knew every nook and cranny of The Plaza, and the members of the staff were like family.

Freud would have had a field day analyzing the way Thompson presented Eloise's parents. "The father is not only not seen, but never mentioned," Hilary Knight noted. "The mother is talked about, but always away somewhere. It was Kay's choice not to have her visible."

Pre–Kay Thompson:
Kitty Fink, sweet 16, 1925.

In black wig for *Ten Nights
in a Bar-Room,* Washington
University, St. Louis, 1929.

Kitty Fink morphs into
Kay Thompson, Hollywood, 1933.

Kay and the Three Rhythm Kings,
The Bing Crosby–Woodbury Show,
CBS, 1933–34.

The *Fred Waring–Ford Dealers Show*, CBS, 1935: Back row: Sisters Blanche, Kay, and Marian Thompson. Front: Priscilla Lane, Fred Waring, Tom Waring, and Rosemary Lane.

With Lennie Hayton, Fred Astaire (21 years before *Funny Face*), and Charles Carlisle, *The Lucky Strike Hit Parade*, NBC, 1935.

Kay Thompson Ray Heatherton
Rhythm Singers

CHESTERFIELD RADIO PROGRAM ∼ COLUMBIA NETWORK COAST-TO-COAST ∼ EVERY WEDNESDAY AND FRIDAY

Promotional postcard for CBS's *Chesterfield Radio Show*, 1936.

7

8

9

Kay leads her Rhythm Singers, 1936.

With Rhythm Singer Al Rinker, fiancé
Jack Jenney, and conductor André
Kostelanetz. *Chesterfield Radio Show*, 1936.

The wonders of airbrushing. 10

Kay and bandleader Hal Kemp co-host
It's Chesterfield Time, CBS, 1937. 11

With protégés Ralph
Blane and Hugh Martin.

12

13

Performing "Down With Love" in the Boston tryout of Vincente Minnelli's *Hooray for What!* October 28, 1937. Kay was fired on November 5.

14

With Ed Wynn in *Hooray for What!*

With director John H. Auer and Joe DiMaggio on set of *Manhattan Merry-Go-Round*.

Kay's movie debut, 1937.

Manhattan Merry-Go-Round: Jack Jenney, Joe DiMaggio, Kay, John H. Auer, Henry Armetta, and Thompson's Rhythm Singers.

18

Kay's first husband, bandleader-trombonist Jack Jenney, 1937.

19

20

Kay and her Rhythm Singers in *Manhattan Merry-Go-Round.*

At the *Manhattan Merry-Go-Round* premiere, 1937.

21

Advising Lena Horne, *Till the Clouds Roll By*, MGM, 1945.

Kay demonstrates her arrangements for *Till the Clouds Roll By*. Ringsiders: Jerome Kern, Lennie Hayton, Lucille Bremer, Arthur Freed, and Roger Edens.

Coaching June Allyson, *Good News*, MGM, 1947.

For Arthur Freed's birthday in 1945, Roger Edens and Kay posed with his cake and a potpourri of favorite things.

With Judy Garland and Vincente Minnelli at premiere of *The Yearling*, 1946.

27

With radio producer-
director Bill Spier
(Kay's second husband)
and Judy Garland the
night Judy guest-
starred on *Suspense*,
November 21, 1946.

29

28

With Howard Duff
(of Spier's *Adventures
of Sam Spade*) and Ava
Gardner, 1948.

Spier directs Lena
Horne and Frank Sinatra
in episodes of *Suspense*,
1944–45.

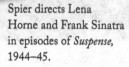

30

31

Dreaming of movie stardom, circa 1945.

32

Self-anointed Balinese princess, 1945.

33

Hopes dashed: Kay's cameo role as "The Matron" was cut from *The Kid from Brooklyn*, RKO, 1946. In this lost sequence, she inspected Goldwyn Girls Karen X. Gaylord and Vonne Lester.

34

Kay and the Williams Brothers (left to right): Bob, Kay, Dick, Don, and Andy (seated below, age 19), 1947.

Beverly Hills, November 1948.

37

With the Williams Brothers at Ciro's, Hollywood, October 1947. Ringsiders: Vincente Minnelli, Judy Garland, and Don DeFore (who later played Mr. B. on TV's *Hazel*).

Secret lovers: Kay, 38, and Andy Williams, 20, 1948.

Rehearsing with the Williams Brothers, 1948.

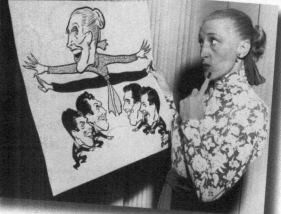

Breaking records, 1948.

Pondering caricature by Jack Lane, 1948.

Danny Kaye in drag as Thompson, with Jack Benny, Jack Carson, Van Johnson, and George Burns spoofing the Williams Brothers. Hollywood Press Photographers' Ball, Ciro's, October 16, 1948.

With Danny Kaye, Stork Club, New York, November 2, 1948.

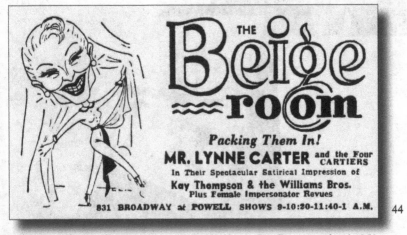

Mr. Lynne Carter's "satirical impression" of Kay's act, San Francisco, April 1953.

45

46

Jack Benny, Esther Williams, and Clark Gable celebrate Kay's million-dollar deal to appear at Arnold Kirkeby's hotels, November 13, 1948.

48

Backstage visitors Judy Garland and Spencer Tracy at Café de Paris, London, April 1951.

47

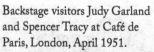

49

50

Kay and her trio: Buzz Miller (top), Lee Scott (left), and George Martin. November 1949.

Caricature by Don Freeman, London, 1951.

51

Carried away by George Martin, Buzz Miller, and Jimmy Thompson at Les Ambassadeurs, Paris, June 1950.

52

Cheesecake wannabe, 1950.

53

In a cloud of cashmere, 1954.

On her perch, hands on hips, 1954.   54

55

Publicity stunt, Grand Central Terminal,
February 1, 1950.

56

Guest-starring on *The Frank
Sinatra Show*, October 28, 1950.

57

In the Persian Room at The Plaza Hotel,
November 1954.

58

Kay's cabaret partner,
Paul Methuen, November 1954.

a 12" *LP* recorded from the sound-track
of the Paramount film-

"Funny Face"

starring

Audrey Hepburn

Fred Astaire

Kay Thompson

Items include:
Overture; Funny Face; 'S Wonderful;
Think Pink!; How long has this been
going on?; Bonjour, Paris!; Clap yo hands;
He loves and she loves; On how to be Lovely;
Basal Metabolism; Let's kiss and make up.
CLP1119

"HIS MASTER'S VOICE"

LONG PLAY 33⅓ r.p.m. RECORD

59   British LP advertisement, 1957.

Atop the Eiffel Tower   60
with Astaire and
Hepburn in *Funny Face*.

62

Upstaging Fred Astaire.

61

In synch with Audrey Hepburn.

63

64

Designing "Fancy Pants" with seamstress Ozel, 1948.

Performing "Think Pink!" in *Funny Face*, 1956.

A slingshot of pink in *Funny Face*, Paramount Studios, Hollywood, 1956.

65

66

Funny Face stars arrive for location shooting in Paris, June 7, 1956.

67

Kay is given a free BMW Isetta for promoting the microcar, 1957.

68

Making a splash in *Funny Face*.

69

Funny Face premiere, Radio City Music Hall, March 28, 1957.

70

Empress of the Eloise Empire, The Plaza, October 1958.

71

In 1956, Hilary Knight and Kay discuss "Eloise in Hollywood," a magazine spread that was never completed.

72

D. D. Ryan (center) convinced Kay to write *Eloise* and recommended Hilary Knight (right) to illustrate it.

73

Future Random House president Robert L. Bernstein (left) and Andy Williams (right) see Hilary and Kay off to France for *Eloise in Paris* research, February 11, 1957.

74

Kay's 1956 Christmas card, drawn by Hilary Knight, though his signature was erased when printed.

75

Eloise honks for Renault, 1958.

76

In December 1956 at The Plaza, Evelyn Rudie poses beside Hilary Knight's *first* Eloise portrait, which was stolen in 1960.

77

On April 17, 1964, Hilary Knight unveiled his *second* Eloise portrait at The Plaza, with Senator Jacob Javits' nine-year-old daughter, Carla.

Playhouse 90 production of "Eloise," CBS Television City, Hollywood, November 22, 1956: Charles Ruggles, William Roerick, Hans Conried, Lennie Hayton, Thompson, Louis Jourdan, Inger Stevens, Mildred Natwick, Jack Mullaney, Evelyn Rudie, Ethel Barrymore, Slapsy Maxie Rosenbloom, Monty Woolley.

79

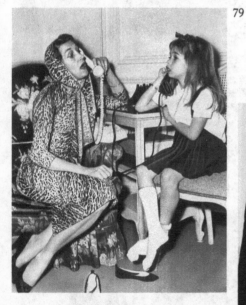

80

With Evelyn Rudie (as Eloise) and Louis Jourdan in the *Playhouse 90* production of "Eloise."

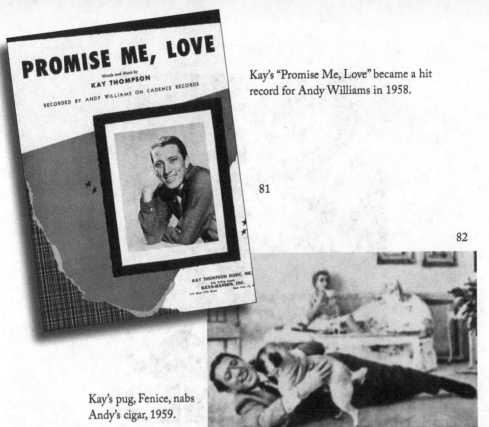

Kay's "Promise Me, Love" became a hit record for Andy Williams in 1958.

81

82

Kay's pug, Fenice, nabs Andy's cigar, 1959.

83

With Judy Garland and 14-year-old Liza Minnelli in London, August 1960.

With Fenice (in her lap) and Judy Garland on flight to the Berlin premiere of *Judgment at Nuremberg*, December 1961.

84

85

With Dick Powell in NBC's *The Dick Powell Show:* "Who Killed Julie Greer?" Studio City, California, June 1961.

86

"Who Killed Julie Greer?": Ronald Reagan, Nick Adams, Mickey Rooney, Jack Carson, Edgar Bergen, Lloyd Bridges, Ralph Bellamy, Thompson, Dean Jones, Dick Powell, and Carolyn Jones (on table).

87

88

Coaching Judy Garland and Robert Goulet for songs in the animated feature *Gay Purr-ee*, Hollywood, November 1961.

89

NOW WHEN I SAY A BEAST
I MEAN A BEAST

Mart Crowley
Rome · 1962

Mart Crowley's renderings for the aborted book *Kay Thompson's The Fox and the Fig: A Bedtime Story*. Rome, 1962.

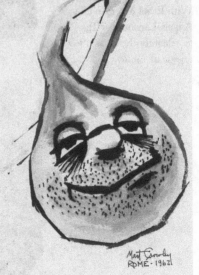

90

NOW WHEN I SAY A FRUIT
I MEAN A FRUIT

Mart Crowley
ROME · 1962

91

92

Marti Stevens, Marlene Dietrich, and Kay at Noël Coward's chalet in Switzerland, Christmas 1962.

Thompson coaches Rita Hayworth for Ian Fleming's *The Poppy Is Also a Flower,* Rome, November 1965.

93

94

With Ethel Merman and Angela Lansbury at The Plaza to celebrate the April 1969 reissue of *Eloise.*

95

Kay throws a party for Sir Noël Coward to honor his knighthood, Sherry-Netherland Hotel, New York, February 1970.

With Peter Allen to make arrangements for Judy Garland's funeral.

With James Mason at Garland's funeral.

Exiting Garland's funeral: Peter Allen and wife Liza Minnelli, Kay, Lorna Luft, and Joey Luft. Campbell's Funeral Home, New York, June 27, 1969.

99

A cross to bear in Halston leatherette: Kay is directed by Otto Preminger for Paramount's *Tell Me That You Love Me, Junie Moon*, July 1969.

100

Thompson, Robert Moore, Liza Minnelli, and Ken Howard in *Tell Me That You Love Me, Junie Moon*.

101

102

With Halston assistant Bill Dugan and Liza at the Palace of Versailles, November 28, 1973.

Directing the opening gala for Bergdorf Goodman, White Plains, New York, September 21, 1974.

104

With Vincente Minnelli for Liza's opening at the Winter Garden Theater, New York, January 6, 1974.

103

With Liza and Lorna Luft at the Minnelli–Mark Gero wedding reception, December 4, 1979.

"Eloise Revisited" by Roz Chast, *The New Yorker*, May 1, 1995.

In Liza's apartment with pal Jim Caruso, mid-1990s.

One early draft, found in the collection of Joan Denise Hill, reveals that when the mother was in town, she kept a busy schedule of "private meetings." Eloise innocently explained, "You can set your watch. There's a lawyer named John who comes at ten. There's a doctor named William who comes at two. There's a doorman named Dudley who comes after four. And the night watchman, Sam, who comes anytime after twelve. I overheard Mabel, the afternoon maid, saying that mother was a nymphomaniac." Ultimately, for the sake of decorum, the mother's promiscuity was left to the reader's imagination.

Early drafts also had Eloise interacting with eight neighborhood boys: Stinky, Junior, Melvin, Nicky, Fenwick, Bruce, Balfour, and Harcourt. As things progressed, however, Kay opted to concentrate all the action in the hotel, where adults would be Eloise's only friends.

Of course, Eloise needed a caretaker, and that character took the form of Nanny, a British au pair.

"I helped her write that," claimed Paul Methuen, Noël Coward's friend who played Kay's British butler in her 1954–55 nightclub act. "I was appearing with her when she was writing it. Of course, I had a darling English nanny when I was young, so I gave Kay all the things an English nanny would say."

When Kay went into her Eloise voice, Paul would pretend to be her nanny and they would improvise endless conversations that Kay would jot down or tape-record for later transcribing.

"My drawings of Nanny," revealed Hilary Knight, "were based partly on Kay and a British actress named Martita Hunt, who played Miss Havisham in *Great Expectations* [General Films, 1946]. But Nanny is very much Kay's personality."

Besides Thompson and Hunt, there was another movie star who came to mind. "Kay and I loved the old Fred Astaire film *Yolanda and the Thief* [MGM, 1945]," Hilary recalled. "In it, Mildred Natwick played an eccentric woman who says everything in threes, like 'Hurry hurry hurry!' and 'March march march!' Kay made Nanny speak like that."

That predilection for speaking in triplets came from one of the movie's writers, Ludwig Bemelmans, author of the *Madeline* children's book series—a precursor and leading rival to the *Eloise* franchise. Kay knew Ludwig when they were both under contract at MGM and she certainly took notice of his work and success. And, there was no question that Mildred Natwick embodied the nanny that Kay envisioned. Not only had Thompson gotten to know

Natwick while working as the vocal arranger on *Yolanda and the Thief*, but later, when it came time to dramatize *Eloise* for television in 1956, Kay would personally choose Mildred to portray Nanny.

Eloise had two pets: a turtle named Skipperdee and a pug dog named Weenie. Kay was very chummy with the Duke and Duchess of Windsor, who famously collected pugs. So, when Hilary suggested the breed, she thought it would be a funny nod to her blue-blooded buddies.

One more likely inspiration was the pug in *Her Highness and the Bellboy* (MGM, 1945), another film for which Kay did the vocal arrangements. The movie took place in a fictionalized version of The Plaza where a bellboy (Robert Walker) takes a stroll through Central Park, exercising a guest's pug—a dead ringer for Weenie.

People were divided over the name Kay gave the pooch. "I didn't want a dog named Weenie," grimaced actress Mariel Hemingway, granddaughter of Ernest. "That was embarrassing to me when I first read it as a child."

More devilish minds relished it. "Any girl who named her dog Weenie was a friend of mine," quipped Cassandra Peterson, aka Elvira, Mistress of the Dark.

Eloise was not going to be sugarcoated. For decades, Kay had been a fan of the adult cartoons that sprinkled the pages of *The New Yorker*, especially those of Peter Arno and Charles Addams, both of whom she knew socially. Their sardonic worldview was just the sort of sophisticated wit to which Thompson aspired for Eloise.

"I took three months off and wrote it," Kay explained. "I holed in at The Plaza and [Hilary and I] went to work. I just knew I had to get this done. Eloise was trying to get out . . . . We wrote, edited, laughed, outlined, cut, pasted, laughed again, read out loud, laughed and suddenly we had a book."

In May 1955, Kay and Hilary decided it was time to see if a publisher agreed. "D. D. brought [*Eloise*] to Jack Goodman, her friend at Simon & Schuster," noted Knight.

"[Jack] recognized and understood Eloise immediately," Kay remarked. Not only did Goodman want to publish the book, he agreed that the target audience should primarily be adults. In fact, he was the one who came up with the clever copy line that emblazoned the top of the dust jacket: "A book for precocious grownups."

Kay's agent, Barron Polan, negotiated the agreement. Dated June 15, 1955, the contract called for a $1,000 advance against future royalties, a final deadline of July 30, and a publication date set for November 28.

"The timing was unheard of," Knight reflected in amazement. "You know, it normally takes a year to get a book out but I can remember doing the color overlays, for the pink and red, with Fourth of July rockets going off."

The division of monies between Thompson and Knight was never mentioned in the original deal, a serious oversight that would be addressed in a March 14, 1956, addendum—months after the fact—retroactively awarding a hefty 66⅔ percent to Kay and 33⅓ percent to Hilary. The industry norm for books of this ilk was a fifty-fifty split between author and illustrator, but evidently nothing was normal in the world of Miss Thompson.

"I totally trusted her," Knight confessed with considerable regret.

Kay was driven by more than mere greed. Though nothing in the contracts mandated it, she managed to maneuver her name above the title in its possessive form: *Kay Thompson's Eloise.* Later, when booksellers created promotional display signage, Kay would call up and complain if her name didn't appear "as part of the title," a prerogative that was manufactured and policed by Miss Thompson alone.

In a significantly smaller font, "Drawings by Hilary Knight" appeared at the bottom of the dust jacket, indicating that any presumed equality between the "authors" was pure fiction (the font size was equalized on editions published after her death). Forever regretting her fifty-fifty deal with the Williams Brothers, Kay was taking no chances. If she could have gotten away with paying Hilary a flat fee as an artist for hire, she would have done so—just as she had done with her trio of dancers and Paul Methuen.

There wasn't any fanfare when the first copies of *Eloise* rolled off the presses in mid-November 1955. Based on tepid advance orders from booksellers of only 4,000 copies, Simon & Schuster's run for the first printing had been set at a conservative 7,500 copies.

But that was before *Life,* the largest-circulation magazine in the country, ran a spread in its December 12, 1955, issue, exposing *Eloise* to millions of consumers in the days leading up to Christmas. Kay was so overwhelmed, she sent a telegram to Simon & Schuster's publicist, Larry Vinick, that read: CONGRATULATIONS. YOU ARE THE END. YOU'RE A COUP D'ÉTAT. THE EDICT OF NANTES. THE LACE ON MY PANTIES. YOU'RE DIVINE, OH LARRY OH LARRY OH LARRY. I'M PRETTY GRATEFUL TO YOU. HUGS HUGS KISS KISS, A PAT AND A SQUEEZE FROM KAY YOUR FRIEND AND ELOISE.

Next, Bloomingdale's department store featured Thompson's character in a *New York Times* advertising campaign for Kalistron Luggage. A steady stream of gushing reviews followed. The *Los Angeles Times* hailed the book as "the *Alice in Wonderland* of the Atomic Age."

One line of the glowing review in *The New Yorker*, however, sent chills down Miss Thompson's brittle spine: "Mr. Knight's drawings give the book at least half its charm." To Kay, any implication that Eloise was not *all* her creation was tantamount to heresy. Consequently, her jealousy of Hilary began to fester.

Not long after her Ciro's gig was done, Thompson flew back to New York to take charge of her baby, taking up residence at (where else?) The Plaza. Within days of her arrival, Kay made her first appearance on *The Tonight Show Starring Steve Allen* (NBC-TV, December 16, 1955) to talk up *Eloise*. She was also joined onstage by her protégé and secret paramour, Andy Williams, to perform one of their old nightclub routines, "Broadway, Street of Dreams," spoofing Gertrude Lawrence and Noël Coward.

As a reciprocal gesture, on December 21, Noël Coward sent a telegram stating, FRANKLY, I ADORE ELOISE, which promptly headlined an advertisement in *The New Yorker*. After that, Kay solicited a slew of endorsements from her many famous friends for a series of ads that quoted Lauren Bacall, Cole Porter, Vivien Leigh, Douglas Fairbanks, Walter Winchell, *The New Yorker*'s Cornelia Otis Skinner, Pulitzer Prize–winning author John P. Marquand, Bennett Cerf (cofounder of Random House, a top competitor of Simon & Schuster), and, most amusing, Groucho Marx, who wrote, "I admire Eloise enormously—and I am very happy that I am not her father."

In the wake of all this, Simon & Schuster ordered a second printing of 9,500, but it was too little, too late. As Christmas approached, *Eloise* books became a rare commodity. With only 17,000 copies in print, frantic buyers rushed from bookstore to bookstore in a futile attempt to locate any remaining copies.

"Booksellers were angry," confessed Simon & Schuster in a mea culpa trade ad. "People . . . took [*Eloise*] home in such quantities that the publishers couldn't print or ship copies fast enough to fill the vacuum."

By early January 1956, a third printing of 15,000 was hitting stores (bringing the total number of copies in print to 32,000)—but the book was just one part of the success story.

On December 20, 1955, The Plaza hosted a cocktail party honoring "Kay Thompson, author of *Eloise*, a brat living in the hotel," attended by Alphonse Salomone, the beleaguered managing director of The Plaza who had just been immortalized in the pages of *Eloise*.

"All the children who come here want my autograph," Mr. Salomone was quoted as saying in *The New Yorker*. "They also want me to bow to the waist, as I do in the book. I oblige on both counts."

"After the first book was published," Kay explained to *TV Times*, "someone phoned up [The Plaza] long distance from Ohio and asked: 'Please may I speak to Eloise?' And the telephone operator, without a moment's hesitation, replied: 'I am sorry. Eloise is on the 13th floor helping with the air conditioning.' Later, calls began to increase in number, so did the operators' excuses . . . 'Eloise is riding in Central Park' . . . 'Eloise is swonking pigeons on the roof' . . . 'Eloise is in the lobby—she has to be in the lobby a lot, you know.'"

Publishers' Weekly confirmed that Thompson personally handled "as many of the phone calls as possible when she was at The Plaza, 'until I realized Eloise was getting more calls than I was,' she says." Not long after that, the hotel had Kay record a telephone message from Eloise that operators would access when callers requested the little girl.

"The success of *Eloise*," noted *The New Yorker*, "has caused [The Plaza] to become a favorite hangout of the pre-teen-age set. The management of The Plaza is delighted with this turn of events and goes out of its way to foster the impression among the impressionable that Eloise really and truly lives there."

When children came to the front desk asking for Eloise, staff played along and made up replies such as, "Oh, I'm sorry, you just missed her. But if you run into Eloise, please tell her we found her missing shoes." To authenticate the illusion, a pair of patent leather Mary Janes would be lifted into view, causing young eyes to widen in amazement. Suddenly, Eloise was as real as Santa Claus and The Plaza was teeming with children on the lookout for her.

"[Thompson] gets letters addressed to Eloise from 6 and 7-year-olds," claimed the *Los Angeles Times*. "It is reported in New York that the small fry set is dropping in on The Plaza in hordes to ask to see Eloise in person . . . The hotel is delighted with the book and sells copies in the lobby, as do other hotels including the Biltmore here [in Los Angeles]. The book has had an enormous effect on hotels."

The Plaza was only too happy to give away promotional postcards that featured Knight's drawing of Eloise saluting the doorman at the entrance to the hotel. To the surprise of the hotel's staff, the demand for this Eloise souvenir far outnumbered requests for traditional postcards featuring The Plaza's facade.

Reacting to the unexpected windfall of free publicity, an incredulous Conrad Hilton (whose company, Hilton International, managed the property) sent a telegram to Mr. Salomone demanding to know: HOW MUCH DID YOU PAY HER?

Of course, Kay's choice of The Plaza as the setting for her book had been completely innocent, devoid of any ulterior motive. Or was it? Once the inherent value of Eloise was clear, Kay demanded and got free accommodations at the hotel.

In short order, Suite 937 was Thompsonized from floor to ceiling. Kay brought in two white chaise lounges and side tables where she displayed eclectic bric-a-brac and clusters of framed photographs (including a handsome 8×10 of Andy Williams). On the walls, she hung magnificent French theatrical posters by the likes of Toulouse-Lautrec.

"These are odds and ends," Kay explained, "that I have picked up from places I have been to . . . Rome and Paris . . . Dallas and Chicago. [Shifting into her favorite Southern drawl] And honey dawlin', I've got some magnolias just to let us know we're all so Southern and Tallahassee and all."

Thompson occasionally conducted interviews in the privacy of her suite, but she preferred to perform for the press in The Plaza's public areas. She'd get more attention that way. "People love to play kid," Kay explained while sipping tea in the Palm Court with newspaper columnist Charles Mercer. A fellow tea-timer asked Kay to "talk Eloise." And with a piercing, high-pitched voice, she did, shrieking, "I am all over the hotel . . . half the time I am lost . . . but mostly I am on the first floor because that's where catering is." Kay's childlike voice, Mercer wrote, "penetrated the four corners of the room and startled customers into unaccustomed silence."

"People are frightened of me only because I talk so loud," Kay reasoned disingenuously. On the contrary, she knew very well that she was making a scene, and she relished every moment of playing a certified nut.

"She cut a wide swath, that dame," marveled Richard Grossman, Thompson's editor at Simon & Schuster. "I mean, I'd known Salvador Dalí for Christ's sake. I'd gone to lunch with him at the St. Regis and I knew what it was like to sweep up the steps with a man in a cape, performing for the world. And Kay had a lot of that."

Indeed, by the 1950s, the real Kitty Fink from St. Louis was buried so deep, it was questionable whether anybody would ever crack the surface of Kay Thompson again. The facade had petrified. And now with Eloise, she had a transformation mask that was one step farther from reality. But who cared what intimate thoughts might be running through Kay's head when there was money to be made on her alter ego?

The Plaza certainly made good use of the opportunity. "Thus the idea of the Tricycle Garage was born," wrote Plaza historian Curtis Gathje. "Carved out of the corner of the Fifty-Eighth Street loading dock and done up in jolly red-and-white candy stripes, the garage opened in May 1956 and provided bike racks and numbered license plates for a fee of fifteen cents a day or three dollars per month. Plaza guests were allowed to use it gratis and were also loaned tricycles for free."

Providing some va-va-vroooom for the opening of the Tricycle Garage was buxom bombshell Jayne Mansfield and her five-year-old pedal-pusher, Jayne Marie.

"The combined success of the garage and *Eloise* has led to some major changes in the hotel," Mr. Salomone explained to *The New Yorker* in May 1956. "For the first time in history, we've issued a children's menu. It has a picture on the cover of Eloise riding a tricycle."

In collaboration with The Plaza's executive chef, Humbert Gatti, Kay came up with a bill of fare that was as tasty as it was humorous. For starters, there was a "Kiddie Kar Kocktail" followed by entrée choices such as "Teeny Weenies" and "Mary-Had-a-Little-Lamb Chop," and side dishes like "Punch and Judy Peas, Purée" and "Jack-&-The Beanstalks, Julien."

"The pièce de résistance was the Tricycle Treat," added Gathje, "a dessert featuring a tiny bike rider cast in vanilla ice cream, riding on a square of sponge cake in a drift of whipped cream doused with raspberry sauce." *The New Yorker* mused that the concoction "must have set Escoffier spinning in his grave."

The very fact that the merits of Eloise desserts were being debated—albeit tongue in cheek—in such urbane forums as the pages of *The New Yorker* was confirmation that Thompson's imp had captured the imagination of more than just children.

Then, Plaza management decided to create an Eloise exhibit on the ninth floor—just down the hall from Kay's private quarters. Decorated like Eloise's room in the book, Room 931 was opened to the public for tours "by appointment only."

"Eloise, of course, was never there," noted journalist Mary Anne O'Callaghan, "but a real-life Nanny hired by the hotel would greet visitors." The young guests were also treated to an unexpected telephone call from you-know-who, usually prerecorded but occasionally live.

"In 1957, I insisted my mother bring me to The Plaza so I could go to the Eloise room and pick up the telephone," recalled *Vanity Fair* writer-at-large Marie Brenner. "And Kay Thompson, herself, still was on that telephone in 1957. And the thrill, at age seven, to hear Kay Thompson's voice saying, 'It's me, Eloise,' I just never—I *still* haven't gotten over it."

Making up for lost time, Simon & Schuster made an all-out push for Valentine's Day—with in-store displays and advertising in newspapers across the country. On February 12, Walter Winchell wrote in his column, "Kay Thompson hit the literary jackpot with her book *Eloise.* 40,000 copies sold."

The true benchmark of fame, however, was notched on Sunday, May 6, 1956, when *The New York Times* crossword puzzle included the following clue for 75 Down: "Kay Thompson's heroine." The answer was a six-letter word beginning with *E*. And, once again, it proved Thompson's point that *Eloise* appealed to grownups.

Thompson was known to storm bookstores that dared to display *Eloise* in the children's section. She would grab the books and haul them to the adult fiction shelves.

"Once Kay left, the books would go right back to the children's section," chuckled Hilary Knight, "but it made her happy."

With or without Thompson's commando raids, the book delighted young and old readers in equal measure. And she certainly did not begrudge the loot being generated from both demographics.

Eloise was not impervious to gusts of backlash. Some people were disturbed by Eloise's lack of parental supervision and felt that she was a dangerous role model. Certain passages were interpreted as subversive—such as on page 51, when Eloise explains the fundamental difference between her mother's lawyer and herself: "Here's what he likes: Martinis. Here's what I like: Grass."

Since 1938, "grass" had been widely used as slang for marijuana—and Thompson was no stranger to the lingo or the weed itself. Alcohol was even more prevalent in Eloise's universe. Not only did her lawyer drink martinis, her nanny imbibed pilsner beer on the job, and, most startling of all, Eloise kept a bottle of gin in her own bedroom—on a shelf right next to her handsaw.

In the 1960s, when substance abuse among minors was on the rise, one concerned mother confronted Kay about her reference to "grass" in *Eloise*.

"Do you know she asked me if I meant marijuana," Thompson related in *The New York Times* in 1968. "I told her 'no' but to read it any way she wanted to."

Kay's feigned innocence did nothing to quell reefer madness. As outrage grew over the years, Simon & Schuster redacted "grass" from new editions starting in 1983, replacing it with the more innocuous "dandelions." And while the publisher was at it, out came an entire vignette, formerly found on page 41, of Eloise flushing a toilet in a public restroom. Oddly, however, Eloise's gin bottle was allowed to stay on that shelf—where it steadfastly remains to this day.

Rather than quash complaints, though, the censorship heightened suspicion about other hidden meanings. For instance, just exactly what was meant by the title of a book on the floor of Eloise's room: *The Little Beaver*? Or what about the line "Sometimes I go into the Men's Room which is very good for playing Railroad Station or something like that"? Taking into account Thompson's wicked sense of humor (as well as early drafts that were even more bawdy), these innuendos had to be intentional. As a result, a small but vocal contingent of do-gooders would continue to protest that *Eloise* was unsuitable for children. As recently as 2008, the ACLU reported that an elementary school in Texas had banned *Eloise* from its shelves.

Kay's defense to all these charges would be that she wrote *Eloise* for adults. It was booksellers who peddled it to kids. Thompson purposefully bombarded her book with mature references to such corporate concerns as AT&T, Kleenex, General Motors, Corvette, and TWA. Aside from The Plaza, Eloise rattled off names of other tony hotels like the Sherry-Netherland in New York and the Roney in Miami. Other topics of conversation included Andover and Buckingham Palace. Even Thompson's favorite department store, Bergdorf Goodman, got a plug. And on page 50, Eloise proclaimed, "My mother knows Lilly Daché" (the famous hat designer), later changed to a more timeless "My mother knows Coco Chanel."

Most of these references go right over the heads of children and are only savored by adults. "I always felt that Eloise was funny on two levels—one for adults and one for children," remarked dancer Marge Champion. "There is something in it for everyone."

Very early on, Kay knew that Eloise could earn money in other mediums. For example, she hoped the "Eloise" song she'd composed for her nightclub act could be turned into a hit single.

When major labels weren't interested in "a novelty record for kids," Kay turned to an old friend, Archie Bleyer, who owed her a favor. Way back in 1941, Thompson had given Bleyer his first big break as her radio conductor, and later got him his first gig conducting a major Broadway show. This led to television in the early 1950s, where he served as Arthur Godfrey's music director. Then in 1952, he formed Cadence Records, a small New York firm that soon generated a remarkable string of hits including "Mr. Sandman" by the Chordettes and "The Ballad of Davy Crockett" by Bill Hayes, the third-highest-selling record of 1955. Because "Davy Crockett" had initially been written off as just "a novelty song for kids," Kay was impressed that Bleyer had seen its potential as a crossover hit. So, naturally, when she asked him to work the same magic for "Eloise," he was more or less obligated to try.

Consequently, on December 2, 1955, the day after Kay's gig at Ciro's ended, Bleyer financed a Los Angeles recording session with Buddy Bregman's orchestra for "Eloise" and, to fill the single's B-side, Kay's bugged-out bongo makeover of Cole Porter's "Just One of Those Things."

At the conclusion of the session, Kay sent this telegram: DEAR ARCHIE, JUST FINISHED. SMASH TIME! MAILING THE TAPES BY AIR TONIGHT TO YOU.

When Bleyer finally heard "Eloise," however, he felt it was too risqué and convoluted for mass appeal, so he convinced Kay to clean up the lyrics and simplify the arrangement. As a result, it became a catchy "call-and-response" bubblegum pop song that began: CHORUS: "Who is the little girl who lives at The Plaza in New York?" ELOISE: "That's me, Eloise. I'm six. I live on the top floor."

In January 1956, the tamed version of "Eloise" was recorded in New York by Bleyer and his orchestra. Thompson performed the voices of both Eloise and Nanny with an impromptu male chorus that included Andy Williams, Ralph Blane, and Simon & Schuster's publicist Larry Vinick.

To promote the song in February, Kay got herself booked again on *The Tonight Show*, where she performed it with Andy. On March 3, Cadence rush-released the "Eloise" single and it rose to No. 39 on *Billboard*'s pop chart—allowing Kay to boast that it had become "a Top 40 hit." Though hardly a smash, it certainly wasn't a dud—and it had legs. According to *Publishers' Weekly*, by year's end, Cadence had "sold out absolutely all the available stock of 100,000 records." Rather than press more copies of the single, Kay convinced Archie to "leave 'em wanting more," insisting that the next step should be an Eloise album. Bleyer went on blind faith that Thompson would follow through with that idea—though ultimately she never did.

As success went to her head, Thompson started alienating the very people who had served her well.

"I set up a publishing company called Kay Thompson Music, Inc., when Kay had written the song of 'Eloise,'" recalled business manager Leonard Grainger. "The deal was that we each owned fifty percent of the publishing company. It really had virtually no value. It only had two songs in it, 'Eloise' and 'I Love a Violin.' I don't think you can find much royalties on either of them. But when I gave her the capital stock to sign, she said she couldn't sign it. I asked her why and she said, 'I just can't share it or give anything away.' Kay and I had made a deal and she reneged on the deal, so I quit. I'm sure she had a great love for me and a great sense of appreciation but she had trouble giving and sharing things. She had to be in control. She was a control freak."

Thompson's agent, Barron Polan, was kicked aside, too. On March 14, 1956, Kay filed papers with Simon & Schuster that eradicated Polan as her agent on the *Eloise* book.

And she certainly took advantage of Hilary Knight. When a drawing from the book was reused on the cover sleeve of the record, for example, Knight received no additional compensation. Had Thompson been consulted, he would not have received credit, either.

"It was quite unusual to have the artist's name on the cover of a record," Knight said, "but they ended up printing my name quite prominently on the jacket—'Drawing by Hilary Knight'—and Kay was furious. I certainly didn't say that my name should be on there. The printer just did that and she was very mad about it."

Even though Knight was not to blame, Thompson remained disgruntled and seemed to be looking for ways to get even. "For Christmas that year," Knight recalled, "Kay asked me to do an Eloise drawing that she could use for her own personal Christmas card. I had signed my name discreetly along the margin of the picture but when the cards were printed, my name was nowhere to be seen. I asked her about it and she said, 'Oh, the printer cut it off. Isn't that awful.' I knew she had done it because that's how she was. With me and with everybody. It was so small of her."

Similarly, when Kay reused Don Freeman's 1951 advertising caricature of her for the cover of her 1954 album, his signature was dropped and he received no compensation.

"I wouldn't put anything past her," concluded British journalist Elspeth Grant. "Nor would I ever wish to get into an argument with her: she seems to have rather more teeth than usual—and all the better to bite your head off with, my dear. Miss Thompson is something to marvel at from a respectful distance."

With the success of *Eloise* came demand for more. "I went to California for the very beginning of the production of *Funny Face*," recalled Hilary Knight, "because Kay had an idea about doing a magazine piece on 'Eloise in Hollywood' while she was shooting the movie. And I did a lot of work on it, a lot of sketches, and I have a drawing of Fred Astaire's toupee in my sketchbook. But that never happened."

The demise of "Eloise in Hollywood" coincided with a falling-out between Thompson and Fred Astaire—which may explain why she redirected her enthusiasm toward a sequel book, *Eloise Abroad*. While Kay was shooting *Funny Face* in Paris, Hilary joined her there to research the sights firsthand, and, eventually, the focus of the book was narrowed to just one European capital— becoming *Eloise in Paris*.

*M*eanwhile, United Productions *of* America (UPA), producers of the highly successful *Mr. Magoo* cartoons, had been negotiating for months to make a series of animated *Eloise* featurettes with Kay providing the voice. Discussions were proceeding quite nicely until her new agent, Wynn Rocamora, among others, advised that the franchise would benefit more if *Eloise* became a live-action, feature-length movie. Acquiescing to conventional wisdom (a rare Thompson occurrence), she went along with the idea as long as she retained creative control. "*Eloise* . . . is being packaged as a motion picture by Kay," revealed Louella Parsons in the *Los Angeles Examiner* on December 22, 1955. "Her choice to play the modern child is that modern young lady, Miss Portland Mason."

The plump seven-year-old daughter of Pamela Kellino and James Mason had a potbelly à la Eloise and a *réputation* to match. The Associated Press claimed that her parents "take her to cocktail parties and nightclubs" wearing "her own fur coat." James admitted that they had "sneaked her into Ciro's" on at least one occasion. In *Daily Variety*, Army Archerd reported a Portland Mason sighting at the Mocambo, where she spontaneously jumped onstage and "did a burlesque dance routine, complete with grinds, which left [Dean] Martin gaping." And when James Mason starred in *20,000 Leagues Under the Sea* for Walt Disney in 1954, he famously got his agent to add "the Portland Clause" to his contract, obliging the studio to lend its films, free of charge, to his pampered offspring so that she could privately screen them at home. Producer Ray Stark, son-in-law of Fanny Brice, had even screen-tested Portland for the proposed television series *Baby Snooks*, based on Brice's alter ego, but nothing had come of it.

Having outgrown Baby Snooks, Eloise was now deemed the perfect starring vehicle for Portland. So, in December 1955, with Thompson's endorsement, James Mason pitched the idea to Twentieth Century-Fox, where his daughter was currently making her feature film debut with Gregory Peck in *The Man in the Gray Flannel Suit* (1956). The powers that be, however, passed on the idea because they believed "kiddie pix don't make money."

All the other major studios passed on *Eloise*, too. But the concerns were not solely based on pessimistic box-office projections. *Eloise* had no plot. The book was a stream-of-consciousness day-in-the-life of a poor little rich girl. Adapting this flimsy premise into a feature-length screenplay was a tall order indeed, made even trickier by Thompson's veto power.

With movies ruled out, television was the next logical stomping ground for the unruly tyke—and Kay's ex-husband, Bill Spier, wanted in on the action. He pitched turning *Eloise* into a TV musical starring Portland Mason as Eloise and Kay Thompson as Nanny, with an original song score by Thompson. After all, Kay had voiced both Eloise *and* Nanny on her hit record, a tune that could now be repurposed as the theme for the television special.

Bill suggested that the dramatization would be a perfect fit for *Omnibus*, the highbrow anthology television series he had created and produced for CBS-TV starting in 1952, hosted by Alistair Cooke. During its summer hiatus of 1956, however, *Omnibus* was in a state of flux. In a dispute over rising costs, its sponsor had decided to move the series to ABC starting in the fall. Before those negotiations were concluded, Spier brought *Eloise* to the attention of CBS chairman William S. Paley, who promptly outbid ABC for the television rights.

In retaliation, ABC snapped up the rights to Ludwig Bemelmans' *Madeline* for live-action dramatization on *Omnibus*—instigating an all-out "War of the Moppets" between rival networks that would be fought tooth and nail to the bitter end.

Eloise didn't come cheap. CBS had to cough up a record-breaking $15,000 to acquire the rights for a single live broadcast (compared to the $1,000 Ian Fleming got for the dramatization of his James Bond novel, *Casino Royale*, on *Climax!*). There was no such thing as reruns back then, so exposure was automatically limited to one performance that could serve as an entrée to Hollywood. In fact, many CBS productions of that era—such as *The Miracle Worker, Judgment at Nuremberg*, and *Days of Wine and Roses*—were later remade into major motion pictures. Even though the dramatization of *Eloise* was a one-shot deal, CBS had the foresight to negotiate options for sequels and a spin-off TV series.

Eloise was assigned to *Playhouse 90*, a new ninety-minute anthology series that promised weekly adaptations of literary works by the likes of F. Scott Fitzgerald, Ernest Hemingway, and William Faulkner. Not only did "Eloise" stand out as the only musical-comedy in an otherwise serious slate of dramas, journalists expressed skepticism over the ninety-minute running time. A humor piece in *Cue* magazine by Philip Minoff, written in Eloise-speak, wondered "what in the world they were going to do with all that time, time, time . . . It took me only ten minutes to read the whole book, for Lord's sake, and I can't even read."

The good news was that anticipation was building. With the combined buzz surrounding *Eloise* and the soon-to-be-released movie *Funny Face*, Kay's stature within the entertainment industry had elevated to new heights, enabling her to demand final creative control over the *Playhouse 90* production of "Eloise."

Unfortunately, producer Martin Manulis was given extremely limited funds with which to work. The standard per-episode budget for *Playhouse 90* was fixed at $175,000, and "Eloise" would be no exception—despite the added challenges a musical presented.

Because the *Playhouse 90* budgets were so modest, Manulis had already instituted a ceiling of $10,000 per actor, no matter how big the star. And, to handle the overlapping workload, he declared that several directors would divvy up the season on a rotating basis, earning $1,000 per week, multiplied by the three weeks it took to put on each installment.

Ralph Nelson, who would first helm the *Playhouse 90* production of "Requiem for a Heavyweight" (CBS-TV, October 11, 1956)—considered by many to be one of the finest television dramas ever—was initially awarded "Eloise" as his follow-up assignment.

On July 19, *The Hollywood Reporter* announced that "Bill Spier, Miss Thompson's ex, is scripting 'Eloise'" for a *Playhouse 90* slot in January 1957.

After years of developing hard-boiled radio noirs for *Suspense* and *The Adventures of Sam Spade,* Spier could not resist the temptation to devise a mystery at The Plaza with nosy little Eloise poised to solve the crime. Though Kay loved whodunits as much as Bill did, she did not see Eloise as a young Nancy Drew, so she rejected his take entirely.

At the same time, Kay had become disenchanted with the idea of playing Nanny, a decidedly nonglamorous role. When she confessed to Manulis that Mildred Natwick was her idea of the quintessential Nanny, he wholeheartedly agreed to offer Natwick the part once they had a suitable script.

Then Cole Porter let it be known that he was "so crazy" about *Eloise* that he'd "like to write the music for it." Unfortunately, there was neither enough money nor time to meet Porter's demands—though it was a tantalizing proposal.

Undaunted, Thompson felt she was perfectly capable of rustling up the song score herself, so she staged a dog-and-pony show for the brass at CBS, reading excerpts from her book and performing her hit song "Eloise."

"Kay had me come over to CBS Television City in Hollywood," recalled Don Williams of the Williams Brothers. "We sat on a couple of stools and I sang, 'Who is the little girl who lives at The Plaza in New York?' and she'd say, 'That's me, I'm Eloise.' And we rehearsed that thing together and then Kay and I did it for Martin Manulis and some other executives so they could get a feel of what Eloise would be like."

Never missing an opportunity, Kay had photographs of the recital dispatched to newspapers around the country, whetting appetites for the special.

Thompson not only announced her intention to compose all the songs, she also pitched her concept for the adaptation—simply a day in the life of Eloise as she crosses paths with an expanded assortment of colorful adults, herself included. She figured she could persuade some of her celebrity friends to play themselves as guests in the hotel.

Kay was given just three weeks to write the score and come up with a viable script—a frightfully short period of time, especially for an inexperienced screenwriter. It soon became apparent that she had bitten off more than she could chew. So, while she focused on the music, Leonard Spigelgass, who had just finished collaborating with *Funny Face* writer Leonard Gershe on the screenplay to *Silk Stockings* (MGM, 1957), was hired for $10,000 to churn out a teleplay.

"Kay *hated* the script that Leonard Spigelgass wrote for 'Eloise,'" recalled film critic and Thompson confidant Rex Reed. She grudgingly endorsed the teleplay, however, assuming there would be plenty of time to make improvements during the rehearsal period.

A number of vignettes came straight out of the book, and the dialogue was sprinkled with familiar Eloise witticisms. The script introduced Kay cleverly: Always scrawling her name as graffiti, Eloise would "autograph" a poster display in the hotel lobby for "Kay Thompson, Appearing Nightly in the Persian Room." This would segue into "3:00 a.m. in the Persian Room," a musical number starring Kay and the Four Singing Busboys (Don Williams, Bill Norvas, Joe Marino, and Hans Conried, modeled after the Williams Brothers) as they clean up the empty nightclub.

Naturally, this appealed to Thompson's ego, but it also satisfied the need for periodic scenes without Eloise, since labor laws limited work for child actors to four hours per day. With rehearsals lasting twelve hours, scenes had to be created among the adult actors to make use of the surplus time.

Standards and Practices decreed that Eloise should have attentive parents and there must be an explanation for their absence from The Plaza. So, although it might have been easier to state that Mom and Dad were on vacation, it was contrived that the parents were steering clear of The Plaza in order to keep reporters and paparazzi away from their daughter during their high-profile divorce and custody battle. It was a very odd way to assuage concerns over family values, but it satisfied the network censor.

*W*hen *ABC announced that* "Madeline" would air on the December 23 installment of *Omnibus*, CBS struck back by switching "Eloise" from January to November 22—beating them by a full month. The upside for "Eloise" was that this new date happened to be Thanksgiving night, when the country would be in the right mood for light family fare. The downside was that many weeks of precious preparation time would be lost.

To accommodate the scheduling change, director Ralph Nelson had to be replaced by twenty-six-year-old John Frankenheimer, who, in addition to directing twenty-six thrillers for *Climax!* had helmed the premiere install- ment of *Playhouse 90* on October 4 (Rod Serling's "Forbidden Area" starring Charlton Heston and Vincent Price) and was working overtime on another one for October 25 (Cornel Woolrich's "Rendezvous in Black" starring Boris Karloff).

Steeped in murder and mayhem, Frankenheimer was certainly an odd choice for "Eloise." The ex–military man would later become famous for directing such muscular political thrillers as *The Manchurian Candidate* (United Artists, 1962), *Seven Days in May* (Paramount, 1964), and *Seconds* (Paramount, 1966). Frothy musical comedy was as far removed from his cinematic vocabulary as one could imagine, especially with a precocious subdebutante as the star. However, it just so happened that, in April of that year, Frankenheimer had become the father of a baby girl—named, similarly, Elise—which may have softened his macho demeanor just enough for Manulis to entrust him with "Eloise."

Taking no chances, Thompson insisted on a conductor of her choosing. She wanted Lennie Hayton, but he was busy conducting the nightclub tour of his wife, Lena Horne. After Kay prevailed upon Lena to share her man, how- ever, Lennie joined the "Eloise" task force.

When it came to populating the program with familiar faces, Thompson suggested Louis Jourdan.

"He's doing a picture with Doris Day," Manulis reasoned. "He's way too hot right now. You'll never get him."

Unfazed, Kay called Jourdan and, in the voice of Eloise, charmed him into doing it. Then Mildred Natwick jumped at the chance to play Nanny. With any luck, Kay's next big "catch" would be Noël Coward. Unfortunately, he was in the middle of an ongoing dispute with CBS over his own contracted specials, so he respectfully declined.

"No worries," Kay said. "We'll just find another old poof."

And that's when they hired erudite character actor Monty Woolley, who, legend has it, introduced his Yale classmate and confidant, Cole Porter, to male bordellos.

The "Eloise" teleplay also called for a famous sports figure to be stay- ing at The Plaza, so boxer Rocky Marciano joined the cast on October 4. A week later, however, he was replaced by heavyweight champion Slapsie Maxie Rosenbloom, whose knockout performance in *Playhouse 90*'s "Requiem for a Heavyweight" (October 11) had just struck a chord with critics and viewers.

By the end of October, the legendary Ethel Barrymore had joined the lineup, too. Since she'd recently been convicted of tax evasion, Ethel's entire fee would go to the IRS. So, Ethel quietly demanded that Manulis cast her son, Samuel Colt, as the bell captain, a peripheral character with only a couple of lines, for which he would be paid the $10,000 guest star rate—a transparent but perfectly legal way to circumvent the IRS lien. In exchange, Ethel accepted minimum union scale for her time—severely limiting the amount she would forfeit to the government.

Others in the cast would include Inger Stevens, Charles Ruggles, and Plaza bigwig Conrad Hilton.

Even actress Marion Marshall, the wife of *Funny Face* director Stanley Donen, appeared in an uncredited cameo. "We were at dinner one night," Marion recalled, "and Kay said, 'Oh, you've got to play Eloise's mother! Come on and do this for me.' So I did. It was really nothing. No lines. You never see my face, only parts of my body."

For the all-important title role, Portland Mason suddenly faced formidable competition from Patty McCormack, whose about-to-be-released movie, *The Bad Seed*, was the buzz of the industry. Thompson insisted on auditioning both potential candidates before making a decision.

So, James and Pamela Mason brought their seven-year-old daughter all the way from London and finagled a timely profile in the September 28 issue of *Collier's* magazine entitled "L'Enfant Terrible." Unfortunately, there was no getting around the fact that Portland had become more portly than ever, several sizes larger than the pleasantly plump silhouette of Eloise.

Patty McCormack's figure was more pleasing, but at age eleven, she was a bit long in the tooth to be cast as a six-year-old.

After rejecting both girls, Kay decided to hold an open casting call, organized by Ethel Winant, a dynamo who later cast *The Mary Tyler Moore Show*.

Hollywood Reporter columnist Leo Guild immediately recommended seven-year-old Evelyn Rudie. "We've known the youngster for a couple of years," Guild campaigned in his column, "and one time when she scribbled a post card from NY to us—'I hate you because you didn't write. You are an ogre and I won't kiss you anymore.'—we figured this little girl really had something."

Rudie's credits were certainly promising, boasting appearances in eighteen television shows and seven movies, including the role of John Wayne's daughter in *The Wings of Eagles* (MGM, 1957), directed by John Ford.

"I remember going in and meeting Kay Thompson," Evelyn recalled. "I can't remember who else was in the room because when Kay was in a room, no one else was in the room. Kay was a bright light. And she started asking me questions. And I started telling her stories about my dolls and my life and about my parents."

"I called her mother," Kay recalled, "and asked if I could take the child for a ride."

"And so we went into her gorgeous car," Evelyn said, "which was a Jaguar XK125, still my favorite car to this day, the most beautiful car in the world! And we went driving around town and we went to lunch. She spoke to me of her hopes and dreams, of how Eloise really was her in many respects, about her excitement that a larger audience would finally be introduced to Eloise, and that little girls everywhere would be able to see that they didn't have to fit into any particular mold."

"Girls can be whatever they want to be!" Kay told Evelyn. "Just look at me!"

Soon afterward, Rudie was awarded the part. "Kay became like a second mother to me," Evelyn added. "That week, she invited me to Saks Fifth Avenue in Beverly Hills and took me shopping for Eloise clothes. The next thing I knew, they were adding padding for a proper potbelly and they bleached my brunette hair blond. My missing front teeth would have been replaced if my father hadn't put his foot down."

On Friday, October 26, a fully made over Evelyn and her parents, along with Kay and John Frankenheimer, were whisked to the East Coast for research and photo ops at The Plaza, where they stayed for free. American Airlines comped their round-trip tickets in exchange for a mention on the program.

"It was my first plane trip," Evelyn remembered. "Eleven and a half hours of horrible turbulence and I got very airsick. When we landed, Kay and I moved to the door of the plane and they were getting ready to open it."

The flight attendant looked out the window and remarked, "My goodness, there are hundreds of photographers out there."

"Well, that did it," Evelyn said. "I turned to Kay and said, 'I'm gonna be sick.'"

Thompson calmly opened her purse and said, "In here!"

"And I did," Evelyn shrugged. "She actually let me throw up in her handbag. But that is the kind of trouper and the kind of person that she was. She closed the handbag, took my hand, and we walked onto that ramp, the photographers and the flashbulbs flashing."

The resulting spreads in *Life, TV Guide, Cue, The New York Times Magazine,* and hundreds of newspapers across the country turned the marginally known moppet into an overnight sensation brandishing a new, media-anointed middle name: Evelyn "Eloise" Rudie.

The Plaza proved a dizzying playground for the wide-eyed young actress, who, upon arrival, "dashed into the revolving doors and propelled two strangers into the same cubicle."

"I'm beginning to think I should write my next book and call it *Evelyn*," Kay quipped.

The headliner at The Plaza's Persian Room that week happened to be Eartha Kitt. "Kay introduced me to Eartha in the hall one time as we were walking through," Evelyn recalled, "and we had a brief conversation."

"So this is the new little Eloise," Eartha growled in her distinctive feline timbre.

"Kay sort of blanched at that for a moment," Rudie observed. "I remember the reaction, but didn't realize what it meant until later on."

Obviously, Kitt's remark had been intended as a compliment. But from Thompson's perspective, it was the ultimate insult. To Kay, there was only one Eloise—and Evelyn Rudie was *not* her. From then on, Thompson made certain that interviews focused on herself—even if her attempts to finesse control were blatantly transparent. *Cue* magazine journalist Philip Minoff made light of the fact that his time with Evelyn Rudie had been cut short "because Miss Thompson sent her into another room just after we sat down, and we never saw her again. If we don't see her on TV November 22nd, someone ought to call the police, for Lord's sake. The room is 937. There's only one person I've ever known who could match Miss Thompson's love for children—W. C. Fields."

Minoff also noted that whenever he asked questions about Eloise, Thompson's eyes lit up "like two griddle-cakes" and she conversed in the screechy, high-pitched voice of the little girl. When he lamented "what a shame it was that she wouldn't be able to talk Eloise's part on television," Kay shot back in her own voice that he was "not to worry about *that*."

True to her word, when rehearsals commenced in Hollywood on November 1, Thompson announced that she herself would provide the voice of Eloise. Under any other circumstances, the folly would have been summarily dismissed, but because Kay had been granted contractual creative control, there was nothing anyone could do about it.

"So every time I had a line, I had to cover my mouth," Evelyn explained. "I had to hold a book up; I had to turn away from the camera; I had to have a doll in front of my face. And Kay had to hide behind furniture or be in a little cubbyhole and speak in the direction of the microphone."

They quickly discovered that it would be impossible for Kay to provide the voice for Evelyn while on-screen herself. One dilemma led to another and soon the entire teleplay was in flux.

"No one was happy," Evelyn confirmed. "There were hushed conversations between Kay and Frankenheimer, or not-so-hushed conversations between everyone and everyone. There was a lot of 'What if we tried this?' and 'Do you think that might work?'"

With many problems still unsolved, Thompson took time off to fly to New York for a prime-time television interview on *Person to Person with Edward R. Murrow* (CBS-TV, November 9, 1956), broadcast live from her suite at The Plaza. The chain-smoking Murrow himself was on assignment in the Near East, so Jerry Lewis had been recruited to take over his ashtray for the night. The pairing of these two entertainment giants was described by *The Hollywood Reporter's* television critic, Leo Guild, as "sprightly."

Behind the scenes, it was a different story. "Kay was *furious* that she didn't get to be interviewed by Edward R. Murrow," Hilary Knight remembered, "and she didn't like Jerry Lewis. Absolute disgust."

On camera, however, Thompson kept her cool and conveyed the sort of air-kissy camaraderie all Hollywood stars are supposed to have for each other. At least that was the case until Jerry asked Kay if she had received his holiday greeting card yet, insisting that she go digging through a pile of mail on her desk to locate it.

"And then when she finds it," Knight observed, "she dismissively hurls it over her shoulder. That is the most typical kind of Kay put-down. She did things like that all the time."

On the subject of nightclubs, Jerry asked, "Do you remember Chicago when we worked in opposition of one another?"

"Oh Jerry, I do so well," Kay responded. "1947. I was at the Blackstone . . . the most plush, the most elegant, the most *marvelous* place. You were in Grant Park playing with pigeons."

Then, in an obvious setup, Thompson went to a piano and said she'd play something if Jerry agreed to sing. Naturally, he suggested his new single, "Rock-a-Bye Your Baby with a Dixie Melody," the first serious recording of his career.

As Jerry started singing, Kay mischievously ad-libbed a jazzy scat—"a booba da, booba da, boob de ahhh . . ."—which caught him off guard.

"Where did you find *that* part in the number?" he said, wincing, between verses.

Nonetheless, it worked and America was introduced to a whole new side of Lewis. "I never expected what happened next," Jerry noted in his memoir.

"The single rose to No. 10 and remained near the top for almost four months, eventually selling a million and a half copies."

"I'm still waiting for my commission," Thompson later told friends, only half joking.

Aside from Jerry's stolen moment, however, the rest of *Person to Person* was an Eloise infomercial. Kay recited passages from the *Eloise* book, sang a verse of the "Eloise" song, took viewers on a tour of the Eloise Room, and unveiled an enormous Eloise portrait that Hilary Knight had painted as a birthday gift (Thompson turned forty-seven the day of the broadcast). And, of course, she plugged the imminent *Playhouse 90* presentation of "Eloise" as though it were the Second Coming.

Immediately after the show, Kay hopped a plane back to Hollywood to resume rehearsals for the main event. One week before the airing, she appeared with the all-star cast in a live, three-and-a-half minute "coming attraction" commercial. Just as they had rehearsed, Evelyn patiently held an *Eloise* book in front of her mouth while Kay spoke all the Eloise lines off camera. Disastrously, however, the young actress lowered the book before the last line of dialogue was finished, shattering any illusion that she was doing the talking herself. The flub demonstrated just how precise the cues had to be to pull off Kay's ventriloquist act. And yet, despite the embarrassing omen, Thompson's hubris was indulged until the wee hours of Thanksgiving, the very day that "Eloise" was to air.

"At one o'clock in the morning, my parents got a phone call from Martin Manulis," Evelyn remembered.

"It's not working," Manulis confessed to Rudie's mother and father. "I've got Johnny Frankenheimer here with me and we've been in conference all night. It just doesn't work. It sounds wrong. Do you think it's possible that Evelyn can learn the lines by tonight? We'll get her a coach. We'll do anything it takes."

Evelyn's father replied, "Well, let's do a run-through in the morning and let's see."

"When you're working on a show for three weeks," Evelyn reasoned in hindsight, "you learn the lines anyway, even if you're not speaking them. I came in the next morning, we did a run-through, and it worked. It was fine. It was *good.*"

Everyone was relieved—with one exception. "No sooner was the dry run finished than Kay appeared on the set with a cadre of lawyers and piles of new contracts," Evelyn explained in *The New York Times.*

If Kay agreed to allow Evelyn to speak the part of Eloise for this one-time-only broadcast, CBS would have to surrender all future rights. There would be no sequels, no TV series, nothing. Furthermore, Rudie's parents and representatives "had to agree that while [Evelyn] could say in her publicity materials that she had *played* Eloise, she could never say that she *was* Eloise." And never again could she be referred to as Evelyn "Eloise" Rudie.

"I am Eloise," Kay roared. "No one else. Ever. Not as long as I live."

"Shortly after the infamous meeting with the attorneys," Evelyn recalled, "I was in a corner, going over my lines, when I overheard a conversation between Kay and John."

"I know it's not your fault," Thompson whispered to Frankenheimer. "It's that Martin. And that little girl."

"Don't worry about it, Kay," Frankenheimer replied. "It's going to be okay. Everything's going to be okay."

"Maybe, maybe not," Kay shot back. "Just make sure when this is over that you never have anything to do with her again."

If Evelyn felt like roadkill in the wake of Kay's megalomania, she was hardly alone. In an atmosphere of forced congeniality, the show went on as scheduled. Thompson's twenty-year-old niece, Julie Hurd (daughter of Kay's older sister, Blanche), was a guest observer of the live broadcast at Television City and accompanied Kay afterward to a viewing party of the delayed West Coast broadcast, held at the home of Inger Stevens' boyfriend, Robert Horton. Tellingly, Frankenheimer and Manulis were nowhere in sight. Apart from Inger and Kay, the only other "Eloise" cast member Julie recognized among the crowd was Monty Woolley. When asked if Evelyn Rudie was there, Julie said, "No. Kay hated her. Every time Evelyn showed up on-screen, the crowd would boo. They'd boo to the TV whenever *anybody* came on they did not like—especially when Conrad Hilton blew his line."

Thompson's vitriol, however, was tame compared to that of the critics. "Pretentious chaos . . . that was dull, dull, dull . . . awful, awful, awful . . . and sad, sad, sad," bemoaned Harriet Van Horne in the *New York World-Telegram and Sun*.

"Instead of worrying about the monopolistic economics of television," wrote Jack Gould in *The New York Times*, "Congressional committees shall serve the public interest and find out how 'Eloise,' the musicalized evisceration of Kay Thompson's story about the little girl at the Hotel Plaza, got on the air."

Equally stinging was *TV Guide*'s assessment that "Eloise" was "among the worst flops of the electronic age."

· · ·

The humiliation was not easy to live down when 26 million people had witnessed the train wreck. Furthermore, the sole aspect of "Eloise" that everyone seemed to like was the very thing that Kay had tried to silence.

"Only one member of this splendid cast emerged with dignity intact," declared the *New York World-Telegram and Sun.* "That was 7-year-old Evelyn Rudie who played Eloise. She had poise and authority, plus a zest for the eccentric." And *Variety* enthused, "The show's real delights came when six-year-old Miss Rudie was on camera."

Suddenly, the youngster's career was on fire with offers for movies, television, and Broadway. "Hottest name in TV at the moment is seven-year-old Evelyn ('Eloise') Rudie," observed *The Hollywood Reporter*—a middle-name reference that made Thompson's blood boil.

Then, on the December 9 installment of *The Dinah Shore Show,* Dinah told her audience that the following week's guest would be "Evelyn 'Eloise' Rudie." That's when Thompson lost it. She fired off a telegram to NBC "demanding the network desist from referring to Evelyn Rudie as 'Eloise,'" or else she would file for an injunction.

Just when Kay thought things could not get any worse, ABC announced it had signed Evelyn for the title role of the *Omnibus* production of "Madeline"—the latest skirmish in the "War of the Moppets," with Thompson's ex-husband among the perpetrators.

If this didn't keep Kay awake at night in her Plaza suite, the fact that Evelyn checked into the very same hotel to begin rehearsals for "Madeline" certainly did. When asked if she had run into Kay, Evelyn replied, "No, but I had my picture taken standing next to the new Eloise portrait."

Hilary Knight's enormous watercolor painting of Eloise, unveiled on *Person to Person*, was now on permanent display in the lobby of The Plaza, where it had become a hot destination for tourists to have their picture taken. Leading the pack was none other than Evelyn, who brazenly posed next to her verboten doppelgänger.

Timed to coincide with the "Madeline" airing on December 23, ABC's publicists got *TV Guide* to run a new feature story on Rudie—and yet the article ended up being titled "Eloise Is For Real." The "Madeline" broadcast fared no better, barely making a dent in the ratings. It was such a nonevent, newspapers did not even bother to run postmortem reviews. In the "War of the Moppets," Eloise may have come out battered and bruised, but Madeline was down for the count.

As the New Year got under way, Thompson was relieved that all the fuss was finally over. However, there was still one more ulcer-inducing addendum to the saga. On February 16, 1957, it was announced that Evelyn Rudie had been nominated for a Best Actress Emmy Award for her performance in "Eloise"—the youngest nominee in the Television Academy's history. When the awards were presented on March 16, Evelyn lost to Claire Trevor, but she had won in the court of public opinion. "As a result," Rudie proudly stated, "I received my star on the Hollywood Boulevard Walk of Fame in 1958, the year it was started."

As for Kay, her words on the *Playhouse 90* experience have been few. When *The New York Times* dared to broach the subject in November 1957, Thompson pleaded the Fifth: "Listen, have a heart. Let's forget it. I'm trying to."

What really mattered to Kay was her treasured book which by year's end had sold 130,000 copies, ranking it the fifth-highest-selling fiction book of 1956. Amplified by her Top 40 hit record and the massive surge in business at The Plaza, no one could deny that Eloise was the biggest debutante to hit New York since the Statue of Liberty.

Chapter Nine

SLACKS FIFTH AVENUE

From "Fancy Pants" to *Funny Face*
(1930–65)

The heterogenesis of *Funny Face* is quite a saga in itself,
full of hair-raising suspense, and completely Horatio Alger.
—*Roger Edens*

I've always loved fashion," Kay Thompson told *Women's Wear Daily* in 1974, "and had friends in fashion like Diana Vreeland and [*Life* magazine fashion editor] Sally Kirkland."

In fact, a fashion magazine was responsible for Thompson's emancipation from St. Louis in 1930, when she was still known as Kitty Fink.

"I got a copy of *Harper's Bazaar* and picked out all the ritzy western girl's camps as my prey," she explained. She wrote them all, landing a counselor job at Camp Toyon on Catalina Island, within spitting distance of Hollywood. From there, she springboarded herself to stardom as Kay Thompson. Had she not been so involved as a musician, entertainer, and Empress of the Eloise Empire, Kay would have pursued a full-time career in fashion.

From the get-go, Kay was a clotheshorse. In the 1930s, she insisted that her radio Rhythm Singers dress as snazzy as they sounded—even though they would be seen only by the studio audience. To shop for a dozen new dresses every week, she recruited the world's foremost fashion critic, Lois Long, to do the job. Long moderated her own CBS Radio talk show on fashion, heard by millions coast to coast. She also wrote an influential column called "On and Off the Avenue: Feminine Fashions" for *The New Yorker* (where her husband, Peter Arno, was a contributing cartoonist).

Though Lois was the expert, Kay was not shy about voicing her own dos and don'ts. "The clothes I like best of all are simple, with good lines and in plain, solid colors," she said in 1937. "The black and white combination is my favorite . . . Pinks and oranges and lavenders are simply color poison to me."

When Kay's radio chorines did not live up to her brand of chic, she took matters into her own hands. "One day at rehearsal," Elizabeth Rinker recalled, "Eula Jernigan wore a funny little hat made out of oilcloth and Loulie Jean Norman had a flat white piqué hat that matched her piqué coat. When everybody went to lunch, Kay and I were there alone in the room and she just picked up both of those offending hats and threw them out the window. To this day, I can just see them sailing across Madison Avenue."

All this attention to glamour soon paid off. In 1937, *Radio Guide* declared, "Kay's girls are the best known, and the best looking of all radio choirs."

And, long before it was acceptable for women to wear pants, Thompson was bucking tradition. On August 1, 1936, *Radio Guide* featured a photo of Kay in androgynous white gabardine jodhpurs and black leather boots.

"I was the first to wear pants and simple shirts," Thompson later told Rex Reed, "because they were easier to move in."

Adding to her tomboy mystique, Kay was very athletic. While most women sported skirts when playing tennis, Thompson wore regular shorts. On the golf course, she was always in slacks. And, according to a 1936 article in *The Washington Post*, one of Kay's favorite pastimes was horseback riding in Central Park, wearing jodhpurs.

"Side-saddling in skirts is strictly for the birds," Kay proclaimed.

At a 1939 premiere, fashion journalist Mary Jacobs observed that Thompson stood out in a room full of major stars. "You didn't notice any of them," Jacobs wrote. "Immediately the tall, lanky figure of Kay Thompson, in an ultra-smart, ultra-simple navy blue tweed suit, with an all-over ticked white blouse, stood forth. There's something startling, dramatic about Kay and her lean, intense face with its network of freckles, its amazingly frank blue eyes and generous mouth. From beneath a smart navy beret her softly waved red hair peeped."

While working behind the scenes at MGM during the 1940s, Thompson turned heads on the lot with her striking ensembles.

"Kay had all her clothes custom-made by a seamstress named Ozel," recalled Angela Lansbury. "She made these incredible thin silk garments for Kay. They just clung to her body. Kay was very thin. She had just incredible legs. Everything was long. Her nails were out to here. And high heels? *Ah!*"

When Kay became a nightclub star in 1947, she pumped up the volume. To make sure repeat customers never saw her in the same thing twice, she commissioned Don Loper to churn out twenty-five different stage ensembles, based on her dictates, described by *Time* magazine as "sleek slack-suits."

Equally trailblazing was Kay's promotion of "three-quarter-length" pants. According to the fashion history books, Prussian designer Sonja de Lennart introduced the style in her 1948 "Capri Collection," named after the Italian isle; others credit Emilio Pucci, who in 1949 opened a boutique on Capri and coined the name "Capri pants."

While debate has raged over who came first, the fact is that Kay beat them *both* by introducing "three-quarter-length" pants into her nightclub ensemble in 1947, with Ozel manufacturing custom knockoffs for Thompson's celebrity pals.

"I started designing them," Kay declared defiantly, "and now you see them everywhere but they are called Capri pants."

The rest of America was a bit slow on the uptake. Capris would finally take off in the early 1960s, largely mainstreamed by Mary Tyler Moore, who caused a sensation sporting the style every week on *The Dick Van Dyke Show* (CBS-TV, 1961–66).

Back in the 1940s, however, a woman wearing pants of *any* length was still considered shocking. On August 2, 1947, Katharine Hepburn made headlines for "creating quite a to-do in London, dining at Claridge's in slacks," defying the restaurant's strict dress code for women. But Hepburn wielded enough power to do as she pleased. Thompson, on the other hand, was out there in the trenches bucking the system—not always victoriously. Columnist Mel Heimer reported, "Kay was going to the Venice Ballroom in Long Beach, California, to hear Benny Goodman's band, and she had on a chic pair of gabardine pants, along with a long evening coat and an armful of diamonds and pearls. 'You can't come in here with those on,' the doorman said. Miss Thompson looked around, stunned, at the big and glittering and noisy dance hall which wasn't quite El Morocco. 'Here?' she asked in disbelief. The doorman nodded, with tight lips, so she went over to the rollercoaster instead."

Thompson's pants caused problems during daylight hours, too. In July 1948, she sported "a black faille pair of pants, along with a ducky white sweater and lined coat" for a day at the races at Chicago's Arlington Park Racecourse. When she and the Williams Brothers tried to enter the plush Turf-and-Field Club, the maître d' said, "I can't admit a woman wearing slacks." In a "devil-may-care mood," Kay marched out on the clubhouse lawn, placed a $10 "win only" bet on the least likely horse to win, and collected a $300 jackpot.

"*Both* underdogs got the last laugh," she gloated.

Even when Thompson appeared in the January 1948 edition of *Vogue,* her fashion-forward thinking was speed-bumped. Editor in chief Edna Woolman Chase assigned photographer George Platt Lynes to capture Thompson's essence, yet the point was missed entirely when her fancy pants were nixed in favor of a traditional silk evening gown by Hollywood designer Howard Greer that sucked the wind right out of her strut.

Columnists such as Dorothy Kilgallen criticized Thompson for wearing pants: "She traipses about the stage in an outfit that is a combination of Hepburn-ish slacks and grandpop's old long underwear, and on her it looks like *Harper's Bazaar* because she is built like a swizzle-stick."

In *The Washington Post,* Jack Gaver complained, "Miss Thompson has made herself look like the most freakish woman . . . with a clinging all-white ensemble featuring slacks . . . that gives her the appearance of having just been plucked."

With a bit more diplomacy, *The New Republic* noted that Kay resembled "a blade-like instrument" in "a pair of ultra-chic black slacks . . . The effect of this costume is not masculine; it suggests the feminine with a deftly epicene touch. 'Sliced Steel' would be a fitting title."

A few, like columnist Danton Walker, dared to cheer her on: "La Thompson, who suggests a cross between a polo player and a Chinese Chippendale goddess, wears slacks with more chic than any other woman living."

Slowly but surely, Thompson was making headway. "[Kay] told me her trip to Boston was very amusing," Hedda Hopper wrote in 1949. "The good ladies there were appalled at her slacks, and a week later, the same ladies were asking for the pattern."

By 1950, Kay's pants were such a trademark that any variation warranted national coverage. *Time* reported that at Manhattan's Versailles nightclub, "some of her admirers demanded that she wear a dress. Her compromise solution: a new outfit she described as 'pedal pushers surrounded by a split skirt.'"

Responding to Thompson's new look, *Boston Daily Record* critic George W. Clarke observed, "Pretty? Far from it. Ugly? No-o-o, but certainly smart, sharp, suave, subtle, sophisticated and very, very soigné."

Kay also introduced catsuits into her stage ensemble, custom-made for her by an aspiring young designer named Nolan Miller.

"I wasn't even in the fashion business back then," recalled Miller. "I was working for Stanley Medeiros, a florist in Beverly Hills, and we did flowers for Joan Crawford, Barbara Stanwyck, and everybody at MGM like Don Loper and Roger Edens. Roger is the one who introduced me to Kay. She wanted somebody to make catsuits for her long before other people started wearing skintight catsuits. She explained in great detail exactly what she wanted, I did some little sketches, found the fabric—black wool jersey—and I made catsuits for her. She came for two, maybe three fittings at Ozel's, and that was it. She didn't fool around."

Though the job seemed inconsequential at the time, Nolan would not forget it. In 1962, Aaron Spelling asked him to come up with wardrobe ideas for a new character he was developing for Anne Francis named Honey West, who was introduced on a 1963 episode of *Burke's Law*, then spun off into her own series, *Honey West* (ABC-TV, 1965–66).

"Anne Francis was very feline," Nolan recalled, "and I could just see her in those black catsuits I had made for Kay. So I made some sketches with that in mind and Aaron sold the show to the network using my sketches. A couple of years later, that's all Diana Rigg wore on *The Avengers*. I was way ahead of my time." Which would place Thompson somewhere in the light-years-ahead category.

When Kay played Paris in the summer of 1950, French critic Henri Larrive thought she looked like "a Salvation Army nurse," but he begrudgingly admitted her innovation of wearing catsuits underneath a split skirt was "*croquignolet*." Translation: "cute."

One important designer sat up and took notice. Pierre Balmain was so inspired by Thompson's innovative use of pants, he created a custom ensemble that she modeled in the November 1950 issue of *British Vogue*, photographed by Cecil Beaton, with a caption that explained she was wearing "a Balmain pantaloon-line dress in nut-coloured taffeta; the irregular skirt, swathed below the knee into trousers."

Back in America, though, Kay was still fighting an uphill battle. Columnist Earl Wilson quipped, "Seeing her in slacks, many men will say, 'She ain't my cup of she.'"

And when Thompson appeared on *The Frank Sinatra Show* (CBS-TV, October 28, 1950), her predilection was the butt of jokes.

"Who's your tailor?" Frank asked sarcastically. "I *must* have a pair of those pants."

"Some people might disagree," Kay responded, "but I believe if the occasion calls for it, a woman has a perfect right to wear trousers. Or, for that matter a man should wear skirts!"

"Not without a set of bagpipes he shouldn't," Sinatra scoffed.

$\mathcal{A}$s it happened, a Broadway musical was in the works that would combine Thompson's talents as entertainer and fashionista. Wedding Day, by Leonard Gershe, was a Pygmalion-like story set in the world of high fashion, loosely inspired by the courtship between photographer Richard Avedon and his first wife, model Doe Avedon. Having served with Avedon in the Merchant Marine during World War II, Gershe had followed his career with keen interest.

Through Avedon, Gershe had become friends with Dorinda "D. D." Prest Dixon (later known as D. D. Ryan), a twenty-two-year-old junior fashion editor at Harper's Bazaar under fashion editor Diana Vreeland.

"D. D. would feed me expressions and things that Vreeland said," Gershe recalled, "like . . . 'Pink is the navy blue of India.'" Vreeland also created her own jargon, like the word "pizazz," which she coined in her March 1937 "Why Don't You . . . ?" column in Harper's Bazaar, meaning "the quality of being exciting or attractive."

For his libretto, Gershe named his editor Dana Prescott. "Dana" was a shortened version of "Diana," Vreeland's first name, while "Prescott" was a lengthened version of "Prest," D. D.'s middle name. He also decided her favorite byword would be "bazazz," a clever amalgam of "Bazaar" and "pizazz."

After Gershe completed his libretto, he recruited composer Vernon Duke and lyricist Ogden Nash to write the songs for the musical. Then, in the fall of 1950, Clinton Wilder, producer of the Broadway hit Regina, optioned Wedding Day with hopes of opening it the following year. It was Wilder's idea to offer the job of direction and choreography to Bob Alton, a choice Gershe heartily seconded. Alton liked the project but would commit only if Kay Thompson agreed to play the fashion editor.

In the show, Kay would get to sing no fewer than six big production numbers, including "I Hitched My Wagon to Harper's Bazaar" and "I'm Glad I'm Not a Man." However, Thompson's response to the libretto was only lukewarm and she liked the songs even less. So she turned it down.

With Broadway plans going nowhere, Gershe's agent, Sam Jaffe, submitted Wedding Day to MGM on July 13, 1951, as a potential movie musical.

Serendipitously, in August 1951, Diana Vreeland assigned Richard Avedon to do a photo session with Thompson in Los Angeles, introducing Kay to the real-life counterparts of the characters in Wedding Day. And then, as if to emphasize the point, the following year, Vreeland got Avedon to shoot Kay again, this time with the Williams Brothers for the September 1952 issue of Harper's Bazaar.

These premonitory confluences began to ruminate and, before long, Thompson had charmed Vreeland via her alter ego. Kay later told writer Stephen M. Silverman that Diana would frequently call and say, "I wanna speak with Eloise." And the conversations proliferated from there, with Vreeland wrapped around Eloise's pinky.

In the meantime, Thompson was moving ahead with plans to market her own "Fancy Pants."

"Selling Bibles to the Hell's Angels would have been an easier sell," recalled Robert Evans, the future head of production for Paramount Pictures, then a salesman for Evan-Picone, Inc., the clothing manufacturer.

But Kay was a snake charmer. "You know how women catch on to a look," observed Robert's brother, Charles Evans, cofounder of Evan-Picone. "Well, a *lot* of women wanted to wear 'Kay Thompson' pants. Kay was a great talent, tall, slim, and full of rhythm. Certainly you would not describe her as a pretty woman, but by singing and dancing with the Williams Brothers, she carved quite a niche for herself. People started paying attention to her style and everyone loved the pants Kay wore—no crease, great simplicity. That was a distinctive part of her act. Adam Gimbel, chairman of the board of Saks Fifth Avenue, knew Kay Thompson socially. She said to him, 'So many people want to buy my pants, why shouldn't we sell them?'"

As a result, Gimbel negotiated an exclusive deal for Saks to carry "Taper Pants designed by Kay Thompson," nicknamed "Kay Thompson's Fancy Pants."

"Being the good merchant that he was, Adam told Kay, 'We'll get the best pants manufacturer and it'll be great,'" Charles Evans continued. "So, that's how my life coincided with Kay Thompson because Evan-Picone was the best manufacturer of men's pants."

Located in Manhattan at 1407 Broadway (between Thirty-eighth and Thirty-ninth streets), Evan-Picone, Inc., had been founded in 1949 by Joseph Picone and Charles Evans. They needed help selling their wares and so, after dabbling in acting and modeling, Charles' twenty-one-year-old brother, Robert Evans, joined the company as a salesman in 1951. The following year, along came Thompson and suddenly Evan-Picone was manufacturing women's slacks.

"I'm in ladies pants," Robert Evans salaciously quipped to friends.

At first, the whole idea was treated as a bit of a joke, just a passing fad. Picone expressed concern that the respected Evan-Picone name might, in some way, be tarnished by Kay's outlandish garments, so he formed a shell company named Diva Manufacturing, Inc.

Starting October 17, 1952, an expensive, yearlong advertising blitz was launched in a dozen major markets where Saks stores were based, including big display ads in *The New York Times* and the *Los Angeles Times*.

"We manufactured thousands of them," said Charles Evans. "Our factory in Union City, New Jersey, could barely keep up with the orders. We had a good reputation and we became the best supplier of slacks for women at Saks Fifth Avenue—all because of Kay."

In November 1952, syndicated fashion critic Phyllis Battelle opined, "The slickest lounging pants of the season are the creations of chanteuse Kay Thompson, who wouldn't be caught either singing or snoozing in a skirt. She has designed gabardine and velvet 'tapered trousers' which are slightly ballooned out over the sitting portion of a lady's figure, and tapered to fit snug at the ankles. Because of their bell top, they fit almost any woman from the waist measurement alone—and they're flattering because the shape is subtly deceitful."

Tastemaker Arlene G. La Rue noted, "Follow through with your shopping and likely as not you will end up with Kay Thompson pants, Greta Garbo hats, Marilyn Monroe nighties and slave girl jewelry."

In October 1952, Kay brazenly showed up at New York's Stork Club wearing a pair—and cunningly brought along Ethel Merman for support. At the time, Merman was the mistress of owner Sherman Billingsley, so an observant doorman waved the ladies right inside without a fight. It was a momentous breakthrough. Flabbergasted, Ethel proclaimed, "Boy, you're the first dame who ever got into this joint in a rig like that." And, of course, Kay made sure the victory was reported in all the papers.

Unjustly, Yves Saint Laurent is often given credit for introducing high-fashion slacks for women. "If it were not for Saint Laurent," wrote *Los Angeles Times* fashion critic Booth Moore in 2008, "who sent pants down the runway in 1962 and again in 1966 . . . Giorgio Armani might not have an empire and Hillary Rodham Clinton might not have a uniform."

The truth of the matter is that Thompson beat Yves Saint Laurent by a decade or two. In October 1952, columnist Mel Heimer declared, "Kay has done more for pants in the last 10 years than Fleming did for bread mold." And there could be no greater judge to set the record straight than "the Empress of Seventh Avenue," Eleanor Lambert, who established the Best Dressed List in 1940; created the biannual New York Fashion Week in 1943; and founded the Council of American Fashion Designers in 1962.

"Kay was most influential, I think, with her nightclub act," Lambert declared in 2002. "Every star in the universe came to see her shows and she always wore her own pants and casual clothes—which gave everybody something to think about. Back then, restaurants wouldn't let women come in with pants on and Kay was one of the main reasons that eventually changed. Unfortunately, she didn't want to license the production of her pants in a bigger way that might have made her clothes more available to the general public. Saks Fifth Avenue only had a few stores back then, so the impact was more among the movie stars and high society who adopted her style, and Kay never really got the credit she deserved."

It is true that Thompson's designs were available only at Saks, but she promoted them to millions of women on *The Buick-Berle Show* (NBC-TV, February 23, 1954)—at that time, the most popular television program in America. When Kay sauntered out in zebra-print trousers, Milton Berle grimaced. "Where'd you get them? At *Slacks* Fifth Avenue?"

Milton soon discovered that Kay's maid and butler were sporting the exact same trousers, and before the comedy sketch was done, Berle had slipped into a pair, too.

Debate raged in the media. *Hollywood Reporter* critic David Newman declared that Kay's slacks were "ridiculous," while *San Francisco Chronicle* columnist Marjorie Trumbull argued that they "looked marvelous."

The association between Thompson and slacks had entered the national consciousness, but after all her accomplishments in music and entertainment, was she happy when *The New Yorker* described her in 1954 as "the girl who made lounging pajamas famous"? Would this be her epitaph?

*W*hile all this was going on, *Wedding Day* finally began to percolate at MGM because of an office romance between Roger Edens and Leonard Gershe. In 1953, while collaborating on "Born in a Trunk" for Judy Garland in *A Star Is Born* (Warner Brothers, 1954), Roger and Leonard had become, as Kay liked to call them, "sweethearts." So, for insiders, there seemed to be intentional innuendo behind *The Hollywood Reporter*'s announcement on March 29, 1955, that "Leonard Gershe has checked into MGM to start scripting his original *Wedding Day* for producer Roger Edens."

Edens agreed with Thompson that the Vernon Duke–Ogden Nash score was inferior, so the first thing he did was replace it with several standards by George and Ira Gershwin—including "Funny Face," "'S Wonderful," "He Loves and She Loves," and "Let's Kiss and Make Up" from the 1927 Broadway musical *Funny Face,* starring Fred Astaire (though the story line had nothing in common with *Wedding Day*). To fill gaps where none of the Gershwin catalog felt apropos, Roger and Leonard would come up with their own songs.

For the beginning of the movie, for instance, they decided to build a song around Miss Prescott's latest *couleur du jour* for *Quality* magazine.

In the script, Miss Prescott sweeps into her office "like a gust of wind" and declares, "Yellow is to be the theme of the entire issue. Contact Revlon and find out if they can bring out a yellow nail polish. Tell them no matter what they hear from *Harper's Bazaar* or *Vogue, Quality* says yellow is the color this summer."

Hence, Roger and Leonard began writing a song called "Hello Yellow"— then decided that the color was all wrong. Instead, they went for the jugular and spoofed an actual campaign that *Harper's Bazaar* had promoted around the color pink.

"I think the 'Sunset Pink' promotion is what cost me my editorial mainstay," blushed *Harper's Bazaar* editor in chief Carmel Snow in her autobiography. "The Budd Company, one of our important advertisers, built for the Southern Pacific Railroad a new train called the 'Sunset Limited' [christened August 20, 1950] that we were persuaded to promote by pushing 'Sunset Pink' fashions. Bags, gloves, coats, fabrics—everything but the train—were dyed Sunset Pink, and pages of *Bazaar* had to be devoted to them."

Snow concluded that the entire endeavor had been "the height of absurdity." And now, thanks to Edens and Gershe, that ignominy would come back to haunt her. In mid-May 1955, the men came up with a wicked opening anthem called "Think Pink!"

Was it just a fluke that during the very same period Thompson settled on pink as the primary color for her new *Eloise* book?

"It's a great coincidence," Hilary Knight said. "I'm not entirely sure how that came about or whose idea it was. Maybe Kay said, 'Let's do it pink.'"

Cross-pollination was certainly possible. While Roger and Leonard were composing "Think Pink!" they were also collaborating on three new songs for Judy Garland's 1955 summer concert tour. And guess who was in the middle of it all, tweaking vocal arrangements, making suggestions on the choreography, and standing in the wings for support on opening night? Our First Lady of Fancy Pants.

It was this summer of teamwork that afforded Kay the opportunity to finally bond with Leonard Gershe—and decide that she wanted to play Miss Prescott after all.

"Don't tell anybody, Katie," Edens warned. It wasn't going to be easy to make their casting wish fly at MGM because Roger rarely saw eye to eye with the new studio chief, Dore Schary.

Kay agreed. "When L. B. [Mayer] left, it was a different studio," she lamented, calling Schary "an idiot."

On September 14, 1955, it was announced that Stanley Donen, co-director of *Singin' in the Rain*, had been signed to direct *Wedding Day*. He agreed whole-heartedly with Edens that Thompson was the ideal choice for the role of Miss Prescott. "I never considered anyone else for the part," Donen told *Vanity Fair*.

Dore Schary was another matter. Schary did not agree on *any* of the creative choices. For instance, Edens wanted Richard Avedon to serve as a visual consultant, but Schary refused to okay the expense. And when Edens initiated discussions with Hubert de Givenchy to design the haute couture for the film, Schary insisted the costumes be made economically, in-house.

For the lead role of Jo Stockton, the Doe Avedon–like model in training, Schary wanted Cyd Charisse. Somehow Edens convinced him to cast Carol Haney, Gene Kelly's former assistant choreographer, who had just won the 1955 Best Featured Actress Tony Award for *Pajama Game*.

For the role of the photographer, Gene Kelly's name had been bandied about during early stages of development, but despite their marvelous collaboration on *Singin' in the Rain*, he and Donen had since fallen out. Then Frank Sinatra was approached, but ever since he'd won the Oscar for *From Here to Eternity* in 1954, his schedule had been logjammed with projects and his asking price had gone through the roof. Schary was not willing to wait in line nor to meet his demands. He decided, instead, to hire Dan Dailey on loan-out from Twentieth Century-Fox. Edens was not happy because he was counting on a bigger box-office star to offset the fact that Carol Haney was a newcomer.

Naturally, when Edens brought up Thompson for the role of Miss Prescott, Schary was churlishly resistant. After some serious arm twisting from both Edens and Donen, however, Schary finally agreed to screen-test her on September 28, 1955.

In the sequence, Kay tells her staff, "Banish the black, burn the blue and bury the beige. From now on, girls, think pink!" This segues into the song "Think Pink!" with a unique arrangement that cleverly blended several bars of "'S Wonderful."

"They're all agog at MGM over Kay Thompson's test for the fashion editor in *Wedding Day*," noted *The Hollywood Reporter* on October 6.

Well, not exactly "all." Kangaroo Court Judge Schary firmly vetoed Thompson and instead assigned the part to studio contract player Dolores Gray. Embarrassed and humiliated, Kay prayed that the November publication of *Eloise* would not be a bust, too.

Meanwhile, complications plagued the production. Carol Haney discovered that she was three months pregnant about the same time Dan Dailey was hospitalized for "a neck injury suffered in a fall from a horse." Making matters worse, Edens had reached an impasse in his negotiations with Warner Brothers for the rights to the Gershwin songs. And so, as the Christmas holidays approached, *Wedding Day* was, in Stanley Donen's estimation, "dead in the water."

But then came the first of several miracles. Donen received a letter from Broadway director George Abbott, asking if he might be interested in codirecting Warner Brothers' film version of *The Pajama Game* after he completed *Wedding Day*. Donen recalled, "I said to Roger, 'Here's the deal . . . I'll get my agent to make an agreement that says Warner Bros. can have my services *if* MGM gets the rights to use [the Gershwin songs].'"

It worked. However, bagging Gershwin chestnuts did not a picture make. *Wedding Day* was still minus a bride and groom.

In the interim, Gershe stumbled onto a magazine interview with Audrey Hepburn in which she declared her passionate desire "to do a musical one day" because she had grown up idol-worshipping the films of Fred Astaire and Ginger Rogers.

When Gershe reported this intelligence to Edens and Donen, they were excited by the prospect—though it seemed a long shot. First, the Oscar-winning actress was arguably the hottest star in Hollywood; second, she was under contract to Paramount; and third, even if a loan-out could be negotiated, she would not come cheap.

In mid-December 1955, shortly after completing *War and Peace* with her husband, Mel Ferrer, Audrey was holed up in Paris at the Hôtel Raphaël, poring over screenplays, trying to decide on her next movie—and there was no shortage of juicy projects from which to choose.

The odds of her selecting *Wedding Day* were ridiculously slim, but, with no stars other than Dolores Gray, Roger and Stanley were in desperate need of some marquee razzle-dazzle to keep their project afloat. So they pitched the project to Hepburn's agent, Kurt Frings, and demanded a fast answer. "She's at the Raphaël in Paris," Frings told them. "Send her a copy of the script and send one to me."

The agent received his copy first and read it immediately. "Kurt Frings hated it," Gershe admitted. "He kept saying how embarrassed he was that he had told Roger and Stanley to send it to Audrey, because he couldn't stand it." It was too late to stop Audrey's copy of the script from being delivered to her hotel, but Frings informed the crestfallen filmmakers that he would be advising his client to pass.

While the script was still making its way across the Atlantic, Edens attended a Christmas party at the Beverly Hills home of Clifton Webb. Spotting his old friend Fred Astaire, Roger had an epiphany: "Why not Fred?" Though the fifty-six-year-old actor was a bit long in the tooth for the role of the thir-tysomething photographer as written, an open mind, a little squinting, and a judicious dose of desperation led Roger to confront Fred with the opening line "What are you doing?"

Fred explained that he had just signed a two-picture deal with Paramount, the first of which would be *Papa's Delicate Condition*, set to start preproduction after the first of the year.

Emboldened by a few cocktails, Roger pitched *Wedding Day* and lied through his teeth: "Audrey Hepburn likes the script and will do it if we get you!"

"Say that again, please!" Astaire whiplashed. "Audrey Hepburn? That's the dream of my life!"

That was all Roger needed to hear. He cabled Audrey that Fred Astaire would be her leading man if she came aboard *Wedding Day*.

"Audrey usually takes about three days to read and consider a script," Mel Ferrer told *Photoplay*. "This one she finished in two hours. She burst into the room where I was working and cried, 'This is it! I don't sing well enough, but, oh, if I can only do this with Fred Astaire!'"

Elated, Audrey sent a telegram to Roger Edens that read: THIS IS THE ONLY THING I WANT TO DO FOR MY NEXT PICTURE.

However, Paramount head honcho Barney Balaban flatly refused to play ball. With *Papa's Delicate Condition* ready to start preproduction, he had no intention of postponing it. And, the idea of loaning Astaire *and* Hepburn to MGM was simply out of the question.

"I was repeatedly told that there was no chance to put the deal across," Astaire wrote in his memoir. "However, I knew that Audrey wanted to make the picture and sooner or later they would all come around—because Audrey is a lady who gets her way."

And she did—by bringing the mountain to Muhammad. After conten-tious negotiations, Schary agreed to sell Paramount the entire *Wedding Day* package (Gershe's script, Donen, Edens, and the Gershwin song rights) for a cool $350,000. In exchange, MGM would gain the right to hire Audrey for *Green Mansions* and Fred for *Silk Stockings*.

Rechristened *Funny Face*, the movie would start filming on April 9 at Par-amount Studios in Hollywood, followed by location shooting in Paris during the month of June.

One important piece of the *Funny Face* puzzle that was *not* included in the complex transaction was Dolores Gray, who remained exclusive to Metro and was immediately reassigned to *The Opposite Sex* (MGM, 1956).

This left the door wide open to reinvite Thompson to the party, but by then, she was busy in New York promoting her runaway bestseller, *Eloise*, as well as rehearsing for a mid-February nightclub gig at The Plaza's Persian Room. Roger flew to New York to meet with Kay and simply refused to take no for an answer.

"It would be wonderful to do because we were so close," Kay said. "Roger and I were just one, into one."

So, with a wave of her arm, she blew off the Persian Room date and on February 7, 1956, the front-page headline of *Daily Variety* heralded: "Kay Thompson in FUNNY Twist, Winds Up In Role."

She would be paid $1,600 per week with a guarantee of fifteen weeks, raised to $2,000 after that—for a total of $30,667 by the time she wrapped on July 3.

By contrast, Audrey would make $195,049, plus 5 percent net profits; and a guarantee that Hubert de Givenchy would be retained to design her high-fashion ensembles—all of which she would get to keep. Astaire would earn a flat $165,000 with no perks. Metro's original projected cost of $1,898,205 would ultimately balloon to $3,164,000 when all was said and done.

"I suppose you might say I'm the result of Hollywood's quest for new faces," Kay joked in a Paramount press release. "New! That's a good one. I've been around so long I remember when it was safe to walk across Hollywood Boulevard."

In the latest draft of Leonard Gershe's script, dated January 20, 1956, there was a highly developed courtship between Miss Prescott and a Christian Dior–like fashion designer named Pierre Duval (to be played by a major French star like Jean Gabin or Jean Servais). In fact, *My One and Only* (George Gershwin–Ira Gershwin) had been planned and licensed as a romantic duet for these characters and, during the finale, they were supposed to be married in a double wedding ceremony along with Jo and Dick.

When Thompson was signed to play Miss Prescott, however, the decision must have been made that her strident and masculine aura did not lend itself well to this lovey-dovey subplot, because in the next re-write it was nowhere to be found. Duval's relationship with Miss Prescott became strictly business and his scenes were significantly reduced (the role was ultimately cast with the economical character actor Robert Flemyng).

Conversely, Miss Prescott's scenes were beefed up as a sexless third wheel to Jo and Dick. In place of the Prescott-Duvall duet, for instance, it was decided that Kay's screen time would be much better spent performing a song with Audrey. So Edens and Gershe composed a new number entitled *On How to Be Lovely* during which the novice is taught the fine art of modeling by the worldly fashion editor.

Somewhat less savvy was Thompson's real-life decision to have the bags under her eyes removed and to undergo her *fifth* rhinoplasty—which, unfortunately, resulted in complications. The following November, after *Funny Face* was in the can, columnist Dorothy Kilgallen revealed, "Only a few friends know that during the shooting of the picture Kay was suffering all kinds of tortures, mental and physical, because of an unsuccessful plastic surgery job on her nose."

As a result, Kay had to be caked in heavy makeup and photographed from a becoming distance, rarely closer than a medium head-to-waist shot. And all her publicity stills from the movie were extensively retouched.

Also, upon close scrutiny, one cannot help but notice that in certain scenes, Kay seems slightly hunched forward like a vulture. "By then, Kay had developed osteoporosis and was very self-conscious about it," Mart Crowley recalled. "She'd do her best to stand straight up but it didn't always work. And she thought Edith Head's clothes did nothing to disguise the hump on her back."

Edith Head was Paramount's resident fashion chief, with an army of Oscars to her credit and an ego to match. On the surface, it seemed logical that she would be assigned to *Funny Face* because she had previously won Academy Awards for two Audrey Hepburn films, *Roman Holiday* and *Sabrina*. For the latter, however, Hubert de Givenchy deserved to share the Oscar for designing Audrey's most memorable couture. Astonishingly, he had not been included on the ballot, and Edith had no qualms about taking home the prize with nary a word of thanks to the snubbed French designer. Not so this time. Before signing his contract for *Funny Face*, Givenchy demanded contractual clauses that would ensure prominent attribution in the main titles and, in the event of an Academy Award nomination, shared credit with Head. And because *Funny Face* was about the world of haute couture, Givenchy would design all of Audrey's high-fashion ensembles, leaving Head to do her dowdy, pre-supermodel attire—which had to be purposefully ugly for the sake of contrast.

Adding to the tense atmosphere was Kay's highly vocal campaign to have Givenchy design *her* wardrobe, too. She argued vociferously that Miss Prescott was the editor of the monthly bible of the fashion trade and should be dressed accordingly. But Head fought tooth and nail to keep Thompson under her jurisdiction—and won—though it turned out to be a Pyrrhic victory.

"Kay was very, *very* upset about her wardrobe in *Funny Face*," recalled Marion Marshall, then the wife of Stanley Donen. "She didn't think that Edith Head had done a good job for her—which I can't disagree with."

"[Kay] persuaded Roger Edens to call the egomaniacal, implacable Edith Head while she listened on the extension phone," recalled Rex Reed. " 'Kay is playing a fashion editor based on Diana Vreeland,' [Roger] said, 'so we need a wardrobe that is very Coco Chanel.' Dead silence, followed by, 'Roger, go fuck yourself.' Kay said, 'Don't worry, I'll do my own clothes,' and she did."

Marching right into the Paramount wardrobe department, Kay dictated her vision to Edith, who later described the Prescott designs as the result of a "happy collaboration" with Thompson: "In *Funny Face*, [Kay] had a code: two-piece costume with a short, short skirt and a long, long jacket, a tiny sailor collar at the top. She wore this from tweeds to chiffon. It became a long skirt for evening wear. The point of the uniform was that here was the editor who told every woman what to wear—'Everybody must wear pink!'—but for herself, 'I wouldn't be caught dead in it.' She announces that every woman must wear different clothes for different moods, and then proceeds to wear her two-piece suit."

Though Edith had been reduced to a seamstress like Ozel following Kay's instructions, the dressing-down was softened by Kay assuming her Eloise voice, making light of each directive—a routine Edith later described as the "squeaky voice of a little girl 'shot with arsenic.'" Head could have put up a fight, but with Edens on Thompson's side, she did not relish eating crow. "Kay is completely Kay," Edith acquiesced philosophically.

Whereas Head had envisioned Miss Prescott wearing either skirts or dresses, Kay could not help but slip in a pair of black Capri-style slacks from the latest "Kay Thompson's Fancy Pants" collection. And she persuaded Audrey to wear them, too, during her "Basal Metabolism" dance in the beatnik club, as well as during her duet with Kay, "On How to Be Lovely."

However, the young star had not yet cottoned to the new Italian fashion trend and was not keen on the idea of exposing her ankles. So when it came time to film the sequence, Audrey covered every inch of her lower extremities with black socks and black ballet slippers that essentially turned Kay's fashion-forward Capris into standard-issue leotards.

Stanley Donen took one look at the ensemble and concluded that instead of black socks, she should wear white ones. Otherwise, she would not stand out in the darkly lit café.

"Absolutely not!" Audrey cried. "It will spoil the whole black silhouette and cut the line at my feet!"

"If you don't wear the white socks," Donen reasoned, "you will fade into the background, there will be no definition to your movement, and the dance sequence will be bland and dull."

"She burst into tears," wrote biographer Donald Spoto, "and ran into her dressing room but later regained her composure, wore the white socks, returned to the set and continued."

Later, upon seeing the brightly lit set for "On How to Be Lovely," Audrey went right back to wearing those black socks. Kay, on the other hand, wore high-heeled sandals that showed off her feet and ankles—which grabbed all the attention.

In hindsight, after comparing the two dance numbers on-screen, Audrey wrote Donen a note: "You were right about the socks—Love, Audrey." (The concept was later championed by Michael Jackson.)

When it came to accessorizing, Kay decided to don a steady stream of Cristóbal Balenciaga hats, a staple of Carmel Snow. The invoices were sent to the production and, thanks to Roger Edens, Kay was reimbursed without incident.

Obsessed with shoes, Kay selected her own footwear for the movie, too. From Capezio, Kay special-ordered a pair of sandals costing $131, and just because she was in a generous mood spending Paramount's money, she ordered a duplicate pair for her secretary. From Bergdorf Goodman, Kay requested a custom-made pair of heels costing $103, but when they did not fit properly, she gave them as a gift to Richard Avedon's then wife, Evelyn Franklin.

Thompson subscribed to her own adage: "If the shoe *doesn't* fit, *don't* wear it." In a 2002 interview, Lena Horne recalled, "The funniest Kay story was about Monsieur [René] Mancini, the custom shoemaker who made the most expensive shoes in the world. She was always fighting with Monsieur Mancini. Finally he got fed up with her saying the shoes didn't fit. 'Madame,' he said. 'God made your foot, I only make the shoe. Don't blame me, blame God.' Kay loved the story."

When it came to footgear, Kay was beyond compare. "The Wicked Witch of the East, North, West, and South" was how fashion illustrator Joe Eula remembered her. "Because all you had to do was look at her shoes. I mean, Kay always wore the wildest shoes in the world. Pointy. And my dear, they could stomp you to death. Those heels could crush anything."

Inspired by Thompson's footwear fetish, Avedon designed Thompson's credit tableau in the opening title sequence with a high-heel shoe silhouetted on black with single strips of pink and red fabric forming a *T* for "Thompson."

Kay became so renowned for her shoes that she was named on Michael Efremidis' International Ten Best Shod People List for 1957, alongside such well-heeled types as of the Duke of Edinburgh, spouse of the Queen of England.

So, when Kay had suggestions about shoes, or anything else regarding fashion, she threw her weight around. Privately, Edith wanted to choke her, but publicly, she toed the party line.

"[Kay is] a designer's dream," Edith gushed disingenuously to columnist Erskine Johnson. "You sketch her gowns and when she puts 'em on, she looks just like your sketch."

In actuality, every single one of Head's designs for Thompson was either radically revised or jettisoned altogether.

The songs for *Funny Face* were prerecorded from March 28 through April 6. Three-time Oscar winner Adolph Deutsch was hired to compose the incidental score, conduct a ninety-piece symphony orchestra, and assemble a team of Hollywood's best arrangers to divvy up the songs: Conrad Salinger ("He Loves and She Loves," "'S Wonderful," "How Long Has This Been Going On?"), Van Cleave ("Bonjour, Paris!"), Alexander Courage ("Funny Face," "Let's Kiss and Make Up"), Gus Levene ("Think Pink!" "On How to Be Lovely"), and Skip Martin ("Clap Yo' Hands")—all of whom had worked with Thompson in the past.

Though she received no credit, Thompson did the vocal arrangements for all her own numbers, and there is considerable speculation that she conducted the sixteen-member choir (eight men, eight women) throughout the score—just as she had done on so many MGM musicals in the 1940s.

"Kay and Fred were old hands at recording," Edens recalled, "but Audrey had never been before that frightening monster the microphone." In Kay's words, "The poor thing was doing something monumental in a hurry."

Just as Kay had coached Garland, Sinatra, and a hundred others, she was now called upon to work her magic on Hepburn. Realizing that Audrey had, as Donen put it, "a thin little voice," Kay would downplay her limitations, favoring simplicity and heartfelt sincerity. According to biographer Barry Paris, Kay instructed the young thrush "to employ a parlando style of speech-song and to concentrate on the lyrics."

"I am fairly proud of my voice in *Funny Face*," Hepburn later reflected. "A lot of people don't realize the movie wasn't dubbed. But Kay persuaded me I could hold my own. I'm so glad she did."

"Fortunately, the songs were perfect for her [range]," Kay explained. "She was very serious, very professional . . . [and] she loved it."

The move from MGM to Paramount had not only resurrected Edens' desire to cast Thompson in the film, now he was free to hire Richard Avedon as "visual consultant."

Before signing a contract in early February, however, Avedon made sure *Funny Face* got an official "blessing" from his bosses at *Harper's Bazaar,* Carmel Snow and Diana Vreeland, who had employed him steadily since 1945.

"We were all at Roger Edens' house," recalled Marion Marshall, "and we had these important women from *Harper's Bazaar* coming in and he was very nervous because he really wanted it to go well. Fairly sober, he went into the kitchen for something and came out absolutely falling-down drunk. It just *hit* him. I remember Kay got up to save the evening and took over the piano and started singing the songs with Lennie Gershe. It was like an *I Love Lucy* episode. And Kay was absolutely *furious* with Roger."

Ignoring Roger's drunken display, however, the fashion matriarchs were impressed and decided to cooperate with the production. Privately, Diana Vreeland told Avedon that she did not like the first name of Dana Prescott being so close to her own. So, Avedon sent a telegram to Paramount's legal department, dated February 7, 1956, strongly advising a name change. That's why, as of March 2, Thompson's character became known as Maggie Prescott.

Oddly, Avedon was not exclusive to Paramount, because on the very same date that he officially began work on *Funny Face,* he also commenced work as the "production creator" for CBS's *General Electric Theatre:* "Judy Garland Musical Special," to be broadcast live, Sunday, April 8, 1956—the night before shooting started on *Funny Face.* Judy's most trusted advisors—Thompson, Edens, and Gershe—had their hands full prepping *Funny Face,* and yet they still found time to help Garland and Avedon plan the TV program.

The first scenes Kay shot for *Funny Face* were the ones in the *Quality* magazine headquarters, requiring seven actresses to portray her brigade of assistants, including Ruta Lee as Lettie, her girl Friday.

"Kay was very cute about one thing," Ruta recalled. "At the time, the hot rage in the fashion world were these very flat little shoes like a dance slipper but they had these perforations in the top and two or three little straps that crossed. Stanley Donen got a bug up his ass saying that all of us girls were going to wear these shoes. So when we went in for fittings, Kay took one look at all of us waddling in these things and said, 'Tell you what, girls. When you show these flat shoes to the director and the producers, waddle in and slump down. Slump like *crazy.* And then, go put on your cute little shoes with heels and march right back in—shoulders up, chest out—looking like *fabulous* models.' And that's exactly what we did and we did *not* have to wear those friggin' little shoes. Thank you, Kay Thompson!"

For her big opening number, "Think Pink!" Kay wanted to roll a bolt of pink fabric toward the camera—sort of a "rolling out the red carpet" motif that would become one of her trademarks.

"We rehearsed with bolts of cheap muslin material," Ruta remembered. "But when we finally shot the scene, they replaced the muslin with this expensive pink fabric that rolled out at a much faster rate of speed—which took Kay and the rest of us by surprise. It took some getting used to—and quite a few takes."

Meanwhile, dance rehearsals were not going smoothly either. For the job of choreographer, Kay had wanted Bob Alton, with whom she'd collaborated so brilliantly on her nightclub act. But he and Edens had grown to detest each other. Audrey wanted Eugene Loring, with whom she had worked on *Sabrina,* and Fred wanted Hermes Pan, with whom he had worked on nearly everything. Naturally, Hepburn got her way.

Eugene Loring's assistant choreographer, Bruce Hoy, recalled, "Kay was very receptive and very open to anything and would try anything and offered her own suggestions. If she didn't like something, she would be very diplomatic about it and she would sometimes speak in her Eloise voice as a gimmick to erase tension. Her big dance number was 'Clap Yo' Hands.' We spent a lot of time on that."

As a lead-in for "Clap Yo' Hands," Miss Prescott and Avery (Astaire) don disguises and deep-fried Southern drawls (inspired by Thompson's routines) to crash a party at the home of the lecherous Professor Flostre (Michel Auclair), in order to save Jo (Hepburn) from his clutches.

According to the script, Prescott and Avery would sing and dance a "happy Southern spiritual with a beat" as they nonchalantly maneuver themselves upstairs where Jo is sequestered. In mid-March, Kay had an epiphany and recommended "Clap Yo' Hands," George and Ira Gershwin's upbeat showstopper from the 1926 Broadway hit *Oh, Kay!* Edens loved the idea, so Thompson collaborated day and night with orchestrator Skip Martin to work out the jazzy arrangement.

"Fred knew Kay was going to upstage him," Hugh Martin recalled, "and he did everything in the world to prevent it. He put in an understudy to work with her during rehearsals, trying to throw her."

"Fred was not happy with the number," Bruce Hoy confirmed. "There was a little ego problem."

Astaire called in reinforcement, at his own personal expense—overriding Edens' authority in the process. "Fred had his own choreographer around for 'Clap Yo' Hands'—Hermes Pan," Hoy recalled. "And there was friction back and forth between the two choreographers and Fred."

"Everything was a fight," Kay said, bluntly describing the fracas. "'Well, what do you want me to do?!' 'What is she doing over there?' It was that kind of thing."

"I remember Kay getting really upset when Fred was on the floor, scrounging around with his guitar," remembered Hoy. "Kay said, 'What the hell am I supposed to be doing while you're doing *that*?' And Fred said, 'Oh, you'll figure something.' And she did."

On May 23, when it came time to shoot "Clap Yo' Hands," tensions had reached a boiling point. Everyone was irritated because Fred had been in makeup for two hours getting his fake beard put on. Killing time on set, Kay suggested to Stanley that she could start the scene at the piano, where she could improvise a few piano chords as accompaniment to Fred's guitar intro.

"Stanley said to me, 'All right, Katie, go to the piano,'" Thompson recalled. "Fred came [onto the set] and . . . Stanley said, 'Okay, let's roll 'em.' I started [playing the piano] . . . 'La da da . . .'"

The piano chords came as a surprise to Fred so he interrupted the take, glared at Kay, and asked to start again. Take 2. As Kay started playing the piano a second time, Fred stopped and shouted, "Stanley, come here!"

"Stop the cameras," Stanley said. "Cut!"

"What is she doing at the piano?!" Fred chafed.

"She's doing what I asked her to do!" Stanley snapped back.

A hush fell over the set. Stanley called for a break while Fred retreated to his dressing room to stew. Kay found Audrey, vented every detail, and fumed, "I'm going to wipe the floor with that man."

After the time-out, shooting resumed. When the song ripped into its up-tempo beat, Kay took the lead vocal as if it were a rallying cry, relegating Fred to strum a guitar in the background. Fortunately, a break in the number slowed things down to a leisurely tempo—"Roses are red, violets are blue . . ."—allowing Fred to regain his footing. But the respite was brief. After only a few seconds of his quaint little soft-shoe routine, Kay bellowed, "LET'S-GET-THIS-SHOW-ON-THE-ROAD!" As the tempo shifted into hyperspace, Thompson surged forward to the staircase as if it were the invasion of Normandy, leaving Astaire in the dust.

"[Fred and I] had to go up these stairs [singing] 'Come a-long and join the jubi-*leeeeee*,'" Kay recalled. "We got to the top, turned around and Stanley said, 'Cut! Print! That's it!'"

Furious that the director was satisfied after only a couple of takes, Astaire could no longer bite his tongue. He grabbed Kay by the arm and sputtered, "Where did you learn balance?!"

"I just could have shot him," Kay recalled, "but didn't . . . I mean, it wasn't even worth a reply. You know, we can't waste the time."

It took two-and-a-half excruciating days to get "Clap Yo' Hands" in the can. The final result would *not* go down in history as Fred's most memorable turn, but as a showcase for Kay's underutilized talents, it was nothing short of bravura.

Before heading to Paris for location shooting, Kay took a red-eye to New York, arriving the morning of May 30. She resumed residence in her free suite at The Plaza for fifty-six hours—during which time she did a little *Eloise* biz, had a medical exam regarding the complications with Nose Job No. 5, and presumably paid a visit to Dr. Feelgood to load up on fresh supplies. On June 1, she flew to Paris and checked into Suite 11 at the Hôtel Raphaël, where twenty-two cast and crew transplants had set up camp for the summer.

Though Audrey and Fred were international icons, French reporters seemed most curious to speak to Kay because *Eloise* was being serialized in nine weekly issues of *Jours de France*, the French equivalent of *Life* magazine. By popular demand, Art Buchwald, who wrote a daily column for the Paris edition of the *New York Herald Tribune*, invited Kay to be a guest columnist on July 4, 1956, to relate—in Eloise style—her adventures at the Hôtel Raphaël. The essay began, "My name is Kay. I live at a hotel in Paris . . . Here's what I can do in the lobby. I can wait for Fred Astaire . . . or I can look in the mirror or I can practice smoking or I can talk to the concierge or wait for a taxi."

Just like Eloise, Kay was ready for adventure at every turn. Comic actor Paul Sand recalled meeting Kay in Paris at that time—when he was just a twenty-year-old student of Marcel Marceau. "I taught Kay that the greatest way to look at the Eiffel Tower is by standing on your head!" Paul noted. "She *did*, while I held her ankles!"

The Eiffel Tower was just one of thirty-eight exterior locations scheduled for *Funny Face* that June. Unfortunately, Mother Nature was not on their team.

"It rained almost the entire time we were there," Kay lamented.

While the filmmakers fretted, Kay turned the cloudy outlook into a bright opportunity. She convinced Stanley and Roger that it would be prudent to add rain gear to her ensemble for the "Bonjour, Paris!" montage. They agreed but pointed out that it was far too late for Edith Head to create something at Paramount and ship it to France.

"What a pity," Kay replied, raising her eyebrow. "I guess I'll just have to make do with something I find here in Paris." As Stanley nodded, Roger smiled knowingly.

Thompson jumped in a taxi and burned rubber all the way to the House of Givenchy, where Audrey was busy with last-minute fittings supervised by Hubert himself. Explaining her predicament, Kay persuaded the couturier to come to her rescue, resulting in the elegant camel-colored raincoat that she gladly wore *over* her clothes, concealing every last stitch of Head's duds throughout "Bonjour, Paris!" Thompson could barely contain her glee.

Tensions on set, however, continued to mount. "When Audrey, Fred, and Kay were at the top of the Eiffel Tower," related Mart Crowley, "Kay told me that they had to get off the elevator arm in arm on the same beat, but they never could get the right step out the door. And Fred said, 'It's Audrey's fault. She doesn't know what she's doing.' Kay turned fiercely to defend Audrey and said, 'It's not her at all. It's *you*.' She tore him up. Fred moved off to the side, dejected, and sat down on an apple box, leaned his chin on his umbrella, and said, 'Oh well, I guess I'm just an old queen.' And Kay said, 'You can say that again.'"

It didn't help that they were forced to spend so much time together. As Kay explained, "The three of us—Audrey, Fred and I—had to go in the *same* car, to go to the *same* hotel, so when [any one of us] wanted to say [in a huff], 'I'm leaving!', we couldn't do that because we had to wait until the car was coming and the three of us went home with your grievances—*all in the same car!*" (Their chauffeur was a diminutive Asian named Koki, whom Thompson immortalized in *Eloise in Paris* as the driver for Eloise and Nanny.)

Feigned congeniality made the car rides tolerable, but once they got behind closed doors in their individual hotel rooms, frustrations could no longer be contained. "I called [Audrey] after [Fred] had done this yelling," Kay confided, "and Audrey said [in her soft and polite voice], 'Yes, well, it *'tis* a bit of a strain.'" Thompson thought Audrey's response was "pure heaven" and often quoted it.

Fred's room was directly above Roger's and, each night, Astaire would keep him awake by clomping around the floor, rehearsing his dance steps until the wee hours of the morning. Roger later discovered that Astaire was holding secret rehearsals with Hermes Pan—who had surreptitiously come to France on Fred's dime. When Pan was spotted leaving early one morning, Astaire insisted the choreographer was in Paris by coincidence.

While Fred and Hermes were colluding at the hotel, Kay painted the town pink—often at Maxim's—with the likes of Doris Duke, Noël Coward, Ethel Merman, Anthony Quinn, Gina Lollobrigida, Zizi Jeanmaire, Billie and Stanley Marcus, and Gloria Swanson.

Thompson was also granted a private audience with the mayor of Paris, Pierre Ruais, and she presented him with a case of California wine. "I shall sip it with pleasure," he said, "after it has been chilled." In return, he gave her a silk scarf. As the meeting came to an end, Ruais "handed a 'Friend of Paris' diploma to Miss Thompson," which was all very exciting until he instructed, "Give that to Fred Astaire, *s'il vous plaît*."

If looks could kill, Thompson's must have been radioactive.

After sixty-two days of principal photography, Kay, Audrey, and Fred were gratefully wrapped on July 3, 1956.

Thompson attended the first screening of *Funny Face* at Paramount on October 5, 1956, with a guest list that included David Niven, Tony Martin and Cyd Charisse, Agnes Moorehead, Vincent Price, Rosemary Clooney, Jose Ferrer, Ann Sothern, Gloria Stuart and Arthur Sheekman, Don Loper, Betsy Blair (Mrs. Gene Kelly), Arthur Freed, Michael Kidd, Leonard Spigelgass (then writing the *Playhouse 90* adaptation of *Eloise*), Donen, Edens, Gershe, Ira Gershwin, Edith Head, and the inspirations for the leads, Richard Avedon and his ex-wife, Doe Avedon.

"Caught the sneak preview of *Funny Face*," wrote Hedda Hopper in the *Los Angeles Times*, "which should be retitled '*A Star is Born* with Kay Thompson.' She is sensational."

Mike Connelly wrote in *The Hollywood Reporter*, "Audrey Hepburn looks like a very, very cool million . . . And the screen really comes alive when Kay Thompson dances 'Clap Yo' Hands' with Astaire."

"Kay Thompson steals many a scene," reported Dorothy Kilgallen, "even from such formidable talents as Fred Astaire and Audrey Hepburn."

On February 4, 1957, *Funny Face* was screened for the first time on the East Coast, attended by Kay, Roger, and a large contingent of staffers from *Harper's Bazaar*. As the film unspooled, it was clear that the audience was eating up Thompson's fierce impression of Diana Vreeland—with one exception.

"A stony silence emanated from the direction of Vreeland," wrote biographer Penelope Rowlands.

At the conclusion of the movie, Diana's assistant editor, Barbara Slifka, recalled, "Mrs. Vreeland marched out saying, 'Never to be discussed.'"

An article about *Funny Face* in the British edition of *Harper's Bazaar* took the position that much of the film's depiction of the fashion magazine world was fiction: "Some of the frantic antics we recognize: the pictures lying about on the floor tend to be old *Harper's Bazaar* covers; but the pink doors and the uniform twittering young ladies are not true to office life. Kay Thompson, on the other hand, is anyone's idea of a fashion editor." No one could accuse the fashionistas of sour grapes, but the praise was so faint, it practically evaporated from the page.

Icy relations thawed *rawther* quickly, though. Before the year was out, Vreeland and Snow allowed Thompson to write a humor piece for the December 1957 issue of *Harper's Bazaar* entitled "Eloise's Christmas List."

Outside the fashion world, *Funny Face* was very well received. At the screening that left Vreeland cold, for instance, cheers erupted from Frank Sinatra, Judy Garland, Van Johnson, and Norma Shearer. Gloria Swanson requested a print for private viewing, then wired Edens that she thought it was "exquisite."

Lucille Ball hosted a screening party at her home in Beverly Hills with Thompson as guest of honor. Turner Classic Movies host Robert Osborne was there that night: "When 'On How to Be Lovely' came on, Kay got up and did the number. So, she's up on the screen with Audrey Hepburn *and* she's in front of the screen doing the number live. And I thought, 'Well now, *this* is fabulous.'"

Samuel Goldwyn was so impressed with the film, he sent a fan letter to Paramount's grand pooh-bah, Barney Balaban, declaring, "*Funny Face* is, by all odds, one of the finest musicals I have ever seen—on stage or the screen . . . Fred Astaire and Audrey Hepburn are simply marvelous . . . and Kay Thompson has opened up a new career for herself." The praise was so generous, especially coming from the competition, Paramount took out ads in *The New York Times* and *Daily Variety*, reprinting the letter in its entirety.

The charity gala world premiere of *Funny Face* was set for March 28, 1957, at New York's Radio City Music Hall to benefit the Hospitalized Veterans Service of the Musicians Emergency Fund. Exhausted from nonstop work, Audrey had decided to take a year off. With its primary star MIA, Paramount asked Astaire to escort Thompson to the opening but he flatly refused, preferring to take his sister, Adele, instead.

Upon hearing this, Kay decided it would be best to follow Audrey's lead and let the film speak for itself. At the time, Thompson was back in France with Hilary Knight doing additional research for *Eloise in Paris*, so she changed her return flight to several days *after* the premiere, creating the convenient excuse that she was "unavailable, working abroad."

Edens interceded by appealing to Thompson's ego. Audrey's absence, he argued, would allow Kay to become a major focus of the push behind the film. Otherwise, he added shrewdly, the publicity would end up being all about Fred. Enough said. Kay cut short her Paris trip and attended the premiere at Radio

City and the lavish after-party at the Waldorf-Astoria, covered via live remote hookup on *Tonight! America after Dark* (NBC-TV, March 28, 1957), the interim version of *The Tonight Show* between the reigns of Steve Allen and Jack Paar. Astaire did some *Face* time but steered clear of his costar, doing his best to ignore her.

"I saw him at the party," Kay recalled, "and he just looked at me like, 'Do we know each other?'"

After that, Kay was sent on a personal appearance tour to Boston, Philadelphia, Baltimore, and Washington, D.C., and became the spokesperson for Angelique Perfume, which launched a new fragrance, Pink Satin, as a tie-in between *Funny Face* and *Seventeen* magazine.

And, in exchange for a free automobile, BMW featured Kay in advertisements for its Isetta 300, the "microcar extraordinaire" with the door that opened in the front—like the one she and Fred had driven in *Funny Face*.

"With no other place to put it," noted the *Los Angeles Daily News*, "Kay Thompson parked her German midget car in The Plaza's tricycle garage." Gratis, of course. And in response to Kay's drumbeating, Elvis Presley bought one for himself and another for Colonel Parker.

On the morning of the *Funny Face* premiere, Kay was interviewed by her former flame, Dave Garroway, on *The Today Show* (NBC-TV) and, on April 14, she guest starred on *The Ed Sullivan Show* (CBS-TV). Kay was still in Paris when she learned that she was booked on the latter, so she decided to shop for something special to wear.

"Kay was very friendly with Pierre Balmain's *vendeuse*, Ginette Spanier," recalled Hilary Knight.

"She had a creep of a husband, Dr. Paul-Emile Seidmann," noted Kitty D'Alessio, former president of Chanel. "Ginette had a *real* relationship with Nancy Spain."

Spain was "a flamboyant society lesbian, writer, journalist and broadcaster," wrote Caroline Mitchell in her book *Women and Radio*, "often found at the social gatherings of the rich and famous, invariably wearing men's trousers and shirt or a suit." While Nancy exuded the stereotypical attributes of a "bull dyke," Ginette was a classic "lipstick lesbian."

Mocking her femininity, Thompson often referred to Spanier as "Muggsy," after Muggsy Spanier, the jazz musician. So, when Kay decided to get a dress for *The Ed Sullivan Show*, she simply rang up Muggsy and made an appointment.

"I went with Kay to Balmain," Hilary Knight recalled. "Balmain made for her—and *gave* her—this beautiful beige silk and chiffon evening dress."

"She went to many fittings at Balmain and finally the dress was ready," Mart Crowley related. "Kay took it back to the hotel and put it on but thought it was too stiff. So, she filled the tub and threw the Balmain into the water to soften it up a bit. A brand new Balmain!"

"She just wanted an excuse not to wear it," Knight concluded, "and so, after soaking in the bathtub, it shrank and it was completely ruined. She ended up wearing a suit. I'm not sure where she got that."

Wisa D'Orso, one of the regular dancers on *The Ed Sullivan Show*, recalled, "For rehearsal, I used to wear riding pants because they gave. Kay *loved* them and asked, 'Where'd you find those?' I said, 'Oh, at a store across from the Madison Square Garden'—back when the Garden was at Fiftieth Street and Eighth Avenue. She ran right there and bought herself a pair."

Rehearsed and coiffed within an inch of her life, Kay hit the Sullivan stage to perform one of her nightclub standards, "Quel Joie" (Kay Thompson), and a brand-new song entitled "Bazazz" (Kay Thompson–Ralph Blane), inspired by Miss Prescott's catchword in *Funny Face*. Taking advantage of the tie-in, "Bazazz" was rush-released as a single by Verve Records, the same label that was distributing the soundtrack album for *Funny Face*.

The opening day gross of $23,000 at Radio City Music Hall broke the house record, and according to the April 26 front page of *The Hollywood Reporter*, the fourth week's take of $214,777 was "the biggest one-week gross of any movie at any theater anywhere in the world in all history."

Thompson was unanimously heralded in all *seven* of New York's major daily newspapers as the hottest "newcomer" in showbiz. However, it was Elspeth Grant, critic for London's *Tattler and Bystander*, who most eloquently summed up the general consensus: "Miss Audrey Hepburn's performance in the title role of *Funny Face* is a complete ravishment—yet it is not the one I shall remember in stunned admiration whenever I think of this admirable musical. No: I shall remember Miss Kay Thompson as the ferociously efficient editress of a fashion magazine called *Quality*. Miss Thompson streaks comet-like into the cinema firmament—a luminary from the Outer Space of cabaret—and beside her the familiar stars look pale. She is the most dominant female personality to have struck the screen for quite a while and she handles every situation, every line, every song and every dance routine that comes her way with dazzling virtuosity."

Roger Edens collected the raves and sent copies to Audrey, who, on April 12, penned the following response: "Dearest Rogé . . . Hurray! Hurray! Please congratulate Kay for her fab reviews (and so they should be); may it mean many more successes for her."

"Kay Thompson's the happiest gal in New York over her success in *Funny Face*," wrote Hedda Hopper on April 5, "and has offers from every top TV show."

In May, *Funny Face* was presented at the Cannes Film Festival as one of the four official American entries. But while the majority of spectators ate it up, French movie critics spit it out. *The Hollywood Reporter*'s Samuel Steinman was a witness to the perplexing dichotomy, noting, "No film during the festival has received as much applause during its screening, but none of the French reviews was favorable." When the jury, led by Jean Cocteau, announced their award selections on May 17, *Funny Face* was snubbed in every category.

Somehow, the bubble had burst back in the States, too. As the movie spread to smaller, less sophisticated markets, the box-office receipts were nowhere near the bonanza generated in New York. Ultimately, the film grossed $3 million—a moderately successful amount in its day—but, given the picture's $3.1 million–plus budget, the thinking around the studio had gone from pink to red.

And then things got worse. Allied Artists decided to release its new Audrey Hepburn picture, *Love in the Afternoon*, on June 30, 1957. Suddenly, three-month-old *Funny Face* was yesterday's news. Theater owners wanted to exhibit the *latest* Audrey Hepburn movie, not her last one.

When Oscar nominations were announced on February 17, 1958, even without much support from its studio, *Funny Face* was cited in four categories: Best Screenplay (Leonard Gershe), Best Cinematography (Ray June), Best Costume Design (Edith Head and Hubert de Givenchy), and Best Art Direction-Set Decoration (Hal Pereira, George W. Davis, Sam Comer, Ray Moyer). But its absence from the Best Picture and other major categories spoke volumes about the apathy that had developed.

After Kay had been deified by nearly every critic in the land, it was especially astonishing that she had been overlooked in the Best Supporting Actress category. And in the end, the movie failed to win anything.

*E*ven though the *Funny Face* luster had faded, there was serious talk of a derivative television series built around Thompson. In early 1958, producer Ted Granik engaged two of Sid Caesar's top comedy writers, Mel Brooks and Michael Stewart (*Bye Bye Birdie, Hello, Dolly!*), to write *Pilot for Kay Thompson*, for which they were collectively paid $3,000.

According to the twenty-eight-page teleplay, Thompson was to portray Kay Baxter, editor of *Style* magazine, juggling her business affairs in Manhattan with domestic duties in Westchester, where her husband, two children, and a stuffy housekeeper constantly complain about her "gallivanting off to the city every day."

In this pilot episode, Kay is vying for exclusivity over "The Bag," a new collection of dress designs by France's top designer, "Jacques Deauville"—spoofing Yves Saint Laurent's recent "sack" dresses for the House of Dior.

"Think, if you will, of a common ordinary shopping bag stuffed full of dirty potatoes," Jacques explains. "You take *out* the potatoes and put *in* a lady!"

"The bag. The *bag*!" Kay paces excitedly, à la "Think Pink!" "I can see a whole issue devoted to it! Eight full-pages, and the cover! We could even have one of the dresses cut and made-up by Monday afternoon . . . in time for The Fashion Academy dinner at The Plaza Hotel."

Sound familiar? Perhaps too much so. NBC was gung ho for a while, then CBS, but the project never emerged from the depths of development hell. It was probably a blessing in disguise. The last thing Kay wanted—or needed— was to be typecast.

But that's what continued to happen. For instance, on *The Garry Moore Show* (CBS-TV, February 28, 1961), Thompson was asked to spoof her *Funny Face* duet with Audrey Hepburn. So, in a comedy sketch called "Frumpy Face," Kay sings "On How to Be Lovely" while transforming Carol Burnett from ugly duckling to fashion victim.

For laughs, Kay wore a positively outlandish ankle-length dress with matching jacket, spike heels, and a ribbon wrapping her hair up in the shape of a pillbox hat. But even though the wardrobe was supposed to be an over-the-top joke, Thompson took every detail very seriously. She told the costume designer, Robert Mackintosh, that the jacket must be "burgundy and no other shade! A silk velvet—thin, thin, thin! Balenciaga and definitely not Chanel."

The reverberations of *Funny Face* were far from over. After Warner Brothers struck gold with its enormously successful 1964 release of *My Fair Lady* starring Audrey Hepburn, Paramount rereleased *Funny Face* with posters and ads that proclaimed, "She's the Fairest Lady of All!" Box office results were so brisk, NBC snapped up the television rights and *Funny Face* was given a splashy prime time premiere on October 12, 1965. It was on this night that *Funny Face* finally found its mass audience. And Thompson, for better or worse, was lionized in the role with which she would forever be identified.

Chapter Ten

KAY'S FRANKENSTEIN MONSTER

Eloise Runs Amok
(1956–61)

I'd hate to call her a Frankenstein, but she scares me, just the same.
—Kay Thompson

"M iss Thompson is of the type which not only would launch a thousand ships but first would design and build them," declared *The New York Times* in 1957.

When it came to merchandising Eloise, however, Thompson couldn't do it all by herself. Richard Grossman of Simon & Schuster introduced her to another S&S executive, Robert L. Bernstein, who later became president of Random House. "Bob was a very sharp guy and he had been very instrumental in the development of both Golden Books and Golden Records at Simon & Schuster," explained Grossman. "I thought with his savvy, he and Kay would make great partners."

"So, Kay and I set up a little company called Eloise Limited," recalled Bob Bernstein, "and we started to merchandise the character. For about a year, I was allowed to moonlight for Kay while I was still working at Simon & Schuster. They gave me permission to do it."

Thompson named herself president and Bernstein was given the title of executive vice president. "She took sixty percent and I took forty percent," Bernstein recalled. "I think it was a three- or five-year deal."

In the fall of 1956, Kraft Foods, Inc., contacted Eloise Limited with an extraordinary proposal. "They wanted to use Eloise in all their advertising for Kraft Caramels, the way that Kleenex was using Little Lulu," said Bernstein. "They were going to guarantee us a quarter of a million dollars against whatever they spent."

But Thompson demurred: "Bob, we can't take the deal because Eloise doesn't like Kraft Caramels."

"Kay, for a quarter of a million dollars, she could really learn to love them," Bob argued.

"You just don't understand Eloise," Kay sniffed. "Eloise loves Rosemarie chocolates. Could you make the deal with Rosemarie?"

Rosemarie de Paris Chocolate Shops were the crème de la crème of ritzy tearoom sweeteries, but there were only a few locations, mainly in Manhattan. Bernstein tried to reason with Thompson. "They're not about to spend money for a national advertising campaign," he said. "Can Eloise adjust?"

"No, she can't," Kay insisted.

"So, we didn't make the deal," Bernstein concluded with a laugh. "It was tragic, but that was Kay."

Consequently, as of January 1957, Eloise Limited had zero earnings, making it difficult for Bernstein to justify his involvement. With sales of the book starting to ebb, there was growing pressure for Kay to deliver her sequel, *Eloise in Paris*, which had been languishing since the summer of 1956.

Eloise in Paris was to be the first in a series of "Around the World with Eloise" adventures. In interviews, Kay rattled off future book ideas such as *Eloise in London*, *Eloise in Rome*, *Eloise in Venice*, *Eloise on the Orient Express*, *Eloise in Hollywood*, *Eloise in Las Vegas*, and *Eloise Goes to Washington*. Thompson was only half joking when she quipped *Eloise in Phoenix, Arizona* ("It's such a strange place"). But for now, Eloise would explore the City of Lights.

According to illustrator Hilary Knight, "Kay didn't think we got enough material the first time in Paris."

Simon & Schuster refused to foot the bill for a *second* trip but that didn't stop Kay. Inspired by the product placement of TWA in *Funny Face* and American Airlines in the *Playhouse 90* production of "Eloise," Thompson got Bernstein to negotiate a "swap deal" with Sabena, the national airline of Belgium. In exchange for four round-trip tickets to Paris via Brussels, Kay would devote three full pages of *Eloise in Paris* to the airline. Furthermore, media outlets were supplied with photographs showing Kay and Hilary boarding a Sabena carrier on February 11, 1957, with Andy Williams and Bob Bernstein on hand to wave them off.

The freebies did not stop there. For Eloise's official Parisian home away from home, Kay finagled gratis accommodations at the Relais Bisson, where she and Dave Garroway had stayed in the summer of 1950. À la the Leaning Tower of Pisa, the Relais Bisson slanted to the right, so with no elevator, guests had to carefully navigate six flights of oblique stairs. They also had to put up with the hotel's cantankerous matron, Madame Dupuis, who is depicted quite accurately in the book.

"I would do documentary research with a camera and with a sketchbook," Hilary Knight explained. "And then we'd have meetings in Kay's hotel room and go over things. After we got back to New York, we'd meet in her apartment or mine."

Once the text and preliminary sketches were completed, it took Knight several weeks to draw the final illustrations. This freed Thompson to focus on merchandising. At the top of her agenda: a doll.

"We had a very hard time getting anybody interested in doing the Eloise doll," Bernstein recalled. "Most people regarded it as much too small a market. It wasn't Mickey Mouse."

After being rejected by Mattel, Madame Alexander, and American Character Doll Company, they finally secured a deal with an up-and-coming New York firm called Hol-le Toys, a partnership of Inez Holland House (the "Hol") and Morris Levitch (the "le").

In a 2001 interview, Hol-le's lead designer, Vilma Kurzer, recalled, "I usually worked in the factory in the Bronx, but Mr. Levitch called me down to the showroom in Manhattan, at 200 Fifth Avenue, to meet Kay Thompson and Hilary Knight. They showed me their book called *Eloise* and when I saw the pictures of this little girl, I said, 'Oh boy, let me get my hands onto this.'"

In late April 1957, Thompson collapsed at a restaurant and had to be rushed to the emergency room at New York's Mt. Sinai Hospital. In his column, Walter Winchell downplayed it as "just sheer exhaustion," but Earl Wilson gravely reported she had suffered "a stroke." When asked about it in 2002, Andy Williams recalled it as "a heart attack," but Vilma Kurzer agreed with the claim in *Daily Variety* that it was "an acute gall bladder attack" that required an emergency cholecystectomy.

While convalescing from whatever it was, Thompson conducted business meetings from her bed at Mt. Sinai. "When I was finished with the first sample of the Eloise doll," Vilma Kurzer explained, "I had to take it to her in the hospital for approval. She must not have been feeling too much pain because when she saw the doll, she jumped out of bed and started dancing with it." Manufacturing would move ahead for an October launch to support the November publication of *Eloise in Paris.*

Then, on July 23, 1957, Kay received word that Simon & Schuster vice president Jack Goodman, Thompson's main editor, had died suddenly of a cerebral hemorrhage at the age of forty-eight. In the wake of this tragedy, Nina Bourne, who had written wonderfully clever jacket and ad copy for *Eloise,* was assigned to finish editing *Eloise in Paris.*

"I tried to make it less hostile to Paris," Bourne recalled, "but Kay very agreeably undid most of my editing."

It hardly mattered. Published on November 14, 1957, *Eloise in Paris* flew out the door in record numbers, prompting ad copy that queried, "Does anybody know the French for *runaway?*" Within three weeks, the number of copies in print had to be increased to 100,000. It had taken five months for the first *Eloise* book to reach that plateau.

To the pleasant surprise of critics, Thompson had overcome the sophomore jinx with aplomb. "*Le brat magnifique,*" raved *Time* magazine. "Eloise observes the French scene with a sharp eye that would have done credit to Voltaire or Art Buchwald."

For trivia buffs, there were many interesting details. For instance, Alphonse Salomone, The Plaza's managing director depicted in the first book, had recently been transferred to the Caribe-Hilton in San Juan, Puerto Rico. So, for the second book, Thompson substituted general manager Gene Voit.

There was another new face, too. On page 10, a physician named Dr. Hadley makes a house call at The Plaza to administer a shot to Eloise—presumably an inoculation for her trip abroad. There is a chilling illustration of Eloise hiding under a pillow as the doctor forcefully clenches her arm, poised to strike with his hypodermic "zambo sting sting stinger."

In light of the fact that Kay was regularly receiving Dr. Max Jacobson's "pick-me-up" injections, this episode takes on an added layer of creepiness. Even the red flower on the doctor's lapel parallels Thompson's tradition of giving a rose to Jacobson every time they met.

When asked if the connection was deliberate, Hilary Knight said, "You could be right but it wouldn't have registered with me at the time. I knew many, many people who went to Dr. Jacobson and so it doesn't surprise me that Kay was involved. But nobody knew what amphetamines were back then."

On a happier note, the book is littered with surprise appearances. Just as Alfred Hitchcock popped up in his own films, Thompson and Knight appear on page 59, seated in a red banquette at Maxim's. There are also depictions of Kay's famous friends—in one case, without her knowledge. On pages 36–37, at Fouquet's sidewalk patisserie, you can spot Lena Horne and her husband, Lennie Hayton, as "extras" seated near Eloise.

"Kay was furious when she found out I had done that without consulting her first," Knight confessed. "She should have seen it in the proofs but she didn't notice it until after it was published. Kay never liked *anything* she didn't instigate but, of course, Lena and Lennie were absolutely thrilled by it."

Other celebrity cameos included Richard Avedon as Eloise's passport photographer. "That was planned," said Hilary. "So was the Christian Dior page, which was based on an actual visit we made to his salon."

On page 51, Dior is seen designing a dress for Eloise. Nearby, an unnamed twenty-one-year-old protégé holds a sheath of pink fabric. The young man turned out to be Yves Saint Laurent.

Also on the Dior page is a bejeweled lady in a turban who ponders the unsightly state of Eloise's flyaway hair. Some readers jumped to the conclusion that this must be Eloise's elusive mother, but she was, in fact, Madame Germaine "Mitza" Bricard, Dior's "empress-muse," a high-society *vendeuse* "never seen without her turban and pearls."

In a case of life imitating art, Dior had just created the black evening gown Kay wore on *The Standard Oil 75th Anniversary Show* (NBC-TV, October 13, 1957). Just ten days after the broadcast, Dior died of a heart attack. Kay flew to Paris to attend the funeral alongside the Duchess of Windsor, Jean Cocteau, Coco Chanel, Hubert de Givenchy, Pierre Balmain, Pierre Cardin, Cristóbal Balenciaga, Carmel Snow of *Harper's Bazaar*, 2,500 other mourners inside the church, an overflow of 7,000 outside, an ocean of flowers, and two humongous wreaths sent by Marlene Dietrich and Olivia de Havilland.

By the time *Eloise in Paris* was published three weeks later, Yves Saint Laurent had been named head designer for the House of Dior. While newspapers scrambled to find pictures of the heir apparent to the fashion throne, Kay and Hilary had already immortalized him in *Eloise in Paris*. Talk about au courant.

Thompson had also turned product placement into an art form long before Madison Avenue got on the stick. In addition to the pact with Sabena Airlines, she signed a one-year "swap deal" with Renault, the French car maker, for Eloise to be a spokesperson for the company's Dauphine automobiles. Seven different illustrations of the car appeared in *Eloise in Paris* and the automobile was mentioned twice in the text.

Reciprocally, Eloise starred in advertisements for Renault Dauphine in *Esquire, The New Yorker, National Geographic,* and *Holiday.* In lieu of monetary compensation, Kay got a free Dauphine, but because she already owned a Jaguar XK125 and a BMW Isetta microcar, she sold it to Noël Coward.

Eloise in Paris was chock full of other promotional plugs for Balmain, Hermès, Maxim's, the Ritz, Macy's, the Irving Trust Company, Gristedes Market, Johnnie Walker Black Label scotch, Perrier, the *New York Herald Tribune* (Paris edition), Band-Aid bandages, Hoover vacuum cleaners, and, of course, The Plaza.

In support of the book, a whole array of Eloise merchandise was ready to hit the stores, including Eloise French Postcards (which folded out like an accordion) and an elaborate Eloise Emergency Hotel Kit—a ten-inch hat box stuffed with such necessities as a "Sleep with Me Eloise" pillow; an Eloise "Do Not Disturb" sign; a picture of the house detective ("who is Mr. Matthews, just in case"); and a wooden resting block ("for exhausted chewing gum").

"We got different companies to contribute their products to be in the kit," Bernstein noted. These included Crayola crayons, Jujubes candy, Bazooka bubble gum, and ten thousand travel-size tubes of Pepsodent toothpaste. "We sold about eight thousand kits, so we had about two thousand tubes of toothpaste left over," Bob laughed. "For the next several years, I was giving them away at Halloween at our house in Scarsdale. We were not popular."

To go with the new Eloise dolls, Kay designed "Eloise Fashions," a line of doll clothes and matching life-size versions for young girls. According to *Good Housekeeping,* the breast pocket of the Eloise Car Coat had an embroidered Renault automobile emblem patch that made it "perfect for tricycling through the halls of The Plaza." It also helped justify the freebie automobile.

Naturally, the Plaza gift shop and the neighboring FAO Schwarz toy store were on board as outlets for Eloise products—but that was just the tip of the iceberg. When a deal with Rosemarie de Paris failed to congeal, Schrafft's became the official sweetery for Eloise, with merchandise available at checkout counters. Of even greater value, the entire line of Eloise products would be carried by several major New York department stores, including Saks Fifth Avenue, Lord & Taylor, Bonwit Teller, Best & Co., and, most amusingly, Bloomingdale's, which gave all its employees a special "Eloise's Guide for Bloomingdale's Sales People" written "in Eloise's *rawther* unusual style."

With New York setting the pace, more than one hundred trendsetting department stores around the country jumped on board, including Neiman-Marcus of Dallas, based on Thompson's long-standing personal friendship with Billie and Stanley Marcus.

On page 16 of *Eloise in Paris,* Kay included the following quote: "My mother has a charge account at Neiman-Marcus." This little mention helped instigate a grand annual tradition that would reverberate for the next thirty years. As it happened, 1957 marked the store's fiftieth anniversary, and to commemorate this milestone, Stanley Marcus wanted to organize a cause célèbre in October, a fête that would attract consumer and media attention. In his search for a theme, Kay's timely love affair with France rubbed off, because the extravaganza evolved into "The French Fortnight" with Thompson, "star of *Funny Face* and author of *Eloise in Paris*," crowned "Special Guest of Honor" and behind-the-scenes "Creative Consultant."

To salute the event, Coco Chanel and a hundred other dignitaries from Paris were flown in on a chartered Air France plane, the first international flight to land at the Dallas Airport. The October 1, 1957, issues of both the American and French editions of *Vogue* devoted thirty-five pages to the bazaar, with full-page ads from A to Z representing name-brand sponsors: "A is for Air France," "B is for Baccarat," "C is for Chanel," "D is for Dior," etc.

Time called the $400,000 event "the biggest birthday party ever attempted by any U.S. department store." Amid Gallic art, decor, food, and haute couture, Eloise got her own three-dimensional in-store and window displays. Plus, fashion shows featuring the latest collections of Dior, Balmain, and Nina Ricci were upstaged by surprise intrusions of mischievous youngsters wearing Thompson's embroidered "Je Suis Me" smocks, "Allo Cherie" aprons, and "Renault Dauphine" car coats. The *Denton Record-Chronicle* reported, "Kay Thompson was in the audience and made entertaining comments when little girls modeling Eloise dresses appeared."

Beyond everyone's wildest expectations, the expo drew World's Fair–like hordes of tourists and opinion makers from around the globe. Long before the event was over, Stanley Marcus was being asked the same question everyone was asking Thompson: "What country are you going to feature next year?"

And so, by popular demand, Neiman-Marcus began hosting annual Fortnight expositions—Britain was chosen for 1958—while Thompson told *The New York Times* that for her next Eloise adventure, "I think she'll visit England." Synergy, anyone?

Three days before the official publication of *Eloise in Paris*, Bob Bernstein left Simon & Schuster, freeing himself to focus all his energies on Eloise Limited while the iron was red-hot.

"I talked The Plaza Hotel into giving us a free office on the first floor above the lobby, Room 107," Bernstein recalled.

Bernstein brought along his secretary, Jill Herman, to be publicity director. "Kay immediately nicknamed me Jilloise," Herman said, "and, aside from legitimate Eloise business, she had me picking up cosmetics, taking shoes to the shoemaker, you name it. Nothing was off-limits."

That included walking and/or babysitting Kay's brand-new pug dog—a real-life manifestation of Eloise's Weenie. Thompson dubbed him Fenice ("feh-NEE-chay")—Italian for "phoenix"—named after Teatro La Fenice, the historic opera house in Venice, Italy.

"That dog was her child," recalled Jill Herman. "Absolutely. She tried to take him just about everywhere she went—even into restaurants that didn't allow dogs. She could talk her way into anywhere and anything."

Her "darling baby boy" was spoon-fed braised chicken liver and constantly rewarded with Chuckles jelly candies. "The green lime ones are his favorites," she'd dote.

In order to escape Eloise during her off-hours, Kay decided to give up free accommodations at The Plaza and rent an apartment three blocks north at 9 East Sixty-second Street, a brownstone building just off Fifth Avenue, one block south of Andy Williams' bachelor pad. "There was only one bedroom," recalled model China Machado, "but it had a huge living room, all with twenty-foot ceilings. There were two beautiful antique chests that she'd painted orange and I said, 'Oh my God?! How could you do that?!' And she said, 'You can have them.' You know, I can't even begin to tell you how crazy she was, but I *adored* her. She was just so fantastic."

Sales expectations for Eloise products were high, but none of the manufacturers were prepared for the level that Thompson was about to generate. Consumer awareness detonated with the November 20, 1957, installment of *The Today Show* when Dave Garroway introduced Thompson and her Eloise dolls to millions of home viewers. Kay also appeared on many other television and radio programs, including a December episode of *The Helen Hayes Story Circle*, a syndicated radio series broadcast each week from Miss Hayes' landmark mansion, Pretty Penny, in Nyack, New York.

Having just read *Eloise in Paris*, Hayes observed, "You're getting to be quite a traveler these days."

"Yes," Kay replied in the haughty voice of Eloise. "I am *rawther* a *voyageur*. Here's where I've been: Central Park and Paris, France. And now, Nyack. I do quite a lot of traveling."

A December ad campaign for Cannon sheets featured the Eloise doll, FAO Schwarz included the doll in its Christmas mail-order catalog, and magazine coverage was unprecedented. Four Eloise dolls adorned the cover of the

December issue of *Good Housekeeping*; inside was a full-color pictorial entitled "Fashions for Eloise," featuring a young girl modeling the new line of Eloise children's clothes in familiar poses around The Plaza.

That same issue of *Good Housekeeping* introduced an all-new Eloise adventure entitled "Kay Thompson's Eloise at Christmastime," an exclusive four-page spread with fresh drawings by Hilary Knight and text by Thompson written in rhyming verse—an Eloise first. A sample stanza: "There's quite a bit of racket, but here's the thing of it: Mr. Voit, the manager, doesn't mind a bit."

Kay also wrote a one-page advice column in the December issue of *Harper's Bazaar* called "Charge It, Please—Eloise's Christmas List." It was essentially Eloise's guide to Christmas shopping, with such advice as "Will you kindly send over a little petite of quelque chose gift wrapped for me Eloise? And charge it please and thanks a lot."

And then, for the third time in two years, in its December 9, 1957, issue, *Life* magazine devoted a spread to Eloise showing a young girl surrounded by Eloise dolls, clothes, hotel kits, and, most spectacularly, two forty-three-inch, life-size Eloise dolls that Hilary Knight later joked were "a little scary."

Singer Nat King Cole ran into Kay and asked where he could get one of those humongous Eloise dolls for his seven-year-old daughter. Thompson told him mass production had been put on hold so that the factory could concentrate on the smaller ones. Nat seemed so disappointed, until a delivery arrived later that day from Kay, containing one of the gigantic prototypes (of which only seven were made).

Natalie Cole said it was her favorite present ever, and that she identified with Eloise's Plaza antics. "Her primary delight in life was raising hell with the staff, roller-skating in the hallways, pushing all the buttons in the elevator, and in general making a pest of herself—like me that Christmas morning."

With the onslaught of media coverage, Hol-le Toys was suddenly deluged with orders for the regular-size Eloise doll.

"The factory was small, only about forty-five people," noted Vilma Kurzer. "So we stayed open around the clock, three shifts. But the manager wasn't capable of running a big production and we couldn't make enough for all the deliveries that were demanded for Christmas. I remember the chaos. It was *unbelievable*."

In the midst of this bedlam, Bernstein told Thompson he'd gotten an offer he couldn't refuse—to become sales manager at Random House under Bennett Cerf, effective January 1, 1958.

"You can keep your Thompson thing," Cerf told Bernstein. "We just want you here."

"It turned out to be the greatest break in my life," Bernstein reflected, "because I eventually became president of Random House in 1966."

To ensure she would not be forgotten, Thompson devised a secret plan of attack.

"On my first day at Random House," Bernstein explained, "I opened the door to my office and four pigeons flew out. There was a gigantic sign on my desk that read, 'Welcome to Random House,' signed 'Eloise.'"

"Okay, Kay, where are you?" Bob called out.

The door to the closet creaked open and out stepped Thompson with a devilish grin.

"Kay, it's my first day," Bernstein shrugged. "Could you get those goddamn pigeons out of here?!"

"Now calm down, Bob," she said with a smirk. "You don't think these are ordinary pigeons, do you? These are *showbiz* pigeons. I have their owner right here and they'll be back in their cage in a few minutes because they are trained."

Famous last words. "Three hours later," Bernstein recalled, "the man was still chasing these pigeons all over Random House. I became instantly very well known."

Meanwhile, the folks at Simon & Schuster were marketing *Eloise in Paris* full steam ahead. By year's end, having sold nearly 125,000 copies in a mere six weeks, *Eloise in Paris* ranked as the No. 6 bestselling fiction book of 1957.

As 1958 got under way, Bob Bernstein was devoting more and more of his time to new business at Random House—including the hot new series of children's tomes by Dr. Seuss (the pen name for Theodor Geisel) published by the Beginner Books division. Dr. Seuss' most recent works, *The Cat in the Hat* and *How the Grinch Stole Christmas!* had both been unleashed in 1957, posing serious threats to *Eloise in Paris* during the highly competitive holiday season.

"I've worked myself into an absolute frenzy thinking about merchandising Dr. Seuss," Bernstein wrote in a memo to his new boss. The timing could not have been worse for Kay because she desperately needed Bob's undivided attention.

The unprecedented demand for Eloise dolls had brought Hol-le Toys to its knees. "It got so bad that the owner, Morris Levitch, had a nervous breakdown and disappeared," recalled Vilma Kurzer. "His wife, Betty Gould, tried to run the company and carry on, but it didn't work. The whole company went out of business within six months. Betty and Mr. Levitch ended up divorced. It was catastrophic."

In addition to this crisis, there were a number of pending deals that needed to be finalized, including a line of Eloise Easter bonnets designed by the world-renowned milliner Mr. John (formerly of John-Frederics) and "an Eloise radio show with Eloise starring as disc jockey." But without the concentrated follow-through that Bernstein had provided in the past, Thompson managed to bungle these deals by making unreasonable demands. With the future of Eloise Limited in crisis, it was obvious that Kay's ying needed Bob's yang. To truly justify his involvement, though, Random House needed to be a beneficiary.

"I said to Kay, 'I would love it if you would come here,'" Bernstein remembered. "And she said, 'Fine. We'll do our next book at Random House.' Needless to say, Simon & Schuster was furious."

With no option clause for sequels in her Simon & Schuster contract, Kay was free to go wherever she pleased, and it just made more sense to have Bernstein overseeing all things Eloise. Business was business.

Kay had already announced *Eloise in London* as the next sequel, but extensive research and development in England had not yet been done. Bernstein did not want to wait; he needed something to come out in time for the Christmas buying season of 1958 to help drive merchandising deals.

"We had already done a short version of *Eloise at Christmastime* in *Good Housekeeping*," Hilary Knight recalled, "so it was already all laid out—at least roughly."

Under pressure, Kay agreed to delay *London* for instant gratification. On May 2, 1958, Random House announced that it would publish *Kay Thompson's Eloise at Christmastime* on September 22 with a first printing of 100,000 copies.

In order to make the publication date, *Christmastime* would have to be completed in record time. Complicating matters, Knight had another project on his drawing board, *The Wonderful World of Aunt Tuddy* (Random House, 1958), by Jeremy Gury, about a "slightly cracked" spinster who spends "six or seven hours a day" in a department store "buying practically nothing." The book was "based on an idea by Max Hess," owner of Hess Brothers department store in Allentown, Pennsylvania—which just happened to be the exclusive local outlet for Eloise merchandise. Hess was hoping that Aunt Tuddy might do for department stores what Eloise had done for hotels. In both cases, the books' heroines were strong-willed individualists who tested the patience of the staff of their respective domains.

"I was working on *Aunt Tuddy* at the same time for the same publisher," Knight recalled, "and Kay was not pleased about that."

Because *Eloise at Christmastime* was such a rush job, detailing was kept to a minimum, with only one celebrity cameo (Rita Hayworth) and two corporate sponsors (Guinness Stout beer and The Plaza).

It was a bit of a miracle, but *Eloise at Christmastime* hit stores right on schedule, poised to jump-start merchandising machinations well in advance of the holiday season.

In the wake of Hol-le Toys' demise, American Character Doll Company, which had previously rejected the Eloise doll, was only too happy to come to the rescue of the now-established goldmine. At the same time, a brand-new collection of Thompson-designed "Eloise Fashions" was introduced, in doll and life sizes, including the White Christmas Tree Apron Dress, the Think Pink Rose Dress (with "the Longest Long-Stemmed Rose Belt"), and the White Terry Robe with three "What-Goes-Where Pockets" embroidered "Brush," "Soap," and "Mitt" (featuring "Skipperdee's Turtle-Shaped Puppet Scrub Mitten").

There was a lot to promote, yet just four days after *Eloise at Christmastime* hit bookstores, Kay made the surprise announcement that she was leaving for England.

Lagging one year behind their respective American release dates, the Eloise books were being published in the United Kingdom by Max Reinhardt, Ltd. (no relation to the Austrian director). The first book had become a huge bestseller on British soil, and, according to historian Judith Adamson, it had gotten an "enthusiastic" endorsement from Queen Elizabeth, who "had read the book to her children"—nine-year-old Prince Charles and seven-year-old Princess Anne.

Anticipation was building to a fever pitch for *Eloise in Paris*, due to be launched in the UK on October 6, 1958. So, when Reinhardt invited Thompson to come to England for an all-expense-paid publicity tour, she readily accepted—especially since the trip would conveniently double as research for *Eloise in London*.

Media coverage of Kay's advent rivaled a papal visitation. With the blessing of Buckingham Palace, the Foreign Secretary of Great Britain, Baron Selwyn-Lloyd, was dispatched to London Airport for a ceremonial greeting amid a phalanx of paparazzi and gawkers. One of Selwyn-Lloyd's bodyguards was assigned to protect Thompson from the waiting mob.

Amid an explosion of flashbulbs, Kay joked, "I love this hick town!"

Then she was whisked via Rolls-Royce motorcade to the Savoy, where, dressed to kill in black Dior, she held court at a press conference in the illustrious Lancaster Ballroom—site of the 1953 Coronation Ball for Queen Elizabeth.

Tirelessly, Thompson toured stores in and around London for book signings and readings. Merchants created elaborate displays with Eloise dolls, bottles of French champagne, extralong loaves of French bread, and live Skipperdee the Turtle petting exhibits.

Kay also did a slew of radio and television shows. The most prestigious was on October 8, 1958, when she appeared on the live debut broadcast of *Riverside One* (BBC-TV), a top-drawer variety show produced by British showman Francis Essex and regularly hosted by actress Margaret Lockwood (star of Hitchcock's *The Lady Vanishes*). Sharing the guest roster with actor Trevor Howard and several others, Kay performed "I Love a Violin" and "Eloise."

"Kay was the most expensive guest we had on the entire series, by a wide margin," Francis Essex related in 2008. "I still have the cost reports right here, which show that I paid Trevor Howard £262 [U.S. $733] for his appearance; Margaret Lockwood, the regular host, was paid £210 [U.S. $588] per show; and all the other guests that first week were paid around £190 [U.S. $532]— except for one person: Kay Thompson. She cost me £750 [U.S. $2,100] off my budget! Kay was in a class by herself."

Having succumbed to Thompson's chicanery, Brits were simply head over heels for Eloise, with the venerable *London Times* jointly placing *Eloise* and *Eloise in Paris* among its "Top 10 Literary Pleasures of 1958." The newspaper's year-end round-up declared, "For sophisticated amusement they cannot be easily bettered."

At the end of her British tour, Kay wrote in *TV Times* (the British equivalent of *TV Guide*), "I am going to swoosh back to America with strict instructions from my publishers to write *Eloise in London,* which will be great fun." According to her preliminary notes, Eloise was destined to cross paths with Nanny's brother, "a bobby in Piccadilly Circus."

By mid-October, Kay was back on native soil to resume promotional duties for *Eloise at Christmastime*. In addition to large display ads in metropolitan newspapers, Eloise merchandise infiltrated many major Christmas catalogs, including FAO Schwarz, Bullock's, Best & Co., Roos/Atkins, and Robinson's (which made Eloise its cover girl).

The most anticipated catalog every year, however, was that of Neiman-Marcus, and for 1958, the store devoted a full page to Eloise. Neiman-Marcus was famous for its "His & Hers" merchandise; as a clever send-up of that tradition, the store was offering exclusive Eloise Bath Towel and Washcloth sets and Eloise Two-Legged Christmas Stockings, all embroidered "Mine."

Hallmark broached the idea of putting out a line of Eloise Christmas cards, but, typically, Kay botched the discussions. And her negotiations with Cadence Records for an Eloise album went no better. Unable to come to terms, she bought back the rights to the "Eloise" single. Her plan was to record the rest of the songs with her own money and shop the entire LP to other labels.

One tangible result of this work in progress was "It's Absolutely Christmastime" (Kay Thompson), performed by Thompson (as Eloise) with a male chorus led by Andy Williams. A one-sided promotional single was pressed in limited quantities for broadcast on radio shows promoting the book *Eloise at Christmastime*. Otherwise, Kay possessively held the song in abeyance for inclusion on the *Eloise* LP—if that ever materialized.

Despite these missed opportunities, media hype was in full swing. At the office of Eloise Limited, surrounded by Eloise products, Kay posed for publicity photos and granted interviews for virtually every major publication. For television, she made guest appearances on *The Garry Moore Show* (CBS-TV, December 2, 1958) and on *three* installments of *The Tonight Show Starring Jack Paar* (NBC-TV, September 22, December 9, and December 19).

But the reviews of *Eloise at Christmastime* were decidedly mixed. "Her bite isn't so sharp as it was," noted Ellen Lewis Buell in *The New York Times*, "even though she is still very funny to watch in Hilary Knight's pictures."

Kay was devastated. More than ever, Hilary's drawings had upstaged her verbiage. Making matters worse, several critics chose to jointly review *Eloise at Christmastime* along with *The Wonderful World of Aunt Tuddy*, which shifted the spotlight toward those books' common denominator: Hilary Knight.

Anne Nicholson of the *Chicago Daily Tribune* felt that Thompson's text "on its own would sink," but, like *Aunt Tuddy*, was "rescued" by Knight, who "has given [both books] their glories."

The blow was somewhat softened by the fact that, at year's end, *Eloise at Christmastime* was declared the No. 6 bestselling fiction book of 1958—beaten only by *Doctor Zhivago* by Boris Pasternak (No. 1); *Anatomy of a Murder* by Robert Traver (No. 2); *Lolita* by Vladimir Nabokov (No. 3); *Around the World with Auntie Mame* by Patrick Dennis (No. 4); and *From the Terrace* by John O'Hara (No. 5).

That was heady company, but unlike the first two Eloise books, which had flourished well beyond Christmas, *Eloise at Christmastime* had a built-in expiration date. And, after December 25, there was just no market for the Eloise Christmas Tree Apron Dress and the Eloise Two-Legged Christmas Stocking.

As sales screeched to a halt, Jill Herman announced she was leaving Eloise Limited to get married. And Bernstein was becoming more and more consumed with other Random House concerns, especially the Dr. Seuss franchise, which, with a considerably more cooperative author, was transformed into an enduring, multimillion-dollar empire.

When asked if Thompson felt threatened by the attention Bob was lavishing on Seuss, Bernstein replied, "Maybe . . . but she never said anything." Her actions, however, spoke louder than words.

The New Year of 1959 had barely gotten off the ground when Richard Grossman convinced Kay to return to Simon & Schuster. Rather than the expected *Eloise in London,* though, he endorsed the idea of doing *Eloise in Moscow.*

"I mean, what a lark!" Grossman chuckled. "The juxtaposition of this indolent child of the rich and pampered going to a socialist republic was just too irresistible. And it really caught Kay's fancy."

Jumping into action, applications were submitted in January 1959 to send Thompson and Knight to Russia for four weeks to soak up atmosphere for their new book. The Soviet propaganda machine discouraged negative portrayals of its country and so, instead of promoting the satirical sociopolitical implications of Eloise blowing the Iron Curtain wide open, Thompson tactfully claimed on her visa application that she would be visiting Russia as "a tourist," curious "to learn how entertainers work and live in that country." Permission granted.

"Kay decided she should wear nothing but fezzes, so she went to Mr. John, the famous hatter, and he made ten fezzes for her," Hilary recalled. Then she bought this big, red fur coat. It looked like fox but it was vicuña."

On February 16, 1959, at a dramatic press conference held in the Eloise Room at The Plaza, Kay made a grand entrance modeling this Bolshevik winter coat, "clutching its big woolly collar tightly up over her ears." And the following day, the diva made an even grander exit—with a bon voyage party that included her sister Blanche (who'd come up from Virginia just for the occasion).

"I hired what was then the only Rolls-Royce limousine service in New York," remembered Richard Grossman, "run by a black man named Roosevelt Zander. I thought this was the offbeat way Kay and Hilary should be taken to the airport and she loved it."

Traveling with Kay and Hilary was Howard Haines, thirty-three, a high-powered press agent for Arthur Jacobs Public Relations, whose clients included Garland, Dietrich, Monroe, Elizabeth Taylor, and Princess Grace.

After changing planes in Paris, the threesome arrived in Moscow during a snowstorm. "We walked into the terminal *loaded* [with luggage]," Kay said. "There were no porters, so between the two Italian bags I had, the tape recorder, the typewriter, my purse which was heavier than my head, bongos . . ."

Bongos?!

"Yes, bongos,"Thompson reiterated. "I thought I might run into some cats."

"We were taken to the Hotel Ukraina," Hilary said, "which was a charmless marble mausoleum in a town painted shades of ochre and mustard."

The following morning, they were introduced to Aida, a short and stout battle-axe who spoke broken English in a heavy Slavic accent. Ostensibly assigned to be their "guide," Aida worked for Intourist, a division of the KGB that monitored "foreigners' access to, and travel within, the Soviet Union." Aida did not look the part of a Russian femme fatale out of an Ian Fleming novel, but she was a spy nonetheless.

"Every place we went had to be cleared with Aida ahead of time," Knight explained. "She would tell us what IS POSSIBLE and what IS NOT POSSIBLE." And this is exactly how Aida would be depicted in *Eloise in Moscow*—though her name would be changed to Zhenka to save them from POSSIBLE EXTERMINATION.

"YOU WILL SEE EVERYTHING," Aida barked.

"'DA!' we chorused, and we did," Hilary noted.

Aida took them on a tour of the Kremlin and other government buildings—which were all very nice but not the sort of entertainment Thompson was craving.

Then, on February 25, Kay got wind that there was going to be a gala command performance of *Romeo and Juliet* by the Bolshoi Ballet for Soviet Premier Nikita Khrushchev and the visiting Prime Minister of Great Britain, Harold Macmillan. By happenstance, Macmillan was accompanied by Baron Selwyn-Lloyd, Britain's Foreign Secretary, who, just four months earlier, had personally welcomed Thompson to London.

Refusing to accept "IS NOT POSSIBLE," Kay explained that she was a friend of Selwyn-Lloyd. Then, as if by magic, three of the best seats in the house were suddenly "POSSIBLE."

"We were on the fourth row," Thompson marveled, "surrounded by all kinds of press—America, British."

"Khrushchev slept through most of the ballet," said Howard Haines, "but he'd be awake during the intermission for all the cameras and photographers."

Mingling with the press, Hilary discovered that one of his childhood chums was residing in Moscow. "Nancy Jones was a neighbor and classmate of mine in the 1940s," he recalled. "Nancy had married Irving R. Levine, the famous NBC news broadcaster who always wore a bow tie. At the time, he was the Russian correspondent for NBC so he and Nancy were living at the National Hotel. We looked them up and Kay and I had tea with them."

Through Levine, Thompson swiftly befriended other members of the U.S. press corps—all of whom used the National Hotel as a hub of operations. By contrast, Thompson was squirreled away in the Ukraina, not the favored meeting ground for free thinkers.

"We've *got* to be at the National," Kay declared.

"IS NOT POSSIBLE," was Aida's blunt response. "TO MOVE HOTELS YOU MUST LEAVE MOSCOW AND RETURN."

So be it. Off they went on a five-day side trip to Leningrad, where they visited the Hermitage Museum, a one-ring circus, the subway, and *another* gala for Britain's Prime Minister Macmillan and Foreign Secretary Selwyn-Lloyd—a ballet, *The Stone Flower*, starring Maya Plisetskaya (later a girlfriend of Warren Beatty).

Late Sunday night, March 1, they boarded an overnight train back to Moscow. "On the train," Hilary recalled, "Kay was assigned a cabin with this man none of us knew—and she *panicked*. She said to Howard, 'You've got to let me stay with Hilary. You have to sleep with this man.' She was petrified."

The incident inspired the sinister drawing in *Eloise in Moscow*, on page 57, of the nosy man leaning over the top berth to leer at Eloise.

As promised, they were now allowed to check into the National, described by Knight as "a hotel with nothing but old-world charm and mystery." Located in Red Square across from the Kremlin, the landmark is revered for its facade of ornate stonework depicting everything from nymphs to train engines. And the lobby is a breathtaking display of marble and larger-than-life statuary. This was more in keeping with the storied splendor Thompson had in mind.

With renewed determination, they hit palaces, mosques, cemeteries, museums, zoos, parks, and the tombs of Lenin and Stalin. "Their corpses were on display," Knight recalled, "stretched out for the world to see. They were so spooky-looking—and Kay was really upset by it."

Then Thompson explored GUM (Glavnyi Universalnyi Magazin), a massive shopping mall with hundreds of merchants. "I went to one beauty shop and I might just as well have stayed out," Kay said, "because the soap isn't good and your hair is less divine for having gone in."

There was, however, one pleasant surprise. "I'd been looking all over for jazz," Kay explained, "and the best of the lot was at GUM Department Store that played for the fashion show . . . this little quintet played the overture, like

'Mack the Knife.' Real fast—you can't *believe* how fast. Then . . . like Dior models from a long time ago, they came in rapid fire order . . . and the band played George Shearing's stuff."

They attended the Obraztsov State Central Puppet Theatre; circuses; magic acts; ballets, including *Carmen* at the Bolshoi Theatre; operas, including *Anna Karenina* at the Moscow Art Theatre; and the troika races at the hippodrome.

On March 6, they visited Mosfilm, the largest and oldest film studio in all of Europe, where they witnessed scenes being shot for *Belye nochi* (*White Nights*), adapted from the short story by Dostoyevsky. The film was being directed by Ivan Pyryev, "the high priest of Stalinist cinema," and the winner of six Stalin Prizes (the Russian equivalent of the Oscars). Less winning were his social graces.

"He was very sassy and a smart aleck," Knight recalled. "He asked Kay, 'What did you think of *The Defiant Ones*?'—the movie with Tony Curtis and Sidney Poitier as escaped convicts chained together. He was trying to find out if Kay liked 'the black actor' or 'the white one'—and who did she think was better—trying to see if she had Communist leanings, embracing black people. It was very deliberate and Kay didn't like his attitude."

Thompson was next introduced to director Mikhail Kalatozov, who had seen *Funny Face* at the 1957 Cannes Film Festival, where his own film, *Letyat zhuravli* (*The Cranes Are Flying*), had been presented out of competition. Refreshingly, he was gracious and complimentary.

Though she had no local celebrity status in Moscow, Thompson managed to make quite a fashion statement. According to *Vanity Fair*, she "deliberately wore a dress 'inside out' to a wedding." In Hilary's words, "The town was totally freaked out by Kay. She appeared in this great fuzzy fur coat and a fez and she looked stylish and never took it off. She had a black knitted dress and black knitted gloves that were covered with dog hairs from her pug, Fenice—even though he'd been left behind in New York."

Between public excursions, Hilary would be summoned for creative meetings in Kay's suite at the hotel, where he found her brimming with ideas and energy. "We wrote, sketched, pasted, and laughed a great deal," he recalled.

There was something unsettling, however, that hung over them like a dark cloud. "At the Puppet Theatre," Knight remembered, "we met this very attractive Polish man who first said he was a builder and then, later, he changed his story and said he was a gymnast. He was asking all kinds of questions, which Kay didn't like, and she got very nervous. She thought he was a spy sent to spy on us. She thought *everybody* was a spy."

"Kay always thought her room was tapped," Howard Haines confirmed.

"I looked everywhere," Thompson explained. "I looked in the chandelier—only dead moths up there. I looked under the carpets. I looked every place I could look in cupboards. And I saw none. *But* . . . I heard from some of the British press that there were microphones."

"And the phone would ring at 3 a.m.," Howard added, "just to see if you were there. Someone would say something in Russian, then hang up."

"You were told not to lock your door," Kay said. "I didn't trust *les girls* at the desk. You have a definite feeling you are being watched."

"Kay was really spooked by it," Richard Grossman said. "She had a conspiratorial view of the world anyway, so naturally, Moscow really got her paranoia going. She visualized herself being spied on, and she may very well have been. Who knows?"

Although the side effects of Dr. Feelgood's "vitamin cocktails" often induced paranoia, Thompson was not imagining things. Intourist operatives routinely kept close watch over foreigners, tracking their every move, listening in on phone calls, reading outgoing and incoming mail, maintaining voluminous dossiers. Knowledge was control—and the Soviets armed themselves by gathering information. It was 1984 in 1959.

Nevertheless, the ever-resourceful Thompson transformed the unnerving situation into a game of hide-and-seek for *Eloise in Moscow*. As a running visual gag, a mysterious man in a trench coat would be lurking somewhere in every illustration—and it was up to the reader to spot the spy on each page.

The device was not entirely original, though. In Vincente Minnelli's *Hooray for What!*—the show from which Thompson had been fired—Le Grande Hôtel de l'Espionage was filled with statuary and paintings that camouflaged eavesdropping spies. Similar tricks had popped up in countless movies—most often real eyes peering out of holes in canvas portraits. And there were precedents in print as well—such as Al Hirschfeld's tradition of embedding his daughter's name, Nina, in all of his drawings, or the editors of *Playboy* hiding the bunny logo on the magazine's covers. But Kay certainly synthesized and reinvented these visual teasers for *Eloise in Moscow* and, in doing so, ushered in a whole new subgenre of kids' books—including Hilary Knight's *Where's Wallace?* (Harper & Row, 1964), with a hidden ape on every page, and Martin Handford's *Where's Waldo?* (Little, Brown and Company, 1987), with a hidden man on every page.

"Kay wanted everything in *Eloise in Moscow* to be gloomy," Knight explained, "and so, when a sudden burst of spring weather began to melt the snow, she was ready to go."

On March 15, the evening before their departure, Kay was given a bon voyage party by the U.S. Ambassador to Russia, Llewellyn E. Thompson. The fête was held at the historic Spaso House, an opulent manor that served as the official residence of all U.S. ambassadors.

The highlight of the evening was a showing of *Funny Face* in the mansion's private screening room, where, during the "On How to Be Lovely" number, Kay got up and performed the song along with her image on the screen (the routine she'd perfected at Lucille Ball's house).

"When we were packing to leave our hotel," Hilary said, "Kay gave everything to the maids. She just emptied her suitcases. So these little Russian ladies are probably very, very rich women in Russia today."

What Kay now valued was all the research they had accumulated—which she feared might be confiscated by customs agents if they were not vigilant. "We came out of Russia with our notes stuffed in pockets, shoes, pinned to underclothes, anywhere," Howard explained, "afraid that Russian authorities might not let critical writing pass."

As a gift to herself, Thompson had acquired a six-string balalaika, a triangular Russian guitar with a mandolin-like sound.

According to Walter Winchell, she also smuggled out several cartons of Ruskie cigarettes, which she awarded to certain deserving newsmen. "They have the longest filter," Kay said, "but terribly strong tobacco—I could only go a couple of them."

Thompson had planned to bring back cans of Russian caviar as homecoming gifts, but every sample she tried nearly made her retch. On the way home, they stopped in Paris, Hilary recalled. "She said, 'Let's go straight to the caviar bar [at the Petrossian Boutique & Café]!' And when she tasted it there, she said, 'Um! Much better!'"

Kay checked into the Hôtel Queen Elizabeth with creative juices on overflow. "I'd planned to go to Lisbon to meet up with a friend of mine," Hilary explained, "but Kay said, 'No, we have to work.' She hired a secretary named Annie Yip to take dictation and type up drafts of the text."

They started work in the afternoon, took a break for dinner, then resumed working until around 1:30 a.m. "I would be so tired, I'd go to bed," Hilary said. "But then she would stay up *much* beyond that."

One night, Kay and Hilary dined at a Chinese restaurant called L'Empire Céleste, where they ran into *Pickpocket* star Martín La Salle and his fiancée, China Machado.

"China was a big model for Avedon," Hilary recalled, "half Chinese, and very good-looking. And Kay was absolutely *fascinated* with her."

The highest-paid runway model in Europe, Shanghai-born China Machado had actually worked on *Funny Face*. "I did not appear in the movie,"

China explained in 2008, "but I'll tell you something that very few people know. I'd just started working as a model for Givenchy and, by sheer coincidence, I had the exact same body as Audrey Hepburn, and so all of her clothes for *Funny Face* were made on me. I was the fitting model. We went to the opening in France but I never got to meet Dick Avedon or Kay Thompson until a couple of years later when I came to New York for three months in the fall of 1958. I was hired by Dick Avedon and he really launched my career as a model for photo shoots. And it was Dick who introduced me to Kay. She took an immediate liking to me and was really fantastic. She invited me to do things all the time and introduced me to everybody. I remember she took me to 21 with Lena Horne—and, you know, this was beyond my wildest dreams. But then I went back to Europe and, I assumed, that was that."

Four months later, Thompson and Machado found themselves dining at the very same restaurant in Paris—as if drawn together by fate.

"I could tell Kay was absolutely *fascinated* by China," Knight continued. "And it was the *only* time I would ever say that I saw anything that would even suggest a kind of attraction to another woman—which, of course, could really mean nothing."

"You know what I think?" China offered. "Kay was so enthusiastic about people that she fell in love with them—kind of had a crush when she met them. Dick Avedon was the same way. When he met someone he liked, he could fall in love with them without being physically involved with them. It was always a big, intense crush. He wanted to see them all the time and get everything from them. I think that's what Kay was like."

Eventually, Kay and Hilary made it back to New York and reported in to headquarters—Simon & Schuster—where the publicity department hailed their Russian deployment as a rousing success.

"Eloise went to Moscow . . . played in the snow . . . and created an incident or two," Thompson teased in a radio interview.

While Hilary worked on the final illustrations, Kay shifted focus.

"Kay's planning to record a musical score on the book in Moscow," reported Hedda Hopper in the *Los Angeles Times* on June 5, 1959, "and former partner Andy Williams was asked to do the voice of an American boy. Kay plays Eloise, natch."

That elusive Eloise album was, once again, on the front burner. Andy had already involved himself by singing backup vocals on "Eloise" and "It's Absolutely Christmastime," but Kay now wanted him to develop his own alter ego to go along with Eloise—based on characters he'd been doing just for kicks for years.

"When Kay would talk in the voice of Eloise," Andy said, "I played two characters: Melvin, a good kid, and Junior, who was a very naughty boy. And we used to just play this to the hilt. We'd go on and on in these voices and crack each other up, and it was so much fun."

Kay saw this as a launching pad for two spin-off characters with their own line of books and merchandise—a companion industry for boys to complement the success that Eloise was having with girls.

But Kay was not about to abandon her core audience—precocious grown-ups. To that end, Thompson decided to record an extemporaneous Q & A on her experiences in the Soviet Union—the first of a series of spoken-word "Kay Thompson Party" albums she had in mind.

"It was kind of a ridiculous concept just to listen to Kay Thompson talk about her trip to Russia but I was the one who suggested it," admitted Thompson's latest manager, Mace Neufeld (the future mega movie producer). "I said to Bob Thiele, 'You know, Kay is such a great conversationalist and raconteur. She's just come back from Russia, so why don't we put together a party and we'll record it?' Bob said, 'Great!'"

Having already put out an album of beatnik Jack Kerouac reading his poetry, Bob Thiele and Steve Allen signed Thompson to their offbeat, fledgling label, Hanover-Signature, in the summer of 1959. It is hard to imagine that they really thought there was money to be made on a gabfest about Russia. The future prospect of an Eloise album was the carrot that clinched the deal.

"It was a nice party at her apartment," recalled Neufeld. "It was just a fun thing. We produced the album, and they put it out."

The twelve-inch vinyl LP was entitled *Kay Thompson Party, Volume 1: Let's Talk About Russia.* On the cover was a misleading photo of Kay holding her balalaika—even though there would not be a note of music. The photo would have been much more appropriate for the two Russian-themed novelty songs Kay decided to compose, record, and release as a single. To help her write the lyrics, she recruited Simon & Schuster's Nina Bourne.

"She thought I was a good rhymer," Nina recalled, "so I spent several evenings collaborating with her in her teeny-tiny apartment. I've never been so at sea working with anybody in my life. It felt as if I were swimming through honey or glue. So, eventually, the meetings just stopped."

Kay then gave her editor, Richard Grossman, a shot. "She'd always said to me that I'd make a good lyric writer because I could put things into short phrases," he remembered. "I was a 'word merchant' as she called it. And so, over the course of the summer of 1959, I used to go up to her apartment on Sixty-second Street off Fifth Avenue and we'd sit around—she had a Russian guitar—and we wrote a couple songs: 'Dasvidanya (Until We Meet Again)' and 'Moscow Cha Cha Cha.' I did write the lyrics largely but we would bat them back and forth, and then she would sing it one way and then another way and ask me which I liked best, like an eye doctor saying is it better with this lens or that."

Once Kay was happy with the compositions, she developed the arrangements and set a session date at A&R Recording Studio (112 West Forty-Eighth Street) around August 1959.

"It was an all-night recording session," Grossman remembered. "Kay, of course, with her tremendous network of music people, got the studio, got the musicians, got her old friend Ralph Blane to sing backup on the record. The conductor was Sid Ramin, who did *The Milton Berle Show* for years. He said, 'Jesus, I can't let my name be on this because I'm not following the union stuff. I've gotta use a pseudonym.' I said, 'Fine, I'll make one up for you.' And I made up the name Nicholas Zarr—a play on the word for a Russian czar. We were up all night and Kay was a masterful producer. She'd make those guys play it fifty times and love it."

When both the album and the single tanked, Thompson lost all faith in the label's ability to handle an Eloise album—so it went no further. Regrettably, it marked an inauspicious end to Kay's otherwise remarkable career as a recording artist—her voice would never again be commercially released on vinyl.

While Kay was spinning wheels, Hilary dutifully completed his illustrations for *Eloise in Moscow* so the book could be published on October 30, 1959.

As if Thompson had planned it, Khrushchev came to the United States that September for a highly publicized cross-country tour that included Twentieth Century-Fox studios in Los Angeles, where Kay, Frank Sinatra, Judy Garland, and a hundred other stars held a VIP luncheon in his honor (boycotted by Ronald Reagan). Afterward, Khrushchev visited the set of *Can-Can*, where Shirley MacLaine and Juliet Prowse demonstrated their bawdy dance routines. The Soviet premier was so offended, he stormed out and, for the gathered members of the press, denounced his hosts in a rambling, vodka-fueled forty-five-minute tirade. His indignant mood was not helped by the fact that his last-minute request to visit Disneyland had been denied for security reasons.

To Thompson's glee, the internationally publicized contretemps put a much brighter spotlight on the imminent publication of *Eloise in Moscow*. Not only was it the exact antithesis of Khrushchev in Hollywood, it was equally farcical. Seizing the opportunity, Simon & Schuster took out an ad in *The New York Times* declaring *Eloise in Moscow* to be "the most daring of all Russo-American cultural exchanges."

"Never before have those Red squares been exposed to anyone as hip as Eloise," reported *Time* magazine—an unmistakable jab at Khrushchev. "She is, of course, an irrepressible capitalist ('The Rolls is the only sports car I will drive in a Russian blizzard'), shows dangerous bourgeois-individualistic tendencies by riding her tricycle on the frozen Baltic, and utters subversive observations ('Everybody watches everybody in Moscow'). But she makes up for it by getting right into the thick of cultural exchange, playing chopsticks in F at Tchaikovsky Hall, and doing a 'rawther unusual' ballet with three elderly snow sweepers, which cries out for choreographer Jerome Robbins."

Good Housekeeping splashed *Eloise in Moscow* on the cover of its November 1959 issue. Inside, a multipage excerpt whetted appetites for more.

Beaming with confidence, Simon & Schuster upped the first printing order to 75,000 copies and bought a spate of ads in *The New York Times* and *The New Yorker* with copy that read, "Russian to your bookstore for Eloise's magnificent mission to Moscow. It's caviar. It's *kultúrny*."

Thompson hit the promotional trail, unveiling the book at the Sheraton Hotel in Dallas, Texas, at a special luncheon sponsored by the Dallas Fall Festival of Music, Art, and Drama, attended by one thousand dignitaries, including opera diva Maria Callas, the Duke of Bedford, playwright Moss Hart and his wife, actress Kitty Carlisle, and, of course, Billie and Stanley Marcus.

On the topic of *Eloise in Moscow* versus Khrushchev in Hollywood, Kay was grilled on a slew of radio and television talk shows, including *The Today Show* (NBC-TV, October 30, 1959)—by Dave Garroway, of course—and *The Tonight Show Starring Jack Paar* (NBC-TV, September 24, 1959). The latter was happily repeated on November 9, 1959, the date of Kay's fiftieth birthday (though not even the KGB knew her age for sure).

There had been plans in the works for a line of Russian-flavored "Eloise Fashions for Winter by Mr. John," but with coats and fezzes to be made of real fur, the costs were prohibitive, so it never happened.

Without any new Eloise merchandise, stores were being asked to cross-promote the *Eloise in Moscow* book with the same Eloise doll they'd been stocking for two years. The timing could not have been worse, because as of March 9, 1959, there was a new girl in town who knocked the Eloise doll on her ass: Barbie. In the wake of an unparalleled Barbie doll invasion and the phenomenal success of Dr. Seuss, Eloise no longer warranted the prime display space she had once dominated. There was also the very basic problem that anything having to do with Russia was a serious turnoff to most Americans. Consequently, *Eloise in Moscow* went over like a lead Sputnik.

"Eloise amid the Soviets isn't the sprightly brat you either wanted to kill or take home," read the all-important critique in *The New York Times*. "She has become just a dull little girl in a travelogue that is pretentiously presented. Fie on Kay Thompson."

Adding insult to injury, the *New York Herald Tribune* observed that "Eloise's escapades in the Soviet Union are somewhat slim . . . Only Hilary Knight manages to extract the fullest delight from the onion-domed city, and his fur-hatted and coated heroine."

Once again, Hilary had emerged smelling like a rose—and thus, Kay's resentment continued to fester.

Sales numbers for *Eloise in Moscow* were nowhere near what the previous books had achieved, with many remainders collecting dust on store shelves.

On March 19, 1960, a keen observation concerning the dismal state of Eloise appeared in John Falter's cover artwork for *The Saturday Evening Post*. Barely visible amid the hubbub of Fifth Avenue at Fifty-ninth Street was a tiny "forlorn figure of Eloise, gazing down from her perch at The Plaza."

The Plaza was in a sorry state, too. By the time Conrad Hilton's management contract expired on March 31, 1960, all his valued executives—including Alphonse Salomone and Gene Voit—had been systematically transferred to other Hilton hotels, leaving The Plaza in the lurch and in serious decline.

"We were desperately concerned over whether we could bring the hotel back," recalled Paul Sonnabend of Hotel International Corporation, owner of the property. "The place was going to seed."

Hence, the new general manager, Neal Lang (former husband of Martha Raye), conducted a ruthless housecleaning to revitalize and spruce up the aging hotel, physically and administratively. The "Lang purge" resulted in the unceremonious cancellation of free office space for Eloise Limited and the immediate closure of the Eloise Room—to the great displeasure of our Miss Thompson.

The coup de grâce, however, occurred five months later. On the night of November 23, 1960, the Eloise portrait mysteriously disappeared from the lobby of the Plaza—all but erasing her from existence.

"The following morning, I was in my apartment," Kay explained, "and somebody from the hotel called to say, 'Eloise is missing.' And I said, 'I'll be right there.'"

Immediate suspicion fell upon the twelfth annual Debutante Ball of the New York Junior League, held the prior evening in the Terrace Room. It was presumed that drunken teenagers had stolen the portrait as a prank, a theory that was already gaining momentum as the accepted version of the crime. The press had gotten wind of the abduction and a flurry of reporters descended on Thompson when she arrived at the hotel.

"I was interviewed," Kay explained, "and I just couldn't wait to talk to Walter." As in Cronkite, CBS News.

Going along with the hotel's explanation, Thompson postulated, "I think it was school boys and I keep seeing coonskin coats. You know, *that* kind of act. Just needless." And to a reporter for United Press International, Kay speculated that the famous painting "now may be gracing the wall of some fraternity house or dormitory room of a college campus."

But how did a five-by-three-and-a-half-foot painting, mounted in a heavy wooden frame, manage to slip by the doormen unnoticed?

"She was kidnapped and came through the window in the Persian Room," Thompson dramatically hypothesized. "Through the window, on the Fifty-eighth Street side. The door is locked there. And the dance was going on . . . So they just slid that through the wide windows in the Persian Room, and out the window into a car and away you go." She had certainly thought this one through—in startling detail.

"It made the papers," Knight said, "and there was *a lot* of publicity."

"There it was, *everywhere*," Kay recalled. "And the [evening] papers were out by 6 o'clock . . . Walter Cronkite was on at 7 o'clock and his announcement, of course, was—to the entire world—'Eloise kidnapped from Plaza Hotel.'"

Eschewing the "drunken teenage prank" account, however, the *New York World-Telegram and Sun* broke the case wide open, suggesting an entirely different theory. The newspaper's society columnist, Frank Farrell, managed to track down Alphonse Salomone at the Caribe Hilton in Puerto Rico. Salomone suspected "either Savoy Hilton manager Gene Voit or Waldorf banquet manager Clyde Harris" because "both Voit and Harris were execs of the Hotel Plaza while Eloise was becoming famous there" and "she became the center of so much attention that neither of these two Hilton execs could conceivably leave such a little darling behind when they changed jobs."

Given the hostile transition of the new administration, it would seem that the disappearance of the Eloise portrait was more than just a random act of vandalism. And the rapidity with which the hotel's management abandoned concern was only matched by the apathy of the police department. By year's end, the case had essentially been dropped and forgotten.

Frustrated, Kay took matters into her own hands. On January 4, 1961, Dorothy Kilgallen reported in her column that Thompson was "offering a reward." But weeks went by with no leads. On February 18, United Press International issued a follow-up story stating that "officials at the Hotel Plaza are still puzzled by the disappearance." Subsequently, for nearly half a century, "the Unsolved Mystery of the Stolen Eloise Portrait" remained a cold case. Until now.

"Some time later," Hilary Knight admitted, "I got a mysterious, anonymous phone call. The voice on the phone told me the portrait was in a dumpster in a dark alley somewhere, if I wanted it."

Knight went to the appointed location and retrieved the painting from the trash. Though no longer in its frame, the artwork was still more or less intact, having sustained only minor damage.

Instead of restoring it and having it rehung at The Plaza, Hilary decided to quietly bury the artifact in storage, where it has remained all these years. When asked why he did not report this to anyone, he sheepishly admitted, "It is a little embarrassing because the thieves were apparently after the *frame*, not my artwork. And, frankly, I made that first portrait for Kay, never imagining it would be put on permanent display at The Plaza. I never really liked it—I did it in a rush—so I was not unhappy when it disappeared."

So, if the artist ended up with the goods *and* had a motive for the portrait's suppression, doesn't that earn him a spot in the lineup of prime suspects? Perhaps. But, in addition to the perfectionist illustrator, the megalomaniacal hotel manager, disgruntled ex-employees, scheming frame filchers, drunken teenage vandals, and maybe even Colonel Mustard, there is one other person of interest in this whodunit who cannot be ignored: the possessive copyright holder.

In unpublished portions of a 1993 interview with Stephen M. Silverman, Thompson confessed, "I found her [the Eloise portrait] on Eighty-something Street . . . torn up. It was torn up and put in one of those baskets, you know, the silver baskets . . . A trash thing."

How was it that Kay just so happened to stumble upon this amazing discovery? Why didn't she take possession of it? Did she place the call to Knight, disguising her voice? Or did she put someone else up to the task? Why did she claim the painting was "torn up" when it was later recovered intact? Indeed, this was curious behavior for an innocent victim.

It's just too delicious *not* to imagine Thompson acting out an Eloise-like kamikaze heist, dressed in one of her black Nolan Miller catsuits, raiding the lobby of The Plaza in the wee hours of the morning, accompanied by Henry Mancini's theme from *The Pink Panther*. Yet even that cinematic set piece falls apart in light of the reward money Kay offered for the return of the portrait.

Or was that just a ruse to throw off suspicion?

The one thing we do know is that if there were an Academy Award for acting in mysterious ways, Thompson would certainly have taken the prize. Annually.

Switching channels from film noir to courtroom drama, we come to Polan v. Thompson, a 1961 lawsuit that, according to *Variety,* was "brought by agent Barron Polan against Kay Thompson" for commissions allegedly due on all "peripheral rights" to Eloise, including sequels, merchandising deals, television and movie rights, and any other exploitation of the character.

To defend her in the case, Kay hired Horace Manges of Weil, Gotshal and Manges, the high-powered New York law firm that represented Random House and a dozen other top publishing companies. At a strategy meeting, Manges said, "Kay, all I ask you is while we're there [in court], don't say anything. We just go easy and you don't have to worry about a thing."

Of course, going "easy" was not one of Thompson's strong suits. On the day of the trial, the double doors to the courtroom were flung open by a diva who was ready for her close-up. Think Dietrich in *Witness for the Prosecution*—and then some.

"I had on my new white Givenchy coat and *whoa!*" Kay gloated. "I could not have looked less like who I was going to be in this scene."

New York Supreme Court Judge Samuel C. Coleman called Thompson to the witness stand. Pointing to Exhibit A, Polan's attorney, Jack Pearl, asked, "Did you write this book?"

"Of course I wrote this book," Kay testified.

"What book?" Judge Coleman queried.

"It's a book about Eloise," Thompson said.

And then, out of nowhere, a screechy, high-pitched voice suddenly announced, "I am Eloise and I am six, and here's what I am. I live at this hotel."

For an instant, the entire courtroom looked around, trying to spot the surprise witness who had just interrupted the proceeding—then realized that the voice of Eloise was, in fact, emanating from the mouth of Kay. Manges shot Thompson a warning glance to zip it.

"But the judge was really ready to hear who Eloise was," Thompson rationalized. "He *wanted* to hear all about this."

Looking back and forth between Polan and Thompson, Judge Coleman said, "You two people are friends. You don't want to—"

"Well, *he* may want to," Eloise squawked, pointing an accusatory finger at Barron, "because you know what his name is? His name is Stinky, and he named his own self."

The courtroom erupted in laughter; even the judge cracked a smile. "And Barron then knew he was very sorry that he had come into this barbwire," Kay later reflected.

"He named himself Stinky," Eloise repeated. Then, looking straight into the judge's eyes, she said, "Who are *you*? And who do *you* want to be?"

That's when all hell broke loose. Guffaws . . . pandemonium . . . gavel beating . . . "Order in the court!"

When things finally settled down, a few basic questions managed to get answered seriously and Thompson was sent back to the table for the defense. Horace whispered, "I told you not to . . . but I'm so glad you did it."

Next up, Polan took the stand but the wind had been sucked right out of his sails. The judge asked a few cursory questions and then simply dismissed the case. "At the same time," reported *Variety*, "the Court ruled Miss Thompson was entitled to recover $619.14 overpayment by the book's publisher to Polan."

Magnanimously, she gave Barron a great big hug on the courthouse steps and then, with Givenchy coattails flapping in the breeze, she sashayed down the street in a blaze of glory.

Though Kay seemed to relish this sort of high drama, deep down she was becoming very weary of her creation. "I don't know how Eloise managed to grow so big, so fast," Thompson told a reporter for the Associated Press. "I'd hate to call her a Frankenstein, but she scares me, just the same. I just can't seem to keep up with Eloise. If I had known all the things she would get me into, I'm not sure that I ever would have had her." She was only half joking.

To Stephen M. Silverman, Kay candidly confessed her misgivings about all the Eloise sequels. "What is [Eloise] doing in Moscow?" Thompson asked rhetorically. "You know, she has no business there." When asked what she thought of *Eloise in Paris* and *Eloise at Christmastime*, Thompson grimaced. "Those were just so rotten. *Eloise at Christmastime* was a piece in a magazine . . . it *wasn't* a book . . . What's next? *Eloise in Mexico* and then *Eloise in Barbados* and then *Eloise in East Hampton*. This has nothing to do with her . . . She's *not* the girl with the hat on in Mexico, you know, smoking a cigar."

Was Kay burned out on her own creation?

In 2008, Liza Minnelli offered a more positive explanation during an interview for *New York* magazine: "[Kay] conquered everything, then moved on. She was the greatest person ever at MGM, then she got tired of that. She did a nightclub act that was the greatest nightclub act that had ever been seen, then she got tired of that. Then she wrote the best children's book in the world. She lived her life!"

Kay's philosophy had always been "Leave 'em wanting more." And it would be no different with Eloise. Her mind made up, Thompson pulled the plug on Eloise Limited. American Character Doll Company stopped making the Eloise doll and no merchandising contracts were renewed or sought. With no author-supported promotions, and no Eloise portrait or Eloise Room at The Plaza to keep the flame alive, sales of all four books dwindled and Eloise gradually faded from the marketplace, ending the gravy train not only for Thompson, but also for Hilary Knight—who very much wanted to continue the franchise but was powerless to do so on his own. Out of sight and out of mind, Eloise was dead.

Part Five

BEHIND THE SCENES

Chapter Eleven

GURU IN THE WINGS

From Sinatra to JFK

(1947–62)

Kay's a Thompson submachine gun.

—*Jack O'Brian*

$\mathcal{A}$s passionately as Kay sought the limelight herself, she could not resist the urge to help other stars—a continuation of the work she had been doing at MGM in the 1940s. She was a case study in love-hate ambivalence: a woman who was supportive and jealous of her colleagues in equal measure. As selflessly helpful as she may have seemed on the surface, Kay relished lording over the very stars she envied, feeding a sense of superiority that was as addictive as stardom itself.

Once the Kay Thompson and the Williams Brothers act knocked the nightclub circuit on its ear, every star in Hollywood wanted Kay to create the same magic for them, including Judy Holliday, Peter Lawford, the Gabor Sisters (Zsa Zsa, Eva, and Magda), Lisa Kirk, Julie Wilson, Jimmie Garland (Judy's sister), Pepper Davis and Tony Reese (a musical-comedy team), and June Havoc (the wife of Kay's ex-husband, Bill Spier)—just to name a few.

A typical example was Van Johnson, who in April 1953 got a lucrative offer to play the Sands Hotel in Las Vegas. There were three basic problems, however. One: He had no act. Two: He'd never done this sort of thing before. Three: He had debilitating stage fright. His savior was Thompson.

"Kay rehearsed with him every day," orchestrator Buddy Bregman recalled. "Nick Castle did the staging of the dancers but Kay did all of Van's movements. Kay would say, 'Go 'round the stage, honey!' Kay and Roger Edens wrote a great opening number called 'It's Good to Be Home Again.' I just got chills. That is a *great* opening number and Kay had a lot to do with it. Fucking brilliant."

Van's fashion trademark was wearing red socks with his tuxedo, which inspired the *Hollywood Reporter* pun "Van Johnson in Sock Café Debut." Embracing the gimmick, Kay got all the waiters at the Sands to sport red socks and then "his bobby-soxer fans in Las Vegas promptly snapped up the idea" and made "a fad of it."

After his success in Vegas, Johnson took the show on the road and, on May 2, 1955, appeared on an episode of *I Love Lucy* during which Lucy bamboozled her way into his act.

Another benefactor of the Thompson touch was Marlene Dietrich, who, for several weeks in 1953, audited rehearsals of Kay Thompson and the Williams Brothers as well as Kay's coaching of Van Johnson.

"Marlene was always dressed in Army fatigues," said Buddy Bregman. "She looked like a Marine. She just wanted to be there, like a fly on the wall, just soaking it all up. She would occasionally say, 'Oh, I like that,' but mainly just watched. During breaks, Kay and Marlene would huddle for a while. They were best friends. They might have had something going."

Perhaps. But it seems more likely that Dietrich got chummy with Thompson because the Sahara Hotel in Las Vegas had offered Marlene a record-breaking $30,000 per week starting December 15, 1953.

The first order of business was to hire a music director, so Kay recommended Peter Matz, the whiz kid she'd broken into the business earlier that year. Marlene wanted to mix naughty barroom numbers like "Makin' Whoopee" with wistful standards like "Falling in Love Again." But with a foggy baritone voice forever in search of a pitch, she needed to offer something more.

Jean Louis, who designed sumptuous dresses for Columbia Pictures, was retained to come up with a showstopper and he did not disappoint. *Time* magazine exhaled, "The sensation of her act, eclipsing her off-key warbling, was her getup: a $3,000 black net gown which, from the waist up, was transparent, except for an occasional sequin or rhinestone. The blasé gambling crowd gasped. Asked what she had on underneath the opaque part, Marlene purred: 'A garter belt.'"

Though the act was devoid of Kay's trademark choreography, Marlene did adopt at least one Thompson signature. "[Dietrich] announced 'Falling in

Love Again' as 'the last one and the inevitable one,'" wrote biographer Steven Bach, "and when it was over, it was over. She chided the audience when they clamored for encores, 'I told you that was the last one.' They were left wanting more." Sound familiar?

Kay helped Noël Coward reinvent himself as a nightclub performer, too—first following her footsteps at the Café de Paris in 1951, but then, most lucratively, in June 1955 at the Desert Inn in Las Vegas, where Coward earned $35,000 per week, breaking Dietrich's record.

When Noël's own accompanist, Norman Hackford, was turned down for a U.S. work permit, Kay naturally recommended Peter Matz. From that day on, Coward requested Matz's services on everything he did.

Kay's vocal arrangement for the time-honored Scottish folk song "Loch Lomond" was an absolute killer. After the conventional opening verse, the song ripped into a jazzified Thompsonian frenzy that simply stopped the show. And if that were not enough to turn heads, the defiantly gay lyrics certainly did: "For there with my honey, my bonny hi'land laddie . . . he's my new love, my true love, my little sugar daddy." This was Coward at his most wicked—spurred on by his mischievous accomplice.

The following month, Thompson was flown to a vacation home in Bermuda by Metropolitan Opera star Patrice Munsel, who was scheming her own assault on Vegas.

"The audience is going to expect you to be 'longhaired' and dignified," Kay told Patrice. "So you've got to take 'em by surprise."

Kay wanted Patrice to open the show in a beautiful Cinderella ball gown and sing Mimi's aria from Puccini's *La Bohème*. Then, Munsel would curtsy and step behind a dressing screen. Seconds later, she would emerge in a pair of "pink satin, jeweled toreador pants and a low-cut halter top," and rip into Thompson's brassy arrangement of "It's All Right with Me" from *Can-Can*.

"Kay and I had a *ball*," Patrice recalled in 2006.

Thompson had too many projects on her plate to hang out in Bermuda all summer, so, after the broad strokes had been decided, she got Peter Matz on board as arranger-conductor and brought in twenty-eight-year-old choreographer Herbert Ross to fine-tune the show (decades before he directed such hit movies as *Footloose* and *Steel Magnolias*). The result came to fruition at the New Frontier in Las Vegas in October 1955, paving the way for her own television series, *The Patrice Munsel Show* (ABC-TV, 1956–58), for which Thompson appeared as a guest star on January 24, 1958.

"Kay was just incredible," Patrice reminisced. "There was nobody on stage like her. She gave me such inspiration."

Things didn't always go so swimmingly. In early November 1957, Ginger Rogers was offered $28,000 per week to christen the Copa Room at the brand-new Havana Riviera Hotel and Casino in Cuba, opening December 10.

Having seen the Kay Thompson and the Williams Brothers act on many occasions, Ginger envisioned herself surrounded by four male dancers—a no-brainer for Thompson to stage in a hurry. With trusty Peter Matz as accompanist-orchestrator, Kay helped Ginger narrow down a list of standards, including "Embraceable You," the Gershwin song Rogers had introduced on Broadway in *Girl Crazy*.

The Havana Riviera was controlled by Meyer Lansky, the mobster—and Frank Sinatra crony—who had employed Thompson at many of his gambling outposts over the years. Figuring they'd earn points with Lansky, Thompson arranged a medley of Sinatra hits.

But Kay also wanted to include some original songs. With her extraordinary nose for talent in the making, she was drawn to a young songwriter who had just gotten his first big break writing the lyrics for Leonard Bernstein's *West Side Story*. His name was Stephen Sondheim.

In 2007, Sondheim explained how he became involved: "I had seen Kay Thompson performing at The Plaza with the Williams Brothers. And then I met Kay a couple of times at parties thrown by D. D. and Johnny Ryan. One day D. D. said, 'Kay would love it if you would write something for Ginger Rogers' nightclub act.' And I said, 'Sure.' So Kay came to see me up at my father's apartment at 1010 Fifth Avenue. I just remember her sitting there on a couch and talking about it. And then I remember I wrote 'Night Is the Best Part of the Day' and I gave it to her. I may have gone to a rehearsal to play it for Peter Matz but I never met Ginger. I just handed the manuscript in to Kay and that's the last I heard."

During rehearsals, Meyer Lansky turned to Kay and snapped, "Ginger can wiggle her ass but she can't sing a goddamn note!"

Nobody really wanted to hear Ginger sing anyway; they expected to see her dance—which was exactly what Kay figured would be the "meat and potatoes" of the show. To everyone's dismay, however, Ginger was hopeless at learning the steps, leaving Kay no choice but to simplify her routines and let the chorus boys do the heavy lifting.

Columnist Shirley Eder raged, "How dare Ginger not dance a step?" And *Variety* complained: "Kay Thompson apparently had the most to do with the act. Her trademark is strongly registered upon Miss Rogers' offerings . . . [but] the audience came to see Ginger Rogers and not Kay Thompson."

Though Rocky Marciano, Johnny Weissmuller, and Ernest Hemingway were among the opening-night glitterati, near-hurricane conditions prevented Marilyn Monroe, Jane Russell, and many other expected guests from attending. Earl Wilson noted that those who did brave "the stormiest weather in years" took their lives in their own hands as "ocean waves crashed over nearby highway walls." Hemingway added "with a restrained shiver" that he had not seen weather this bad in Havana since the 1930s, when he was bunkered in writing *To Have and Have Not*.

Then, as *Variety* reported, "A pipe feeding water to the air-conditioning plant burst over the registration desk." When Ginger tried to get from the elevator to her dressing room, she discovered that the lobby was submerged in four and a half inches of water. "My audience practically had to swim to see me," Rogers shrugged while the local weatherman joked, "They might have been better off booking Esther Williams."

According to publicist John Springer, while squishing through the sodden lobby, Nicky Hilton queried, "Where is all the water coming from?"

Kay, who happened to be sailing by at that very instant, quipped in the high-pitched voice of Eloise, "Here's the thing of it. I might have left the water running in the *bawth*."

The ad-lib not only got a laugh, it sparked the idea for a potential sequel book, *Eloise Takes a Bawth*.

*N*ightclub *acts were not* Kay's only specialty; her expertise was also highly valuable to television. At a time when female directors were nonexistent, she helmed *The Standard Oil 75th Anniversary Show*, NBC's most expensive variety special to date. Set to be broadcast live from the network's studio in Brooklyn on Sunday, October 13, 1957, the ninety-minute program was a test of Thompson's skills—and patience.

For her services as a performer and creative director, Kay earned $50,000, her biggest single payday ever. Her first hire was Richard Avedon, who would visually style the opening production number for $10,000.

To highlight Standard Oil's diamond anniversary, Kay and Richard proposed the idea of opening the show with Marilyn Monroe performing her signature song, "Diamonds Are a Girl's Best Friend," from *Gentlemen Prefer Blondes*. A formal offer was made to Monroe in July 1957, reinforced by a telegram from Avedon, who had recently photographed her: OUR PLANS ARE BEING HELD BREATHLESSLY FOR YOUR DECISION. THERE MIGHT NEVER BE A MOMENT SO PERFECT, SO LISTEN, BABY, CALL ME . . . FONDLY, DICK AVEDON.

On August 2, Kay attended a soirée at Clifton Webb's Beverly Hills home, where she cornered Marilyn for a little arm-twisting. However, the timing could not have been worse. Marilyn's 1956 marriage to playwright Arthur Miller had sparked a fixation on intellectual pursuits—studying at the Actors Studio, reading books on philosophy—which put a serious damper on her "material girl" image. What's more, Monroe had just terminated a dangerous ectopic pregnancy and was profoundly depressed. She not only declined the TV appearance, she didn't make another movie for a full year.

Second choice was Carol Channing, who had originated "Diamonds Are a Girl's Best Friend" on Broadway, but she was already signed for *Chrysler Shower of Stars* the very same month on CBS—which NBC considered a conflict of interest.

To host the special, Thompson suggested Dick Powell. The sponsor agreed, adding that it would be even better if Powell brought along his wife, June Allyson, to do several segments—including the opener.

June "Peter Pan Collar" Allyson singing "Diamonds Are a Girl's Best Friend"? Thompson was fit to be tied. But she bit her tongue as an offer of $100,000 was made for the pair. Powell turned it down because of a scheduling conflict but, to Kay's horror, Allyson signed on for her half of the payday before anyone could balk. Thompson made little effort to hide her displeasure, turning a deaf ear on every suggestion June made. Three weeks later, Allyson took a hike, saying she "didn't like the material submitted to her."

Having gotten rid of June, Kay persuaded her old friend Tyrone Power to host the special, and with the help of her address book, she secured "a jungle of high-priced talent" including Jimmy Durante, Bert Lahr, Jane Powell, Donald O'Connor, Marge and Gower Champion, and Duke Ellington.

Dancers Wisa D'Orso and Hugh Lambert (Frank Sinatra's future son-in-law) would perform a spaced-out ballet to a fusion of jazz by Alec Wilder and electronica by Louis and Bebe Barron of *Forbidden Planet* fame.

There would also be an animated short by British cartoonist Ronald Searle, disingenuously promoted by the network as an Eloise-like romp. In reality, it was nothing more than a "through-the-ages" history lesson on energy.

Newsweek noted that "as the morale booster and liaison girl between performers and their various superiors," Kay was accustomed to having "her flexibility tested."

"We don't have problems to contend with so much as hurdles," Thompson stated tactfully. "Maybe I'll say, 'Hey, I've got a great idea—a bit at a tea party.' 'Superb' someone will answer. 'Don't waste time. Get started . . .' Then suddenly there's word that the sponsor or the agency doesn't get it. They want it explained. So I think about it and then I say 'I didn't mean a tea party at all, I meant a country club.' And off I go again."

Although Tyrone Power was the primary master of ceremonies, he would be briefly relieved by columnist Art Buchwald. It was Kay's caprice to ship her old pal Art all the way from France for a half minute of face-time introducing a medley of Parisian songs. For weeks following the special, humorists bandied about the estimated cost per second for Buchwald's participation. Art made light of it, too, recalling, "When I arrived on the set, the only direction Kay gave me was this: 'When you get back to Paris, go to the shop next to George V and ask them what happened to the sweaters I ordered six months ago.' Upon my return, I went there and saw the manager of the store, who said they weren't ready yet. He was surprised. 'I didn't know it was a rush order.'"

With time running out, Thompson decided to perform the kickoff herself. Concerned that "Diamonds Are a Girl's Best Friend" was too identified with Monroe and Channing, however, she substituted her own signature opener, "Jubilee Time," which was still in keeping with the celebratory theme of the show. Thompson was decked out in a scrumptious black satin, ankle-length evening gown by Christian Dior, a fur stole by Fredrica, stilettos by Delman, and a million dollars' worth of jewelry from Van Cleef & Arpels.

"Kay was wearing so many real diamonds, there were two detectives following her everywhere," Marge Champion said with a chuckle. "They would even follow her into the ladies' room. She got so upset."

With new technological advances for split-screen compositing during a live broadcast, Avedon played tic-tac-toe with multiple subframes floating on colored backgrounds. Squares with Kay's face, snapping fingers, and tapping feet gave way to a full screen, revealing a swirling grand staircase, a ballroom floor painted as the face of a clock, and a magnificent chandelier shaped like a multilayered birthday cake.

Though most Americans only had black-and-white TV sets, brand-new color technology allowed Thompson and Avedon to one-up their "Think Pink!" opening from *Funny Face* by drenching "Jubilee Time" in rich hues of green and yellow. As the corporate muckety-mucks in the control booth cheerfully raised their champagne glasses to toast the launch of the show, however, Jack Rathbone, the president of Standard Oil, stood up and shrieked, "Green and yellow?! Those are the colors of British Petroleum!"

Immune to such corporate concerns, critics hailed "Jubilee Time" as the highlight of the show. The rest of the broadcast? Not so much. Still, *The Standard Oil 75th Anniversary Show* was seen by 40 million people, one of the highest-rated shows of the season.

A week later, Kay was hired to save *The Big Record* (CBS-TV, 1957–58), a weekly musical hour hosted by Patti Page that was getting trounced in the ratings by *Wagon Train* (NBC-TV, 1957–65).

"One of Kay Thompson's first suggestions for improving the program was, 'More Patti!'" wrote columnist Earl Wilson. Kay also insisted the show be "youth-enized" by dumping older guests like "The Incomparable Hildegarde" in favor of under-forty popsters like Andy Williams, Teresa Brewer, and Bill Haley and the Comets.

"Many artists had not really performed on TV before and they needed a lot of help," Patti Page recalled in 2006. "That's where Kay was involved, behind the scenes. She tried very hard to change *everything* on our show for the better, but they didn't change *Wagon Train*, so we only lasted one season."

Subsequently, Kay was often hired as a "creative consultant" on variety specials such as *Ford Startime*: "Ethel Merman on Broadway" (NBC-TV, November 24, 1959) and *A Toast to Jerome Kern* (NBC-TV, September 22, 1959), starring Carol Channing, Lisa Kirk, and Patrice Munsel.

In 1959, she signed with NRB Associates, Ltd., a boutique agency co-headed by Mace Neufeld, thirty, long before he produced such blockbuster movies as *The Hunt for Red October*.

"I first met Kay when she appeared on *The Ed Sullivan Show*," Neufeld recalled in 2008. "We struck up a friendship and I would stop over at her apartment on the way home from my office and we'd have some drinks and talk and try to cook up songs and shows. I remember writing a song with Kay. As soon as we finished it, she jumped up and said, 'Let's sing it to Frank.' I said, 'Frank who?' She said, '*Sinatra!*' She picked up the phone and dialed Sinatra and we sang the song to him on the phone. Nothing ever came of it but, eventually, I was formally managing her."

Kay and Mace collaborated on other projects, too. "We tried to put together a TV show with Peter Ustinov as the host," Neufeld explained. "Kay wanted to call it *Manet, Monet and Jacques*, which was a play on Manny, Moe, and Jack of the Pep Boys Auto Supply Centers. Unfortunately, Ustinov's availability was up in the air because of all the movies he was doing, so it never happened."

Kay also worked behind the scenes on a surprising number of stage shows. During a London gig in 1951, she got very involved coaching Noël Coward's lover, Graham Payn, for his participation in *The Lyric Revue*, a variety show that opened that May at the Lyric Theatre in Hammersmith.

To help him get over his insecurities, Kay said, "Graham, if I can make June Allyson sing, I can make you sing." As Payn recalled in his memoir, "She wrote a strong number for me, called 'Lucky Day,' about a gambler who loses on every race he bets on. It was very much in Kay's distinctive 'never-stop-singing-for-a-second-and-while-you're-singing-keep-moving' style."

After a year of SRO business, *The Lyric Revue* moved to the Globe Theatre in the West End on July 10, 1952, where it was renamed *The Globe Revue*. To freshen things up, Kay wrote another song for Graham entitled "Kiss the Girls Goodbye," and the show ran two more years.

Back in the States, Thompson began secretly coaching Bette Davis in mid-September 1952 for her Broadway-bound musical revue, *Two's Company*. With a frog's croak for a voice and no dance experience whatsoever, Davis was hopelessly miscast yet stubbornly determined to prove the naysayers wrong. In desperate times like these, Thompson always suggested "reciting the lyrics" rather than trying to carry the tune—advice Davis thankfully took to heart.

On opening night of the Boston tryout, Kay sent Bette a confidence-boosting telegram that read: YOU ARE NATURALLY MAGNIFICENT. SO.

Unfortunately, Davis came down with what appeared to be a serious case of influenza and the Broadway opening, scheduled for December 4, 1952, had to be postponed because of "an acutely infected larynx" and exhaustion. On December 8, *The New York Times* reported that her recovery was "coming along very well" under the care of "Miss Davis' physician, Dr. Max Jacobson." No one knows exactly who recommended Dr. Feelgood, but it could easily have been Kay or the director of the show, John Murray Anderson, who also happened to be one of Max's patients.

With methamphetamines injected directly into her throat, Bette was able to open *Two's Company* on December 15. However, speed did nothing to help her *real* problem, which turned out to be a severe wisdom tooth infection that caused osteomyelitis of the jaw, a life-threatening inflammation that would have spread to the brain without immediate surgery. Luckily, Dr. Stanley Behrman was brought in for a second opinion before it was too late. Consequently, the revue closed on March 8, 1953, and Bette's rehabilitation kept her out of work for the next two years.

An eerily similar situation occurred when Kay coached Lucille Ball for her Broadway musical debut in *Wildcat*, which opened December 16, 1960—financed by Ball's own company, Desilu Productions. Not only had Ball relied on Thompson's coaching for over a year, she wanted Kay to be a major creative component and guest star on *Lucy Goes to Broadway*, a CBS-TV special Desilu was developing as a fictionalized spin-off, to be filmed in Manhattan throughout April 1961. The comedy would feature the Lucy Ricardo character from *I Love Lucy* experiencing many of the funny things that Lucille

Ball had experienced herself. It would feature a constellation of stars playing themselves (Kay among them), and the cast would also include *I Love Lucy* regular Vivian Vance, Thompson's understudy from *Hooray for What!* who had usurped her role during its Boston tryout in 1937. Was the idea of Kay and Viv sharing screen time in a spoof about Broadway someone's idea of a sick joke? Or was Thompson plotting to exact her revenge with some merciless upstaging of her own?

Alas, we'll never know. Plans for the special were derailed when Ball suffered a near-collapse from chronic vocal cord injuries and exhaustion. Witnesses recalled "a constant influx of needle-wielding doctors promising miracle cures," suggesting that the ubiquitous "Miracle Max" was likely in the mix. Ball's condition worsened, forcing the early closure of *Wildcat* on June 3, 1961.

Slightly less traumatic was Kay's work on Jule Styne's production of *Mr. Wonderful* starring Sammy Davis Jr. Styne wanted Kay to collaborate on the score with composer Jerry Bock and lyricist Larry Holofcener.

"Jerry didn't really want Kay Thompson in there with us," Holofcener explained. "So, over a weekend, he and I got together without her and wrote four songs for *Mr. Wonderful.* On Monday, we played them for Jule and Kay. Kay was aghast. She said, 'My God, where did you get these? Were these in your trunk?' We said, 'No, no. We wrote them over the weekend.' And she said to Jule, 'Well, they don't need me. These boys can write the score, no problem.' And that was that."

Then it was announced that Kay would choreograph the show—until Sammy Davis insisted on doing his own dance moves. Nonetheless, she remained involved, advising Styne on all aspects of the production. "Kay Thompson does everything well and knows about everything," Styne enthused on a radio show in 1957.

Shortly after *Mr. Wonderful* was up and running, Kay began helping Ethel Merman with her self-financed Broadway musical, *Happy Hunting,* featuring songs by newcomers Harold Karr and Matt Dubey. When Kay beefed up some of the vocal arrangements, however, the composers objected.

"Miss Merman," Dubey complained during a rehearsal, "if I wanted the song sung that way, I'd have written it that way."

"Merman never spoke to Dubey thereafter," wrote theater historian Ken Mandelbaum, "and he was not permitted to speak to her." By association, Karr got the cold shoulder, too. "During the tryout," Mandelbaum added, "Merman's original opening song, 'The International Set, Yet,' was replaced by a terrific Merman introductory number, 'Gee, but It's Good to Be Here.'"

Exactly how the Karr-Dubey brain trust had suddenly gone from mediocrity to brilliance had always been something of a mystery. George Martin, Thompson's former dancer who was featured in *Happy Hunting*, claimed, "Kay came in and she secretly wrote that new opening number for Merman. She came to Philadelphia when we were in previews and that's where it happened. Just listen to it. It's typical Kay. Like 'Madame Crematante' in *Ziegfeld Follies*, it has Merman addressing a bunch of reporters—and I was one of the reporters. But Karr and Dubey were given the credit because their contract or the union made it difficult not to."

In any event, it was the one song in the show that Merman relished, and according to Mandelbaum, she kept it "in her repertoire for the rest of her career."

When *Happy Hunting* failed to win a single Tony Award, Merman demanded that two of her weakest songs be replaced by new ones. With Dubey and Karr no longer on the payroll, Ethel announced to the world that Kay Thompson had written two new songs for the show: "Just a Moment Ago" and "I'm Old Enough to Know Better and Young Enough Not to Care." Actually Thompson had collaborated on both songs with Roger Edens, but because he was still exclusive to MGM, he could not be credited.

Sometimes Thompson's involvement in a project would be more at arm's length. For instance, at a party at Clifton Webb's home in August 1957, Lena Horne asked Kay for advice on her upcoming Broadway debut in *Jamaica*, the new Harold Arlen–Yip Harburg musical. Privately, they went over all the songs (including "Napoleon's a Pastry," revived and updated from *Hooray for What!*), fine-tuned the vocal arrangements and phrasing, and called in Peter Matz to compose some supplementary dance music and write additional lyrics. The effort paid off. *Jamaica* was nominated for seven Tony Awards, including Best Musical and Best Actress in a Musical.

Then, Horne's daughter, Gail benefited from Thompson's guidance. The precocious little girl Kay once teased for "being adept at ordering room service" had grown into a lovely twenty-two-year-old Ivy Leaguer on the cusp of making her off-Broadway debut in Sandy Wilson's musical comedy *Valmouth*, set to open October 6, 1960, at the York Playhouse.

The second-generation angle was big news. Gail was splashed on the cover of *Ebony* magazine, and columnist Earl Wilson scooped, "Kay Thompson, who once coached Lena Horne at MGM, is now coaching Lena's daughter, Gail Jones."

While the publicity had a positive effect on advance ticket sales, it also raised impossibly high expectations that Gail was the next Lena Horne.

"I was very timid about singing," Gail Jones Lumet Buckley recalled in

2002. "So, Kay put on records of the Hi-Lo's and Ethel Merman. Then she turned the volume up very loud, almost deafening, and she said, 'I want you to sing along with these people—*loud!* Sing out so that the head and the chest come together. You've got to sing *through* it!' It wasn't a pretty sound to begin with, but she got me to make my voice bigger. Then she worked with me to make it sound better."

Regarding Thompson's teaching fee, Gail explained, "There was never any money exchanged. It was just gratis. Kay was a pal. I didn't get bad reviews but, frankly, I'm not a dedicated performer. Luckily for me, the show didn't run very long and I eventually went into journalism."

Kay occasionally coached friends for movies, too, including Rosalind Russell for "If You'll Only Take a Chance" and "My Hillbilly Heart" in *The Girl Rush* (Paramount, 1955)—numbers featuring male backup dancers (choreographed by Bob Alton) that simply screamed Kay Thompson and the Williams Brothers.

When her ex-husband, Bill Spier, made his directorial debut with *Lady Possessed* (Republic Pictures, 1952), Thompson gamely coached James Mason to warble "More Wonderful Than These" (Kay Thompson–Bill Spier), the weekly sign-off theme for *Kay Thompson and Company* (CBS Radio, 1941–42), which Spier had produced.

Time magazine described the movie as "foolish," but noted the "outstanding novelty" of watching Mason, "usually typed as a glowering heavy, blithely crooning."

*K*ay *became very political* on January 2, 1960, when Senator John F. Kennedy announced he would run to become the Democratic nominee for president. She had known Jack since 1945 and was convinced that he was destined for greatness. Aside from Thompson, Kennedy received immediate support from many other showbiz friends, especially Frank Sinatra and, of course, Peter Lawford, who was married to Kennedy's sister, Pat.

After the 1957 death of Holmby Hills Rat Pack leader Humphrey Bogart, Sinatra had kept the flame alive with his own rowdy bunch of ring-a-ding ding-dongs, now simply the Rat Pack: Dean Martin, Peter Lawford, Sammy Davis Jr., and Joey Bishop. In addition to the usual carousing, they'd gone professional as an all-star act in Vegas and as the ensemble cast of the hotly anticipated new heist movie, *Ocean's Eleven*, set to begin shooting in January 1960.

The gang's roster extended to "Rat Pack Mascots" (aka "Satellite Charleys") including Jack Kennedy (nicknamed "Chicky Baby"), Judy Garland, Tony Curtis and Janet Leigh, Shirley MacLaine, Angie Dickinson, Marilyn Monroe, Robert Wagner and Natalie Wood, David Niven, and, of course, Thompson, who'd been Sinatra's on-and-off "vocal guru" since 1943. And so, when Sinatra pledged his support of JFK, he brought a legion of Hollywood clout to the party—a fiercely loyal faction that became known as the "Jack Pack."

Blending the JFK crusade with showbiz, Kay served as a creative consultant on *The Frank Sinatra Timex Show: To the Ladies* (ABC-TV, February 15, 1960) with guests Lena Horne and Eleanor Roosevelt. She helped coax the best out of Sinatra and Horne for a critically acclaimed medley of Harold Arlen songs, cited by *The New York Times* as the "highlight" of the program.

The most unusual segment, however, was Sinatra's sit-down chat with Eleanor Roosevelt, who received some tips from Thompson before the taping began on February 9. Kay recommended that rather than attempt to sing, Mrs. Roosevelt should "recite" the lyrics to "High Hopes" (Sammy Cahn–Jimmy Van Heusen), Sinatra's Oscar-winning hit from *A Hole in the Head* (United Artists, 1959).

However, unbeknownst to Mrs. Roosevelt, exactly two days earlier, Sinatra had been carousing with Jack Kennedy at the Sands Hotel in Las Vegas, where it had been decided that the senator's new official anthem for the presidential primaries would be "High Hopes," to be rerecorded by Frank, featuring customized lyrics such as, "K-E-double-N-E-D-Y, Jack's the nation's favorite guy." Kay helped brainstorm the new words and arrangement with Cahn, Van Heusen, and conductor Nelson Riddle, and coached Frank for the hush-hush recording session on February 9—just hours after Eleanor had left the building.

Since Mrs. Roosevelt had already pledged her support to Adlai Stevenson for the Democratic nomination, her performance of JFK's campaign song became a huge embarrassment.

"My recitation of the song has no political significance," Eleanor Roosevelt angrily protested at a February 12 press conference—three days before the broadcast of her pretaped appearance on the Sinatra special would imply just the opposite. "I didn't know anything about it being [Kennedy's] campaign song."

By the time the Democratic National Convention kicked off on July 11, 1960 (at the Los Angeles Sports Arena), the Kennedy camp was tense because their man had not yet secured all the delegates needed to clinch the nomination.

"Frank Sinatra would've done anything to get Jack elected," Peter Lawford recalled. And if that meant glad-handing every undecided delegate in the stadium, Frank was determined to do it. He gathered his troops—including Kay, Judy Garland, and the rest of his "Jack Pack"—and hit the floor poised for battle.

"They prowled the aisles restlessly," Kitty Kelley reported, "wanting to be a part of the Kennedy power-brokering . . . [wandering] at will from one delegation to the next, impervious of barriers and restrictions."

The next day, with the nomination still uncertain, Kay and Judy flew to New York, where, in Thompson's apartment, they gathered Lena Horne, China Machado, and others to watch the final delegate count on television. Amid cheers and tears of joy, Kennedy won his party's nomination, and on Election Day in November, he prevailed by the slimmest of margins, winning "by only 118,550 votes out of 68,832,818 cast."

Many believe that the election results were swayed by the Mob. Sinatra's own daughter, Tina, admitted in her memoir that her father "had served as a liaison between Joe Kennedy and [Sam] Giancana on a mission that may have swung the 1960 presidential election." But the Jack Pack had certainly done its part to help the cause.

And it is worth noting that Jack Kennedy and Kay Thompson had more than friends in common. According to FBI records, Dr. Max Jacobson had begun administering his methamphetamine-laced "vitamin cocktail" to JFK the week of his September 26, 1960, television debate with Richard M. Nixon.

Jack was so impressed by the euphoric blast of energy, he summoned Max to his home in Hyannisport shortly after the election for more of his "pick-me-up" boosters. Although there is no evidence that Kay had anything to do with connecting Jack with Max, the mutual association may have drawn them closer.

"By the summer of 1961, [the President and the First Lady] had both developed a strong dependence on amphetamines," reported C. David Heymann in *A Woman Named Jackie*. According to Heymann, Robert Kennedy asked the FBI to analyze the contents of five vials Jacobson had left at the White House: "The subsequent FBI report showed the presence of amphetamines and steroids at high concentrated levels." Confronted with the lab results in 1962, Jack raged, "I don't care if it's horse piss. It works." It was a sentiment shared by Thompson and many others.

After Kennedy's victory Sinatra volunteered to organize the John F. Kennedy Inaugural Gala, an all-star fund-raiser for the Democratic Party, to take place at the National Guard Armory in Washington, D.C., on January 19, 1961, the night before the inauguration. Although Sinatra and Peter Lawford would be the figureheads of the event, three *Funny Face* colleagues—Thompson, Roger Edens, and Leonard Gershe—were drafted to respectively direct, produce, and write the extravaganza. They had the enthusiastic blessing of the President-elect and especially his wife, Jackie, who was a big fan of *Funny Face*. (Further channeling the movie, Jackie made immediate arrangements for Richard Avedon to photograph her for *Harper's Bazaar* in the Oleg Cassini gown she would wear to the Inaugural Gala.)

"Kay Thompson flew to Washington last Friday [January 6, 1961] in the Kennedy plane," reported columnist Leonard Lyons. Arriving at the Butler Aviation terminal at National Airport, Kay disembarked the twin-engine *Caroline* with a posse that included Sinatra, Lawford, Edens, and Thompson's pug dog, Fenice, sporting "a smart black sweater."

Preparations and preliminary rehearsals would take place at the Statler Hilton Hotel where Thompson and company set up camp. Plans called for a three-hour show with thirty stars working for free, including Gene Kelly, Jimmy Durante, Milton Berle, Tony Curtis and Janet Leigh, Ella Fitzgerald, Nat King Cole, Bette Davis, Laurence Olivier, Sidney Poitier, Harry Belafonte, plus a seventy-five-piece orchestra alternately conducted by Nelson Riddle and Leonard Bernstein.

Aside from directing, Thompson would appear in the extravaganza, too, leading the cast in an all-star parade that would open and close the show singing "Walking Down to Washington"—another Kennedy campaign song.

Trolling for more star wattage, Kay boldly suggested Ethel Merman—an idea that seemed absurd because of her tireless campaigning for Richard Nixon. But, when the offer was floated, Ethel earnestly told reporters, "It would be an honor to entertain *any* President, Democrat or Republican."

There was one major catch. The Merm was starring in *Gypsy* on Broadway, and producer Leland Hayward refused to underwrite the $12,000 it would cost to go dark for the night. But now that Kennedy had high hopes about Merman's participation as "a show of unity," Sinatra turned to Thompson and said, "I don't care how you do it, just make it happen."

Through the grapevine, Kay knew that Leland Hayward was trying to sign up stars for his latest television special, *General Electric Theatre:* "The Gershwin Years" (CBS-TV, January 15, 1961), but, so far, only Ethel Merman had committed. According to journalist Peter J. Levinson, "Kay called Leland and said, 'Look, if I can get you Frank for free, will you let Ethel do the gala?'"

Booking Sinatra for a TV special would normally have cost in excess of $100,000—so, if all it would take was $12,000 to close *Gypsy* for the night, Hayward was in. Now it was up to Thompson to deliver Sinatra.

"If anyone else had asked Frank to do that, he would have flipped," Levinson insisted. "But coming from Kay? It carried a different weight."

Sinatra acquiesced to the trade-off but strictly limited his time to one four-hour videotaping session in New York on January 9 "with Kay Thompson on hand to supervise each of the numbers." Taking a break from planning the gala, Kay and Frank flew up from Washington on Kennedy's plane, and shortly after one o'clock, they marched into CBS Studio 52 at 254 West Fifty-fourth Street (later the discotheque Studio 54).

"I noticed Kay stayed right by his side all afternoon," *Newark Evening News* reporter Tom Mackin recalled in 2008. Levinson concurred: "They huddled by the playback monitor after each take and he obviously hung on her every word. They seemed very intimate." Until Merman showed up. Upon seeing Ethel, "Sinatra smirked and said, 'Vice President Nixon,'" noted Mackin. "It broke everyone up, including Kay Thompson."

With the gang in good spirits, the taping session was completed a half hour ahead of schedule and Thompson and Sinatra jetted back to Washington to resume preparations for the main event.

On the first day of rehearsal, all the stars were present except for Merman, who could not travel to D.C. until the day of the show. To fill in for Ethel singing "Everything's Coming Up Roses," Kay did a dead-on impression that had everyone in stitches.

"It was parody, it was camp, it was brilliant," bellowed fashion illustrator Joe Eula, on assignment for the *New York Herald-Tribune*. "We all were gasping for air when it was over. Strike me dead, but Kay did Ethel better than Ethel did Ethel."

To Kay's chagrin, Mahalia Jackson did not know any of the words to "The Star-Spangled Banner," and because she couldn't read, cue cards were not an option.

But that was the least of their worries. On the big day, it began to snow and by evening, eight inches had accumulated.

"It's an absolute catastrophe," Thompson declared, gawking at the blizzard in disbelief. "Just wretched, positively kooky."

"Confusion we have seen before," observed *The Washington Post*, "but this was gilt-edged, mink-lined, silk-hatted, 10-gallon, 100-proof, classic and absolutely capital chaos. It snowed—*sideways*."

"The original schedule called for a 9 o'clock curtain," explained *The New York Times*, "[but] at that time the hall was virtually empty and even the President-elect, despite motorcade escort, was slogging through stalled traffic downtown."

When the Kennedys finally arrived at 10:40 p.m., Leonard Bernstein "raised his hands for a fanfare."

"Hooray, hooray! Come join the jubilee," Kay sang while leading the parade of stars in a "Walking Down to Washington" procession to the stage. When the cast had settled, Mahalia Jackson stepped up to the podium to perform "The Star-Spangled Banner," but all of Thompson's coaching had been for naught. Nervous and forgetful, the singer frequently glanced down at a cheat sheet on the podium.

"What the hell is she looking at?!" Thompson hissed. "She can't read!"

The rest of the show went considerably better and, near the end, the President-elect stepped up to the podium and said, "The happy relationship between the arts and our long history, I think, reached culmination tonight."

For the grand finale, the program booklet instructed the audience, "Please join in," with lyric sheets for "Walking Down to Washington" distributed to everyone in the house. Overflowing with pride and optimism, enhanced by the communal ordeal of just getting there, thousands sang along. Of all the superchoirs Kay had ever conducted, this one couldn't be topped.

There were, however, a couple of sour notes. First, drug abuse was as prevalent as the driven snow. According to *A Woman Named Jackie*, Dr. Max Jacobson was in Washington for the festivities "as a guest of Florida Senator Claude Pepper and his wife," patients of Max since the late 1940s. It is not known exactly who got what and when, but the participants in the Inaugural Gala read like a sign-in sheet from Jacobson's Manhattan waiting room.

The other problem was a clash over billing. The official credits in the Inaugural Gala program read "Staged and Directed by Roger Edens; Associate to Mr. Edens: Kay Thompson." Yet *The Washington Post* seemed completely unaware of any contribution by Edens to the show "which the tireless Kay Thompson's been rehearsing all week."

Asked about the discrepancy in 2002, Janet Leigh said, "I don't even remember seeing Roger there. Kay was in charge of everything I did—and as far as I could tell, she was in charge of everything that everybody else did, too."

When the program credits were read to Joe Eula, he hit the ceiling: "That's insane! All I know is that Kay was the fuckin' *boss*! She was blazing around in her Wicked Witch shoes, clicking those heels all over Washington, honey. And *nobody* was telling her what to do. She did the whole thing. She was up there *doin'* it. She was the bandleader. She was John Philip Sousa."

In the month leading up to the gala, it had been announced that Thompson and Edens were forming a partnership to launch "a TV production company," but, in the wake of the credit flap, those plans fell by the wayside. The bond they had shared was never quite the same after that, though Kay remained superficially friendly.

"You never know when he might prove *useful*," she reasoned with brutal pragmatism. According to a number of acquaintances, she used that same callous criterion whenever deciding who to "cut off at the ankles" or to "keep on the list."

As her friendship with Edens cooled, Kay's love affair with Camelot intensified, extending well beyond the First Family. On June 17, 1961, Kay sang "The Trolley Song" with Judy Garland and Ethel Merman at Bobby and Ethel Kennedy's eleventh anniversary dinner dance, accompanied by Lester Lanin and His Orchestra. Thompson's long association with Peter Lawford resulted in several visits to the Kennedy Compound in Hyannisport, where she hit it off with Sargent and Eunice Kennedy Shriver.

Despite never-ending distractions, Kay always found time to coach Judy Garland on nearly everything she did, including her landmark *Judy at Carnegie Hall* concerts in 1961—which spawned a live double LP that spent thirteen weeks at No. 1 and collected five Grammy Awards including Album of the Year.

"Kay not only advised Judy on the songs," recalled Mort Lindsey, music director for *Judy at Carnegie Hall,* "but she did her choreography, too. When Judy did 'Chicago,' for instance, she had a routine all worked out, where her feet were going to go, exactly when her feet were going to stamp. She did it each time identically, and this was what Kay had worked out with her very specifically."

When Garland had a studio album to record, Thompson was usually there—for better or worse. During the 1958 sessions for *Judy in Love,* for instance, Kay brought along Fenice, who caused quite a commotion during the recording of "Do It Again."

"Right at the bridge, the damn thing *farted*," Garland howled, "and everybody went—Mmmwwwrrr-AAAAAH!! Let's get *outta* here!"

Kay was Judy's "security blanket" throughout the filming of "Born in a Trunk" for *A Star Is Born* (Warner Brothers, 1954) and for all her numbers in the animated feature film *Gay Purr-ee* (Warner Brothers, 1962).

Garland also called upon Thompson to be a "creative consultant" on her television specials, including *The Judy Garland Show* (CBS-TV, February 25, 1962), featuring guests Frank Sinatra and Dean Martin, and directed by Norman Jewison, long before his big-time movie career.

"When we went to California to shoot the special, Kay went with us," recalled Jewison. "If you can imagine, I got on that plane with Kay, Judy, all three of her kids—Liza, Lorna and Joey—Mort, the music, the arrangements, the clothes, and that bloody dog of Kay's, Fenice, whose farts were enough to clear out the first-class compartment of any airplane. I'm telling you, it was a circus and we were coming out west to conquer television."

Thompson knew the drill all too well. She told Jewison to schedule all of the sequences involving Frank and Dean on the first day of the three-day shoot, and to forgo the live audience on that day. She knew Frank would not want spectators and that they would get more out of him without that distraction. Conversely, the remaining two days would be spent shooting Judy's solo numbers with a studio audience because she fed off the adulation.

"Judy and Kay and I worked on the arrangement for the opening number, 'Just in Time,'" recalled conductor Mort Lindsey. "We must have worked about eight hours figuring out how to do this thing. It's a spectacular layout because Kay wanted to modulate every eight bars."

"When Mama did her television show with Frank and Dean all that dialogue they say was written by Kay," Liza Minnelli recalled. "It was very casual but all so *charming*. Mama was so attractive and she felt so pretty around Kay. Kay brought out the side of Mama that was really feminine, funny, smart, and sophisticated."

"Kay was just fabulous," Jewison reflected. "She brought a lot of bazazz to that show and she was an anchor for Judy. I don't know what the relationship was between Frank and Kay, but I remember his enthusiasm just *blossomed* around Kay, and he ended up really helping with the number he did with Judy and Dean."

When the show aired on February 25, 1962, it garnered a 49.5 rating—making it the highest-rated special in CBS-TV's history up to that date. Consequently, the network ordered a weekly Garland series for the 1963–64 season. Thompson was asked to work on it, but she declined. "We did a wonderful show," Kay said. "Let's not spoil something that was so wonderful."

Throughout the 1950s and early 1960s, Thompson kept her own ego fully nourished by making guest appearances on a slew of variety shows and, in the wake of her star turn in *Funny Face,* she suddenly had the aroma of a "bankable" Hollywood star. Taking full advantage of this scent, she wrote a letter to Noël Coward: "Why don't you write a marvelous script for a marvelous movie for you and me?" Noël felt they would make a bigger splash on Broadway and so, with that in mind, he began working on *Sail Away,* a musical comedy set aboard a luxury cruise liner.

Flash forward to December 1960 when Kay threw a head-spinning sixty-first birthday soirée for Noël. "It was *the* most extraordinary party I'd ever been to in my whole life," China Machado recalled. "Everybody on Broadway came *before* their performances, *between* their performances, *after* their performances. Then they stayed until dawn the next morning. If they had bombed that studio, there'd be no more Broadway—or Hollywood!"

"It started with near disaster," Noël recounted, "as [Kay] had forgotten to order any food at all! [We] were all famished so we sent out to Steuben's and ultimately all was more than well."

"Kay had rented two grand pianos," China explained, "which she had put together facing each other. She was on one piano and Lennie Hayton was on the other—and they were singing songs to each other. And then Noël Coward sang, Lena Horne sang."

"Richard Burton sang his Welsh songs," recalled model Carmen Dell'Orefice, "and Laurence Olivier ended up in his boxer shorts and bare feet up on top of the piano, pretending to toe-dance."

Thompson explained the key to her "hostess with the mostes" success: "There are two ways to attract people—have a secret everybody's dying to know, or play the piano. And when you have both of them, you're practically Perle Mesta."

Noël was so inspired by Kay's éclat, he stepped up efforts to launch *Sail Away* as her Broadway debut. On January 7, 1961, he noted, " 'Mimi Paragon' is certainly a marvelous part for Kay Thompson. I hope to God she plays it and doesn't make a fathead of herself which, I fear, she is quite capable of doing."

The following month, his worst fears were realized. "Kay came to dine on Monday and *raved* about everything, but doesn't want to play Mimi because she has a complex about appearing on Broadway . . . This, of course, is irritating."

Yes, Kay's dismissal from *Hooray for What!* was traumatic, but in the *quarter century* that had passed since then, she had become one of the most lauded performers in the realm of live entertainment. Her tiresome "complex-about-appearing-on-Broadway" no longer held water. In truth, she was constitutionally unable to commit to anything unless she could rule the roost. Flummoxed, Noël settled on Elaine Stritch instead.

Similarly, Kay flirted with the idea of playing "Vera Charles," the acid-tongued best friend and comic foil of Rosalind Russell in the movie version of *Auntie Mame* (Warner Brothers, 1958). However, after weeks of ever-increasing demands, Rosalind and the producers began to wonder just who was the star of this picture. Ultimately, Coral Browne, a lesser-known actress with a more manageable ego, was cast in the role.

In August 1958, Kay spent some time in Palm Springs, where Roger Edens was developing a musical update of the old Irene Dunne screwball comedy *Theodora Goes Wild,* as a vehicle for Doris Day—with a fresh new title, *Who Is Sylvia?* The movie would also star Thompson, Glenn Ford (the No. 1 Box Office Star of 1958), and Kim Novak in a guest appearance as herself. David Miller (*The Opposite Sex*) was attached to direct; Leonard Gershe was adapting the screenplay; and the score was being composed by Hugh Martin and Ralph Blane (though, according to Martin, Blane's participation was in name only). Edens would have to share his producing credit with Doris' husband, Martin Melcher, as a condition to secure her services.

Who Is Sylvia? would tell the story of Emily Pritchett (Doris Day), a writer from a prudish New England village called Pritchett Falls, who, under the pseudonym Sylvia Storm, has written a lurid romance novel called *Babylon Falls,* a thoroughly sexed-up version of her hometown.

After receiving the manuscript in the mail, New York's most enterprising literary agent, Annabelle Grant (Kay Thompson), convinces Adam Campbell (Glenn Ford), president of Campbell Publishing House, that *Babylon Falls* "will be the next *Peyton Place.*" When Adam asks for the true identity of Sylvia Storm, Annabelle replies that it's a secret.

"It's a good gimmick," Adam agrees. "When the book comes out, the whole country will be asking, 'Who is Sylvia?'"

Cue the musical number "Who Is Sylvia?" sung by Annabelle and her four male assistants—à la Thompson and the Williams Brothers. A montage of vignettes chronicle the overnight sensation of *Babylon Falls*—with everyone around the country joining in the chorus, "Who is Sylvia?"

Everything is rolling along just fine until Adam announces, "I've got a million-dollar offer from Hollywood—they want it for Kim Novak."

When Annabelle fails to get Emily's signature on the contract, Campbell offers a five-hundred-dollar reward to anyone who reveals Sylvia Storm's true identity. A media frenzy ensues and soon Emily's picture is emblazoned on the cover of *Time* magazine as the town of Pritchett Falls is invaded by a Hollywood movie crew for the filming of *Babylon Falls* starring Kim Novak. The chaos escalates from there.

At least on paper, the project seemed like a sure-fire winner, playing to the strengths of all concerned—especially Kay, who would have had a ball bringing Annabelle Grant to life. And, with Edens and Gershe in her court, there would be no shortage of showstopping moments for Thompson. In addition to owning the title song, Kay would also perform a frothy duet with Doris Day entitled "What in the World Do They Want?" which included such clever lyrics as: EMILY: "I've been Novak, enchantingly tawdry." ANNABELLE: "I've been Garland with tears from every pore." EMILY: "I've been Hepburn, both Katharine and Audrey." ANNABELLE: "I've been Ga Ga like Zsa Zsa Gabor."

And the studio wanted even *more* Kay Thompson added to the recipe. "Annabelle ought to be doing a number when she walks down the corridors of that office building in Scene 1," decreed Columbia Pictures executive James Crow in a memo to Edens.

So why did the movie never get made?

According to biographer David Kaufman, Doris nixed the project "because she did not want to undertake another comedy on the heels of *Pillow Talk*." However, that reasoning doesn't wash, since her next picture was *Please Don't Eat the Daisies* (MGM, 1960).

When asked what *really* happened, Hugh Martin said, "To tell you the truth, I think Doris refused to do the movie because my songs were not up to my standard. I was too busy having fun in Palm Springs and not really focusing on my work the way I should have."

Whatever the reason, Edens did not give up his dream to team Doris Day and Kay Thompson in a movie. His next attempt would take him back to MGM on an old pet project that just wouldn't die: *Billy Rose's Jumbo*, based on the 1935 Broadway musical with songs by Richard Rodgers and Lorenz Hart.

Ever since Judy Garland and Frank Sinatra sang a duet of "My Romance" from *Jumbo* on Danny Kaye's radio show in 1945, MGM had planned to team Judy and Frank in the movie version. However, by the time Edens got assigned to produce the film in 1951, both Garland and Sinatra had been fired by the studio.

Roger got Leonard Spigelgass to write the script and, in 1952, announced that Debbie Reynolds and Donald O'Connor, both hot off *Singin' in the Rain*, would be reteamed under the direction of Stanley Donen, with Kay Thompson and Jimmy Durante in supporting parts. Unfortunately, the project got stalled in development due to "restrictive clauses in Billy Rose's contract which prevented tampering with the book and score."

Flash forward to the end of the decade when Edens returned to MGM to resurrect *Jumbo*—now with Doris Day, Richard Burton, Kay Thompson, and Red Skelton in discussions to star, and Charles Walters set to direct from a newly revamped screenplay by Sidney Sheldon.

The story now revolved around the Wonder Traveling Circus, owned by Pop Wonder (Red Skelton), which is in financial trouble because of his gambling debts. The stars of the circus are his aerialist daughter, Kitty Wonder (Doris Day); a fortune-teller named Lulu Bellula, "the Great Indian Mystic" (Kay Thompson); and last but not least, a beloved elephant named Jumbo. Sam Rawlins (Richard Burton) arrives on the scene supposedly to help save the circus from financial ruin, but unbeknownst to all, he is plotting a hostile takeover. Sam's scheme grows complicated when he genuinely falls in love with Kitty.

As preparations began in earnest, however, the supporting cast started to unravel. Richard Burton opted to replace Stephen Boyd in the troubled production of *Cleopatra*, while, in a peculiar flip-flop, Boyd would take over Burton's role in *Jumbo*. Then, for reasons unclear, Red Skelton was dropped in favor of the original choice, Jimmy Durante.

Kay would get to sing a duet with Doris called "Why Can't I?" (Rodgers-Hart; borrowed from *Spring Is Here*) and join the cast for two big production numbers: "Circus on Parade" (Rodgers-Hart) and "Sawdust, Spangles and Dreams," a new finale composed by Roger Edens. There was also going to be a solo number for Lulu but perhaps Doris felt threatened by the prospect of being upstaged by the formidable Miss Thompson. Certainly it was not unusual for Day to make her desires known.

"If Doris didn't like something about somebody," recalled her personal assistant, Barbara Flicker, "she'd give this big sunny smile, then go to her dressing room, and tell [her husband] Marty, 'Get rid of them.'"

Sensing another Fred Astaire situation might be brewing, Thompson was not the least bit interested in locking horns with Doris Day. And, after her run-in with Roger over credit for the JFK Inaugural Gala, she could no longer trust him to protect her best interests. So, when her solo number got nixed during prep, Kay bailed and Martha Raye replaced her.

Considering the enormous impact Thompson made in *Funny Face*, it was a scandal that it took five years for her to act in front of a camera again. The project that finally caught her fancy and follow-through was a made-for-television murder mystery entitled "Who Killed Julie Greer?" presented September 26, 1961, on the premiere installment of NBC's new anthology series, *The Dick Powell Show*, produced by Four Star Television (founded by Dick Powell, David Niven, Charles Boyer, and Ida Lupino).

From an original script by Frank Gilroy (who later won a Tony and a Pulitzer for *The Subject Was Roses*), "Who Killed Julie Greer?" was a standard-issue whodunit that executive producer Dick Powell wanted to goose up with a dozen well-known stars. To get things started, Powell cast himself as Amos Burke, an independently wealthy Los Angeles chief of detectives who solves crimes while being chauffeured around town in his Rolls-Royce. His associate investigator would be played by Dean Jones. The producer of the show, Aaron Spelling, got his wife, Carolyn Jones, to play Julie Greer, the murder victim who gets bumped off in the first few minutes—co-opting the gimmick of Janet Leigh's early demise in *Psycho*. And then there was an impressive school of red herrings to be interrogated by the detectives, including Ronald Reagan, Mickey Rooney, Lloyd Bridges, Ralph Bellamy, Nick Adams, Jack Carson, and Edgar Bergen.

Powell's wife, June Allyson, was going to play Mrs. Pierce, a blind landlady who has heard the murderer's voice and is called upon to identify the culprit by listening to a lineup of suspects. However, Allyson was already signed for a subsequent installment of the same series, so the network decided it would be better not to overexpose her. Consequently, Powell began looking for a replacement among his friends.

"I saw Dick in New York," Kay recalled, "and he asked if I ever wanted to act, and I said, 'Sure,' thinking he was kidding. He told me about the blind part and then went off to Europe. I thought no more about it until he called from Hollywood and asked if I was coming out. This man was serious, honey-darling, and I took the next plane. I didn't ask about the money. I still don't know if it's three dollars or not. Either way, it's O.K. with me."

Next to the thrill of snatching a coveted role away from June Allyson, what most appealed to Thompson was "the chance to stretch." Unlike Miss Prescott in *Funny Face*, Mrs. Pierce was quiet, unassuming, and unfashionably dressed, and had no musical numbers. Plus, as Powell very shrewdly pointed out, it would require "serious acting chops" to pull off the illusion of being blind. Thompson was a sucker for a challenge.

It also didn't hurt that her entire commitment would be just two days: one for a table reading of the script and a group photo shoot for *Life* magazine; and the other for filming all three of her scenes. That was it.

Each star would work for the same "favored nations" rate of $1,000, plus, according to Aaron Spelling, "a beautiful gift from Dick Powell." Billing would be alphabetical and each would be chauffeured in a Rolls-Royce limousine to and from the Four Star lot in Studio City where the show was filmed in June 1961.

"Kay was 'Queen for a Day,'" recalled director Robert Ellis Miller, a veteran of *Perry Mason* and *Peter Gunn*. "She was a terrific pro. She knew how to play blind because she had prepared herself. But I remember telling her, 'Just touch the back of the chair, because then you'll know exactly where you are in the room.' Something as simple as that made all the difference and she smiled because she got it immediately. She nodded and she did it. She was a pleasure."

Reviews were generally upbeat, and *The New York Times* noted that Thompson's "little old blind lady" was a highlight among the "succession of intriguing small character portraits."

Ratings were so impressive, Powell's rich detective character, Amos Burke, was spun off into a series called *Burke's Law,* but, tragically, before production began on the series in 1963, Dick died of cancer and had to be replaced by Gene Barry.

"Historically, 'Who Killed Julie Greer?' really started that thing of putting a famous actor in every part," recalled Dominick Dunne, then a vice president at Four Star Television.

A whole subgenre of all-star murder mysteries was born. Movies like *Murder on the Orient Express* and television staples like *Murder, She Wrote* all trace back to Powell's original high concept.

"And Aaron Spelling applied the idea to shows like *Love Boat,*" costume designer Nolan Miller added. "Because of 'Who Killed Julie Greer?' every aging actor and actress in this town got a chance. If they didn't do *Love Boat,* they were dead."

Nevertheless, it sure seemed like a colossal waste of Thompson's real talents after five years of waiting for her follow-up to *Funny Face.* In the same way she allowed Eloise to hijack her life, Kay had fallen into a rut of creating opportunities for stars other than herself.

Chapter Twelve

MAD ABOUT ANDY

Pygmalion Redux (1949–62)

Kay was Andy's guru. It was a Svengali thing.
—*Norman Jewison*

When Kay Thompson and the Williams Brothers broke up the first time in the summer of 1949, many assumed that Kay's love affair with Andy Williams had ended, too. Far from it. When she took three dancers out on the road that fall, Andy quietly traveled with her, and, during off-hours, they developed an entire act for his first solo flight at Manhattan's Blue Angel in November 1949.

"Andy sang his ass off," recalled Bill Harbach. "It was marvelous, but his act was just a boy singer, like Perry Como, singing at a microphone. No choreography."

"I thought I was going to be Noël Coward," Andy told writer Ben Alba. "So I spent about two years in supper clubs singing 'Mad Dogs and English-men' and doing George Gershwin medleys and that kind of thing."

His repertoire also included a catchy new love song Kay had written for him entitled "(The Birds Are Talkin') 'Bout You 'n' Me," about a clandestine romance that had turned into hot gossip. When Thompson released her own version of the song on Decca Records—with Andy singing backup—it insti-gated another flurry of romance rumors.

The Thompson-Williams affair became such a pervasive topic of discussion, it actually inspired a romantic musical entitled *Two Tickets to Broadway* (RKO, 1951). "The idea came from the success of Kay Thompson and the Williams Brothers," admitted the film's director, James V. Kern. "Reversing it, writer Sammy Cahn thought it would be the basis of a good story if a man were teamed in an act with four girls." The story would focus on the May-December romance that develops between the older headliner, Dan Carter (the Thompson-like star), and the youngest member of his backup quartet, Nancy Peterson (the Andy Williams counterpart).

Howard Hughes, then head of RKO, "liked the idea and bought it" as a vehicle for his latest obsession, Janet Leigh, in the role of Nancy Peterson.

"I had to share my good news with Kay Thompson," Janet wrote in her autobiography.

Thompson offered to give Leigh voice and dance lessons—an idea enthusiastically rubber-stamped by Hughes. Unfortunately, Kay was only intermittently available, so during her absences, Harriet Lee was brought in as the vocal cord drill sergeant; and Marge and Gower Champion were borrowed from MGM for dance instruction.

While Leigh was kept busy rehearsing from January to September 1950, Ann Miller, Gloria DeHaven, and Barbara Lawrence were hired to flesh out the distaff version of the Williams Brothers quartet. And, after Danny Kaye, Bob Hope, Sid Caesar, and Bing Crosby turned down the Thompson role reversal, Hughes offered the part to Frank Sinatra.

"Sinatra would like to do a picture at RKO," Hedda Hopper reported on May 29, 1950. "Said he'd play a male Kay Thompson in it. We both roared." The setup was so ripe, punch lines weren't even necessary. But just days after meeting with Hughes, Sinatra's vocal cords hemorrhaged during a performance at the Copacabana in New York. His recovery was going to take months and Hughes was unwilling to wait.

Ultimately, Tony Martin was signed in July 1950 for ten weeks that grew into six months. "The reason it lasted so long," Martin recalled in his memoir, "is because Hughes developed a crush on the girl star, Janet Leigh, and kept it going so he could be around her more."

In November 1950, Kay breezed into town for some last-minute polishing of the musical number "Big Chief Hole-in-the-Ground."

"[The set] was rigged on the largest stage at RKO and was about four stories high," noted Theodore Taylor in *Jule: The Story of Composer Jule Styne,* "with a winding circular staircase. It was so mammoth that some of it projected outside the stage. Even Busby Berkeley would have been envious of this awesome Gog and Magog."

Then word came down that Howard Hughes wanted to see the work in progress, but plagued by debilitating phobias and superstitions, Howard refused to set foot on his own RKO lot because he thought it would bring him bad luck. So he ordered a full-fledged dress rehearsal on the Samuel Goldwyn lot, including the completed set. In two days.

"The production department was stunned," wrote Taylor. "Carpenters and grips sat down, weak from the thought of it. Did Mr. Hughes know what it meant to dismantle a four-story set, truck it three miles, and rebuild it in forty-eight hours?"

They had no choice but to make it happen. "Promptly at one o'clock, Mr. Hughes made his entry, along with a covey of assistants," Taylor continued. "He observed the number and quickly reacted by firing Kay Thompson. A few minutes later the Champions were fired, without explanation. By 6:00 p.m., composer Jule Styne had quit, along with lyricist Leo Robin."

The "Big Chief" set was hauled back and re-erected at RKO, and Busby Berkeley was hired to take over the choreography. Filming progressed slowly until the day Janet announced she was engaged to Tony Curtis. "Instead of more delays," recalled Tony Martin, "now suddenly they told us we'd have to wrap the picture that midnight."

The final film was forgettable, but like all her colleagues, Thompson made out like a bandit and never looked back.

Meanwhile, Thompson and Williams were still seeing each other as regularly as their schedules allowed, and they adopted a pair of "kids."

"Kay got two boxers," Andy explained. "One we named Barnaby and the other we named Cristóbal. They were siblings."

Cristóbal went with Kay, but she didn't keep him for very long because she was traveling so much. Barnaby, on the other hand, remained Andy's sidekick until he passed away in 1960. "All my companies were named after him," Andy explained. "Barnaby Publishing, Barnaby Records, and Barnaby Productions."

In 1950, Andy took the dog with him on the road when he played solo gigs in cities such as Pittsburgh and Boston.

"I did some of the hotels where Kay Thompson and the Williams Brothers had played," said Andy, "but nobody knew who I was . . . and when I played, nobody listened."

An appearance on *Ed Sullivan's Toast of the Town* (CBS-TV, August 20, 1950)—his television debut—and a regular role as a singing undergrad on the

Chico Marx musical-variety series *The College Bowl* (ABC-TV, 1950) did little to reverse Andy's anonymity.

By the winter of 1951, he was playing small dives in unglamorous cities, making so little money, he was practically down to his last dime. One night, in a dingy motel room, Andy ended up sharing a can of Alpo with Barnaby.

"If I needed a wake-up call," Williams reflected, "a dose of dog food certainly supplied it."

Neither Andy nor his brothers had found much success on their own, so the idea of a reunion of Kay Thompson and the Williams Brothers sounded mighty fine. A tour was mounted and, for the next two years, they earned top dollar playing the A-list clubs—just like old times.

When the act was dissolved once and for all in 1953, many wondered if Kay and Andy's relationship had finally run its course. Not in the slightest.

Marti Stevens, who lived directly under Thompson's Los Angeles flat at 1364 Beverly Glen, remembers seeing Williams "scampering up the steps to Kay's apartment, at all hours of the day and night. Very often. Now, I can't tell you details. I wasn't hiding under the piano. But Andy practically wore a path up those stairs. They were very close."

In the summer of 1954, Williams did his very first solo sessions for RCA's Label X in Hollywood. Of the seven songs recorded, two were composed by Thompson: "(There Is a Time) A-O-Lee-O," an early example of rock 'n' roll, with a Persian flavor; and "Ground Hog," a fusion of jazz and rock 'n' roll with a call-and-response children's choir. Two singles with non-Thompson compositions were released but the records went nowhere, resulting in the rest of the songs being shelved. "(There Is a Time) A-O-Lee-O" finally surfaced in 1971 on the Camden Records album *Andy Williams*, and, in 2006, was faithfully covered by the British indie rock band Vatican Jet. Sadly, "Ground Hog" has never been released (though it still exists in RCA's vault).

With his recording career a bust, Andy's luck turned when NBC's Pat Weaver ordered a brand-new late-night series called *The Tonight Show Starring Steve Allen*, produced by Kay's former aide-de-camp, Bill Harbach.

"Billy called one day," Kay explained in a BBC Radio interview, "and he said, 'Listen, we need a singer. What do you think about Andy? Do you think he can do it?' And I said, 'Bill. Of *course* he can do it!' He said, 'Well, he's gonna have to audition for Steve.' And I said, 'He'll be there. No doubt.' So I called Andy and I said, 'Come over here!' I said, 'I think maybe you ought to do a medley . . . I'll put these two songs together . . . 'All I Do Is Dream of You' and 'You're My Everything.' And by God, he went over there and got it, of course."

The Tonight Show premiered September 27, 1954, and became an instant hit—still going strong today—but there is an untold part of the success story.

"Kay helped me arrange songs to perform on that show, just as a friend," Andy confessed. "She did quite a few of those—uncredited, unpaid, and without the knowledge of the show. Kay would teach me her arrangements and she got Peter Matz to do the orchestrations. Peter was going to a shrink and the shrink was charging him twenty-five dollars a session. So I paid him twenty-five dollars per orchestration. Then I'd come in to work on the show and everyone was so amazed that I had these amazing arrangements. I never told anybody that it was Kay. I wanted them to think that it was me. It was one of the reasons why they kept me going on that show for nearly two-and-a-half years."

There was one instance when a Thompson arrangement proved to be a bit embarrassing. "Andy sheepishly remembered the night they did a tribute to Richard Rodgers," wrote Ben Alba in *Late Night*. "He sang Rodger's classic 'Spring Is Here,' a song he frequently performed in his nightclub act, but didn't realize that the opening verse he had been doing was something extra that had been written especially for him by Kay Thompson and incorporated into his arrangement of the song. When he sang Thompson's verse in front of Rodgers, 'Richard Rodgers was looking at me like, *What the hell is this?*' chuckled Andy. 'And then he told me later, *I didn't write that first part!*'"

With a regular paycheck coming in, Andy could afford to rent a $129 per month apartment at 5 East Sixty-third Street, right off Fifth Avenue—just four blocks north of Kay's suite at The Plaza.

He decorated nearly every inch of his walls with framed artwork. "[Andy] is a budding art collector," wrote columnist Dick Kleiner in 1958. "Although no painter, he likes to surround himself with nice paintings, generally modern impressionists. This started when he was with Kay Thompson."

Buoyed by his ongoing *Tonight Show* exposure, Andy felt the time was right to get a record deal. "I told Kay that I really wanted to get a contract with Cadence Records because the label was churning out a lot of hit records for the Everly Brothers and others," he explained. "Kay said, 'Oh, well I know the owner, Archie Bleyer.' And I said, 'Listen, if you can get me a contract with Cadence, I will give you half.' And she basically took me up on that offer."

Having helped Bleyer launch his career in 1941, Thompson had every reason to believe he'd return the favor. "Kay and I went over there," Andy recalled. "She played piano for me and I sang. A man of few words, Archie said, 'Do you want to make some records?' I said, 'Yeah.' He said, 'Fine,' and gave me a contract."

As a result, Thompson demanded 50 percent of Williams' royalties, an onerous deal that he would live to regret. Aside from the money, the provision magnified Kay's sense of entitlement over Andy.

For instance, when Kay gave up her suite at The Plaza in 1956, she moved into an apartment at 9 East Sixty-second Street, just around the corner from Andy's flat on Sixty-third. It was very convenient when they were working together, but when he needed a little space, it was a bit too close for comfort— especially when he began dating other women.

Andy's breakthrough came when his third single at Cadence, "Canadian Sunset," climbed to No. 7 in August 1956. But his follow-up, "Baby Doll," stalled at No. 33. This disheartening development was followed by the news that Steve Allen was leaving *The Tonight Show* on January 25, 1957, which meant Andy was out of a job.

Andy's mellow style, it seemed, was not in tune with the hottest trend in music: rock 'n' roll. Williams recalled the day in January 1957 when Bleyer played Charlie Gracie's latest rock 'n' roll single, "Butterfly," for him: "I listened to the record and I thought, 'Boy, that doesn't sound like me at all.' He said, 'Well, if you want a hit . . .' And I said, 'Yeah, I do want a hit.' And he said, 'Well, then we oughta do this song.'"

"I got an Elvis Presley record, and I listened to it a lot, and I went and did the same thing," Williams later told Larry King.

In the spring of 1957, Williams' version of "Butterfly" soared all the way to No. 1 on both the U.S. and UK charts. There was nothing "Andy Williams" about it, but who could argue with success?

Thompson was not surprised. "I love Elvis Presley," she proclaimed on CBS-TV's *Person to Person* in November 1956, a declaration later reinforced when she sang one of Presley's hits, "Stuck on You," on *Perry Como's Kraft Music Hall.* Thompson was fascinated by Elvis's androgyny, calling him "a sort of butch Lolita."

Following "(There Is a Time) A-O-Lee-O" and "Ground Hog," Kay had continued dabbling in rock 'n' roll songwriting, her latest being "You Gotta Love Everybody," with lyrics by Bill Norvas, which was recorded by such artists as Della Reese, the Sun Spots, and Ray Ellington. Even Danny Kaye gave it a whirl, but his label, Capitol Records, declined to release it.

Once Williams got on the bandwagon, Thompson wasted no time writing an Elvis sound-alike for him called "Stop Teasin' Me," which she submitted to Bleyer under the nom de plume Y. Des Louvettes—which looked French, but when phonetically pronounced with a heavy Southern drawl, it came out "Why, they love it."

"Stop Teasin' Me" became the B-side of Andy's next Cadence rocker, "I Like Your Kind of Love," which peaked at No. 8 in May 1957. After years of positioning himself as a crooner of show tunes, Andy hit pay dirt doing Elvis. Go figure.

Sticking with the trend, Andy's seventh single featured two more guitar-laden rock 'n' rollers: "Lips of Wine" and "Straight from My Heart," the latter composed by an emboldened Kay Thompson, no longer hiding behind a pseudonym.

On September 9, 1957, Andy performed the new songs on Dick Clark's *American Bandstand,* but apparently kids just weren't buying it. It was one thing to *hear* Andy copy Elvis on the radio, but quite another to *see* him masquerading as a rock 'n' roller on TV. No amount of vocal hiccups and pelvic thrusts could cover the fact that Andy was simply out of his element. Sales of the single stalled.

Sure, copying Elvis may have worked in the short term, but to build a career with longevity, Andy needed sincerity. So, fittingly, his next Cadence single was entitled "Are You Sincere?"—a passionate ballad that was squarely in his comfort zone. When the single shot to No. 3 in February 1958, it proved that there was, after all, a market for the *real* Andy Williams. There were sighs of relief all around, especially from Kay, whose bank account got a nice infusion of cash.

For his next single, Kay wrote a midtempo pop ballad, "Promise Me, Love," that marked Williams' first A-side of a Thompson composition. In September 1958, the song rose to No. 17, followed shortly thereafter by "Hawaiian Wedding Song," which reached No. 11 and snagged a Grammy Award nomination for Best Male Vocal Performance.

With his pop crooner status on the rise, Andy hosted three consecutive summer replacement series in 1957, 1958, and 1959, with Kay working as a "creative consultant" most intensively on the last one. *The Andy Williams Show* was broadcast on CBS-TV, from July 7 to September 22, 1959, directed by Norman Jewison.

"Kay was Andy's guru," Jewison recalled. "It was a Svengali thing, and she had a lot of say on what we did."

Her influence on the show stretched far beyond the music. "I want *Harper's Bazaar,*" she demanded, "not Ed Sullivan!"

"Kay had worked quite a bit with Avedon," recalled art director Gary Smith, "and she was very keen on *Vogue*-like imagery. She helped us set a whole new standard for a TV variety show. The 'all-white' look. No one had seen anything like it. It was revolutionary."

"White on white," Jewison concurred. "I suggested that we paint the floor white going into gray and then blend it into the cyclorama at the back and then lighting it in such a way that they were endless in space."

"I will never forget one particular number Kay had us do that just bowled everybody over," Smith remembered. "Way in the back of the all-white stage, in the infinity, was Andy Williams wearing a Panama hat and something rolled up at his feet that was about five feet wide. It was a roll of gray paper and he kicked it and it rolled right down to camera. And then he just snapped his fingers, singing 'Look down that lonesome road,' walking down this path he made. It was so simple and yet the hair on the back of my neck stands up just thinking about it."

On another installment, Thompson created an Asian arrangement for Gershwin's "They Can't Take That Away from Me," featuring the Peter Gennaro Dancers dressed in Kabuki costumes.

"Gimmicks like that were Kay's ideas," Smith observed. "Pure Kay Thompson."

Helped by his weekly television exposure, Andy's next single zoomed all the way to No. 5: "Lonely Street," backed with a new Thompson composition called "Summer Love."

If there were any doubts that Kay was still hung up on Andy, the melancholy, lovesick lyrics of "Summer Love" put those to rest. Reinforcing that notion to millions of Americans was the Williams spread in the September 1, 1959, issue of *Look* magazine, with Andy sprawled out on the floor of Thompson's apartment, rough-housing with Fenice as Kay observes the shenanigans from a nearby sofa. Domestic bliss practically leapt off the page.

If Kay wanted Andy all to herself, however, she was in for a lot of heartache. *TV Guide* wrote that the thirty-one-year-old bachelor was "quite content to play the field," and gossip columnists would soon link Andy to a whole string of starlets, including Ann-Margret, Kathleen Nolan, Hope Lange, Pippa Scott, Carol Lawrence, and, most seriously, Claudine Longet, whom he began dating in August 1960, when she was a seventeen-year-old dancer for *Les Folies Bergere* in Las Vegas.

The ratings and reviews for *The Andy Williams Show* were so terrific, suddenly all three networks were bidding for Andy to headline his own series during the regular television season. However, the only time slots being offered were of the sacrificial lamb variety—in competition with such ratings stalwarts as *Gunsmoke*. Skittish, Thompson reminded him of what happened to Patti Page's *The Big Record* when it went up against *Wagon Train*.

Andy took the advice to heart, choosing to stay in the public eye by hosting network specials and by appearing in top nightclubs—which were not only risk-free but highly lucrative.

During a gig at New York's Copacabana, Williams came down with a serious case of laryngitis. "I'd heard about the miraculous healing powers of Dr. Max Jacobson from Kay," Andy recalled. "Archie Bleyer also went to him. So, I went to him to help me. He said, 'Do you want to sing higher or lower?' I said, 'I don't care. I just want to sing.' He gave me a shot. I went outside and hailed a taxi. 'Take me to 5 East 63rd Street.' By the time I got halfway home, I was talking a mile a minute, so fast I couldn't control myself, like Donald Duck. I told the cabbie, 'Now-wait-a-minute-take-me-back-to-where-you-picked-me-up!' And I was like, 'Let-me-out-here-okay-thank-you-very-much!' And I raced back in and said, 'Wait-a-minute-what-the-hell-is-wrong-with-me-what-did-you-give-me-I-can't-stop-talking-so-fast!' Then Jacobson poked a needle right in the middle of my stomach and my speech wound down like a battery was running out. It was scary, but, I have to say, I went back to the Copacabana and I didn't have any laryngitis. I got through it fine."

On the recording front, Andy took a chance releasing a religious song, "The Village of St. Bernadette," which went all the way to No. 7 during Christmas week of 1959. Its surprise success motivated Bleyer to fast-track an entire album of inspirational songs. Andy asked Kay if he could include her special version of the Twenty-third Psalm, "The Lord Is My Shepherd," which she had written in 1948 with Andy in mind but had never recorded.

"I don't think so," Thompson replied. "I want to save that for Leonard Bernstein and a full orchestra."

Andy was crushed. "I couldn't believe that she wouldn't allow me to perform the song," Williams recalled in his memoir. "I had been with her when she wrote it, and I had sung it for her many times in her apartment. I guess that was Kay; she was possessive about everything she worked on."

Nevertheless, Andy hung on to that arrangement and, after Kay's death, sang it at the 2003 funeral of his eldest brother, Bob.

As consolation, Kay composed "Sweet Morning" for the album *The Village of St. Bernadette,* and Andy magnanimously recorded it—though it must have been with a heavy heart.

Positive reaction to the album cheered him up, especially when he received a commendation from the Vatican.

Emboldened by this experimentation, Andy persuaded Archie to let him self-produce his next album, *Under Paris Skies,* a collection of French-flavored songs, including a new Thompson composition entitled "Au Revoir, Paris," her wistful answer to "Bonjour, Paris!" from *Funny Face.*

Partly for authenticity but also, more important, to remove himself from Bleyer's cocoon, Williams recorded the album in France with an up-and-coming conductor named Quincy Jones. The resulting album was nothing short of exquisite, showcasing Williams' dazzling vocals and Jones' lush orchestrations—with "Au Revoir, Paris," representing the very best of Kay's compositions for Andy.

With Williams' reputation building as a recording artist and television star, it wasn't long before Hollywood came calling. In August 1960, Hedda Hopper announced that Andy had been cast to star in the movie version of *Bye Bye Birdie* at Columbia Pictures. The role had been originated on Broadway by Dick Van Dyke (Andy's sidekick in his 1958 summer replacement series), but at that time Williams was considered more of a household name. Contractually, however, shooting could not start until the Broadway musical had run its course.

In the meantime, Kay felt Andy could use some experience doing a stage musical—quietly, off the beaten path, beyond the glare of New York critics. As a result, he signed up to star with Julie Wilson in a summer-stock tour of *Pal Joey* for the Kenley Players theater circuit in Columbus, Dayton, and Warren, Ohio, throughout July 1961—with Thompson on board as his coach.

"Kay traveled with Andy," recalled theater owner John Kenley in 2005. "By the time they arrived, we had the musical all laid out and we had to get it on in five days, including the dress rehearsal. It was boom, boom, boom."

Nevertheless, Thompson insisted on adding a number from *Gypsy*, "All I Need Is the Girl" (Jule Styne–Stephen Sondheim), for Andy to sing "as the first-act curtain number."

"Kay was absolutely brilliant," Kenley remembered. "She brought out the best in Andy and was highly respected by all."

Williams came away with more confidence to handle the *Bye Bye Birdie* movie challenge. Unfortunately, two months later, *The Dick Van Dyke Show* premiered on CBS-TV and became an instant smash. By the time *Bye Bye Birdie* went into production, Columbia Pictures dumped Andy for Dick.

At the same time, Andy's relationship with Kay was coming to a predictable climax right out of *Pygmalion*. The inevitable declaration of independence occurred in October 1961, when Andy signed with Columbia Records, thereby eradicating Kay's fat commission.

"Fifty percent was a pretty harsh deal," Andy reflected in 2002. "It represented hundreds of thousands of dollars. I really, in the back of my mind, sort of expected Kay to give back that money at some later date. But lo and behold, that never came to pass. She kept it. And that was that."

Two months later, Andy effectively severed any lingering romantic ties between them when he married Claudine Longet.

"I have compassion for Kay," remarked Marti Stevens, "because, at a certain age, young lovers inevitably strike off on their own and it's a killer. Her feeling would have been that she was dumped . . . and used and betrayed."

"Looking back on our affair with the benefit of hindsight," Williams reflected in his memoir, "I wonder whether it was not only Kay who attracted me but also the glamour and aura that surrounded her, the artistic and literary circles she moved in, and the famous people she knew. Whatever it was, I loved everything about her."

On the rebound, Kay got back together with Dave Garroway, but by then he was a broken man. The April 1961 suicide of his second wife triggered a downward spiral that resulted in Garroway being fired from *The Today Show* on June 16, 1961. Soon afterward, Dave reconnected with Kay, but his mood swings and his long-term addiction to codeine short-circuited the affair before the year was out. (Garroway's mental state never fully recovered; he died in 1982 from a self-inflicted gunshot wound.)

While on this emotional roller coaster, Kay was also mourning the sudden death of her beloved younger sister, Marion, who had succumbed to cervical cancer on April 1, 1960. With Marion gone, the only remaining blood relative from her immediate family was her older sister, Blanche, but they had grown apart over the years. The heartbreak left Kay feeling more alone and vulnerable than ever before.

In the summer of 1961, Thompson got another kick in the stomach. "While Kay was away from New York," China Machado recalled, "her maid, Sarah, and her boyfriend went to live in Kay's apartment and drank all the liquor that was in the house, got drunk, and totally trashed the place. She wore all of Kay's clothes and ruined them. Kay came back unexpectedly and this is what she found. Kay just let the woman go and said to me, 'Oh God, I'm so disappointed.' It soured her feelings about the entire apartment and she no longer wanted to live there."

It was the last straw. She dumped her New York flat and sprinkled her oddball possessions among friends "on permanent loan."

"I didn't want anything," Kay remarked. "Let it all go, I said. Travel light. I just grabbed my pug dog and headed for Rome."

Part Six

THE DOYENNE

Chapter Thirteen

THE ROMAN SPRING OF MISS THOMPSON

Eloise on the Tiber

(1962–68)

Dear Eloise, We wish we could hold your hand, yeah, yeah, yeah.

—*The Beatles*

*I*n April 1962, Kay Thompson arrived in Rome, hell-bent on embracing *la dolce vita*. The self-appointed welcome wagon for visiting showbiz royalty was an American businessman named Lee Engel, vice president of International Latex (makers of Playtex bras), who had recently been transferred to Rome. Having served in the Merchant Marine with Richard Avedon and Leonard Gershe, Engel shared many of their friends, including Thompson. Though gossip columns reported flings with Janis Paige and Doe Avedon, intimates knew Lee was gay. That did not stop our heroine from falling head-over-heels for him.

"Kay Thompson found her Great Love in Rome," claimed Walter Winchell. "An American exec."

What Kay and Lee shared was a passion for exploration, sightseeing, and treasure hunting in curio shops. They even collaborated on business ideas.

"Kay actually designed a Playtex bra or wrote an ad campaign for them," recalled journalist Roland Flamini, at the time a correspondent for Reuters. "There was a lot of talk about bras."

With Engel's help, Thompson leased a three-level maisonette atop the Palazzo Torlonia (at the bottom of the Spanish Steps), the royal palace of Prince Alessandro Torlonia (great-uncle of actress Brooke Shields) and his wife, Beatriz, Infanta of Spain and aunt of Juan Carlos I, the future King of Spain.

"Juan Carlos—who was then in his twenties—would come over and visit Kay from time to time," remembered Flamini. "They were very friendly."

The first time Thompson saw her spectacular view of a scarlet sunset over Rome, she wept. "It is a wonderful place to sit and think about all the things you've done right and wrong in life," Kay waxed philosophical for a minute or two.

But, then there was work to be done. To clean the apartment twice a week, she hired Engel's housekeeper, Concetta. Because she always raised her arms, dramatically shrieking "Señora, señora!" Kay called her Edith Piaf or Anna Magnani, depending on the level of hysteria.

Thompson's decorating flourishes were equally over-the-top. For the rooftop garden, she used an old porcelain toilet as a flower pot—and stored her sheet music in the rear tank.

"Kay discovered minimalism," marveled Mart Crowley, Natalie Wood's former secretary, who had just arrived in Rome hoping to find work as an art director on movies. "This was pre-Beatles, so nobody was sitting on harem cushions on the floor at the time, but that's what Kay wanted."

The ceilings were magnificently high with windowed French doors that opened onto a green-tiled terrace. She had the rooms painted aquamarine blue and hung flowing blue curtains that billowed in the breeze. Mirrors and bold artwork went up on the walls. Crowley recalled that her office was lined with "kitsch paintings of priests, dressed in birettas and cassocks, doing unlikely things like walking a tightrope or swinging on swings in a playground." For the living room, Kay splurged on an original oil, *Rouge et Noir*, by Antoni Clavé, the renowned abstract expressionist and Oscar-nominated art director and costume designer.

"She had a three-fold screen," noted choral director Ray Charles, "like the Oriental ones, except hers was just a bare wood frame with chicken wire on it."

"Well, you know what it needs now?" Kay said to Crowley. "The *zebes*."

"That's what she called her treasured zebra skins that she used as rugs," Crowley translated. They were later used as set dressing for *The Boys in the*

Band, William Friedkin's movie adaptation of Crowley's groundbreaking off-Broadway play.

Then she bought ten unfinished wooden Chinese side tables, twelve inches high, that she decided to paint red.

"Kay *loved* the color red," recalled Kitty D'Alessio, then an advertising executive, before her ascendency to president of Chanel. "One time, very late at night, Kay made me sneak with her to the Elizabeth Arden salon that was down on Piazza di Spagna, and—with me as her lookout—she scraped a little paint off the Red Door into an envelope and said, 'This will be my *campione'*—her 'sample.'"

Crowley picked up the story: "Kay and I went to a drugstore and she found this exact shade of red in a Revlon fingernail polish and bought out their entire stock. Then the two of us start painting the tables with these tiny nail polish brushes that are attached to the inside of the little screw-top lids. Well, the wood hadn't been primed, so it just soaked up all the paint and it took forever."

"I helped her," recalled Robert Wagner, who, having just filed for divorce from Natalie Wood, was in Italy to lick his wounds and to film Vittorio De Sica's *The Condemned of Altona* with Sophia Loren. "But we kept running out of nail polish, so then we'd have to go out and find more of it."

"Then she got a grand piano," said fashion illustrator Joe Eula. "But they couldn't get it up the spiral staircase, so they sawed off the legs and lowered it through the skylight."

"Put it on the floor," Kay ordered. "That's how I want it."

"She'd sit cross-legged like a Japanese Genkō," Eula continued, "and play the piano to serenade that damn dog of hers, Fenice."

"Kay was a world-class eccentric and everyone gravitated to her," Roland Flamini mused. "She'd have dinner with Pat Kennedy, Gregory Peck, Elizabeth Taylor. She was a port of call for Americans of a certain type in Rome."

"Rita Hayworth was always flying her places because she had Karim Khan's plane," added Mart Crowley.

Noël Coward often visited Kay, too. "We dined peacefully," Coward wrote in his diary, "and sat afterwards on the Via Veneto and had ice creams while we watched the gay throng of hustlers, pimps, queens, faggots, priests and tourists ambling past."

And when her old friend Perry Como arrived in 1966 to record his latest album, *Perry Como in Italy,* Kay wined and dined him and his entourage.

"Kay got us to improvise a parody of 'I Believe,'" recalled the album's choral arranger, Ray Charles. "It went, 'I believe in homo-sex-u-ality, for man and beast. I believe that it deserves le-gal-ity to say the least.'"

"One of her favorite places to go was the Blue Bar at the Osteria dell'Orso," said Kitty D'Alessio. "One night, we were there with Lee Engel, Bobby Mackintosh, and Lennie Gershe. Kay sat down at the piano and began to play 'My Funny Valentine.' Then she became the vocal director and made this group sing this, and that group sing that, and then she put us all together. It was just magical."

Roland Flamini related, "My former wife, Janet, answered a classified ad in the *Rome Daily American* to be the assistant to somebody who turned out to be Kay Thompson. At the time, Janet was very young, very calm, very proper, and, above all, very British. All of that appealed to Kay so she hired her."

"For her breakfast at noon," Janet Flamini remembered, "I always was required to bring a papillon biscuit—in the shape of a butterfly. She had a nickname for everybody. Mine was Janetini."

"Kay's nickname for Lee Engel was Fellini," added Kitty D'Alessio, "because he was always photographing everybody with his Polaroid camera."

It wasn't long before the *real* Fellini came into Kay's life. She claimed that the director once made a pass at her—a tale that seems mighty tall—but he did, in fact, offer her the bit part of a pushy fashion magazine reporter in his latest movie, *Federico Fellini's 8½*. (Kate Hudson played a younger, sexier version of the character in the 2009 musical adaptation, *Nine*.)

"Fellini had seen Kay around Rome and was fascinated by her," said Hilary Knight. "She told me that he summoned her to his office to discuss playing this particular part. He sat her in a chair in the center of a room and walked continually around her, talking to her all the time while staring at her and observing her. She was flattered and totally intrigued by the idea of someone like Fellini being interested in her. She also knew that what he had in mind was to turn her into one of his grotesques—another freak in the freak show. She was smart enough to see that and declined. But she enjoyed having this important director wooing her and she played along with it for a while before turning him down."

Instead, Kay got Fellini to cast Gilda Dahlberg, the colorful aunt of Peter Matz, now a fabulously wealthy widow residing in Rome. Gilda showed up on set wearing sequined and feathered "leftovers from her days as a Ziegfeld girl."

On the social scene, Thompson reconnected with Marion Marshall, who, after divorcing *Funny Face* director Stanley Donen in 1959, had moved to Rome with their two children (Peter and Josh), and, like Kay, was in search of a fresh start.

"When I arrived in Rome," Robert Wagner recalled, "I took over Lee Engel's old apartment at 7 Via Adda—he'd just gotten a bigger place—and he introduced me to Marion." (Mart Crowley crashed there, too, until he could find work).

"When I was going with Robert Wagner before we were married," Marion Marshall Donen Wagner recalled in 2004, "he was shooting a movie at Tirrenia Studios in Livorno, which was on the beach, so I moved up there for the summer of 1962 with the kids, and Kay came up, too. We went to a dime store called Standa and, for five dollars every day, we would completely outfit ourselves in some wild shirts, hats, and beads, and then we would arrive on the beach, all decked out in our latest ensembles."

"RJ [Robert Wagner] had a four-door Jaguar sedan," Mart Crowley recalled, "and he drove Marion, Kay, and I around in it everywhere. He would pay for everything. Kay never offered to pay but, in return, she did buy RJ the most outrageous, expensive gift. It was a collapsible wooden 'butterfly' chair with real zebra skin. She bought it at Gucci."

She could be generous in other ways, as well. In June 1962, for example, Kay attended a Frank Sinatra concert in Rome to benefit the Boys Towns of Italy orphanage. A choir of orphans performed during the show, and afterward, Frank introduced the boys to Kay. Moved, she volunteered to be a guest choir director from time to time. And Marion Marshall recalled a related charitable impulse. "Kay and Lee Engel found a less fortunate boys' orphanage on the way to Naples. They took over and supplied blankets, clothes, shoes, and threw these lavish annual Christmas dinner parties with Kay performing for the kids."

Although Thompson boycotted the United States, she frequently visited France, Switzerland, and England. In late July 1962, for instance, she flew to London to coach Judy Garland in *I Could Go On Singing* (and to emotionally prepare her to file for divorce from Sid Luft, which she did soon after the shooting of the movie was completed).

Then Kay got the itch to write a screenplay. It all started when she was seated on an airplane next to the great jazz vibraphonist Lionel Hampton (whom she'd known since 1937 when they performed on *The Saturday Night Swing Club*). He had just taken part in a cultural exchange arts festival in Lagos, Nigeria, where he discovered a local thirteen-year-old prodigy named Mike Falana "who could play trumpet like Miles Davis."

According to Dorothy Kilgallen, "Kay made shorthand notes and was so enthralled . . . she wrote a screenplay based on them . . . titled *The Pebble*." Unfortunately, in a quagmire of revisionitis, the manuscript stalled in her Olivetti.

In the fall of 1962, a cat burglar caper entitled *The Pink Panther* was gearing up for shooting at Cinecittà Studios on the outskirts of Rome. Hot on the heels of *Breakfast at Tiffany's*, Blake Edwards was set to direct the picture, with the hands-on producer being his former agent, Martin Jurow, who had coproduced *Tiffany's*.

Oscar winner Maurice Richlin (*Pillow Talk*) came up with the basic story line about "a detective who is trying to catch a jewel thief who is having an affair with his wife." The main object of the thief's desire is a rare, priceless diamond with a pink flaw shaped like a panther.

Though *The Pink Panther* is remembered for introducing the bumbling Inspector Clouseau, spawning an enduring movie franchise, in this first film outing Clouseau was only a supporting character among a large ensemble that, originally, was to include David Niven (the jewel thief known as "the Phantom"), Audrey Hepburn (Princess Dala, owner of the Pink Panther diamond); Peter Ustinov (Inspector Clouseau); Ava Gardner (Simone Clouseau, wife of the inspector); and Robert Wagner (the thief's playboy nephew).

There was one more delicious role that beckoned for a casting coup: Angela Dunning, a social climber modeled after real-life "hostess with the mostes" Perle Mesta and society columnist Elsa Maxwell. Because the Phantom stages all the jewel robberies during Angela's soirees, everyone on her guest list is under suspicion—including Angela herself.

Naturally, Thompson's name came up because she was perfect for the role, pals with all five stars, and a cost-effective "local hire." When the offer was made, however, she played hard to get by demanding a musical performance during her big party scene. Though Edwards was not terribly eager to "suddenly stop the plot to do a number," he granted Thompson's wish.

She offered to sing her own Italian-flavored composition, "Subito," which Steve Rossi had recently recorded for Columbia Records. But Edwards was partial to hit-maker Henry Mancini, who had just won an Oscar for "Moon River" from *Breakfast at Tiffany's*. He phoned Mancini in Hollywood and asked him to compose a "Latin jet-set" number. The result was "Meglio Stasera (It Had Better Be Tonight)," with lyrics cowritten by Franco Migliacci ("Volare") and—with considerable irony—Johnny Mercer ("On the Atchison, Topeka and the Santa Fe").

To stage the number, Kay wanted Hermes Pan, who had come to Rome to choreograph *Cleopatra* and never left. Bowing to Thompson's pressure—again—the producers complied.

Meanwhile, negotiations with Audrey Hepburn hit a snag and she was replaced by a far less costly Claudia Cardinale, fresh off the set of *Federico Fellini's 8½*. "When Kay was cast in the film," recalled Roland Flamini, "she wanted to meet Claudia in advance of the movie, so she threw a dinner party for her—

though I'm sure she had no idea who Kay was." Cardinale's English was so bad, she came with a translator and ultimately had to be dubbed throughout the entire film.

Around that time, fashion wunderkind Yves Saint Laurent was hired to design chic ensembles to be worn in the film by Cardinale and Ava Gardner. Because Yves was a friend, Kay assumed her own wardrobe would be created by him as well. Not so. Edwards purposefully wanted Angela Dunning to be dressed in clownish designs by Annalisa Nasalli-Rocca, one of the resident wardrobe mistresses at Cinecittà.

Thompson would have none of it. "She demanded that Yves Saint Laurent do her clothes and insisted they fly her first-class to Paris for a fitting," related Mart Crowley.

While Thompson waited for a response to her latest ultimatum, Ava Gardner got canned because her own perks had bloated the budget by $100,000. To replace Gardner, the producers went after Elizabeth Taylor, but since she'd been spoiled by *Cleopatra*, her demands were positively Elizabethan. As a cheaper alternative, Charles Feldman, the agent for both Edwards and Wagner, suggested another client from his stable, a thirty-four-year-old model-turned-actress named Capucine.

"They were an item at the time, she and Charlie," Blake admitted.

"The replacement did not please Peter Ustinov," wrote executive producer Walter Mirisch in his 2008 memoir, "who advised us that he did not want to act in the film with Capucine and chose to withdraw from the cast."

The emergency substitute for Ustinov was Peter Sellers, who was flown in from London on Saturday, November 10—just two days before shooting was set to commence. During the ride from the airport to the hotel, he convinced Edwards that Inspector Clouseau should be played more broadly, as an accident-prone buffoon. So, on Monday, Sellers went before the cameras, slapshtick and all, and summarily hijacked the picture.

With the budget awash in red ink, producer Martin Jurow was ready to snap if someone so much as requested a paper clip. So, on Friday, November 16, when Thompson started up again about her wardrobe, Jurow just lost it.

"Kay got a big ramrod up her ass," was how Robert Wagner remembered Martin's tirade. "I was in the makeup department when it all went down. Kay came in and was very upset. She was crushed."

"I can't be in show business anymore," Kay fumed. "I don't have the stomach for it."

"But Kay wasn't just upset about the wardrobe," Wagner added. "It was also the script, which was always being altered."

Originally, there was a major subplot involving Kay's character and three important red herrings: a British novelist, a Greek shipping magnate, and a Chicago Mafia daughter-turned-Hollywood starlet. Once Sellers commandeered more screen time, however, these scenes were truncated or cut altogether. Alarmed that her role was being chipped away to nothing, Thompson confided to Wagner that she was on the verge of walking off the picture.

"What in the fucking hell is the matter with you?!" Wagner pleaded. "Don't you realize this is a great shot?!"

But the die had been cast. According to Louella Parsons, Kay "flipped her wig and left the set."

The party line over Thompson's exit was diplomatic. "A spokesman for the Mirisch film production said the actress-author's departure was by 'mutual consent,'" noted a United Press International news bulletin. "Script changes were made when Sellers agreed to do the role [vacated by Ustinov]. According to a company spokesman, Kay Thompson's role changed along with Sellers' and it was decided that she no longer would be in the picture."

As a result, Thompson's part was split in two. Her musical number was reassigned to a twenty-five-year-old sex kitten named Fran Jeffries (soon-to-be ex-wife of Dick Haymes), who decoratively dropped in and out of the picture with no rhyme or reason. The nonsinging role of the party hostess—what was left of it—was given to Brenda de Banzie, a plump, British thespian whose interpretation was boorish and grating.

"It would have been great if Kay had been in it," Wagner mused wistfully. "She was a *great* character actress and she'd have knocked 'em dead with a song-and-dance routine."

Humiliated and depressed, Kay went into hiding and fell apart.

*W*hen *I saw Kay* in Rome," recalled Marti Stevens, "she had gone from this immensely elegant, completely pulled together, dazzling creature, to someone who looked like a bag lady with unwashed hair and filthy, chipped red fingernails so long that they curled over like a witch's. It was a terrible shock because I wondered what could possibly have happened to go to that extreme. There is no way to quite describe it. Was it the breakup with Andy? All the energy was still there and enough anger to fuel a train."

It was Noël Coward who helped pull Thompson out of her funk. "Kay and I got invited to go to Noël's for Christmas in 1962," Stevens continued. "So we took the train from Rome to his place in Switzerland. She had a dreadful little dog called Fenice who shed all over everything, particularly Kay. She looked so bad that when we got to Noël's, he had to send her down to the village to clean her up for Christmas supper. She got her hair done, got those chipped nails manicured."

That was all it took to restore some of the old Thompson spirit. "Then the thrill and the fun," Marti added. "After dinner, there were double pianos. Kay and Noël started playing and it was heaven. Sitting in the corner, looking bored was Marlene [Dietrich]—and she eventually disappeared because nobody was paying any attention to her. Unfortunately, sometime later, she came back and in her hand she had some records. She interrupted the evening we were simply adoring to say, 'Here, you must play this. These are my applauses.' Records of applause! There was no music on them. Just the applause. And she was determined that we should hear it."

"Wet blanket time" was how Kay later described the situation. "Marlene could be a most humorless human being."

At the recommendation of Dr. Max Jacobson, Kay became a regular patient of Dr. Paul Niehans' Clinique la Prairie in Vevey, Switzerland. Niehans specialized in live cell therapy injections containing placenta extracted from pregnant sheep—inspiring Kay, Noël, and Marlene to sing a chorus of "I've Got EWE Under My Skin." Believed to be rejuvenating, the treatments had become a fad among such jet-set disciples as Charlie Chaplin, Gloria Swanson, and Cary Grant. Of course, this sort of medical experimentation flew in the face of Thompson's Christian Science doctrine—yet wherever there was a syringe that promised some sort of "pick-me-up," Kay seemed to be first in line.

"I remember Kay as a pill popper," Roland Flamini stated. "There was medicine all over the place. In Rome, she saw Dr. Richard Pennington de Jongh at Salvator Mundi International Hospital. When Elizabeth Taylor was doing *Cleopatra*, he was a bit of a Dr. Feelgood, prescribing all sorts of drugs to alleviate her never-ending ailments, many of them imagined."

"There was something like that going on with Kay," Janet Flamini concurred, "but she was very secretive about it."

"She often called Janet at three or four o'clock in the morning," Roland added. "She never had anything pressing to tell her. She just needed to talk. I guess she was lonely but whatever she was taking made her lose all track of time and manners. It was especially rude because we had very small children and it woke them up."

Though she had her low ebbs, Roland remembered that Kay was "usually well turned out, especially in the evenings when she'd wear one of her many Chanel suits."

"At first, she was into beige and actually wore skirts or a cotton sundress," Mart Crowley observed. "Flat sandals or Gucci boots. By the end of the 1960's, though, she was in black, black, black. I think she slept in black."

"With heavily made up eyes," Roland added. "Raccoon eyes."

Reliably outlandish, Kay became a favorite celebrity kook among local fashionistas, including Countess Consuelo Crespi, the Rome editor of *Vogue*, and Irene Brin, the Rome editor of *Harper's Bazaar*.

Turning heads, she showed up with Noël Coward and Merle Oberon at the June 1965 wedding of Princess Olimpia Torlonia and Paul Annik Weiller wearing "a pink Chanel suit and matching pillbox hat that was an exact replica of the outfit that Jackie Kennedy was wearing when JFK was assassinated."

Roland Flamini could not reconcile why Thompson would do such a tasteless thing because she "was just devastated by the assassination of JFK and such a close friend of the entire Kennedy family."

Her notorious style made her a hot commodity among the paparazzi and, consequently, she was invited to appear as a runway model for the House of Micia wearing "hand-loomed knits with peeping-Tom cut-outs." For Ken Scott's groundbreaking 1968 "Burn the Bra and Bury the Girdle" collection, Kay opened the show in a "slinky black and white print with a long, black ostrich boa," then swooped over to a white grand piano and performed "30s songs while the models paraded."

In 1966, fashion god Eleanor Lambert wrote, "At collection time in Rome, [Kay] and her gigantic, snuffly pug dog hold daily reunions with pals in the fashion press. In between she wrote us all lengthy letters about how much she'd like to be in fashion." When asked in 2002 why that never happened, Lambert replied, "She was just too flighty and unpredictable to pin down for more than five minutes at a time."

"I want to open a shop that has a glorious gate and a bell in a cave in Portugal," Thompson told *Women's Wear Daily*. "I'd sell pretty things, go to lunch at noon on a bicycle with some cheese and a guitar player, come back around five and stay open until midnight." What sort of "pretty things" would be in the store's inventory? "Vegetables and ribbon."

The closest she got to that fantasy was becoming the self-appointed marketing maven for La Mendola, a luxury ladies boutique at the top of the Spanish Steps. The store was opened in 1961 by an American gay couple, Michael La Mendola and Jack Savage. To help the boys get noticed, Thompson led all of her famous friends to their doorstep—from Ethel Merman to Ethel Kennedy.

"One day Kay Thompson popped in with Judy Garland," wrote fashion columnist Marian Cristy. "Kay, a thorough extrovert like the fictional Eloise, grabbed a bolt of fabric and did an impromptu song-and-dance routine while simultaneously winding the fabric around her body. Customers broke into applause."

Kay's favors were rewarded with freebies off the racks, but as usual, her interest was ephemeral.

The same was true when it came to acting. Though she had already rejected the role of Madame Arcati in *Blithe Spirit* on two previous occasions, a masochistic Noël Coward tried to convince Kay to finally take on the nutty clairvoyant in a new musical adaptation entitled *High Spirits*, with a score by Hugh Martin and Timothy Gray. After the usual hemming and hawing, she refused—prompting Coward to conclude in his diary that she was "sweet as ever and barmy as ever."

Kay was replaced by Beatrice Lillie, who ended up with *another* juicy role Thompson foolishly blew off—the villainous dragon lady, Mrs. Meers, in George Roy Hill's *Thoroughly Modern Millie*, starring Julie Andrews, Mary Tyler Moore, and Carol Channing.

In 1965, Kay turned down the role of Madame Dubonnet, a wealthy socialite in Terence Young's all-star thriller, *The Poppy Is Also a Flower*, based on a story by Ian Fleming. The cast included Yul Brynner, Marcello Mastroianni, Omar Sharif, Rita Hayworth, and numerous other big names (including Princess Grace of Monaco, coaxed out of retirement for a "special introduction"). Instead of joining the impressive lineup, Thompson recommended her dependable *8½* replacement, Gilda Dahlberg, who wore another one of her glitzy Ziegfeld getups. But her involvement did not end there. When Rita Hayworth was having trouble remembering her dialogue, Kay volunteered to discreetly help her on the sidelines.

Similarly, when Janet Leigh came to Rome in November 1966 for the diamond heist thriller *Grand Slam*, the star asked Thompson to coach her. "Kay advised me on wardrobe choices," Leigh recalled in 2002, "and, on the set, she whispered comments in my ear, sometimes about my performance, but most often a funny remark about someone else. She knew how to put my mind at ease."

Back in America, Kay may have been out of sight, but she wasn't entirely out of mind. For example, when *The Andy Williams Christmas Album* became a No. 1 smash in 1963, it contained his interpretations of "Kay Thompson's Jingle Bells" and her composition of "Holiday Season." This lucrative olive branch from Williams went a long way toward clearing the air with Thompson.

In 1964, Broadway got an injection of that old Kay magic when Angela Lansbury paid homage to her in Stephen Sondheim's *Anyone Can Whistle*. Lansbury's evil character, Mayoress Cora Hoover Hooper, sang a number with four boys called "I've Got You to Lean On" that was, according to *New York Times* critic Frank Rich, "a jazzy, finger-snapping, Kay Thompson kind of number."

"Stephen wanted me to *be* Kay Thompson," Angela Lansbury said with a chuckle. "It was real kind of whoop-tee-doo stuff. Totally Kay and the Williams Brothers."

Meanwhile, on the other side of the globe, Roger Edens hired Kay to write the Rome segment for Irving Berlin's *Say It With Music*, an episodic MGM musical being developed by the Freed Unit and director Vincente Minnelli. It was to star Frank Sinatra as a man who romances Julie Andrews in London, Ann-Margret in Hollywood, Brigitte Bardot in Paris, and Sophia Loren in Rome.

"Kay gave a huge dinner party for Sophia Loren," Roland Flamini recalled. "She was bringing Sophia together with the American producers, which, in Kay's mind, was going to rival the Last Supper."

Thompson also coached Loren's recorded audition, to make sure she could sing well enough.

"Kay loved Sophia and said that she had a good voice," Hilary Knight recalled.

But after a revolving door of writers, directors, and cast replacements, the project was abandoned.

With her cash flow running dry, Thompson reluctantly accepted an advance from Harper & Row for *Eloise Takes a Bawth*, the fifth book in the series, instigated in the fall of 1962 by legendary children's book editor Ursula Nordstrom.

"It's pretty much what the title tells you," Mart Crowley explained. "Eloise is ordered by Nanny into the bathroom to fill up the tub. The tub overflows and it floods the entire hotel, turning the whole place into, shall we say, a Titanic disaster."

Feeling uninspired, Kay convinced Nordstrom to first allow her to do a non-Eloise book called *Kay Thompson's The Fox and the Fig: A Bedtime Story*. It was a Dr. Seuss–like imaginarium in rhyming verse—with lines like "The beastly fox has a great fox tail that flies with the wind like a full fox sail" juxtaposed with "The modest fig, with fastidious care, has a fig leaf to cover whatever is bare."

To illustrate the book, Kay first approached Hilary Knight. "I want you to do this in a Chinese ink brush technique," she insisted. Knight had no desire to work in that medium so he said, "Why don't you get Tomi Ungerer." Remembered today for having designed the poster to Stanley Kubrick's *Dr. Strangelove or: How I Learned to Stop Worrying and Love the Bomb*, Jean-Thomas Ungerer was a celebrated illustrator who was not the least bit interested in taking direction from Kay. And she was not about to give up one iota of creative control. So, that was that. The next artist under consideration was Andy Warhol.

"Andy asked me what I thought about the idea of working with Kay," Joe Eula remembered. "I said, 'You are out of your fucking mind. All she wants is a weak-bellied sister she can push around.'"

Nevertheless, Warhol submitted sketches that were rejected outright for being "too decorative."

Thompson ended up drafting Mart Crowley into service even though he had little experience or ambition to be an artist. Apparently, that was the point, since Kay felt at liberty to dictate every stroke of his brush.

"Sometimes Kay would actually guide my hand with the brush in it," Mart exclaimed with exasperation. "If not that, she would pull the drawing out from under me and, with a pair of scissors, start cutting off a leg or an ear or an eye or God only knows what, and paste it on some other drawing and say, 'This is how it ought to look.' Then one day, I rang on her doorbell at the Palazzo Torlonia and her maid answered that Kay wasn't in. Next day, same thing. After this happened several times, I realized I'd been 'cut off at the ankles.' Then later, once things started to happen for me as a writer, suddenly Kay was back. 'Oh congratulations, Mart. Isn't it just *wonderful*?' That's how she was."

Kay didn't only treat people that way. She was just as capricious about her endeavors—*The Fox and the Fig* being just the latest example. After having toiled madly away on a dozen drafts—none of which were ever completed or made the slightest bit of sense—she suddenly decided to ditch the whole shebang.

"Then she came up with the idea for *Darling Baby Boy*," Joe Eula explained, "a book about that awful, ugly, farting pug, Fenice! Well now, that dog had a life that was extraordinary. Spoiled is not the word. She practically had sex with him."

No joke. "We were sitting outside Piazza Navona one night," Marion Marshall recounted, "and Kay was worried that Fenice was too hot. So she had the waiter bring her a cup full of ice. She turned the dog on his back and rubbed his balls with ice cubes!"

On another occasion, Kay ordered a startled dinner guest to observe the contrast between the dog's "beige fur and his pink erection."

"Kay once asked Marcello Mastroianni's tailor, Vittorio Zenobi, to make a jacket for Fenice," remembered Roland Flamini. "He was highly offended and said, '*We don't dress dogs!*' But, in the end, he did it—because Kay could talk anybody into doing anything."

"*Darling Baby Boy* was all set in Rome," said Eula, "with that little dog having chicken livers and goose up his ass at Passetto's . . . his whole life at the Palazzo Torlonia . . . lifting his leg to take a leak on the crutch of a woman hobbling down the street. It was great, honey. You know me, I went crazy. But then Kay never stopped cutting and pasting these mock-ups. It drove me nuts. By the time Easter came, I realized that I was still sitting there doing hundreds of drawings that were never going to be used. I finally said, 'I have to meet somebody in Africa,' and I took off."

Meanwhile, in New York during the Christmas holidays of 1963, Princess Grace of Monaco brought her two children, six-year-old Princess Caroline and five-year-old Prince Albert II, to The Plaza to show them the giant portrait of Eloise, only to discover it had been stolen.

"I am so disappointed," Princess Grace lamented to the management. "I do hope you'll have the picture back again."

Alphonse Salomone, who had just resumed his old post as general manager of The Plaza, wrote to Kay in Rome, asking, "What'll we do?"

"If you want to have another drawing," Thompson responded, "call Hilary and tell him I said to give you another drawing."

"By telephone and sketches sent to Kay in Rome," Knight recalled, "I did a rough drawing for what would then become an oil painting."

Reminiscent of the Lansdowne portrait of President George Washington, Eloise is depicted in a neoclassical pose, standing by a drawn-back curtain and marble pillar, with Skipperdee and Weenie at her feet.

In connection with the opening of the 1964 World's Fair in New York, the new Eloise portrait was given a ceremonial unveiling in the lobby of The Plaza on April 17. Several high society youngsters made the scene, including seven-year-old Amanda Plummer (daughter of Tammy Grimes and Christopher Plummer), six-year-old Heidi Hagman (daughter of Larry Hagman and granddaughter of Mary Martin), and nine-year-old Carla Javits (daughter of Senator Jacob Javits). Invited but unable to attend, the Beatles wired a congratulatory telegram that was read by Mr. Salomone at the event: DEAR ELOISE, WE WISH WE

COULD HOLD YOUR HAND, YEAH, YEAH, YEAH. THE BEATLES. (A fan, Kay finally met the Beatles face to face when they performed in Rome the following year.)

Postcard reproductions of the portrait were made available at the front desk; Eloise "Do Not Disturb" signs were dangled from every doorknob; and full-page ads were taken out in *The New Yorker* and *The New York Times Magazine*, headlined "For Lord's sake . . . could it be Eloise?"

In the wake of all this publicity, Ursula Nordstrom was more determined than ever to pry *Eloise Takes a Bawth* out of Kay. Having run out of tangents and excuses, Thompson summoned Knight to Rome.

"We must treat this as a movie," Kay told Hilary, envisioning the storyboard system she'd learned at MGM.

"As I finished each drawing," Knight explained, "I'd hang it up on string like a clothesline." But each night, after he had gone back to his hotel, Thompson would stay up until dawn fiddling, rearranging, cutting and pasting. "The next day, I'd return to find that she had changed it all," said Hilary. "Here was this enormously talented woman who excelled at everything and yet the one thing she couldn't do was draw and it simply drove her crazy."

Isolated in New York, Nordstrom optimistically bought the entire front cover of *Publishers' Weekly* on July 13, 1964, to announce that *Eloise Takes a Bawth* was set for publication on October 21.

"When my sketches for the layout were all finished," Knight recalled, "I sent everything to Rome for Kay's approval. She took one look at it and said, 'No. I don't like it.'"

The deadline came and went. Ursula fired off missives to Thompson. In return? Deafening silence. On November 4, 1964, Nordstrom wrote to Thompson once more: "I wonder if I'm dead and don't realize it, and that's why you can't get in touch with me."

An entire year slipped by with no progress whatsoever. "Oh, Hilary, *please!*" Nordstrom begged. "Just finish it!"

"Ursula, Kay has destroyed my *life*," Knight responded. "I can't deal with this . . . *thing*."

"Get over it!" Nordstrom snapped back. "We've got a book to publish!"

So, in 1966, Hilary trudged back to Rome for another round of pulling teeth and, this time, managed to extract a completed manuscript that went as far as blueprint proofs before Kay once again got cold feet.

Hanging Nordstrom out to dry, Thompson telegrammed from Rome: THIS BOOK CANNOT COME OUT!

•　•　•

In 1966, Roland Flamini got appointed *Time* magazine's bureau chief in Vienna, so his wife, Janet, had to give up her position as Kay's assistant. Thompson burned through a few other secretaries until she settled on a full-time houseboy named Juliano.

"Juliano was a hunky, sexy kid who could not have been more than eighteen or twenty at the very most," remembered Mart Crowley. "He was like a street boy, you know, *tough*. He looked like a gay hustler. I thought anything was possible. I wondered at times if there was anything going on between him and Kay, but he was so young and she was not so young. But he was a *very* sexy-looking boy and he was *everything* to her."

If Kay's infatuation with Juliano suggested a midlife crisis, her acquisition of a Vespa scooter kind of cinched it. The sporty two-wheeler, manufactured by Italy's Piaggio & Co., was given to her as a gift by the public relations executive who handled the Vespa account in Rome—Count Rodolfo "Rudi" Crespi, husband of *Vogue*'s Consuelo Crespi. It was Rudi's job to get Vespas product-placed in movies and television, and since Kay traveled in showbiz circles, he used her for traction.

When asked by an American reporter what she did for kicks in Rome, Kay dutifully replied, "I plunk my guitar, race about on my Vespa, and hit the high spots and the low spots with some great Italian men."

In 1968, however, the bloom was suddenly off the rose. When Fenice died of diabetes, Kay could only blame herself for recklessly feeding him a steady diet of lime green Chuckles. Racked with guilt and grief, she became homesick. She was also running out of cash—partly because whenever Judy Garland needed a handout, Kay always "helped with her expenses." If Thompson was expecting something in return, it never came.

"Kay always talked about how she'd had a falling-out with Judy Garland, toward the end of her life, over the drugs and everything," recalled Thompson's physical therapist, Bi-Ko. "She said that Judy had become impossible and there was a lot of anger."

No longer able to support herself, much less Judy, Kay sublet her maisonette to sex symbol Monique Van Vooren, gave her furniture to Juliano, put her other belongings in storage, and shouted from the roof of the Palazzo Torlonia, "Arrivederci, Roma!"

Chapter Fourteen

LIFE WITH LIZA
The Last Hurrah
(1968–98)

Walk like you have ice water in your brassiere.
—*Kay Thompson*

On November 1, 1968, Kay flew back to the United States to face the music. Immediately, she appeared on *The Joey Bishop Show* and *The Hollywood Palace* but, in both instances, was treated as a relic from the past singing her oldie "I Love a Violin." She didn't care; she took the money and ran.

Then, for a hefty ransom, she authorized Simon & Schuster to launch a large-scale reissue of *Eloise* on April 30, 1969, for which she appeared on all the major talk shows.

"I want to see about making an animated film of *Eloise*," Kay crowed. "And I want to make an LP of the book, with songs and music of course. Maybe I can get Burt Bacharach to conduct." Thompson talked up grand designs to relaunch a high-end Eloise doll with Louis Vuitton luggage and a wardrobe designed by Madame Karinska and manufactured by Broadway's Barbara Matera.

None of it happened, of course, but Kay used the buzz to leverage free accommodations at The Plaza—which she refurbished in her own anomalous style. Using pins and Scotch tape, she covered chairs, tables, and lamp shades with zebra-striped Porthault sheets. Then she manufactured a fake fireplace out of leftover cardboard boxes.

To further justify squatter's rights, Thompson sanctioned a new Eloise Room (decorated by the editors of *House Beautiful*), and a new Eloise Ice Cream Corner in a nook of the lobby near the Fifty-eighth Street entrance.

While putting a happy face on selling out, Kay received word of the sudden death of Judy Garland on June 22, 1969. Fulfilling her duty as twenty-three-year-old Liza Minnelli's godmother, Thompson jumped into action.

"Kay did what godmothers do," Liza reflected. "Took charge. And organized it all."

She escorted Liza to Campbell's Funeral Home to choose the casket. "They asked for a white one," wrote columnist Liz Smith. "The funeral people . . . said it was not possible. Miss Thompson spoke right up. 'We're from MGM. We want white. Do it!'"

"Judy had a bracelet given her by Kay Thompson when Liza was born," reported Garland biographer Gerold Frank, "and Judy had given it to Liza and they'd given it back and forth. It was good luck. 'If I go before you go, I want to be wearing this,' Judy instructed Liza about the cherished bracelet. 'I don't care what dress you put me in, but I'd like to be wearing this.'"

Her wish was honored and the bracelet was placed on Judy's wrist, forever linking her to Kay. Their bond would be as eternal as the public's fascination with it.

"The day of the funeral was a *circus*," Lorna Luft recalled. "Kay was the voice of reason. She was the one at the funeral who stood behind us, with her hands around us. And after the funeral, at Liza's place, when all the news reports were on TV and someone said, 'Oh we have to listen to this,' Kay said, 'No we don't,' and turned it off."

Liza recalled, "After about ten minutes of sitting around feeling sad, Kay suddenly said, 'All right, everyone to the piano.' We went to the piano and we sang 'Great Day' with her. And she said, 'Sing! Come on!' And we all sang our brains out. The music grounded us. When the kids left, I looked at her and I just said, 'Thank you.' And she said, 'My darling, that's what I'm here for.'"

But now what? As days passed, Thompson could sense that Minnelli's marriage to Australian singer Peter Allen was a sham. Perhaps Liza needed a little guidance from a godmother with better gaydar. And for her own part, Kay realized that Liza was just the sort of fresh project she needed to get back into the swing of things. Minnelli's first starring vehicle, *The Sterile Cuckoo*, was set to open in October, and with any luck, she just might have a future. Like Andy Williams, Liza became Thompson's next "client."

"Kay was so great because when she came in, she brought a world with her," Liza explained. "She brought this energy, this freedom, this intelligence."

Liza had already begun rehearsals for her next movie, *Tell Me That You Love Me, Junie Moon*, the cheerful story of a girl whose face has been disfigured by acid during an attempted rape. Based on the bestselling novel by Marjorie Kellogg, the film was being directed by Otto Preminger. Kay offered to assist Liza throughout the production as her coach and rock.

Originally, there was going to be a brief bit with a grumpy landlady who rents a run-down house to Junie (Minnelli) and the two friends she met during her hospitalization—Arthur (Ken Howard), an epileptic, and Warren (Robert Moore), a crippled homosexual. Then, later in the story, the trio meets a spoiled young heiress, Gregory (named after Gregory Peck), who invites them to stay overnight in her castle. Gregory sadistically taunts Warren to get up from his wheelchair and walk, but it only leads to him falling on the floor, humiliated and in tears.

When Preminger saw Kay hanging out with Liza, he decided to merge the characters of the landlady and the heiress into one mysterious grande dame named Miss Gregory.

"Otto knew Kay," Liza explained in 2008. "So one day he said to her, 'There's this woman in the picture. Would you do it?' And Kay said, 'All right. Why not?'"

On June 29, 1969, the morning after the Stonewall Riot, it was announced that Thompson had been signed for the movie. Could it really be true that, thirteen years after *Funny Face*, her long-awaited return to the silver screen would finally happen? Without a hitch?

Naturally, she insisted on being "creatively involved" in the development of her character's look and persona. And for every inch Preminger indulged, Kay snatched a mile. Soon, Halston was designing her wardrobe and she was making arrangements to rent a 1925 Rolls-Royce Phantom convertible. "I want the back seat re-upholstered in zebra-striped Porthault sheets," she ordered the art department. Yep, Kay Thompson was back in business.

In early July, Kay and Liza traveled to Gloucester, Massachusetts, where shooting commenced in and around the historic Hammond Castle, which served as Miss Gregory's estate.

"When I was twenty years old," recalled comedy writer–performer Bruce Vilanch, "I was a journalist writing for the *Chicago Tribune* and I was sent on a press junket to the set of *Junie Moon* in Massachusetts. Liza was the star of the picture but *not* the center of attention. Between Otto Preminger and Kay Thompson, it was a draw as to who was the more imperial of the two. Crazy

Otto, we called him—and he was running around screaming at the top of his lungs, 'Miss Thompson! Will you come to the set?!' Kay was heavily scarved the day I met her, with sunglasses. I mean, she was as absolutely Hollywood, New York, as you could be—and I thought I'd met a god. She certainly was to me. I'd grown up idolizing Eloise, for Lord's sake, and I told her so. She gave me the once-over and said, 'How sweet.'"

For her first scene, Miss Gregory arrives in her chauffeur-driven Rolls tourer to meet her new tenants. Dressed in a black leatherette pantsuit with matching skullcap, big black shades, and an Isadora Duncan–length silk scarf monogrammed with the letter *G*, the spider woman rises from her zebra-striped throne, puffs on a cigar, and proffers, "Would you come to dinner tomorrow night? I'll send a car at six."

Honestly, it felt like Kay had dropped in from either *Sunset Blvd.* or *Zorro,* but so what? The dame knew how to make an entrance.

Kay not only stole her own scenes, she Thompsonized one of Liza's, too. At a cocktail bar in Miss Gregory's garden, Junie mixes up a pitcher of "Purple Kazazz" (an amalgam of "Kay" and "bazazz"), while strutting and wriggling a "razzamatazz" jingle: "A little VO, some Grand Marnier, and, oh, I almost forgot the Beefeater." It was Liza channeling Kay à la Judy doing "Madame Crematante."

"It was almost like she took direction from Kay," Vilanch observed. "Unlike Marilyn Monroe, who would always look at her acting coach for approval, Liza didn't make it so obvious. But you could tell that Kay was advising her discreetly."

Thompson referred to Preminger as Eau de B'Otto and snarked, "His reputation precedes him, so we don't need to tell you about that."

Glass houses.

Around that same time, Thompson met Hilary Knight to discuss the possibility of giving *Eloise Takes a Bawth* one more whirl—with talk of *Eloise in Rome* and *Eloise's Wit and Observations* to follow in rapid succession. As he pulled out a pencil and began to sketch an idea, however, Kay's spiderlike talons crawled down and clutched the tops of his fingers.

"She guided my hand, pushing the pencil across the paper, trying to take control and make the drawing her own," Knight said, shuddering from the memory. "That was it. I knew right then and there that it was never going to work. My ego had already been crushed to a pulp by her and I refused to put up with it any longer. I told her to find someone else."

For a time, Thompson boasted that she was in discussions with David Hockney to replace Knight, but everyone knew that would never fly. Kay was a chorus of one in her dismissal of Hilary's contribution to the universal appeal and longevity of the Eloise phenomenon.

Rather than be forced to refund eight years of advances, Kay fulfilled her obligation to Harper & Row with a new book. *Kay Thompson's Miss Pooky Peckinpaugh and Her Secret Private Boyfriends Complete with Telephone Numbers* was a teenager's alphabetical catalog of the boys she has encountered, from "Arthur is awful" to "Zooz is zizzy." The heroine's name was derived from Pookie, Liza Minnelli's sweet and quirky character in *The Sterile Cuckoo*, juxtaposed with the last name of director Sam Peckinpah, aka "Bloody Sam," because of his notoriously violent movies like *The Wild Bunch*.

Each profile had a minuscule drawing by Joe Eula, whose credit was buried on the inside flap of the dust jacket.

"I mean, you know, she was a cunt," Eula exploded. "That's the only word for it and don't be afraid to use that in the book. I always used to say, 'You're not going to fuck me like you did Hilary.' Well, she did on *Darling Baby Boy*. And then she said, 'Well, now I've got this project. Would you do this book?' *Pecky Pickenpooh*, whatever the fuck it was. I said, 'I'll do it under one condition: You stay away from me.' I did it all in three days. And when she said, 'There's a revision . . .' I said, 'Do it yourself.' So she reduced my drawings to the size of postage stamps."

The exhaustive text to *Pooky Peckinpaugh* dominated the layout and became tedious after about page 2. Published in November 1970, *Pooky* was dead on arrival and Thompson's beleaguered editor, Ursula Nordstrom, refused to work with her again.

"When I saw the book," said Eula, "Kay and I had a very, very quick word and I just said, 'You're fuckin' lousy.' We didn't talk for a while until she wanted me to do posters for Liza. Then we made up."

Not long after the filming of *Junie Moon*, Kay got back into her old habit of coaching stars for Broadway shows—with decidedly mixed results. First, it was Gloria Swanson, who was preparing to replace Katharine Hepburn as Coco Chanel in the Broadway musical *Coco*. Kay had Gloria "walking 26 blocks daily to build up her stamina" until Swanson's excessive contractual demands kiboshed the whole affair.

Next, director Hal Prince asked Thompson to coach Alexis Smith for the Stephen Sondheim musical *Follies*. As Mart Crowley recalled, "Kay had Alexis go through some simple vocal exercises, then stopped, turned to her, and said, 'You have no talent at all, and you shouldn't be doing this show. I can't help you.'" Smith ignored the opinion and went on to win a Tony.

When it was announced that Rita Hayworth would replace Lauren Bacall as Margo Channing in *Applause*—the musical adaptation of *All About Eve*—Hayworth moved into The Plaza to be near Thompson.

"My mother really depended on Kay," recalled Princess Yasmin Khan (daughter of Hayworth and Prince Aly Khan). "And Kay was always there for her. They were very, very close. For *Applause*, Kay was coaching my mother, trying to help her with her confidence, but my mom was sick and she couldn't remember anything. So, it was a real drama and turmoil and panic. Of course, none of us knew it was Alzheimer's. Finally, my mother had to pull out."

In 1973, Kay gave singing lessons to Carrie Fisher for her supporting role in *Irene*, starring her mother, Debbie Reynolds. She helped create nightclub acts for Baroness Nina Van Pallandt and Neile Adams (Steve McQueen's ex-wife). She preached style and method acting to Peter Allen. She even taught Prince Albert of Monaco how to sing.

After a shaky audition, Kay told the prince to imagine himself on the balcony of the Hôtel de Paris in Monte Carlo, overlooking the curve during the Grand Prix. "You're wearing a white tuxedo and a scarf," she said suggestively. "A silver Jag pulls up and out comes the most beautiful woman you have ever seen in a multicolored chiffon gown with a gardenia in her hair. Now sing it again." He did—and his vocals improved.

Then Kay was offered, yet again, the role of Vera Charles, Auntie Mame's best friend, in the movie version of the Broadway musical *Mame*. In 1968, there had been discussions of teaming Judy Garland with Kay in the movie (from a screenplay adaptation by Leonard Gershe), but, contractually, "no film could be released before 1971," to avoid competition with the ongoing Broadway smash starring Angela Lansbury.

Flash forward to August 1972 when it was announced that Lucille Ball and Kay Thompson would star in the picture. Unfortunately, negotiations with Thompson hit the usual impasse, and the role went to Bea Arthur, who had won the 1966 Tony Award for portraying the character opposite Lansbury. Kay always felt that she had been sabotaged by the director, Gene Saks—who just so happened to be Bea Arthur's husband.

Ignoring the flap, Ball called Thompson for advice on her own vocalizing for the picture. "Darling," Kay replied, "do not try to sing the songs. Write the lyrics out on paper three times. Then vocalize, sing Da-DA-da-DA-DA!"

Ball told the *Los Angeles Times* that she tried to persuade Thompson to coach her throughout the challenging production. "I mean, bombastic Kay *is* Mame," Lucille enthused, "but Kay finally was not available. I can't sing, no Kay to inspire me! So I'm trying to get out of the whole damn thing."

Still miffed over the Bea Arthur nepotism, Kay refused to have anything to do with the movie. And she must have felt a twinge of schadenfreude when audiences stayed away in droves.

George Roy Hill asked Kay to play a Nurse Ratched type in *Listen to the Silence* but the film never got made. And Louis Malle wanted Thompson for the "really nutty" old hag in *Black Moon,* but she couldn't bring herself to appear in such an unflattering role.

The one film that Kay did make during that period, *Tell Me That You Love Me, Junie Moon,* was not well received. In June 1970, Rex Reed wrote in the *Los Angeles Times:* "Although Liza Minnelli, Ken Howard, Robert Moore and Kay Thompson struggle bravely to make flesh-and-blood characters out of one-dimensional creatures, even good actors need a director."

If nothing else, however, the movie provided an opportunity for Kay to introduce Liza to Halston.

"Stick with Halston," Kay advised. "You'll never go wrong."

"And that's exactly what happened," China Machado observed. "It became Liza's signature look. The Halston look. The hat. The scarf thrown over the shoulder."

When Liza went off to Germany to shoot her next picture, Bob Fosse's *Cabaret,* she was so unhappy with the wardrobe that she got Halston to design and/or retrofit nearly everything she wore in the movie—for which he went uncredited.

"I would talk to Kay all the time on the phone from Germany," Liza recalled. "She had loved a picture called *The Damned* and that was what she felt I should use as inspiration. And it was a great influence on Fosse, too."

Kay not only set the wheels in motion for Liza's attire, she was also instrumental in the overall look that has come to define "Liza Minnelli" through the ages—the Louise Brooks bob, the starburst eyelashes, even the Joe Eula posters for shows like *Liza with a Z* and *The Act.* Minimalist, timeless, and instantly recognizable, it was this consistent branding that helped Liza emerge from the formidable shadow of her mother as an icon in her own right.

For "influential buildup," Thompson introduced Minnelli to Diana Vreeland (by then, the fashion editor of *Vogue*) and China Machado (Vreeland's successor at *Harper's Bazaar*). One example of the campaign appeared in the May 1972 edition of *Harper's Bazaar,* a spread entitled "A Day in the Life of Liza," with five photos of Minnelli and Thompson having a glorious time together at Liza's Fifty-seventh Street apartment, at Halston's showroom, and in The Plaza's Palm Court. (They were a team on *The Mike Douglas Show*, too.)

"Kay knew how to take the essence of someone and bring it to the forefront," observed China Machado. "And not just with singing or fashion. Whether they walked well or had bad posture, she could somehow make it work. She was extraordinary. She brought a confidence to women who didn't have it. Like Judy—or Liza when she first started. I mean, Kay really took what they had and pushed it. She practically put herself into their bodies."

Kay even influenced Liza's interviewing style. For instance, when Rex Reed sat down with Kay for *Harper's Bazaar* in 1972, she told him, "I don't like looking back. Let's keep it crisp as lettuce." Accordingly, Liza abides by the "less is more" philosophy, with a dash of embellishment for maximum crunch.

*M*eanwhile, *The Sterile Cuckoo* earned Liza an Academy Award nomination for Best Actress and she copped the gold for *Cabaret*. But while Liza was basking in glory, Kay's world was unexpectedly torn apart. First, on December 4, 1972, *The New York Times* published an explosive exposé on Dr. Max Jacobson, revealing that his "B-12 vitamin cocktails" were, in fact, heavily laced with speed.

Panic spread among his high-profile patients because the *Times* and other news organizations were naming names. Big ones. JFK, Jackie Kennedy, Truman Capote, and Tennessee Williams, just for starters. It was a miracle that Kay managed to avoid being outed, because she had just blabbed in the November issue of *Harper's Bazaar* that she relied on a "B-12 shot" whenever she "felt tired."

Then, one week later, on her last nerve, Kay got into a heated altercation with John F. Craver, the manager du jour of The Plaza. With no Eloise books or promotions forthcoming, Craver insisted that Thompson start paying for her room.

"She was so angry, she threatened to move Eloise to another hotel," Kitty D'Alessio recalled. "She told him she was going to paint Eloise's little footprints on the sidewalk leading from The Plaza all the way over to the St. Regis."

Craver could not have cared less. That night, an eviction notice was slid under Thompson's door. According to columnist Jack O'Brian, "She was given 24 hours to move out."

Homeless and with no visible means of support, Thompson fled New York and crashed at the Alexandria, Virginia, home of her sister, Blanche—the only surviving member of her immediate family. Perhaps she just needed to get the hell out of town for a while, to lie low until the dust settled. Some friends wondered if she did a stint in rehab.

"I missed her so much, so I called her up," Liza remembered. "You could not offer her anything. There was no such thing as charity with Kay Thompson. So I said, 'Kay, I don't know what to do with my apartment. It needs redecorating. Will you *please* help me.' So she said, 'All right.'"

With her pride still intact, Thompson accepted the "job" and moved into Minnelli's one-bedroom flat on the eighteenth floor of 300 East Fifty-seventh Street (the last New York address of J. D. Salinger before he became a recluse).

"Liza paid the rent the whole time Kay lived there," said Minnelli's former manager, Deanna Wenble. This arrangement lasted from 1973 to 1990, no strings attached. When Liza was in town, she often stayed at her sister Lorna's, or at a hotel, and, eventually, when she realized that Kay really had nowhere else to go, she got a second apartment on East Sixty-ninth Street that became Minnelli's permanent home base.

In the meantime, Thompson took her assignment very seriously and soon the old apartment had been given a wild makeover. The kitchen was lacquered fire engine red. She covered the grand piano—first in brown butcher block paper, then later in red vinyl. The most whimsical addition, though, was a Richard Ohrbach loveseat "in the shape of a great big pair of pouting red suede lips" (a knockoff of Salvador Dalí's Mae West Lips Sofa).

"Kay went to Lamston's and bought tons of red bandannas," recalled Kitty D'Alessio. "She wanted my dressmaker, Mrs. Glass, to sew them together to make bedsheets. Mrs. Glass glared at me and said, 'Thank you very much.'"

Instead of traditional framed artwork on the walls, Kay mounted giant pop art blowups of a "gray and glum newspaper photo of Nixon" and "the Pope eating spaghetti."

"There were two very small closets," recalled Geoffrey Johnson, Noël Coward's U.S. representative. "Inside them, squeezed in tight, were little café tables with ballroom chairs. Each table had a vase with a rose and a wine carafe."

Behind the tables, on the rear closet walls, were scenic blowups of Paris and Rio de Janeiro—two of Minnelli's favorite destinations. Kay told Liza, "Open the door to the third closet and you'll see *my* favorite thing in the whole wide world." When Liza opened the door, she saw a reflection of herself. The closet had been lined in mirrors.

For quite some time in the 1970s, Thompson and Minnelli were inseparable, traveling the world. "Oh, God," Liza exclaimed, "the David Nivens, the Gregory Pecks, they all *loved* Kay! We spent so much time together in the south of France."

Liza relished Thompson's childlike imagination. If they saw a crescent moon in the evening sky, Kay always said, "Look! God's paring his toenails." Or, when the wind was blowing leaves off limbs, she'd say, "The trees are getting their hair done."

"We had two imaginary characters," Liza explained, "and Kay was always making up stories about them. Gabriella and Beatrix—nicknamed Ga and Trix. Kay was Ga and I was Trix—and that's what she wrote in all of her notes to me. She'd sign 'Ga.' She'd just write these wacky stories about these women who traveled around one summer in Europe—in a sports car. You know, she *loved* sports cars!"

"You need to buy yourself a Jaguar XK120 and have a good time," advised Thompson, Queen of Pep Talks. "Enthusiasm and imagination can carry you anywhere you want to go, without Vuitton luggage." "Drink lots of orange juice, eat lots of lobster." "Do it for Donnie and Marie." Instead of saying good-bye, she'd throw both arms in the air and bellow, "Happy *everything!*"

Thompson lived vicariously through Minnelli's whirlwind romances. When Noël Coward died in 1973, for instance, Thompson and Minnelli went to the memorial service in London, where Peter Sellers swept Liza off her feet (resulting in the annulment of her engagement to Desi Arnaz Jr.). Much to Peter's chagrin, however, he soon realized that Liza and Kay were practically joined at the hip.

"Kay Thompson was with them constantly," explained Sellers' son Michael. "My father liked her, but he never got any peace and quiet or privacy . . . and Liza was determined not to give her up."

"If I marry Liza, I'll be marrying Kay, too," Peter confided to friends. "And, if I'm not mistaken, there are laws in this country against polygamy."

After a few weeks of bazazz run amok, Sellers disguised himself in a Nazi officer's uniform and escaped to the home of Joan Collins. A brief reconciliation was botched when Liza yanked Peter's toupee off his head in a crowded restaurant, a practical joke that went over like lead soufflé. The day after the split was final, Kay fumed to a reporter that Peter was "a rotten bastard for the way he treated my beautiful Liza."

With the press in a tizzy, the girls vamoosed to Positano, Italy, where they met up with Tennessee Williams and took refuge at the home of director Franco Zeffirelli and his partner, Pippo Pisciotto.

"The first night we arrived," recalled Minnelli's makeup artist, Christina Smith, "Kay, Liza, and I got all dolled up for dinner but the men were all just looking at each other. They were all gay. So, after dinner, as Kay, Liza, and I were heading back up to our rooms, Kay said, 'Well, that was a bust.'"

Zeffirelli had decided to star Minnelli in a remake of *Camille* from a new screenplay by Hugh Wheeler (Tony winner for *A Little Night Music* and, later, *Sweeney Todd*).

"Franco loved Kay's influence, her point of view, and her sense of style—as did everybody," Liza explained. "So, I was just thrilled she was there because I knew she wouldn't let me *ever* do anything that was wrong."

Franco and Kay marinated ideas for days, and then a screen test was filmed with Liza and Tim Woodward (son of actor Edward Woodward).

"Kay set up how it should look," Smith added. "For Liza's period costume, Kay had her in a big push-up bra. Liza put her head down and was laughing. 'Oh my God, I'm gonna bounce off my boobs!'"

Despite "violent enthusiasm," the financing never materialized. "If the movie had been made," Smith reflected, "Kay would have been involved in some way, either on the screen, behind it, or both."

The next putative project was an authorized biography of Liza, written by Kay, to be published in the spring of 1974. Preview "fragments" of Thompson's text, amounting to fifteen hundred words, were excerpted in the September 1, 1973, edition of *British Vogue* (featuring cover and interior photographs of Liza taken by, of all people, Peter Sellers).

"The biggest influence I believe was her mother," Kay freely associated, "always together . . . sharing the fun . . . and whatever old man trouble was dishing out at the time. Liza sets her own pace . . . strong in a crisis . . . constantly looking through rose-coloured glasses . . . if there's a shadow looks the other way . . . common sense to the core . . . run for your life . . . survival at all costs . . . and as a result Liza has made all the right mistakes."

Thompson's style was quirky and carbonated, and it would have been a fun read, but, living up to her reputation, she got bored and the book idea fizzled.

A historic alliance between Kay and Liza did come to pass in the fall of 1973. It all started one October night in New York. The girls were having dinner at Orsini's with Halston, Joe Eula, Anthony Perkins, and his new wife, Berry Berenson.

"We're giving a fashion show in France at the Palace of Versailles," Halston told Kay. "Liza will be our star and we want you to direct it and produce it."

"*Funny Face* lit up like a big balloon in my head," Thompson recalled, "and suddenly I was singing, 'I want to step out on the Champs-Élysées . . .' and then Liza began singing . . . and Tony Perkins, because he was on the set the day we were shooting it . . . and away we were and the whole Orsini's was going to Paree! It was just darling. We finished it and stood up and, my God, the applause was filled with people and waiters. And I said, 'Well . . . we're going to Versailles.'"

The job offer did not come completely out of the blue. Since her return from Rome, Kay had worked the runway as a celebrity model for Halston, Giorgio di Sant'Angelo, and Robert Mackintosh, and at two annual Coty American Fashion Critics Awards ceremonies. In each case, she had ended up advising behind the scenes and making herself indispensable. To his credit, Halston was the one who really recognized her undervalued potential.

The Versailles exhibition was not going to be just any old fashion show. To raise money for the restoration of the palace, publicist Eleanor Lambert had come up with the novel idea of staging a fashion event in Marie Antoinette's Théâtre Royal du Château de Versailles.

"I called up Baroness Marie-Hélène de Rothschild in Paris," Lambert recalled, "and said, 'If I can get five American designers, can you get five French designers?' So, she organized the French half of the show. She had Pierre Cardin, Marc Bohan for Christian Dior, Hubert de Givenchy, Yves Saint Laurent, and Emanuel Ungaro. And to sing, they had Josephine Baker. For the American half, I got Anne Klein, Stephen Burrows, Bill Blass, Oscar de la Renta, and Halston—with Liza opening and closing. And Kay agreed to direct and produce our half of the show."

Flush with funds from his recent $16 million acquisition by Norton Simon, Inc., Halston was the ringleader and covered many of the expenses. Thus, ground control emanated from Halston's Manhattan headquarters at Sixty-eighth and Madison.

"So in comes Kay to figure out what the hell we're going to do," recalled actor Dennis Christopher, who, along with Bill Dugan and Stephen Sprouse, made up the trio of assistants known as the Halstonettes. "In anticipation, I had gone out to this fabulous little grocer on Madison Avenue and bought kiwi and lady apples—those little tiny apples with a stem and little tiny leaves on them. They're adorable, very expensive, and I bought them for her. So, Kay comes in and looks at me."

"Who is this charming little boy?!" Thompson beseeched, hands thrown high.

"He's my assistant," Halston replied.

"Hiring twelve-year-olds now, are we?" she sneered.

"I was young, but not *that* young," Dennis said, continuing the story. "Trembling, I handed her this bag of fruit that I had gotten her. Halston's eyebrow flew up like 'What are you doing?!' She opened it and gasped. Lady apples were her favorite thing and kiwis were her favorite thing and she refused to eat any of the food that had been prepared by Halston's cook for the lunch meeting that day. All she ate were the kiwis and the lady apples and she insisted that I sit next to her."

Surrendering, Halston said, "Why don't you just take him." Then he shifted his eyes to Dennis and ordered, "You go with her."

So, for the next six weeks, Dennis became Kay's boy Friday–cum–stage manager—six years before his breakthrough movie, *Breaking Away*, earned him a Golden Globe nomination and a British Academy Award. "Not only did I assist her with the show," he recalled, "but I also did other stuff like getting her food, calling her to confirm, 'We're meeting in half an hour. Shall I pick you up in a taxi?' One time, I picked her up at Dr. Feelgood's office, where she had had her B-12 shot—which seemed to be something that she looked forward to and needed."

Thompson would need all the energy she could muster to pull off this fashion Olympics. "I got on the phone," Kay recalled, "and from then on, I never got off the phone."

"She never ate," Dennis observed. "I always tried to force-feed her a yogurt or fruit. She might have a couple of cashews but I never saw her eating a real meal. She lived on cigarettes and Coke—and by that I mean the soft drink."

"She drank Coca-Cola because she loved the red can," noted Jim Caruso. "It was all about the red."

"As odd as it sounds, there were times when Kay looked like a kid," Dennis added. "When an idea came to her, it lit up her face, turning this old crone into a sprite."

Her first decision was to prerecord the entire soundtrack for the show in New York, and to ensure absolute perfection and audio control, Liza would lipsynch. For the opening, Thompson borrowed Paramount's original multitrack recording of "Bonjour, Paris!" from *Funny Face* and replaced the vocals with Liza and a female chorus that included Kay. For the finale, Liza would sing "Cabaret," followed by "Au Revoir, Paris," a cover version of the song Thompson had composed for Andy Williams' 1960 album, *Under Paris Skies*—with Kay on keyboard and Max Hamlisch (father of Marvin) playing the accordion.

To accompany the designers' individual presentations, Thompson selected a startling array of instrumental tracks. For Halston, it was Maurice Jarre's brooding score to *Luchino Visconti's The Damned* (with riffs of Mahler's waltz); for Burrows, it was Curtis Mayfield funk from *Superfly*; and for Blass, it was a medley of Cole Porter songs. For de la Renta, the swirling strings of "Love's Theme" by Barry White's Love Unlimited Orchestra were pumped into the mix—three months *before* the song became a No. 1 smash on the nation's dance floors.

"The music was bold, loud, and *very* eclectic," Eleanor Lambert remembered. "It was seismic. It absolutely changed the way music was used in fashion shows ever since."

"What was really essential," added Oscar de la Renta, "was that we had models who walked to the music. That was the very first time it was done—girls just swinging out to the pace of the music."

"Walk like praying mantises!" Kay ordered them. Forty models would be shared by the designers, plus they would all appear with Liza for the opening and the closing of the show.

"For 'Bonjour, Paris!'" Kay said, "we can do all the day and sportswear and rain wear."

"It allowed for the models to do a lot of movement," Dennis Christopher recalled, "like opening the coats or the umbrellas would go up at a certain point. I had to get a place called Uncle Sam's to manufacture umbrellas in matching fabrics from all the different designers. Kay wanted to start with beiges and progress to more explosive colors toward the end of the number."

For the "Cabaret"/"Au Revoir, Paris" finale, the attire was formal evening wear. " 'Cabaret' started playing," said Dennis, "and Liza came out in front of a scrim as you saw this marvelous tableau behind her—with very dramatic lighting. Everybody was frozen at these café tables—including me and Billy Dugan in tuxedos, because there was a shortage of male models. Then the scrim goes up, and as Liza sang and danced, each person she went by suddenly came to life, so that by the time the song came to an end, the cabaret was in full swing. Kay thought of the whole thing, from concept to choreography. It was unbelievable."

Of the forty models, Kay insisted that ten should be trained dancers. "The dancers didn't know how to model," Dennis remembered, "and the models didn't know how to dance. So there was a lot of hands-on, a lot of molding them. She would say things like 'Elocution with your arms.' 'Vocabulary with your fingers.' 'There's a bird trapped in your hair.' 'Walk like you have ice water in your brassiere.' These far-out haiku statements. She wanted an army of women who were replicants of her."

To upstage the other designers, Halston paid several famous women to appear in his segment, including Marisa Berenson (costar of *Cabaret*), Baby Jane Holzer (Andy Warhol's very first "superstar"), Elsa Peretti (the jewelry designer), and China Machado.

When the traveling satyricon arrived for rehearsal at Versailles, all hell broke loose. Because he'd mistaken metric measurements for inches, Joe Eula's painted backdrops came up short. "Get rid of it," Eula winced. "It looks like Chinese laundry, like everything shrunk in the wash."

Kay insisted that he do a giant rendering of the Eiffel Tower. "So, I just got a huge piece of no-seam paper," Joe explained, "rolled it out on the floor of the halls of the palace, and I got black stovepipe material and a broom and I did the Eiffel Tower in three sweeps, and up it went."

On the night before the show, the French contingent's rehearsal stretched until ten o'clock as the Americans impatiently awaited their turn. When things finally got under way, bad blood began to boil.

"Kay directed Anne Klein a lot," Eleanor Lambert explained. "Anne had cancer then, though none of us knew it at the time. She was ill and nervous that her casual designs would pale beside these elaborate evening dresses of the others. So she kept asking Kay how to make her segment shine. The others were annoyed that this was eating into their precious rehearsal time."

"I was backstage amid all the chaos," China Machado recalled. "Halston was so awful with Kay. *So* awful. And she was very upset by it. And Bill Blass insulted her or something—there was a rather nasty scene. The French were being impossible, too. It was madness."

"Fed up with the viciousness, Kay Thompson walked out," recalled Bill Blass. "Fortunately, she did not go far. Without Kay, in my opinion, we would have certainly perished in flames of amateurishness."

No sooner had Kay been coaxed back into action than Halston took a hike. "He walked out and sat in a car by the sidewalk," Eleanor Lambert remembered. "He wanted the models to retire with him but Liza said, 'Listen, girls. Don't you dare go out. This is show business. We're committed to it.' And so they all turned around and came back."

"Kay was just so glad that everybody was furious," Joe Eula said with a chuckle, "because that's the way she likes things. She said to me, 'It always makes a good performance, my dear. Raw edge.'"

Charged with plenty of it, Le Grand Divertissement à Versailles raised its curtain on the evening of November 28, 1973. Seven hundred and fifty of the world's aristocracy paid $235 per ticket, plus $50 for the lavish blue-and-gold programs designed by Jean-François Daigre.

"The first segment was the French," explained Bill Dugan, "and they had a lot of celebrities in the show like Louis Jourdan, Capucine, Zizi Jeanmaire, Rudolf Nureyev, Jane Birkin, and Josephine Baker. It was all very staged with classical music, a lot of sets, and yet, ultimately, it was kind of staid and not very exciting. It was politely received, followed by an intermission. Then the American segment came on. There were no sets. It was all about lighting, with just Joe Eula's huge brush painting of the Eiffel Tower as the background."

"Kay had the models going *fast*," recalled Christina Smith, "just boom boom boom boom boom! Clean and precise."

"The French portion had dragged on for days," remembered Eula, "and here we storm on and off in exactly thirty-five minutes. It was breathtaking. We *killed*'em. And when it was over, the audience threw fifty-dollar programs in the air like they were confetti."

"There was a frenzy," Dennis Christopher agreed, "which was especially surprising from such a refined audience. These were not kids at a rock concert. These were the wealthiest kings, queens, and royalty of Europe. Princess Grace showed up with her fucking crown on."

"I'll never forget Yves St. Laurent, so long and gangly, coming backstage, picking up Kay and swinging her around," Liza observed. "He said to her, 'The Americans have triumphed again.'"

"Not since Eisenhower liberated Paris have the Americans had such a triumph in France," concluded high-society matriarch C. Z. Guest.

"It was the robbery of all time," raved fashion critic Eugenia Sheppard in the *Los Angeles Times*. "Five American ready-to-wear designers completely stole a joint fashion show from five of the greatest names in world fashion."

"Like a big show on Broadway," assessed Marc Bohan of the House of Dior, "Kay Thompson knew what she was doing."

"Up to that time," Eleanor Lambert explained, "everybody in America went to Paris for inspiration, but this show turned the tables."

"They agree to disagree about where the fashion world's capital should be," wrote William Safire in *The New York Times*, "though most concur that American director Kay Thompson taught them a lesson in sparkling presentation."

Bill Cunningham of *The New York Times* later reflected that the show was "the Valhalla of American fashion—and everything was all downhill after that."

Lambert concluded, "The show was groundbreaking on so many levels—not just introducing American designers—but changing the way fashion shows were presented. And Kay was a very big part of that."

"We did Versailles in November and I didn't come down until February," Kay rhapsodized. "It was just the most exciting, just crazy, wonderful, beautiful stuff."

For the rest of her life, Thompson talked about authoring *Getting It Together*, a coffee table book chronicling the milestone, but true to form, that never happened. However, in 1993, the Costume Institute at the Metropolitan Museum of Art hosted a twentieth-anniversary tribute to the Versailles smackdown as "the moment American fashion came of age."

In the wake of her Versailles victory, Kay virtually became the fashion doyenne she had played in *Funny Face,* opening up a whole new career for herself at age sixty-four.

Soon she was staging a Rube Goldberg–inspired "Exhibition on Escalators" for the opening of Bergdorf Goodman in White Plains, New York, showcasing collections by Halston, Bill Blass, James Galanos, Norman Norell, Pauline Trigère, Donald Brooks, and Kenneth Jay Lane—with Hubert de Givenchy, Prince Egon von Fürstenberg, New York governor Malcolm Wilson, and Pat Kennedy Lawford on hand as guests of honor. The kick-off was underscored with Burt Bacharach's exotic Bollywood ballet, "Sir James' Trip to Find Mata," from the soundtrack to *Casino Royale.*

As *The New York Times* reported, "Twenty-five models, choreographed by Kay Thompson, glided, twirled, reclined and danced as they went up and down" a labyrinth of cascading escalators in a vast three-story atrium under a moonlit skylight.

"I wanted it to look like a waterfall of beautiful girls," Kay explained in the *New York Post.*

"Miss Thompson," *The New York Times* added, "crouched at the bottom and using her hands as a baton to orchestrate the movements, was, to many, a sight equally as mesmerizing as the show."

"Surrounding Kay was a team of Otis workmen," wrote Eugenia Sheppard, "who were making the escalators do tricks."

It was Barnum & Bailey meets Busby Berkeley with Thompson as Houdini. Or, as the *Times* concluded, simply a "smasheroo."

When Anne Klein died of cancer in 1974, her assistant, Donna Karan, became head designer for the company and chose Thompson to direct the presentation of her first collection. When Kay decided to show the tropical resort wear in a grimy, industrial warehouse setting, some of the Klein establishment feared she'd lost all her marbles, but critics and buyers went positively nuts over the unusual juxtaposition. At the conclusion of the show, amid screams of approval, Thompson gave Karan a great big bear hug and said, "You just went out and came back a star."

When Thompson's name was mentioned to Donna Karan in 2008, her eyes lit up and she exclaimed, "Oh my God, Kay! She was so important in my life. She meant so much to me and I wouldn't be here today without her. She was motherly, delicious, and made it all happen."

Liza's next big movie project was a family affair: *A Matter of Time*, directed by Vincente Minnelli, based on Maurice Druon's 1954 French novel *La Volupté d'être* (source of the 1965 British play *La Contessa*, starring Vivien Leigh). Liza was set for the role of Nina, chambermaid to an aging Italian contessa, Lucrezia Sanziani, once the rage of Europe, now suffering from Norma Desmond–like dementia. As the old woman reminisces about the wild exploits of her heyday, Nina fantasizes that the flashbacks are her own.

"Actually, the thing was a love story between the chambermaid and the countess, if you want to look at it that way," recalled the movie's screenwriter, John Gay. "That's really what it was all about."

The contessa character was inspired by the Marchesa Luisa Casati (1881–1957), a scandalous heiress who wore "live snakes as jewelry," paraded "cheetahs on diamond-studded leashes," and employed "nude servants gilded in gold leaf." According to Hilary Knight, Kay was "absolutely fascinated by Casati and campaigned hard to play this fictionalized version of her in *A Matter of Time.*"

Others considered for the part included Luise Rainer, who had won two Best Actress Academy Awards in the 1930s, and Valentina Cortese, who had recently been Oscar-nominated for François Truffaut's *Day for Night*. But the producers insisted on pairing Liza with a bigger star. When Katharine Hepburn demanded too much money, the coveted role ended up going to Ingrid Bergman, hot on the heels of her Oscar-winning comeback in *Murder on the Orient Express*.

Nevertheless, Thompson did not walk away from the project. "Liza's going to do the film in Italy," Kay said during a radio interview. "And I'm going to be a consultant."

"Kay had a certain cadence, a certain melody to the way she wanted me to speak in that picture," Liza recalled, "and it was wonderful because it was exactly what Ingrid Bergman was doing, too. Kay said, 'You have to paint the picture with the melody of the words.' She instinctually understood what needed to be done and she was dead right."

Kay's disappointment over not being able to appear in the picture eventually turned to relief when the distributor cut the film to shreds, resulting in, as Rex Reed put it, "a brainless gumbo of incompetence." It effectively killed the career of Vincente Minnelli; he never directed another movie.

Miraculously, Liza emerged unscathed and Kay continued to advise her through a rapid succession of major motion pictures, starting with *New York, New York*, directed by Martin Scorsese. "They first asked Kay to do the vocal arrangements," remembered Earl Brown, who had sung in Thompson's chorus at MGM. "But she was not feeling well at the time and she didn't want to travel to Los Angeles. So Kay told Liza, 'If you can't get me, get Earl Brown.'"

"We were at MGM shooting the picture," Liza explained. "I was in my mother's old dressing room and I called Kay and said, 'Can you help me? This is all about singing in the forties.' I care about the words so much but Kay said, 'That's not what it's about.' Back then, big-band singers were supposed to be up, no matter what the song was about. Kay said, 'You're thinking too much about the words. Pretend your head is a balloon and there's a string through your ears. Now, just smile and sing.'"

Thompson also instructed Minnelli on phrasing. "I was trying to sing 'You Brought a New Kind of Love to Me' very fluidly," Liza explained, "but Kay told me, 'No. Sing it right on the beat.' And I said, 'Huh?' Then she sang it, 'If a NIGHTingale, COULD sing like you, THEY'D sing sweeter THAN they do . . . Cause YOU brought a NEW kind of LOVE to me.' I said, 'Uh, well, okay . . .' So I sang it that way and everybody thought it was just the hippest thing they'd ever heard and I said, 'Yeah, I know.'"

"On *Arthur*," Liza continued, "Kay put me in black high-tops, jeans, a little striped T-shirt that we'd gotten in Italy, a yellow slicker, a low belt like we always wore, a red cowboy hat, and a bandanna around my head. And from the moment my character came on the screen, you knew exactly who she was. Kay just nailed it."

By then, Liza was the poster child for the hedonistic New York nightlife of the 1970s—and Kay was part of her entourage, a freakish fixture of Studio 54, where she got a kick out of the giant mechanical "Man in the Moon with a Cocaine Spoon."

Lorna Luft observed that Thompson "was fascinated by the Sodom and Gomorrah type of atmosphere going on there."

"Kay was always asking about sex in the balcony and all that," Liza said, laughing. "And I'd say, 'I don't know about *that*, but if you push this button in the lighting booth, you can light to the beat of the music.'"

When Liza married Mark Gero on December 4, 1979, Archdeacon Peter Delaney, who had officiated the Judy Garland–Mickey Deans wedding, came from London to New York to preside. "I expect I didn't come up to scratch in terms of the clothes I was going to wear," Archdeacon Delaney recalled. "So, I had this extraordinary spree for two days with Kay Thompson in black limos, darting from various couturiers I'd never heard of, trying to get some suits that were more stylish. I suppose I was being 'Vogued' by Kay Thompson, for lack of any other expression. Can you imagine anything more splendid?"

In the late 1970s and early 1980s, Thompson was still hot to trot, a habitué of Regine's, an impromptu performer at Ted Hook's Backstage Club, and a staple at every opening.

"I was at Elaine's one New Year's Eve," remembered Randall Wallace, "and in swept Kay with an entourage of pretty boys, looking like something out of *Sheltering Sky*. Bizarre but arresting. She had this elongated black hooded cape thing, with black kohl under her eyes. Very Egyptian."

"When Ethel Merman and Mary Martin appeared together on Broadway, Kay came with us," recalled Geoffrey Johnson. "Everything she wore was black, except an aluminum foil vest. I said, 'Kay, that's stunning. Where did you get it?' She said, 'Oh, do you like it? I made it myself, just for this evening.'"

In 1981, *People* magazine described the always-cloaked-in-black Thompson as "a Bergmanesque dervish." And though she gushed about the plethora of projects on her plate, as far as anyone could tell, she never committed to anything.

"I was working for Harry Warren in 1980 and '81," Michael Feinstein recalled. "Paramount was going to make another musical with John Travolta because of the success of *Grease*, and they were going to do this Harry Warren musical written and directed by Jim Bridges starring Travolta. I called Kay to ask if she would do the vocal arrangements on that film and she said, 'Oh, I'm way past that, darling. I'm doing so many other things now. I'm writing and I'm producing and I'm just so busy, I couldn't possibly go back to that. I love doing it, but it's just so far in my past.'"

As time went on, Kay saw less and less of her goddaughter. Busy with her own life, Liza had collected two more husbands (Jack Haley Jr., and Mark Gero), suffered two devastating miscarriages (if she'd had a girl, she'd planned to name her Kay), kept the tabloids in business with high-profile flings (Baryshnikov, Scorsese, etc.), and, like her mother, had fallen prey to substance abuse that, in 1984, landed her in the Betty Ford Center.

"Liza always thought Kay didn't know what she was doing," observed Christina Smith, "but Kay did know—because Kay would ask me. She would be very upset about it."

Lorna Luft reflected, "When my sister's behavior started to, you know, *whatever*, Kay said, 'Uh-oh, here we go.' Because she knew the parents."

To calm Liza's distress over all the negative press, Kay told her, "The legend is going to build. They're going to build it, you've got nothing to do with it. So don't go out and say, 'But I'm not like that!' because people don't want to hear it."

"Kay always told me I sold papers so not to worry about it," Liza later admitted to columnist Cindy Adams in the *New York Post*. "Sometimes that helped a little."

As the years ticked by, Thompson seemed to become more and more world-weary. Contemporaries were dropping like flies, and with each passing, it seemed that a little bit of Kay's spirit died, too.

Then Vincente Minnelli passed away in 1986. "I immediately called Kay," Liza remembered. "She said, 'Yes, darling, what is it?' And I said, 'Daddy died.' There was a long pause and then she said, 'Well, that's it.' I always wondered why she said that. 'Well, that's it.' I guess, meaning that that whole period of her life was gone."

In many ways, it was. Not long after that, Kay's sister, Blanche, now a widow with failing eyesight, moved into the home of her daughter, Julie Hurd Szende, in Woodland Hills, California, where she could be looked after for the rest of her life. Saddened, Kay feared that someday she might lose her own independence, too.

"One day, I ran into Kay on the street," recalled Leonard Gershe. "People kept looking at her because she looked so ghastly. And she said to me, 'Isn't it incredible what an impact that picture had?' Meaning *Funny Face*. It never occurred to her why they were *really* gawking."

"I was next to her in the crowd at a Broadway opening," recalled Geoffrey Johnson, "and somebody said, 'Oh my God, look! There's Isak Dinesen!' Kay said nothing."

Eventually, she got the message and stopped going out altogether. Like Garbo and Dietrich, Thompson assumed the role of the eccentric recluse. She stayed in touch with the world strictly by telephone—with calls screened by Belles Answering Service (the company that inspired Vincente Minnelli's *Bells Are Ringing*). And she kept those operators very busy.

For weeks on end, Kay conversed as Eloise with Francis Ford Coppola, who wanted to adapt *Eloise* for the silver screen. He eventually realized that Thompson would never be satisfied, so he ended the fruitless discussions with a curt "Well, good-bye to both of you." Undaunted, the director collaborated with his seventeen-year-old daughter, Sofia Coppola, on the short screenplay for "Life Without Zoë," a highly derivative tale of an eleven-year-old heiress who lives with her butler and a dog at the Sherry-Netherland Hotel, diagonally across the street from The Plaza. Sumptuously produced for Coppola's section of the anthology film *New York Stories* (Touchstone, 1989), the forty-minute short was cast with an impressive array of actors, including Giancarlo Giannini, Talia

Shire, and Adrien Brody (in his movie debut). Incensed, Thompson consulted with her lawyers but ultimately could do nothing to stop it. The legerdemain only served to heighten her distrust and obstinacy.

Over the years, Kay entertained a barrage of proposals from Disney and Universal Pictures (for animated Eloise movies); from Robert Wagner (for an Eloise cartoon series); from Mike Nichols, Franco Zeffirelli, Robert Evans, Steve Tisch, Tracey Ullman, and George Hamilton (for live-action Eloise movies); from Jerome Robbins and Geraldine Chaplin (for Eloise ballets); from Knopf (for a Kay Thompson memoir); from Charles Evans (for a Thompson biopic); and from Donald and Ivana Trump (for Eloise promotions at their newly acquired Plaza Hotel). But, like a cat toying with mice before dinner, Kay strung everyone along before "cutting them off at the ankles."

No one was immune to her possessiveness. Not even the person who paid her rent. "You know Kay threatened to sue Liza if she ever sang her songs," Michael Feinstein related. "When Liza and I sang 'I Love a Violin' in Houston in 1985, we had to do it secretly because if Kay found out she would get her lawyer on the case."

Fed up with her behavior, Richard Avedon advised friends to stay away. "She's crazy," he warned. "She'll call you in the middle of the night and drive you absolutely nuts."

One of the few people who actually saw Kay in the flesh was Bi-Ko, a Chinese physical therapist who came to the apartment once a week to administer a combination of Japanese shiatsu massage and acupuncture. One of her other devoted clients was Jacqueline Kennedy Onassis.

"Kay's apartment was always very clean," Bi-Ko observed. "She had a maid come in once a week. She never wore makeup. She dressed casually but always elegant. Her main problem was that she didn't want to see doctors. Her teeth were really bad. She refused to go out and never let anyone come see her—including Liza. They talked on the phone but their relationship seemed strained. Kay was very stubborn. Everything was done on the phone, sent in and delivered."

Although Minnelli continued taking care of the rent, utilities, and other expenditures, Thompson was covering some of her own day-to-day living expenses with money she received from Social Security. Occasionally, she ran out of cash. Kay's former business manager, Leonard Grainger, explained, "Once she called and said, 'Listen, I have a friend of mine who needs a thousand dollars and I just don't happen to have the thousand dollars right now. Would you mind loaning it to him?' And I'd say, 'No, not at all.' So I'd send a check for a thousand dollars, and of course it was for her."

"One time, Kay wanted some money from me," recalled Andy Williams.

"So I gave her $10,000 in exchange for the publishing rights to 'Kay Thompson's Jingle Bells' and 'Holiday Season,' which I published through my own Barnaby Publishing Company."

But what about the royalty checks she was receiving from Simon & Schuster for the never-ending reissues of the first *Eloise* book? According to Hilary Knight, he periodically received payments that were "substantial," so hers would have been twice as much. Apparently, Thompson never kept any of her royalty income liquid. "She had her money invested in stocks," recalled Grainger. "It was strange because when she needed cash, she could have sold some stocks. But she was afraid to sell, I suppose."

When asked if she thought Thompson was under the influence of speed, Bi-Ko replied, "I had a sense about that because she wanted me to come at *very* strange hours. I'd rarely go to see her any earlier than ten or eleven o'clock at night. I'd do her for an hour and then we'd chat and talk and blah-blah-blah until all hours of the morning. She'd pick up the phone in the middle of the night and dial somebody and when they didn't answer, she'd get mad and say, 'Why don't people answer the phone?!' I'd say, 'Kay, who are you calling?' And she'd say, 'Hammacka Schlammacka'—her nickname for Hammacher Schlemmer. She had no idea of time."

Thompson never ceased to amaze with her eccentricities. "One day I came for a session," Bi-Ko explained, "and Kay showed me her leg. 'These are the places that hurt me.' She had put red Magic Marker dots all over her leg but the ink started running. So the next time, she put little pieces of masking tape on all the places."

"Another day," Bi-Ko continued, "she said, 'Would you like a chestnut?' I thought, '*A* chestnut?!' 'Sure,' I said. So I watched her as she picked up a single chestnut with tongs and roasted it over a gas flame. Then she presented me with one roasted chestnut on this beautiful china plate, on a silver tray, with a crystal glass of water, a fine linen napkin, and a fresh rose in a vase."

Then, in August 1990, the fairy tale turned Grimm. Shell-shocked by the recent deaths of Garbo, Sammy Davis Jr., and Halston, the 80-year-old Thompson fell and injured her brittle, osteoporotic bones.

"Kay called me in desperation," Bi-Ko remembered. "I rushed there and she said, 'I think I've broken something. I need you to help me get up onto the bed.' She couldn't walk. I said, 'Let me call the hospital.' She said, 'No, no, no! I'll be fine.' She was afraid that she'd go into a hospital and never get out, or be put in a nursing home. I said, 'Kay, let me call Liza.' And she said, '*Don't you dare!* She's filming a movie in Toronto and I don't want her to know!' She made me promise that I wouldn't tell her."

After Bi-Ko left, Kay refused to let another living soul enter the apartment. On the phone, she acted as though everything was perfectly fine, when in fact she was incapacitated with a broken foot and fractured hip. She could barely drag herself to get food and water, much less caffeine, cigarettes, or "B-12" fixes. It was cold-turkey central. Days turned into weeks. Time blurred. She completely lost her grip on reality. It was like Miss Havisham.

"There were vermin everywhere," related a friend who wished to remain anonymous. "Discarded soup cans, tins, old newspapers. Horrible beyond belief. When she needed to go to the bathroom or whatever, she'd crawl on the floor, beating off roaches with a back scratcher. Then the place flooded. The water destroyed all her manuscripts and things."

Eventually the building's management called Liza's accountant, who paid the rent, and said, "There's a problem. The smell is so bad coming from her apartment that you've got to do something or we're going to evict her."

The complaint caught Minnelli completely off guard. "Liza called me in a panic and asked me about it," Bi-Ko explained. "I said, 'Liza, she should be in the hospital.' Liza said, 'I'm going to take care of it.' Later, Kay called and was so annoyed with me. She accused me of telling Liza. I hadn't. But Kay wouldn't speak to me ever again."

When Liza arrived at the apartment, she was stunned by the nightmarish squalor. And it quickly became clear that Kay was not going to budge without a fight. Shrewdly, Liza invented, "Kay, reporters and paparazzi are on their way over here."

That's all it took. Thompson replied, "Let's go."

Rescued from this *Grey Gardens* hell, Kay was rushed to a hospital, where she was treated for malnutrition and dehydration. Her bones had not mended properly, so, like the cripple she had taunted in *Junie Moon*, she would now be confined to a wheelchair for the rest of her life. If there was a silver lining, it was that she'd finally receive the necessary dental work she'd avoided for eons.

"What day is it?" the doctor asked her, trying to determine her competence.

"You fool, it's Thursday!" Kay barked back defiantly.

She knew what day it was and knew what was going on, but like Howard Hughes, was selectively delusional. When she was well enough to leave the hospital, she was moved to Minnelli's apartment on Sixty-ninth Street, where she was installed in the guest room and provided with a nurse to look after her. The muscle needed to lift Kay to and from her wheelchair was provided by M'hammed Soumayah, a handsome bodyguard-chauffeur formerly employed by the King of Morocco and Halston. And for companionship, Liza gave Kay a new pug dog to spoil, sardonically named Mr. Begelman, after the notorious manager David Begelman, who bilked Judy Garland out of her fortune.

"Liza was marvelous," Joe Eula recalled. "She took care of Kay. I used to go up there and visit her all the time. She was a frail, withered thing in a wheelchair but as tough as ever—all wrapped in a pea jacket and a bright red Halston scarf and a bandanna on her head with three hairs. That dame was a survivor."

"God bless Liza," praised Roni Agress, who was working as Minnelli's assistant throughout the transition. "The circumstances that brought Kay to Liza's apartment were not pleasant, but, I'll tell ya, the end result was a resurrection."

"She was treated like royalty in that home," said Jim Caruso. "Like a queen, living out her last years in absolute luxury. Rigaud-scented luxury. Liza's houseboy, M'hammed, would fix Kay's lunch plate and it was a work of art. A little delicate plate with little flowers painted on it, with ten champagne grapes—those little tiny grapes—with two beautiful crackers with a wedge of something. Little, beautifully put together things. That's what she liked. And a Coke can. Always a can of Coke. It was like a fashion accessory."

"Kay was the ruler of the free world, you know," said Michael Feinstein, "so Liza was indulgent of that. Sometimes Kay would assert herself. Liza was always very deferential yet I know that it was, at times, hard for her."

"It got to be tough," Roni Agress observed. "It's your house, it's nobody's business how you live your life, but there is an extra person in there who will know if you're coming and going, late or early, or this or that."

"There was a wall built," Lorna Luft explained, "so my sister would not have to go by Kay's door and see Kay's eyebrow rise up."

"But Liza adored Kay above all else," Feinstein added, "and she just made sure that she was taken care of. Kay was her last family member, in some ways, of the old guard."

"Liza not only loved Kay as a person," observed George Feltenstein, "she would go absolutely bananas anytime Michael or I would find a rare piece of Kay's music. 'Oh my, just listen to what she did there! The *brilliance* of it!'"

In January 1991, the *New York Daily News* declared, "With Garbo gone, the last recluse in New York is Kay Thompson." But, by the fall of that year, things had normalized to the point where Thompson was ready to brave the public again.

Julie Wilson recalled, "At the premiere of Liza's movie *Stepping Out*, Kay was there in her wheelchair. When she saw me, she threw up her arms and said, 'Julie! How are you?!' I give Liza a lot of credit for getting Kay out of her hiding, to make her a part of everything."

Rekindled, Kay was suddenly up to her old tricks—including the all-too-familiar nihilistic ones. In 1992, for instance, she agreed to let Simon & Schuster reissue *Eloise in Paris*, but after promotional posters had already gone up in bookstores, she pulled the plug.

Meanwhile, Kay was discussing various ideas with John Loring, director of design for Tiffany & Co. "Naturally, the most promising of the bunch was a book to be called *Eloise at Tiffany's*," Loring recalled. "It's not hard to imagine all the possibilities: Eloise breaking things, disturbing nice ladies who were trying to shop, driving the sales people mad. It would have been delicious. From the book would have evolved a whole Eloise Collection at Tiffany & Co.—children's jewelry, piggybanks, dishes, silverware with Eloise and the dog and the turtle as the handles. There would have been no end to it. Unfortunately, she and Hilary Knight just could not see eye to eye and it all fell apart."

But Thompson wasn't done. She said to Loring, "You remember Walter Hoving's book *Tiffany's Table Manners for Teenagers*? Well, I think grownups need a few table manners. Why don't I write *Tiffany's Table Manners for Grownups*?"

"She started coming up with the zaniest things to tell grownups *not* to do," Loring remembered. "Joe Eula had illustrated Hoving's book, so Kay was talking to him about doing her *Grownup* version. But, obviously, that never worked out either. Then she wanted to do a Tiffany fragrance to be called 'Think Pink.'"

None of it came to pass. "Kay had the mind of a grasshopper," Loring reminisced. "Scattered but very determined. Whenever she'd get exasperated with me, she'd go into her Eloise voice and say, 'Well, good-bye. I'm going to play in traffic.' Click! She had a habit of hanging up the phone as an exclamation point at the end of sentences."

While Thompson made a career out of sabotaging Eloise, others had a field day satirizing the character. In 1967, Yves Saint Laurent wrote and illustrated *La vilaine Lulu*, a book about the ghastly adventures of ten-year-old Nasty Lulu who splattered fashionistas with black ink, took hallucinogens, and set homes on fire. Although *The New York Times* wrote that she "does things Eloise would never have dreamed of," she did have a governess and a schoolgirl's uniform that seemed awfully familiar. Then in 1971, *National Lampoon* magazine published "Michael O'Donoghue's Eloise," four years before Michael became the founding head writer for *Saturday Night Live*. The spread explained that due to an economic downturn, Eloise had been forced to move from The Plaza to the grungy Dixee Hotel. "My mother . . . cawn't cawn't cawn't afford Nanny anymore," Eloise said. "My new nurse's name is Carmelita Sanchez. She hooks on the side."

In 1976, O'Donoghue's girlfriend, Anne Beatts, in cahoots with humorist Deanne Stillman, instigated a parody entitled "Eloise Returns," with art direction by John Belushi's future wife, Judith Jacklin. Published in the feminist magazine *New Dawn,* as well as in the book *Titters: The First Collection of Humor By Women,* the spread showed Eloise living at The Plaza, only now, like Pooky Peckinpaugh, she's seventeen years old and getting into the kind of precocious mischief that might get her arrested or pregnant. Provocative graffiti on a wall read "Mr. Salomone was a child molester!"—a punch line that did not sit well with the real-life Alphonse Salomone. In fact, he sued for libel but ultimately could not prove to the New York Supreme Court that his reputation had been damaged by an obvious joke. Remarkably, that landmark decision is still cited today in cases involving parody.

Kay had absolutely no sense of humor about this sort of thing and was frustrated that she had no legal recourse to stop it. She really blew a gasket over Bob Morris' "Delia at the Delano," a humor piece in the February 18, 1996, edition of *The New York Times Magazine,* about "a trendy 8-year-old who lives at the Delano in Miami with a Prada ant farm and a French au pair." Recognizing its Eloisian potential, the Delano's owner, Ian Schrager (of Studio 54 fame), paid Morris to expand the spread into the book *Delia at the Delano,* published later that year. Hot off the presses, Schrager sent two hundred thousand free copies to movers and shakers "to create a groundswell, a buzz."

There was a buzz, all right. Protesting that the book was more copycat than parody, Thompson got Simon & Schuster to send a cease-and-desist letter to Schrager that erupted into a farcical feud, with indignant press conferences and rebuttals, until *Delia at the Delano* had been indelibly "suppressed" right into the public consciousness. By the time the book became "unavailable," it was a hot item on the collector market—although for those who bothered to check, it remained brazenly on sale at the Delano gift shop long after Schrager told *Time* that he had amicably agreed to yank it.

When Kay got wind of the breach, she phoned a fan in Florida to blow the whistle on Delia contraband—a priceless postscript to the saga of the cranky old lady who brought an almighty tycoon to his knees.

Perhaps the most biting of all Eloise parodies was the Roz Chast cartoon published in the May 1, 1995, edition of *The New Yorker.* Entitled "Eloise Revisited," the panel shows a forty-six-year-old recluse in a frumpy housecoat, lying in her Plaza Hotel bed watching TV, surrounded by a mess of magazines, half-eaten room service trays, and other assorted junk strewn about. No one dared show it to Kay because it struck too close to home.

Thompson *did* spend most of her time lying in bed, glued to the television or yapping on the phone. Once a week, she'd call her sister, Blanche, to argue about politics. Although Kay was a staunch Democrat, she never cottoned to Bill Clinton, so she cast an absentee ballot for independent candidate Ross Perot.

She was captivated by real-life mysteries like the Clifford Irving/Howard Hughes hoax, Travelgate, and the peculiar circumstances surrounding the death of her friend Doris Duke.

"During the Claus von Bülow trial that I covered in 1982," revealed true crime journalist Dominick Dunne, "Kay would call me up every night at my hotel in Rhode Island. That was one of the first televised trials, 'gavel to gavel,' and she watched every minute of it. She *hated* Claus. So did I, so we were in absolute accord. She would call me and she would get *so worked up because it wasn't going right!*"

"She was obsessed with the O.J. Simpson trial," Jim Caruso said. "She absolutely thought he was innocent. He was an acquaintance and that was good enough for Kay."

Thompson was an avid—and eclectic—reader. She devoured philosophy books like *Meditation in Action* by Chogyam Trungpa. "He's a guru to a lama," Kay explained to writer Hugh Fordin. "Listen, we need to go to Tibet. I wish it were on the ocean. It may be for all I know."

At the other end of the spectrum, she loved juicy showbiz memoirs like *Haywire* by Brooke Hayward, daughter of producer Leland Hayward and actress Margaret Sullavan. "We were at a party," recalled Geoffrey Johnson, "and Kay was very excited to talk to Brooke about the book, but she just wanted to change the subject."

"There was a book about the Pope called *In God's Name* [by David A. Yallop] that she was quite worked up about," remembered Michael Feinstein. "Transgressions in the church and all the corruption. She said, 'You *must* go out and *immediately* get a copy!'"

When Bette Midler did a sassy children's book called *The Saga of Baby Divine*, reviewers often compared it to *Eloise*. "Kay liked it," Hilary Knight recalled, "which surprised me because anything that even remotely seemed like Eloise, she usually hated. But Kay really liked Bette Midler, so it was okay."

She had other pop culture favorites, including Bernadette Peters, John Travolta, and Whoopi Goldberg. And Liza marveled, "Kay was completely up to date on every piece of music that came out. Everything Annie Lennox did. She loved her. She loved Sting."

When Sting was headed to Broadway in *3 Penny Opera,* Thompson told the show's casting director, Geoffrey Johnson, "Well, I could take Sting in hand and tell him exactly what he's doing wrong and what he can do to make the performance better." Unfortunately, she was never given that tantalizing opportunity.

Jim Caruso remembered, "One day, Kay said, 'I want a record of monks singing.' Of course, nobody had such a thing. Finally, I called one of those scary places downtown like the bookstore in *Funny Face,* except it's records. She would have *loved* this place. They absolutely had an old cassette tape of some crummy old monks in Parma chanting. So I got it for her. Well, she was *thrilled.* Beyond thrilled. She played it twenty-four hours a day. Six months go by and all of a sudden we're reading *The New York Times* and there's a two-page spread of this new CD called *Chant.* It ended up being the No. 1 worldwide selling record of all time, something crazy like that. I immediately called Kay and said, 'What made you think of monks, for God's sake? They're so hot now.' And she said, 'It was just time for monks.'"

She was also wildly unpredictable. "One of my all-time favorite Kay Thompson arrangements is her version of 'How Deep Is the Ocean,'" said Caruso. "One day we were sitting in the kitchen and I said, 'Kay, someday I'd kill to have an arrangement that cool.' Not ever thinking she was going to let me have it. But, all of a sudden, Kay gives me the arrangement. I think Liza's hair almost fell out when she gave it to me—because normally Kay didn't let anybody do anything."

Was Thompson finally softening up in her old age?

"Kay talked about Andy Williams a lot," recalled Roni Agress. "She said they'd had a falling-out at one point. I remember she got in touch with him when he started performing out of Branson because she wanted to send him a painting. I know they had a long conversation and she said to me, 'Things are better now.' She was very happy she had talked to him."

Her relationship with her goddaughter improved, too. One day Liza confided to Kay, "Mama died when she was forty-seven. I always worried that by the time I got to that age, I'd be dead, too. But, now that I'm turning forty-eight, I think that I should celebrate that I'm still here."

So, on March 12, 1994, to commemorate Liza's "coming of age," Kay decided to throw her a birthday party. But this was not going to be just an intimate, cake-and-candles affair.

"A Radio City musical extravaganza" was how Thompson underplayed it to *Variety.*

"The attraction was that Kay would be hosting the party for Liza at The Plaza Hotel," Roni Agress remembered. "It was mythic. The whole history. It was a grand idea."

Enthusiasm mounted, and suddenly the fête was going to be filmed as a Liza Minnelli television special and recorded for an album—with Kay joining Liza "on little bits of it here and there." Donald Saddler, who had danced for Bob Alton and won a Tony for choreographing *No, No, Nanette,* was recruited to join the creative team.

"Kay thought I should stage it," Saddler explained. "We would eat in the kitchen at Liza's apartment and discuss what it would be like. It was very *en familia.*"

Fashion publicist Eleanor Lambert and Tiffany & Co.'s John Loring were brought on board as consultants.

"It was going to take place at The Plaza in the Terrace Room," recalled Loring. "We'd go over there and work in that space. Kay was stage directing the whole thing from a wheelchair. We had recording people and computerized light towers. It was going to be rehearsed for several days but Kay kept repeating, 'It's got to be totally spontaneous, you understand.'"

"Kay was *reborn,*" recalled George Feltenstein, who oversees the MGM vault and archive. "They were going to do 'Madame Crematante' from *Ziegfeld Follies* and 'Ladies' Man' from *Good News,* so Kay called and asked me to get the conductor scores, which I did and I sent them to her."

"Leaving nothing to chance," Loring added, "Kay took a big red magic felt marker and wrote out the invitation, which she insisted we reproduce exactly 'as is,' in red ink on white invitation cards, made by Tiffany & Co., suitable for framing."

The distinctive scrawl read, "Kay Thompson is giving a Surprise Birthday Party for Liza . . . Liza AGREES it's a Good IDEA . . . So Come to the Plaza. WE'LL BE THERE."

Invitations were in the mail when sadly, Kay came down with pneumonia and the whole occasion had to be canceled. But, even though the final presentation never came to fruition, the experience had been a personal triumph. One last heavenly hurrah in the thick of it.

When she was on life support at Lenox Hill Hospital, everybody thought she was a goner—except for her former chorus member Beverly Freeland, who blithely insisted, "Oh, no. Kay's not the type to die."

She was right. Thompson cheated death again and lived four more pampered years at Chez Liza, chatting on the phone, feeding green lime Chuckles to Mr. Begelman, and conjuring up a thousand new projects that went no further than her mind's eye.

"Whenever I'm tired," Thompson told friends, "I just think about the glorious colors of butterfly wings. It's refreshing. I mean, butterflies never get tired—or if they do, we never hear about it."

On May 14, 1998, Sinatra died—a blow that really knocked the wind out of Kay. Then, on June 19, she received an unexpected gift. It was a new CD with a letter that read, "Dear Kay, I like this album of Dave Grusin's. I thought you would like it too. Love, Andy." The music was nice, but it was the note from her long-lost love that made her shoulders tingle.

Shortly afterward, on July 2, at age eighty-eight, Kay joined the choir—where you can bet she's jazzed up the arrangements with "a lot of joy and a whole lot of tra-la-la!"

In the aftermath of her passing, Rex Reed eulogized that she had "a trumpet in her heart" and was "ahead of her time for nine decades."

China Machado reflected, "There is a Spanish song called 'Dramática Mujer'—which means 'dramatic woman'—and that's what Kay was."

For Liza, words were not enough: "It's impossible to describe what a fascinating person Kay was. She's the original 'you had to have been there.'"

BED, *BAWTH*, & BEYOND

The last thing Kay ever said to me was, "I'll see you in the movies."
It still gives me chills.

—*Jim Caruso*

Kay Thompson's pervasive genius still reverberates in movies, music, dance, books, and fashion. But perhaps her most surprising gift was empowerment. Legions of working women have been inspired by her trail-blazing in a man's world—in real life as well as on screen in *Funny Face*. And generations of children have been seminally influenced by the independent spirit of Eloise.

"She was my kind of girl," recalled supermodel Lauren Hutton, who discovered Eloise while growing up in Charleston, South Carolina. "I didn't realize it then, but she became my role model. You know, she escaped from her parents, got to live in The Plaza, and could go around causing trouble. It was a hell of a life. And I did get to grow up and live a lot of it."

As a child in Texas during the 1950s, *Vanity Fair* writer-at-large Marie Brenner was taken with Eloise, too. "We were in the middle of a gray flannel society," Brenner recalled. "Our mothers had station wagons. We were girl scouts. And here was this little girl who could sklonk kneecaps. She could put water in mail chutes. She could do things we didn't *dream* of doing. We would say to our mothers, 'Why can't we live like Eloise?' And I think an entire generation of us tried to."

Another member of that Eloise generation was *Batman Returns* producer Denise Di Novi, who fulfilled a lifelong dream when she instigated two Emmy Award–winning television movies, *Eloise at the Plaza* and *Eloise at Christmastime*, both starring Julie Andrews as Nanny.

"When I was about seven years old," Di Novi explained, "I received the *Eloise* book for Christmas. I've loved her ever since. She was part of the reason I wanted to live in New York and part of the reason I wanted to stay at The Plaza as soon as I had enough money."

"I don't remember a time when I wasn't aware of Eloise," recalled Meredith Vieira of *The Today Show*. "I grew up in East Providence, Rhode Island. Small town, two parents, a picket fence, a perfect, idyllic suburban life. And I would sit there in my room and fantasize about a life at The Plaza. Forget the picket fence. I wanted to live in a big hotel. Here was this little kid who called the shots and it was a *girl*. And she had this attitude—and I wanted some of that attitude. I wanted to be her."

Eloise opened minds in other ways, too. "The vocabulary!" Marie Brenner marveled. "I mean 'zimbering,' 'the zimbering reindeer.' Remember that? And 'I skibbled and skittered.' Ah! For a young girl who was going to grow up to be a writer, these words were a liberation. It showed me the power of words, what you could do with an inventive sentence."

But the impact ran even deeper. "Rereading all the Eloise books," Brenner added, "I realized how powerful she was and how she inhabited our imagination. I really began thinking about her in the most broad cultural terms and I realized that not only had she given me permission to rebel, but that, in fact, she was the very symbol for our generation to usher in the 1960s. There have been other bad girls in children's books but this one felt like the 1960s are coming. You could really feel the beginning of a new era. And then, of course, ten years later, we were all teenagers and we were right in the middle of the youthquake. Eloise's importance as a cultural figure is that she was a liberating force coming in. She was our Holden Caulfield."

The emancipation that Eloise stirred was not limited to girls. Take the case of a young Washington, D.C., boy who was coming to terms with the divorce of his parents. "Eloise," "The Plaza," and "New York City" were mystical "words that pulled at me as if they were music," he wrote in his bestselling coming-of-age memoir, *Ghost Light*. Thompson had made Eloise's parentless life at The Plaza so tantalizing, so *comforting*, it mesmerized him and was a central driving force that drew him to the Big Apple for his adult adventures as the celebrated *New York Times* columnist Frank Rich.

Eloise also spoke to Bruce Vilanch, the comic performer and comedy writer behind Bette Midler, Billy Crystal, and the Academy Awards. "I was a very precocious kid," he recalled. "I was fat, I was ungainly, I was not athletic. I was growing up in New Jersey, so Eloise was about as glamorous as you got. Even at seven years old, I viewed myself as a woman in a black dress with a large picture hat sipping a Manhattan at the bar of the Russian Tea Room. And Eloise just seemed to fit right in. She just called my name. I wanted to be Eloise but I never could wedge myself into that Catholic schoolgirl uniform that they made her wear. But my hair actually was inspired by Eloise, and as you can see, it still is. It gives new definition to the term 'flyaway.'" Rim shot.

"As an adult," Vilanch added, "I cannot tell you how many people in the arts I have run across who read *Eloise* and knew all about her. Bette Midler— to name just one. We'd *all* read *Eloise*. I guess I was hanging out with a more sophisticated brand of child when I got older. That tells you something, doesn't it? We're a hardy band."

And the band plays on, passed down from generation to generation. "After I had given birth to my daughter Lily," noted Meredith Vieira, "the very first thing I did—literally about three days after her birth—I bought her *Eloise* because I wanted her to find this character and love this character and *own* this character the way I had as a little girl."

On September 26, 1998, just a few weeks after Thompson's passing, The Plaza was declared a literary monument as "The Home of Eloise," and was awarded a plaque that is proudly affixed to a front corner of the building. And Hilary Knight's famous portrait of Eloise remains on permanent display in the lobby, where fans from all over the globe gather for photo ops.

Posthumously, Thompson's estate allowed all four *Eloise* books to be reissued by Simon & Schuster. Then, the long-dormant *Eloise Takes a Bawth* was resuscitated and completed. Published by Simon & Schuster in 2002, the book shot to No. 1 on *The New York Times* children's books bestseller list and remained on the chart for six months—a long-awaited, triumphant addition to the Eloise canon.

In addition to her alter ego, Thompson's performance in *Funny Face* resonates through the ages and has influenced a slew of descendants, including Meryl Streep in *The Devil Wears Prada*, Vanessa Williams in *Ugly Betty*, and Anna Wintour in real life.

Similarly, Kay's innovative musicianship permeates the cultural landscape. To hear what the fuss is all about, just sample two comprehensive CD compilations that preserve her bazazz for posterity: *Kay Thompson: The Queen of Swing Vocal & Her Rhythm Singers: 1933–1937* (Baldwin Street Records), produced and annotated by Ted Ono; and, picking up chronologically where that left off, *Think Pink! A Kay Thompson Party* (Sepia Records), produced and annotated by yours truly.

The flame has also been kept alive by Liza Minnelli, who, dismissing the naysayers, forged right ahead with her tribute to Kay—featuring Jim Caruso, Cortés Alexander, Tiger Martina, and Johnny Rodgers as the Williams Brothers, directed and choreographed by Ron Lewis. To hedge her bets, Liza threw in several of her own greatest hits, but the centerpiece of her show steadfastly proselytized the gospel according to Kay—her music, her arrangements, her movement, and her joie de vivre. For nearly two years, Minnelli took the act on the road, playing venues all over the world, honing every nuance until, finally, it was ready for Broadway.

Liza didn't settle for just any theater. It had to be The Palace—the mythic site of her mother's Tony Award–winning concert series in 1951, coached by none other than Kay. There's no place like home.

With all the stars in perfect alignment, *Liza's at the Palace* opened on December 3, 2008. "Electrifying," wrote Rex Reed in *The New York Observer*. "It's sort of a goddam miracle. If you don't know who Kay Thompson was, or what she contributed to the history of show business, now's the time to find out."

On June 7, 2009, from the stage of Radio City Music Hall, broadcast to millions around the world, the Tony Award for Best Special Theatrical Event was awarded to *Liza's at the Palace*. Everything had come full circle and Minnelli's emotional acceptance speech said it all: "I just wanted to thank my parents for the greatest gift they ever gave me: my godmother, Kay Thompson."

Acknowledgments

VIOLENT ENTHUSIASM

*F*irst and foremost, I must thank my mother, Mary Bantly Irvin, for having the good taste, sophistication, and foresight to buy Kay Thompson's four hilarious *Eloise* books (with wickedly mischievous drawings by Hilary Knight) when they were hot off the presses in the 1950s. And I especially want to thank my two older sisters, Janet Crowder and Anne Aspinwall, for not destroying them before I was old enough to be indoctrinated. My sisters were the ones who obeyed my orders and read these books to me at bedtime. Often. These sacred hand-me-downs have proven to be a seminal influence on my life and I cherish their magic to this day.

When I later discovered that the cyclone in *Funny Face* was, in fact, the same woman who had written the *Eloise* books, my fascination grew. There were some old, scratchy records, a couple of faded magazine clippings, a few behind-the-scenes credits on MGM movies, but there were no books about Kay Thompson, so she remained shrouded in mystery and legend. The turning point came when I read Marie Brenner's apocryphal profile of Thompson in the December 1996 *Vanity Fair*. The article was a treasure trove of information and yet, at the same time, it was extremely frustrating. Much to my chagrin (and Brenner's), Kay had refused to be interviewed so there were still sizable gaps in the saga. When Marie wrote, "Very little is known about Thompson's early life," and when she failed to crack the mystery of Kay's best-kept secret—her age—it got my Sherlock Holmesian juices flowing. I just *had* to know more.

After Thompson's death, I was hired to write and direct a documentary on the history of *Eloise*, to be shown at the 1999 Eloise Pink & Black Ball at The Plaza to commemorate Simon & Schuster's reissue of the four *Eloise* books and the launch of Madame Alexander's Eloise dolls, plus other merchandising. In the process of interviewing Hilary Knight, Mart Crowley, Robert Wagner, Jim Caruso, and others who knew Kay, I had an epiphany that a book was just waiting to be written and I was the one with the passion to do it. Kay's niece and nephew, Julie Hurd Szende and John Hurd, recognized my zeal and encouraged me to get started. Had I known then that it would take a decade of painstaking archeology to unlock the secrets and piece together the puzzle of Thompson's astonishing life, I would have been too intimidated to begin. My naiveté served me well as I embarked on what turned out to be the thrill ride of my life.

This book would not exist were it not for the extraordinary kindness and encouragement of Michael Feinstein. He not only agreed to be interviewed but shared so many invaluable leads and helped open so many doors, I've lost count. But all of this pales in comparison to his inspiring friendship, which I value most of all.

I also would have been lost without the incomparable Ned Comstock, archivist at the University of Southern California Cinema & Television Library, who guided me through the Arthur Freed, Roger Edens, and MGM Collections, and subsequently called every single time he came across another tidbit of information related to Kay.

I am extremely grateful to a core group of Thompson enthusiasts who were particularly helpful and supportive: Jim Caruso, Jennifer "The Goddess" Chandler, Bryan Cooper, Mart Crowley, John Epperson (aka Lypsinka), George Feltenstein, Curt Gathje, Eloise Gorski, Meredith Mohr, Kathy Reilly, David S. Siegel, Richard Tay, and Ruth Williamson (who wrote and starred in the stage musical, *Pure Heaven: A Party with Kay Thompson*).

I also want to pay tribute to the late Gary Hill who, in the words of Judy Garland, was "my best critic and severest friend."

My sincerest gratitude goes out to Hugh Fordin (author of *The World of Entertainment! Hollywood's Greatest Musicals*), Stephen M. Silverman (author of *Dancing on the Ceiling: Stanley Donen and His Movies*), and Lisa Jo Sagolla (author of *The Girl Who Fell Down: A Biography of Joan McCracken*) for allowing me to use unpublished portions of the priceless taped interviews they had conducted with Kay Thompson for their own books.

I am forever in debt to the legion of Thompson's friends, family, and colleagues who, over the course of the last decade, so graciously agreed to be interviewed for this book, from A for Andy Williams to Liza with a Z.

In alphabetical order, they are: Neile Adams, Roni Agress, Van Alexander, Margaret Spier Angeli, Lucie Arnaz, Lauren Bacall, Henny Backus, Kaye Ballard, Anne Beatts, Judith Jacklin Belushi-Pisano, Robert L. Bernstein, Bi-Ko, Jerry Bock, Nina Bourne, Ray Bradbury, Buddy Bregman, Marie Brenner, Mel Brooks, Earl Brown, Art Buchwald, Gail Lumet Buckley, David Carradine, Marge Champion, Cyd Charisse, Ray Charles, Marilyn Child, Dennis Christopher, Betty Comden, Ray Conniff, Catherine "Kitty" D'Alessio, Yoel Dan, Bill Dana, Gloria DeHaven, Archdeacon Peter Delaney, Carmen Dell'Orefice, Denise Di Novi, Elinor Donahue, Wisa D'Orso, Bill Dugan, Dominick Dunne, William Engvick, Joe Eula, Charles Evans, Robert Evans, Bob Finkel, Janet Flamini, Roland Flamini, Betty Garrett, Larry Gelbart, Patricia Marshall Gelbart, Guy Gillette, Leonard Grainger, Kathryn Grayson, Adolph Green, Richard Grossman, Virginia Haig, George Hamilton, Bill Harbach, June Havoc, Dick Heimann, Mariel Hemingway, Paul Hemmer, Skitch Henderson, Larry Holofcener, Lena Horne, Ken Howard, Bruce Hoy, Michael "Peanuts" Hucko, Marsha Hunt, John Hurd, Lauren Hutton, Henry Isaacs, Jill Jacobson, Lois January, Carla Javits, Fran Jeffries, John Jenney, Norman Jewison, Geoffrey Johnson, Donna Karan, John Kenley, Princess Yasmin Khan, Greta Spier Kiernan, Jill Herman Kline, Victor A. Kovner, Vilma Kurzer, Perry Lafferty, Frankie Laine, Eleanor Lambert, Lynn Lane, Angela Lansbury, Arthur Laurents, Ruta Lee, Janet Leigh, Peter J. Levinson, Jerry Lewis, Leslie Lieber, Mort Lindsey, Joe Lipman, June Lockhart, John Loring, Alice Ludes, Lorna Luft, Joe Luft, China Machado, Tom Mackin, Ginny O'Connor Mancini, George & Ethel Martin, Hugh Martin, Tony Martin, Barbara Matera, Jack Mattis, Marilynn Lovell Matz, Katie Menz, Paul Methuen, Nolan Miller, Robert Ellis Miller, Liza Minnelli, Walter Mirisch, Meg Mundy, Mace Neufeld, Loulie Jean Norman, Margaret O'Brien, Robert Osborne, Patti Page, Cynthia Lindsay Patton, Graham Payn, Cassandra Peterson, Jane Powell, David Raksin, Sid Ramin, Uan Rasey, Peggy Rea, Rex Reed, Elliott Reid, Elizabeth Newburger Rinker, Julie Rinker, Christopher Riordan, Joan Rivers, Mickey Rooney, Virginia "Ginny" Farrar Ruane, Evelyn Rudie, Donald Saddler, Patrice Munsel Schuler, Robert Scott, Virginia "Jitchy" Vass Scott, Doris Shapiro, Sidney Sheldon, Christina Smith, Jerrie Marcus Smith, Liz Smith, Stephen Sondheim, Mark Spier, Richard Spier, John Springer, Gary Stevens, Marti Stevens, Deanne Stillman, Gloria Stuart, Julie Hurd Szende, Elizabeth Taylor, Sylvia Sheekman Thompson, Louise Tobin, Meredith Vieira, Bruce Vilanch, Larry Vinick, Baroness Marilou Hedlund von Ferstel, Marion Marshall Donen Wagner, Robert Wagner, Bea Wain, Connie Polan Wald, Mike Wallace, Randall Wallace, Lou Weiss,

Deanna Wenble, Margaret Whiting, Phyllis Rogers Whitworth, Andy Williams, Dick Williams, Don Williams, Julie Wilson, and Franco Zeffirelli.

An exemplary supporting cast of generous friends, family, aficionados, archivists, musicologists, collectors, and historians contributed their time and encouragement to help make this dream a reality: Frank Absher, Nancy Allen, Nancy Ruane Arendes, Mike Aspinwall, David & Susan Aspinwall, Scott Atkinson, George & Karen Babos, Steve Beeman, Perry Botkin, Rev. Malcolm Boyd, Nancy Barr-Brandon, Julie Brown, Lauren Buisson, Charles Busch, John Canemaker, Jeff Cason, Maxwell Caulfield, Charles Cochran, Patti Cohen, Paul Colichman, Bill Condon, Tamara Conniff, Alan Cooperman, Paige & Bill Covert, Andreza & Ryan Crowder, Rob Crowder, Robert Cushman, David Demsey, Bill DiCicco, Michael Dolan, Robin & Matt Durawa, David Ehrenstein, Fred Eppenberger, Richard Erikson, Larry Estes, Dan Evans, Margo Feiden, Peter Fitzgerald, Jordon Flakser, Matt Freeman, Roy Freeman, John Fricke, Marc Friend, James Gavin, Samuel Goldwyn Jr., Starleigh Goltry, Kathe Green, Charles Grenata, Phil Gries, Barbara Hall, Marty Halpern, Mark Harrison, Dan Helmerson, C. David Heymann, Edward Hibbert, Daryl & Joan Denise Hill, Dee Hoty, Tim Irvin, Jerry Jackson, JC Johnson, Peter Jones, Meredith Kadlec, Peter Kiefer, Jon Kroll, Christina Krupka, Lance LaShelle, Janet Waldo Lee, Dori Legg, Rick Lertzman, Bob Levy, Michael Lindsay, Malcolm Macfarlane, Leonard Maltin, Howard Mandelbaum, John Manulis, Michael Mascioli, Merrill McLoughlin, Linda Mehr, Harry Miller, Juliet Mills, Jack Morrissey, Eric Myers, Stephen R. Myers, Bill Norvas Jr., Mel Odom, Ted Ono, Bruce Paddock, Stephen Paley, Brent Phillips, Dana & Greg Plog, Ranse Ransone, Bill Reed, Janice Roland, David Rosenthal, Hunter K. Runnette, Robert G. Salomone, Karl H. Schadow, Scott A. Schechter, John Scheinfeld, Michael B. Schnurr, Ed Sikov, Bruce Simon, Jeff Sotzing, Julian Spencer, Don Spradlin, Mike Szymanski, Dace Taube, Lee Tsiantis, Tracy van Straaten, Frank Vlastnick, Cassandra M. Volpe, Frank Watson, Tegan West, Bobby Williams, and Bob Zaldman.

The award for championship goes to my literary agent, Peter W. Bernstein, who tirelessly helped me shape my avalanche of material into something palatable—and managed to get Simon & Schuster on board. I also want to thank his father, Robert L. Bernstein, Kay Thompson's business partner in Eloise Ltd., and a marketing genius behind the *Eloise* books at both Simon & Schuster and Random House during the late 1950s. Bob not only shared hilarious stories, he also suggested I meet with his son for representation—a match that has proven to be "pure heaven."

Words cannot express the gratitude I feel for my editor at Simon & Schuster, the legendary Alice Mayhew, Vice President, Editorial Director. Like Kay Thompson coaching Audrey Hepburn to become a supermodel in *Funny Face*, Alice was my "Maggie Prescott," turning this green first-time biographer into an overnight sensation (well, at least a published author). In our very first conversation, she boiled it down to one haiku mantra: "Keep it saucy." Words to live by, too!

I also want to thank the amazing support team at Simon & Schuster, including Karen Thompson, Associate Editor; Roger Labrie, Senior Editor; Jackie Seow, Vice President, Executive Director of Trade Art; Nancy Singer, Design Director; Jonathan Karp, Executive Vice President and Publisher; Victoria Meyer, Vice President and Executive Director of Publicity; Brian Ulicky, Publicity Manager; Nina Pajak, Marketing Manager; Leah Wasielewski, Senior Publishing Manager; Aileen Boyle, Vice President and Associate Publisher; Jon Anderson, Executive Vice President and Publisher of Children's Publishing Division; Justin Chanda, Vice President and Publisher of Books for Young Readers; Elisa Rivlin, Chief Counsel, Legal Affairs; Marie Florio, Associate Director, Subsidiary Rights; Tristan Child, Managing Editorial Assistant; Gypsy da Silva, Associate Director of Copyediting; and Loretta Denner, Senior Copy Editor.

Full-circle, I absolutely must must must bow down and thank the great Hilary Knight for drawing all those indelible images of Eloise that captured my imagination when I was growing up. I first met Hilary in 1995 at a signing for the 40th anniversary reissue of *Eloise*, but I got to know him much better during our first sit-down interview in 1999. Since then, countless conversations developed into a lasting friendship that I appreciate beyond words.

And last, but certainly not least, I want to thank my partner since 1982, Gary Bowers, for putting up with me and for patiently living through my never-ending journey to document the larger-than-life story of Kay Thompson.

About the Endnotes

$\mathcal{E}$very fact in this book has been substantiated, but the notes are so extensive, the only practical thing to do was to publish all of them online, at www.kaythompsonwebsite.com.

Illustration Credits

$\mathcal{C}$opyright page illustration: by Hilary Knight, from *Eloise*, by Kay Thompson (copyright © 1955, renewed 1983 by Kay Thompson; by permission of Simon & Schuster Books for Young Readers, a division of Simon & Schuster Children's Publishing Division); all rights reserved. Page 87, Part Two photo (Kay and Judy Garland, November 1946): The John Fricke Collection. Page 203, Part Four photo (Kay and Hilary Knight on the set of *Funny Face*, April 1956): Courtesy of Hilary Knight. Photo insert section, by numbers: 1: Courtesy of Virginia Farrar Ruane. 6: Courtesy of Gail Lumet Buckley. 7: Courtesy of Virginia Vass Scott. 12, 20: Courtesy of Hugh Martin. 14, 43, 57, 69, 95, 96, 103: Photofest. 27: The John Fricke Collection. 31: Courtesy of Ranse Ransone. 37: J. R. Eyerman / Time & Life Pictures / Getty Images. 48, 49, 50, 51: Courtesy of George Martin. 58: Courtesy of Paul Methuen. 73: Courtesy of Hilary Knight. 75: Courtesy of Renault. 76, 78, 79, 80: Courtesy of Evelyn Rudie. 77, 93, 94: Photo by Henry Krupka of D'Arlene Studios, Inc.; copyright © C. Krupka. 87, 88: The John Fricke Collection and David Rambo. 89, 90: Courtesy of Mart Crowley. 91: Courtesy Geoffrey Johnson, Noël Coward Collection. 102, 106: Courtesy of Jim Caruso. 104: Courtesy of Archdeacon Peter Delaney. 105: Copyright © Roz Chast / The New Yorker Collection / www. cartoonbank.com. All other images from the author's collection.

About the Author

Sam Irvin is a veteran director, producer, and screenwriter for movies and television. After beginning his career as the assistant to Brian De Palma, Irvin has directed a dozen movies, including *Guilty as Charged* (Rod Steiger, Lauren Hutton, and Heather Graham), *Out There* (Bill Campbell and Billy Bob Thornton), *Elvira's Haunted Hills* (Elvira, Mistress of the Dark), and *Fat Rose and Squeaky* (Louise Fletcher and Cicely Tyson). He wrote and directed *Kiss of a Stranger* (Mariel Hemingway, Dyan Cannon, and David Carradine). He has also directed several seasons of the premium cable TV series *Dante's Cove* (for which he also co-wrote the theme song). Irvin's other credits include co-executive producing Bill Condon's Academy Award–winning motion picture, *Gods and Monsters* (Sir Ian McKellen, Brendan Fraser, and Lynn Redgrave). While researching the life of Kay Thompson, Irvin served as a historical consultant for the Tony Award–winning Broadway show *Liza's at the Palace*, and produced the 3-CD compilation *Think Pink! A Kay Thompson Party* (Sepia Records). He resides in Los Angeles.

INDEX